WOMEN
IN
EARLY AUSTRIAN ANABAPTISM,
Their Days, Their Stories

WOMEN
IN
EARLY AUSTRIAN ANABAPTISM,
Their Days, Their Stories

Second Edition

with a new preface, bibliography, and appendix

Linda A. Huebert Hecht

PANDORA
PRESS

Women in Early Austrian Anabaptism, Their Days, Their Stories.
Copyright © 2009 Pandora Press. 2nd Edition Copyright © 2023.
All rights reserved.

ISBN-13: 978-1-77873-008-5

Cartography by Pamela Schaus.
Layout design by Karl Griffiths-Fulton
Cover Art: Felicitas, a slave-girl in her early twenties in the third century Christian Church, was executed for her faith, in Carthage, North Africa, three days after giving birth to her child in prison. Etching of Jan Luyken in the 1685 edition of the *Martyrs' Mirror*. Mennonite Library and Archives, Bethel College, Kansas, USA.

Published by Pandora Press.
www.pandorapress.com

Anabaptist and Mennonite Studies (New Series)

Edited by Maxwell Kennel

Volume 1. Gary Waite, *Anti-Anabaptist Polemics: Dutch Anabaptism and the Devil in England, 1531-1660*. Thunder Bay: Pandora Press, 2023.

Volume 2. Edmund Pries, *Anabaptist Oath Refusal: Basel, Bern, and Strasbourg, 1525-1538*. Thunder Bay: Pandora Press, 2023.

Volume 3. Cornelius J. Dyck, *Hans de Ries: A Study in Second Generation Dutch Anabaptism*. Introduction by Mary S. Sprunger. Thunder Bay: Pandora Press, 2023.

Volume 4. Linda A. Huebert Hecht, *Women in Early Austrian Anabaptism: Their Days, Their Stories*. 2nd Ed. Thunder Bay: Pandora Press, 2023.

Volume 5. J. Lawrence Burkholder, *Mennonite Ethics: From Isolation to Engagement*. 2nd Ed. Edited by Lauren Friesen. Thunder Bay: Pandora Press, 2023.

Linda Agnes Huebert Hecht is an Independent Scholar and completed a Master of Arts degree in History at the University of Waterloo in 1990. She co-edited the book, *Profiles of Anabaptist Women: Sixteenth Century Reforming Pioneers* with C. Arnold Snyder (Wilfrid Laurier University Press, 1996) which has been reprinted a number of times. She has published articles on Anabaptist women in academic and popular journals as well as in books. A number of grants allowed her to process, her "Data Base on Anabaptist Women in Tirol, 1527-1531" as well as travel to Germany, Austria and Italy to expand her research on these women. Between 1992 and 2013 Linda had several full and part time contracts to work in the Conrad Grebel University College Archives, processing *The Canadian Mennonite Newspaper* (1953 to 1971) Photograph Collection and the Frank H. Epp Collection of Papers. Beginning in 1991 she served on several Mennonite Historical Society boards: the Ontario one, the Canada wide society, and the bi-national Mennonite Brethren Historical Commission. Born and raised in Winnipeg, Manitoba she is now retired and lives in Waterloo, Ontario where she and her husband Alfred have lived since 1972. They have two married children and five grandchildren.

Praise for
Women in Early Austrian Anabaptism

"When Linda A. Huebert Hecht of Waterloo, Ont., ... began to read Anabaptist court records, she was astonished at the number of 'courageous and committed' women mentioned there. She has made it her mission to bring these women to greater awareness, first in *Profiles of Anabaptist Women*, a collection she and C. Arnold Snyder edited, and now in this closer look at those in Austria. Huebert Hecht provides context for each of the years 1527 to 1531, then presents actual court text or summaries of various cases."
    —Dora Dueck, former editor of *Mennonite Brethren Herald*, author of *Return Stroke* (CMU Press, 2022). From the *Mennonite Brethren Herald*, Oct. 1, 2009.

"Huebert Hecht's text is a valuable contribution to scholarship on women and Anabaptism but also easily accessible for the non-specialist. ... Both the translated court records and the fourteen-page 'Index of Women's Names' at the end of the text testify to the involvement and leadership of women in this outlawed religious movement."
    —Patricia Janzen Loewen, Assistant Professor of History Providence University College and Theological Seminary, Otterburne, Manitoba. From *Journal of Mennonite Studies* 28 (2010), 262-63

"Anabaptist women were the mainstay of the early baptizing movement – a fact generally obscured by most historical narratives describing the movement. In this book, Linda H. Hecht opens a unique window through which we can glimpse the life, faith and practice of people to whom history has generally denied a voice. ... This book shines much-needed light on the variety and extent of women's participation in the baptizing movement."
    —C. Arnold Snyder, Professor Emeritus of History, Conrad Grebel University College. Co-edited with Linda Huebert Hecht, *Profiles of Anabaptist From Women Sixteenth Century Reforming Pioneers* (1996). Author of *The Life and thought of Michael Sattler* (1981).

"Hecht has done a formidable job in following the stories of these Anabaptist women through countless court records. ... the book is well written and designed to make it easy to read and to follow."
    —Susan Brandt, Former editor of the *Mennonite Brethren Herald*. From *Rhubarb Magazine*, Fall (October 20, 2009), 47-48.

"This book represents the culmination of a long-term project by one of the very few scholars to focus sustained attention on the subject of Anabaptist women. The result is as detailed a picture as the sources allow of Anabaptist women in the Austrian Tirol from 1527 to 1531, the period when Anabaptism was established there and persecution was the heaviest.

This book matters for several reasons. First, ... traditional sources for studying Anabaptist women have been martyr stories or printed works by exceptional women like the prophetess Ursula Jost. The *Martyrs Mirror* has ... the disadvantage of including only the martyrs and not all who were connected to the movement (the many who fled, escaped, and recanted as well as those who were imprisoned and martyred). Furthermore, geographic coverage in the *Martyrs Mirror* is not balanced as only one Tirolean woman was included, while Huebert Hecht's index identifies more than sixty women martyrs in the Tirol. By looking at court records, which include a range of women's choices and experiences, a more complete picture of women and their role in Anabaptism emerges. The book contains several appendices of translated documents, including ... a confession written by a noblewoman, Helena von Freyberg, one of the few writings left by any Anabaptist woman."

—Mary S. Sprunger, Professor of History, Eastern Mennonite University, Harrisonburg, Virginia. Co-author with Piet Visser. *Menno Simons: Places, Portraits and Progeny*. Masthof Press, 1996. Co-editor with Mark Jantzen and John D. Thiesen. *European Mennonites and the Challenge of Modernity over Five Centuries: Contributors, Detractors, and Adapters*. North Newton, KS: Bethel College, 2016. From *Mennonite Quarterly Review* 85 (April 1, 2011), 325-27.

"It is mentioned that in this time period of five years the names of more than 400 women are on record in government court documents of whom (in turn) 32 were pregnant or nursing mothers. [*Erwähnt wird, dass in diesem Zeitraum von fünf Jahren mehr als vierhundert Frauen aktenkundig wurden, darunter wiederum 32 Schwangere oder stillende Mütter.*]"

—Marion Kobelt-Groch, Associate Professor of History, Hamburg University, Germany. Author of *Aufässsige Toechter Frauen im Bauernkrig und in den Täuferbewegungen* (1998). From the *Mennonitische Geschichtsblätter* 67 (2010), 161-62.

"We owe Huebert Hecht a debt of gratitude for introducing us to these courageous women who played such a significant role in the Anabaptist movement of Austria."

—Elfrieda Schroeder, German instructor, translator and freelance writer. From the *Mennonite Historian* 35, 2 (June 2009), 8.

"Linda Hecht has written a ground-breaking book on Anabaptist women for the years 1527-1531. It is important for two reasons. This is a major contribution to the history of the Reformation, describing not the leaders and their writings and theology, but the life and death of women, most of whom were peasants. It is also important because for the first time ever we can read about hundreds of mothers and working women and their struggle to be faithful in the face of loss of home and often life itself. ... This book should be in every church library and every home."

    —Walter Klaassen, Professor Emeritus of History, Conrad Grebel University College. *Anabaptism in Outline: Selected Primary Sources* (2019); Author with William Klassen of *Marpeck: A Life of Dissent and Conformity* (2008); *Anabaptism Neither Catholic nor Protestant* (2001). From *Ontario Mennonite History* Vol. 27, No. 2 (November 2009), 11.

"The book's treasures lie in the details of the author's narrative and in the records behind them.... She writes of maids and servants, rich and poor women, wives of leaders and single women, widows and pregnant women, all of whom made difficult choices to join or leave the movement. She follows their stories as far as the evidence allows, produces a detailed picture of what it was like to live as Anabaptist women in Tirol during the period, and masterfully articulates how these women negotiated their lives under persecution."

    —Adam W. Darlage, Lecturer in Humanities and Philosophy, Oakton Community College. From the *Conrad Grebel Review* 31, 1 (Winter 2013), 90-92.

Preface to the New Edition

More than twenty-five years have passed since the publication of the widely distributed book *Profiles of Anabaptist Women Sixteenth Century Reforming Pioneers* co-edited by C. Arnold Snyder and myself.[1] When the present book *Women in Early Austrian Anabaptism, Their Days, Their Stories* was published in 2009 my goal was to expand our knowledge of Anabaptist women in Austria beyond the several chapters I contributed to *Profiles of Anabaptist Women*. The process by which the latter took place is described in the Preface of 2008 below.

As stated in the Introduction, the translations and discussions of the first edition of this book are based on the 1972 volume of the German Anabaptist criminal court records which Grete Mecenseffy of the University of Vienna compiled and summarized and in some cases transcribed from the archival Anabaptist court records for the five year period 1527 to 1531.[2] In the sixteenth century court of criminal law, women and men were equal in that each had to speak for themselves. This was in contrast to the court of civil law where only men spoke publicly and men had to speak on behalf of women. Moreover, the court records – being government documents – are not a 'friendly' source of information and neither are they 'insider' sources written by Anabaptists which would have put their actions in a favourable light.

In analyzing the 1972 volume of Anabaptist court records I compiled a list of over 400 women – an extraordinary number – from all segments of society who were accused of involvement in the outlawed, heretical Anabaptist movement. Social historians in general have just begun to uncover the experiences of women in times past. Likewise, historians have only begun to create awareness of women in the sixteenth century Anabaptist movement. Since the Anabaptist court records have only been available in German – a feat in itself – I hope that the translation of some of them into English, giving as much detail as possible, will foster such awareness.

While this book focuses on the choices and experiences of women related to Anabaptism, there are, of course, men named in the court records. Women did not make their religious choices in a vacuum but in the context of their families – fathers, husbands, brothers, sisters, and children – and their everyday lives. To date we have information about some important male Anabaptist leaders in Tirol but not of the experiences of ordinary men who, with the women, formed the basic strength of the Anabaptist movement. In the new edition of this book a second appendix (II) has been added which provides some preliminary figures for the total number of men named in the 1972 court records for the same geographical region, the Austrian territory of Tirol and the same time period as for the women, 1527 to 1531. A few of the men's experiences are also discussed. This new appendix provides a glimpse of how men's participation compared to that of women's, and points to a broader framework within which the experiences of the Anabaptist women in this book can be viewed.

No changes were made in the text of this second edition except for corrections in spelling and vocabulary, but the page numbers remain the same as in the original publication. However, in order to aid the reader and to encourage further research in Anabaptist women's and men's studies in, for example, their beliefs and other subjects, a Bibliography has been added, compiled mainly from the endnotes at the end of each chapter of the first edition.

Finally, it must be noted that the 1972 volume of Anabaptist court records discussed in this book constitutes just one of more than 20 such volumes of court records for different geographic regions of Europe where Anabaptism took root. Historians have delved into various parts of these different collections. However, to my knowledge, no systematic analysis such as is presented in this book has been undertaken to date for other regions. Indeed, the story of Anabaptism in Austria continues from 1532 to 1564 in many more court records compiled by Grete Mecenseffy with the aid of Matthias Schmelzer and published in 1983 (volume three).[3] These too have not been analyzed in depth. However, volume three includes valuable indexes which were used in this second edition to collect information on men's participation.

Regarding this second edition, I heartily thank Christian Snyder who urged me to begin this project and Maxwell Kennel, Director of Pandora Press, who saw it to completion.

Linda A. Huebert Hecht, M.A.
Independent Scholar
November 2023
Waterloo, Ontario

---

[1] C. Arnold Snyder and Linda A. Huebert Hecht, Editors, *Profiles of Anabaptist Women Sixteenth Century Reforming Pioneers* (Waterloo, ON: Wilfrid Laurier University Press, 1996), 438p., seventh impression 2008.

[2] Grete Mecenseffy, *Quellen zur Geschichte der Taufer "Osterreich II Teil* (Gutersloh: Gerd Mohn, 1972).

[3] Grete Mecenseffy, *Quellen zur Geschichte der Taufer "Osterreich III Teil* (Gutersloh: Gerd Mohn, 1983).

Dedication

To all Anabaptist women, past, present, and future
who knew, know, and will know that,
"Jesus Christ is the same yesterday
and today, and forever."

Hebrews 13: 8
(NRSV)

Table of Contents

Author Bio, Praise, and Preface to the New Edition

List of Illustrations	xi
Preface (2008)	xiii
Introduction	1
Map of Tirol	2

Chapter One   29
Introduction to the Records of 1527
Translations from the Court Records of 1527

Chapter Two   41
Introduction to the Records of 1528
Anabaptist Women Leaders, 1527-1531
Translations from the Court Records of 1528

Chapter Three   97
Introduction to the Records of 1529
Use of Torture in Interrogating Anabaptist Women, 1527-1531
Translations from the Court Records of 1529

Chapter Four   141
Introduction to the Records of 1530
Pregnant Women and Nursing Mothers, 1527-1531
Translations from the Court Records of 1530

Chapter Five   179
Introduction to the Records of 1531
Translations from the Court Records of 1531

Epilogue   203

Illustrations	221
Illustration Credits	239
Appendix I	241
Appendix II	253
Bibliography	261
Index of Women's Names	279
Index of Selected Names and Topics	293

List of Illustrations

1. Women in Swiss costume *Froschauer Bible* 1531.
2. Martyrdom of Jephthah, tile by Bartlmä Dill Riemenschneider 1532.
3. "Kreuzigungstafel" painting by Bartlmä Dill Riemenschneider 1533.
4. Rattenberg Castle 1737.
5. Rattenberg town and castle, sixteenth century.
6. Place of execution in Bozen, South Tirol, 1541.
7. Sandstone pulpit in the Bozen cathedral 1514.
8. The Freyberg family tree, sixteenth century.
9. Hohenaschau Castle, Bavaria, 1550.
10. Woman baking bread, fifteenth century France.
11. Pregnant woman, midwife and assistant, 1529, Augsburg.
12. Birthing room, 1529, Augsburg.
13. Birthing stool, 1529, Augsburg.
14. Maid carrying a bowl, detail from 1488 altarpiece.
15. Pröslhof, birthplace of Jacob and Agnes Hutter, South Tirol.
16. Sixteenth century handwriting, July 26, 1530.
17. Butchering in Augsburg, Germany, 1540.
18. Seventeenth century farmhouse, Ziller Valley, North Tirol.
19. Peasant farmer and his wife, South Tirol, 1550.
20. Mint tower of Hall in Tirol.
21. Freundsberg Castle above the mining centre of Schwaz.
22. Michelsburg Castle, Puster Valley, South Tirol.
23. St. Petersberg Castle, west of Innsbruck, Austria.
24. Münichau Castle 1913.
25. Pankraz von Freyberg, painting of 1545.
26. Farmer sowing, *Froschauer Bible* 1560.
27. Ursula of Essen being flogged, *Martyrs' Mirror*, 1685.
28. Felicitas, young slave-girl in prison, *Martyrs' Mirror*, 1685.

29. Man and woman harvesting, fifteenth century.
30. Woman gives bread to a boy, fifteenth century.
31. The Seven Seals, Revelation, Chapter 8, *Froschauer Bible*, 1531.
32. *Froschauer Bible* of 1560, Zurich.
33. Augsburg city hall in Heinrich Vogtherr the Younger (?)'s painting 1540.

Preface

The seeds for this book were sown during my graduate studies in the late 1980s at the University of Waterloo in Waterloo, Ontario. Walter Klaassen, Prof. of History at Conrad Grebel College, gave me the idea of reading through a volume of the German Anabaptist court records to determine what they included about women. I chose to work through Grete Mecenseffy's *Quellen zur Geschichte der Täufer XIII Band Österreich II. Teil* of 1972[1] and was soon overwhelmed by what I discovered. The number of courageous and committed Anabaptist women was extraordinary! It seemed to be an impossible task to process all their difficult and each somewhat different experiences in one short essay, but an attempt had to be made.

I had been inspired to pursue Anabaptist studies by Werner Packull, Prof. of History at the University of Waterloo, through a guest lecture he gave on Melchior Hoffman in one of my undergraduate courses. Later, when I took a course with him, he made me aware of Meceseffy's third volume of court records, published in 1983. These records included new information about the key Anabaptist leader, Jacob Hutter, and also revealed more about the participation of women.[2] At first I thought I would use volume three as well for my Masters essay, but soon abandoned this idea and chose to limit my study to the 1972 sources.

My Cognate Essay advisor, Karin J. MacHardy, Prof. in the History Department, without whom I would not have been able to pursue this topic, assisted me in establishing the format of a computer data base. There I entered all the information available about the 268 women involved in the Austrian Anabaptist movement in its first three years, between 1527 and 1529. The 1972 volume covers a five year period and the records of 1530 and 1531 were also significant for the role of women in Anabaptism, but they could not be processed in the first stage of the research. I included notes in the data base from the secondary literature with the profiles on the women, much of it from my studies with Mary T. Malone on the history of Christian women. At that time, Mary was Professor of Religious Studies at St. Jeromes University in Waterloo, Ontario. She took great interest in the Anabaptist women I was writing about. Studying with Mary was an inspiration to me.

Upon finishing my Masters degree I gratefully received a grant from the Quiring-Loewen Trust in 1991 for the purpose of converting the material in my data base into a manuscript of biographical profiles on Anabaptist women in Tirol. Only three of the women from Tirol were included in the traditional source of information in English on Anabaptist women, the *Martyrs' Mirror*. There were so many stories needing to be told. As I began re-working the data base with material from the 1972 court records, I took a course with Arnold Snyder in the Master of Theological Studies program at Conrad Grebel College. In this course I began writing the biography of one Anabaptist woman in particular, and a very important one, the noblewoman Helena von Freyberg. With Arnold's assistance I translated a piece of her writing, her "Confession," into English which was subsequently published with her biography. My article on Helena and the comments of Lois Y. Barrett at the first Women and Theology Conference, "In a Mennonite Voice: Women Doing Theology," hosted by Conrad Grebel College in the spring of 1992, led Arnold and me to begin collecting the biographies of sixteenth century Anabaptist women from all parts of Europe. This resulted in our co-edited book, *Profiles of Anabaptist Women Sixteenth Century Reforming Pioneers* (1996). The book included several chapters on Anabaptist women in Tirol, but it did not include all of the women I had discovered. I continued to write about Anabaptist women in Tirol and present papers about them on various themes.

I appreciated the grant I received in 2003 from the Mennonite Historical Society in Goshen, Indiana to assist me in expanding the data base to over 400 profiles, covering all five years of the 1972 court records. My hope was that on completing the research on this volume of records, which were arranged chronologically, I would have enough information to tell the story of all the women mentioned there in the form of a Daybook, according to the days of the year. The records themselves speak powerfully and bring the experiences of these women to life and thus I chose to translate excerpts from them into English. These translations, I felt, would give readers another source of information besides the *Martyrs' Mirror*. In 2005 the Quiring-Loewen Trust generously gave me a second grant, making possible a research trip to Austria and Italy during which I visited Helena von Freyberg's castle and many places where Anabaptist women lived in former times in addition to collecting information in libraries and archives.

Over time, the format of the manuscript changed as I began adding narrative text to give some background and a context to the translations. The text provided a springboard for discussing important themes related to Anabaptist women in Tirol such as their leadership roles, their experiences with pregnancy and so forth. It is hoped that the combination of translations and narrative text will make this book useful to both the interested reader and to those studying Reformation History and most of all, will give these Anabaptist women the legacy they so well deserve. In a conversation with Walter Klaassen at a conference in 1997 on the women in the *Profiles of Anabaptist Women* book about whom he had written, he mentioned that he was looking forward to someday meeting them in Heaven. His comment astonished me, but I realized then, that the Anabaptist story is not just about the past but about a future that is still to come. It is the story and the history of all believers' church denominations, all those Christians who believe in the baptism of adults on confession of their faith. It is a story at times hard to read because of the severe persecution which Anabaptists experienced in Tirol. But this story also very much needs to be told. The harshness it reveals makes it no less significant. It is the story of ordinary women who made crucial religious choices, which in some cases led to martyrdom. Today, when women's roles and choices are much discussed, the story of Anabaptist women must be included. Their history is part of my religious roots in the Reformation, which has been one of the factors motivating me in this research. The book has come to include many endnotes which may serve those who want to research the topic further—and there is certainly much that remains to be done on sixteenth century Anabaptist women.

I wish to thank the staff in the following libraries, archives and museums: in Germany, the Stadtarchiv Augsburg, the Kunst-sammlungen und Museen Augsburg, especially Dr. Christoph Nicht, the Staatsarchiv München, especially archivist Frau Frauenreuther, the Staatliche Kunsthalle

Karlsruhe, especially the interim Director, Dr. Siegmar Holsten, the Fürstlich Hohenzollernsche Sammlungen in the Sigmaringen Castle, especially the Curator, Dr. Peter Kempf, for his kind assistance in regard to "The Crucifixion" painting of Bartlmä Dill Riemenschneider; in Austria, the Bildarchiv of the Österreichische Nationalbibliothek in Vienna, the Österreichische Akademie der Wissenschaft, Institut für Realienkunde des Mittelalters und der frühen Neuzeit (Institute for Material Culture of the Middle Ages and Early Modern Period) in Krems, especially the Director, Dr. Elisabeth Vavra who gave permission to use the maid in the "Birth of Mary" painting, and the Alpbachtal Seenland Tourismus in Rattenberg for the 1737 frescoe of Rattenberg; in Italy, the Castello del Buonconsiglio Monumenti e collezioni provinciali in Trent, the Südtiroler Landesmuseum für Volkskunde in Dietenheim/Bruneck, especially Frau Untersulzner who sent museum photographs, and the Archivio Storica in Bozen, especially Dr. Hannes Obermaier, who provided the color illustration of Bozen from 1541; in France, the Bibliothèque Municipale in Angers who provided the manuscript illustration of a woman baking bread; and in the United States, the Mennonite Library and Archives at Bethel College in Kansas, especially Dr. John D. Thiesen, the Archivist and Co-Director of Libraries, for the use of etchings from the *Martyrs' Mirror*.

On my visits to Austria, the assistance of my colleague and friend, Dr. Astrid von Schlachta at the University of Innsbruck has been invaluable, as have the stimulating and informative conversations with Dr. Mathias Schmelzer, who was Prof. Mecenseffy's assistant in collecting the Anabaptist court records for Tirol. I am grateful to Dr. Schmelzer for his transcriptions of some of the court records from sixteenth century into modern German so they could be translated in this book.[3] Dr. Manfred Rupert of the Tiroler Landesarchiv in Innsbruck assisted me in providing original documents a number of times over the years since 1990 when I first met him and most recently, kindly obtained permission from the Director, Prof. Schober, to print part of the document about the miller and the woman preacher, in this volume. Herr Wolfgang Bude, as head of the Tourist Information Aschau im Chiemgau and a member of the local history society, provided a historic photograph of the Hohenaschau Castle and made me aware of new sources on Helena von Freyberg in the Munich archives. I appreciated the conversation I had with Dr. Schürman of the Staats-und Stadtbibliothek in Ausgburg regarding books and publishers of the sixteenth century, especially the wonderfully color illustrated midwives book. In 2005 following my discovery of the Anabaptist artist Bartlmä Dill Riemenschneider in the Castello del Buonconsiglio in Trent, Italy, Dr. Leo Andergassen shared his research with me on this son of the famous south German artist Tyl Riemenschneider. In 2007, Dr. Andergassen gave me a personal tour of Bartlmae's works in the Brixen Museum. Finally, I am grateful to Hanns-Paul Ties who shared his research on Bartlmä with me, in 2017 and earlier. Both he and Dr. Andergassen consider Bartlmä to be the first Anabaptist artist.

Closer to home, I am especially grateful to Sam Steiner, head of the Library and Archives of Conrad Grebel University College, for photographing illustrations from the Froschauer Bibles of 1531 and 1560 for use in this book. Also, Sam supported my work on this manuscript by allowing me a flexible schedule for my contract job in the Conrad Grebel archives.

Arnold Snyder encouraged me in my idea for this book from the beginning. His editorial work is sincerely appreciated and brought many an improvement to the manuscript in its various stages. His suggestions were especially important last December when the project threatened to falter. At that time I changed the format of the book and began adding narrative text. Pamela Schaus, cartographer at Wilfrid Laurier University, deserves special thanks for preparing the map of Tirol. I extend gratitude to the Institute of Anabaptist and Mennonite Studies at Conrad Grebel University College for undertaking to publish this book. I would like to express my thanks to Ted E. Friesen, Judith Dueck, Mary Huebert and Ethel (Rusty) Anderson for some of the financial support.

It has been a long journey to complete this book and many colleagues and friends have provided invaluable support. I wish to thank the following people: Lucille Marr, a long time friend whose interest in my research has been a real encouragement; Ilse Friesen, for her course on the History of European art which I enjoyed very much a number of years ago in my journey back to the classroom and more recently for the very helpful discussions we have shared on sixteenth century art and the Anabaptist artist, Bartlmä Dill Riemenschneider; William Klassen in Waterloo for the many conversations we have had about Helena von Freyberg as he and Walter Klaassen were writing their book on Pilgram Marpeck, and for the copy of Helena's "Confession" from Heinold Fast's *Kunstbuch* collection which he and Walter made available to me; Doris Gascho, with whom I shared some of my first ideas about a book on Anabaptist women; members of the Grace Mennonite Brethren Church who often inquired how the book was coming along; members of the Christian Writers' Club who gave positive critique on early drafts of the Introduction, Pat Adam, Erica Jantzen, Sandra Lavallee, Eleanor McDonald, Ruth Martin, Esther Regehr, Mary Waind and Ruth Zehr; Mabel Hunsberger, Prof. at McMaster University, a friend who volunteered to read a major portion of the Daybook manuscript and gave valuable insights; Ken Reddig of Manitoba; and the following friends for their interest and continuing support, Roma Carlson, Jack and Eleanor Dueck, Nancy Fehderau, Carol Lichti, Marvin and Karen Warkentin, and Alfred Pletsch of Marburg, Germany. I have appreciated the involvement of each one.

Members of my family cheered me on many a time, Marvin and Deborah Hecht of California and Melinda and Albert Hecht-Enns here in Waterloo, my sister Ruth Loewen and aunt, Mary Huebert, both in Winnipeg. And last but by no means least, I wish to thank my husband for his continued faithful support and encouragement.

Linda A. Huebert Hecht
Independent Scholar
September 2008
Waterloo, Ontario

Notes

1. Grete Mecenseffy was a pioneer in Anabaptist studies. She "taught church history and history of dogma at the Protestant Faculty of the University of Vienna, the first woman to hold a chair in the faculty, and one of the earliest Austrian women to be ordained to the ministry (in the Austrian Reformed Church).... During the last 33 years of her life she gathered and edited 1,740 printed pages of Anabaptist documents in three volumes of Austrian *Täuferakten* (Anabaptist documentary sources)." John S. Oyer, "Mecenseffy, Grete (1899-1985)," in *Global Anabaptist Mennonite Encyclopedia Online* (1988). Retrieved 09 September 2008 http://www.gameo.org/encyclopedia/contents/M42.html. Oyer also stated, She had an "infectious enthusiasm for Anabaptist studies." *Mennonite Quarterly Review*, 60 (January 1986), 104.
2. Packull tells the story of early Anabaptism in Tirol admirably well in his book, *Hutterite Beginnings Communitarian Experiments during the Reformation*, (Baltimore, MD: John Hopkins University Press, 1995). It was a valuable source to me in writing this volume.
3. The author is grateful to Dr. Matthias Schmelzer of Bruneck, Italy for transcribing the following original, archival texts printed in Grete Mecenseffy, *Quellen zur Geschichte der Täufer XIII Band Österreich II. Teil* (Gütersloh: Gerd Mohn, 1972) into modern German: documents 280 (Barbara Velcklehner), 349 (appointment of Michel Kürschner), 513 (Balthasar Vest and his wife) and 620 (the Silberbrennerin, Cristan Gschäll and Spitzhamer inventories) and for his transcriptions of the archival document for July 26, 1530 (The Blacksmith's Wife Preaches With the Local Miller) and July 14, 1528 (Explanation of the Sacrament (Communion), Passed on By a Woman) printed in Grete Mecenseffy, *Quellen zur Geschichte der Täufer XI. Band Österreich I. Teil* (Gütersloh: Gerd Mohn, 1964), as well as for his assistance in deciphering the meaning of June 23, 1528 (Women in Styria, Preached and Did Radical Things), also in the 1964 volume, and the October-November 1530 inventory of the Paul Taurer family in the 1972 volume.

Introduction

This book invites you to enter into the religious experiences of women, ordinary in social status, but extraordinary in their actions. They lived their faith during that crucial turning point in Christian history, the Reformation. Their history, the story of how they chose to declare their faith publicly through adult baptism, has until now, for the most part remained hidden. It is presented here in two parts, as story or narrative and in translations from court records, organized by the days of the year on which women accused of Anabaptist involvements were arrested, interrogated, tried and martyred. It gives a voice and historical memory to the women who played a significant role in establishing the Anabaptist movement in Austria.[1]

This history of Anabaptist women in one part of Europe, the sixteenth century Austrian territory of Tirol, is history "from the bottom up." It is part of a newer approach to our past, in which social and cultural historians tell the story of the lower classes, of the hearers and doers of the message, of those feeling the impact of government decrees, not those making them and not those writing Reformation theology and doctrine. This is the story of women making choices in the everyday circumstances of life, circumstances which challenged old ways and promised change.

The Geographical Setting

In the sixteenth century, the mountainous region of Tirol consisted of various secular, ecclesiastical, rural and urban feudal lordships among which were several mining centres. Archduke Ferdinand's "administration and court for these territories presided at Innsbruck." The territory was "subdivided into administrative jurisdictions"[2] or districts. Innsbruck, located on the Inn River, was "situated at the point where the east-west road along the Inn Valley crosses the north-south road over the Brenner Pass, the lowest (4,000 ft.) pass over the Alps."[3] The Brenner Pass was the dividing line between North and South Tirol and North Tirol was further

Map of Tirol

subdivided into the Upper and Lower Inn regions. Three major river valleys, the Inn, the Eisack and the Etsch or Adige divided the mountainous terrain. The broad Inn River Valley in the north included several urban centres east of Innsbruck, namely, Hall, a market town and centre for the salt mines and for the minting of coins, the mining towns of Schwaz and Rattenberg, a border town to Bavaria, Kufstein and the urban centre of Kitzbühel, part of a bishopric administered from Salzburg. The bishopric of Freising extended from Rattenberg to Kufstein. To the west of Innsbruck lay the Ötz Valley and west of that, a separate territory, Vorarlberg, with its administrative centre at Bregenz, on Lake Constance. Ferdinand governed from Vorarlberg to Innsbruck.

Following the north-south route from Innsbruck down the Wipp Valley, the first major centre in the south on the Eisack River was Sterzing important as a market town, followed by Brixen, which was the centre for the bishopric. The Puster Valley extended eastward from the Eisack River Valley and included the urban centres of Bruneck, St. Lorenzen and St. George and the smaller Taufer Valley north of Bruneck. Klausen, a market town and Gufidaun, were two other major centres in the Eisack River valley, to the south of which lay the urban centre of Bozen, with the adjacent centre Gries. The Etsch Valley broadened out to the west of Bozen extending to Meran and the Vintschgau or Upper Etsch Valley, bordering on the Swiss territories. At Bozen, another market town, the Etsch River flowed south toward Trent, and the border of the Republic of Venice. See the map of Tirol on page two for the location of these places.

The Reformation and Anabaptist Beginnings

In the early years of the sixteenth century Europe's inhabitants were experiencing a time of spiritual poverty and a dearth of spiritual care for people at the local level. Monastic life was at a low ebb; many local priests could not even read Latin to conduct a proper mass. At the same time, life was difficult for the ordinary commoner and life expectancy much shorter than today. The carvings and sculptures in their churches reminded them constantly of the prevalence of death but gave them little hope for their future and for life after death. Religious issues were of course intertwined with the larger socio-economic issues of the day, an economy in transition from feudal to capitalist and political hierarchies seeking greater control of local authorities.[4]

When Martin Luther nailed his ninety-five theses on the church door in Wittenberg in 1517, he intended only to initiate some much needed church reform. Instead, his action was like a match flung into a haystack which subsequently erupted in flames. People were ready for and in need of religious change. The recent invention of the German printing press made it possible to disseminate Luther's writings very quickly and despite the fact that the majority of the people were illiterate, a Reformation movement soon took shape. What followed was a time of tremendous upheaval – in German called a time of "Umbruch."

Luther's call for biblical reform brought widespread religious change to all parts of Europe. It included salvation by faith alone (*sola fide*), belief in Scripture alone (*sola Scriptura*) and in a priesthood of all believers. On January 21, 1525, eight years after the events in Wittenberg, a group of Christians was gathered in the home of Felix Mantz's mother in Zurich, Switzerland. They had already accepted Luther's three principles and now took the radical step of baptizing each other on the confession of their faith. The first to be baptized by Conrad Grebel was Jörg Blaurock. They did this in obedience to their understanding of Jesus' words in Matthew 28:18-20 to go into all the world making disciples, teaching and baptizing them, in that order.[5] The authorities soon declared adult baptism to be heretical and "a capital offense against the state."[6] Felix Mantz became the first Anabaptist martyr in Zurich, forfeiting his life on January 5, 1527. The "Anabaptist" or "Re-baptizing" movement – as the baptizers were disparagingly called – was outlawed by all political and religious leaders in Europe, both Protestant and Catholic.[7] This included Archduke Ferdinand I, ruler of the Austrian territories since 1521.[8]

To understand how radical the adult baptisms in Zurich were, it is necessary to remember that in the sixteenth century religion was part of the fabric of life. It affected all aspects of society and the life of every person rich or poor, male or female. As one historian puts it, "reform took place because people were religious rather than irreligious."[9] The baptism of infants was the ritual by which individuals were initiated into the structures of church and society. To negate this sacrament was thus an act of rebellion against both church and state. The grace of God was no longer imparted to the Christian believer through a priest or, as may have been the case for women, through a male guardian. Now anyone could experience the grace of God based on personal choice. The baptism of adults on the confession of their faith was a visible sign of this inner experience and led to the establishment of a visible, gathered church, a community of believers that practiced discipleship. But, allowing such freedom of religion was not in the best interests of the governments of the time. "Sixteenth century political wisdom demanded the monopoly and control of religion by the rulers of any given state."[10]

Anabaptists also negated the sacrament of Holy Communion. For them, communion or the Lord's Supper was simply an act of remembrance. The Anabaptist Hutterite leader Jörg Zaunring wrote in his treatise on the Lord's Supper, that it was contrary to reason or common sense to suggest that Christ's body was in the bread "because Christ in his mortal body was seated at the table when he spoke the words, 'this is my body.'" In speaking these words, Christ was referring to the "congregation of God" on this earth and this ceremony was a remembrance and a sign. "The symbolic breaking of the bread and drinking of the cup, therefore, indicated solidarity with Christ and one another in suffering as his body on earth."[11] Moreover, Anabaptists partook of both the bread and the wine, which differed from the established church of that time.[12] This too was radical behaviour and along with their belief in baptism marked the Anabaptists as heretics. The two most frequently asked questions in Anabaptist interrogations were, "What do you think of baptism?" and, "What do you think of the sacrament?" meaning Holy Communion.

Ferdinand I, Hapsburg ruler of the Austrian territory of Tirol was particularly determined to eradicate dissent and uphold traditional Christianity. He has been called "'an honest fanatic' without virtues of self-doubt" who considered it "his God-given duty to eliminate heresy from his territories" in order to maintain a united Christendom.[13] In discussing the legal position of the sixteenth century Anabaptists, Thomas Winkelbauer relates the following. As the sovereign of Tirol, Ferdinand was responsible to God for his subjects. The decree of 1524 stated, he was to care not only for the physical but also for the spiritual wellbeing of his subjects by ensuring that the holy Gospel and other godly writings would be proclaimed in proper fashion.[14] At the same time, the issue of heresy was a means by which Ferdinand, who like other rulers of the day strove to establish absolute power, sought full control over his subjects and the local authorities. This was resisted by some local rulers sympathetic to the Anabaptists.[15] Moreover, due to the perennial threat of war with the Turks Ferdinand desired to control the Estates. In the latter, in Tirol, the lower classes traditionally were relatively strong politically and the nobility weaker since they were smaller in number compared to other Austrian territories. With the exception of the Sonnenburg nunnery in the Puster Valley women were not represented in the Estates. They shared in the relative political equality of the (middle) burgher and peasant classes indirectly through their husbands and fathers.

The form of land tenure in Tirol promoted attitudes of resistance as well. Many of the peasants were freeholders and not under the direct control of landholding nobles or political and religious authorities.[16] The religious discontent of the time combined with Luther's teachings and the economic crisis led some of the lower classes in all parts of Europe to revolt. In Tirol the Peasants' War was led by Michael Gaismair in 1525 and 1526 but was not successful.[17] Ferdinand saw in the Anabaptist movement which grew in its wake a continuation of the peasant rebellion. In his view, those guilty of listening to radical preachers and suspected of Anabaptism were undermining the political as well as the social and religious orders. For all of these reasons, beginning in 1527, Ferdinand instituted a policy of repression and severe persecution for all women and men who became Anabaptists in the Austrian territory of Tirol.[18]

Anabaptist Membership: In the Beginning there were Women

Despite being outlawed, Anabaptism grew quickly as the new religious ideas provided encouragement and answers for people who felt spiritually deprived. In its first three years, between 1527 and 1529, there are 210 documented cases of baptized women in Tirol, categorized as believers.[19] They comprised forty-six percent or nearly half of the Anabaptist membership[20] and more than one-third, forty percent, of all those who were martyred.[21] (The Introduction in Chapter Three includes details about female Anabaptist martyrs for the five year time period.) Writing in 1959, one of the most important Mennonite historians of the time, Harold S. Bender, concluded that, "The Anabaptist emphasis upon voluntary membership, adult baptism and personal commitment inevitably opened up new perspectives for women." Bender went on to say that after a time this openness was lost.[22] The famous sociologist Max Weber, whose work Bender studied in Heidelberg, Germany,[23] had published this hypothesis in his writings of 1922. Weber analyzed the religion of the disprivileged classes and said they extended religious equality to women only in the early stages of development, in particular in charismatic leadership roles. Once the relationships in the community became routine and regimented there was a reaction and women retained religious equality more in theory than in practice.[24] Bender and Weber's views[25] are confirmed in Tirol by the fact that so many women became Anabaptist members and that, as discussed in Chapter Two, twenty-one Anabaptist women acted as lay missioners, leaders and teachers.[26]

The prevalence of more women in the beginning years of Anabaptism in Tirol, whether they were believers or leaders, is not unique. This pattern is evident already in the New Testament. New spiritual freedom and opportunities for discipleship for women originated with Jesus but appeared to be curtailed by the Apostle Paul. As already shown in the book *Profiles of Anabaptist Women*, greater numbers of women participated in the early years of the sixteenth century Anabaptist movement in all regions of Europe.[27] The pattern can be seen "… in all major religious movements from early Christianity onward…."[28] It is evident among the Beguines, a lay religious community of the thirteenth and fourteenth centuries,[29] in medieval heretical movements such as the Cathars and Waldensians,[30] the Hussites and Lollards,[31] in Pietism,[32] Quakerism,[33] Methodism,[34] the Holiness movement[35] and the more recent experiences of Canadian religious women.[36] Two historians of women in the Christian and Jewish traditions describe it as follows.

> Women's leadership also appears where lay leadership is stressed. Various renewal movements in left-wing Protestantism, as well as Catholicism, have been marked by an anticlericalism that validated

the authority of the entire community to teach, interpret the Bible and evangelize. Those who have the gifts, rather than those authorized by the traditional institution, are acclaimed as leaders. In this situation women too can emerge as leaders. However, in the next generation, as renewal movements settle down and begin themselves to institutionalize, there is a loss of this early freedom. Institutionalized leadership again reverts to the patriarchal pattern, and women are eliminated. One can find this phenomenon recurring again and again in the history of Christianity.[37]

Anabaptist women of sixteenth century Tirol then stand in a long tradition.

That more than four hundred women are documented in the Anabaptist court records for the five year time period 1527 to 1531 may seem surprising. But, as was the case in other turbulent times and in the first years of many other new religious movements, everyone was needed and gender and class were not important.[38] What was true for the fourteenth century Waldensians, the only medieval sect to take root in the Austrian regions bordering Tirol,[39] was true for the Anabaptists as well. For the Waldensians, wider rights for women were caused by two factors:

(a) the return to the New Testament and the consequent emphasis on the spiritual equality of all Christian believers, including women;
(b) the fact that it was a persecuted fringe community, which naturally made for relatively greater equality among the members, including women.[40]

The same was true for Anabaptist women. The focus on the New Testament and reading the Gospels in the vernacular[41] as well as the emphasis on lay participation were key factors for their involvement. The decentralized and informal environment in which Anabaptism grew also made it easier for women to participate. Meetings places were changed frequently due to the persecution. Sometimes they took place in forests but most often in homes, in the women's domain. Chapter Five includes some interesting examples of what happened and what was taught at these meetings.

One additional factor was very significant for women's participation in Anabaptism. Merry Wiesner, the renowned historian of sixteenth century women's history, explains that divine inspiration from the Holy Spirit gave each believer, including women, an inner authority for public speech and action and the freedom to speak out on religious matters.[42] In general, in Anabaptism, "Appealing to the Holy Spirit as the central interpretive agent meant that a spirit-filled, illiterate, or semi-literate woman or man would be a truer exegete of Scripture than would a learned professor lacking the Spirit."[43] This meant that women could be prophets in the same way as men. Ursula Jost and Barbara Rebstock were Anabaptist prophets in Strasbourg.[44] In southern Germany, "Females experienced the greatest equality with men when congregations emphasized the Spirit over Scripture."[45] Reference to the Holy Spirit or the "inner Word" is also found in the writings of Leonhard Schiemer, the Anabaptist leader martyred in Rattenberg, who taught that "the true light of the Holy Spirit is needed which shines in our heart."[46] In February 1528, Ferdinand gave his officials an important clue to identifying Anabaptists. In Tirol they greeted each other in a characteristic way. One Anabaptist would say, "Peace be with you!" and the fellow believer would respond "The Holy Spirit live in you!"[47] The dependence of Anabaptists on the Holy Spirit was emphasized then every time they greeted each other. The Anabaptist emphasis on the Holy Spirit gave women a basis for public speech and action.

Anabaptist Women, Integrally Involved

Women were integrally involved in the establishment of the Anabaptist movement in Tirol. There were the wives of travelling merchants who brought Reformation ideas to Tirol from the north, the wife of exiled Swiss leader Jörg Blaurock who accompanied her husband when he brought Anabaptist ideas to Tirol from the west and the wives of husbands who invited local reformers like Wölfl, the goatherd turned preacher, into their homes. A few Anabaptist women were from the upper class. The Baroness, Helena von Freyberg, joined the movement in its early years and became an Anabaptist leader. The noblewoman Elisabeth von Wolkenstein became a member later but heard the Anabaptist message already in 1527. From the very beginning, wives were always present and many chose to be baptized in the same way as their husbands. Chapter One provides a context for some of these early participants.

The majority of Anabaptist women were married. In the medieval time period the most acceptable form for women's piety had been the celibate life. That changed in the Reformation with the overthrow of the celibate ethic. However, the fundamental social position of women in society did not change.[48] Married women were responsible primarily for childcare and managing the household. In most cases sixteenth century women were engaged in the same work endeavours as their husbands or fathers. "If the male head of the household was a peasant farmer, they worked on the farm; if he was a weaver or a shoemaker, they worked with him in the craft industry."[49] The tendency in the court records was to name the occupation of an Anabaptist only when the person was not a farmer.[50] For Tirol, not many occupations are indicated so we may assume the majority of the Anabaptists were engaged in farming. If their farms were larger, as was the case for a few Anabaptist families, they had several maids in addition to farm labourers. Quite a few families had at least one maid.[51] Young women often left home at age 16 or 17 to work as maids.[52] They assisted with childcare, household duties and the occupational pursuits of the family in a kind of apprenticeship system in which families basically trained each other's children.[53] Of the single women named in the records (54 between 1527 and 1529), the majority were younger women and worked as maids. At times the maids were under suspicion along with the rest of the household and at times they chose to become Anabaptists. In cases where their work separated them from their family, Anabaptism offered young single women a caring community. Anabaptist wives may have exercised "the highest calling" for a woman at that time, that of being a wife and mother, but were willing to risk life and limb as well as their families for the sake of their faith.

Women's central involvement in Anabaptism threatened the institution of the family, and indeed some women left their children behind when they were forced to flee. Others joined the movement on their own, without their husbands or, adult daughters joined with their mothers or brothers or with other members of their household if they were maids. The persecution affected everyone, women as much as men. Often the members of one's family were the first group to be evangelized. In some families this strengthened the family ties, but in others it caused division.[54]

For women who were pregnant there was the additional fear of death in childbirth. Their physical condition may have heightened their concerns for their souls and attracted them to Anabaptism. As a rule, the trials of pregnant women were postponed until they had given birth. However, those Anabaptist women whose actions merited greater punishment had to spend their pregnancy in prison. Chapter Four includes a discussion of pregnant Anabaptist women.

In order to discuss the choices which Anabaptist women made, four categories of direct participation were used with the following results. The majority of the female Anabaptist members were believers, the next largest group were martyrs and the smallest number were lay missioners and lay leaders. Women categorized as Indirect Participants were only involved in the movement indirectly and it is not clear if they had been baptized. Indirect Participants were named and at times arrested because members of their family were Anabaptists or because they were sympathizers and gave assistance to members of the movement. The index of this book lists each woman's involvement by category and includes 418 women's names. Numbers do not tell the whole story, but without a doubt, whatever role women had in Anabaptism, their participation was crucial in making it possible for the new religious movement to take root. As the Quaker historian Roland Bainton has said, if women had boycotted religious reform, there wouldn't have been a Reformation.[55]

The names and stories of sixteenth century Anabaptist women need broader recognition and need to be more widely available. All "believers' church" denominations such as "present-day Mennonites, Hutterites, Amish, and some groups of Brethren, such as the Mennonite Brethren, the Church of the Brethren and the Brethren in Christ"[56] as well as Baptist denominations have their roots in Anabaptism. In the widely used traditional source for the history of Anabaptist women, the *Martyrs' Mirror*, first published in the seventeenth century, one third of the Anabaptist martyrs are women – a high percentage given the patriarchal society of that time and compared to other religious groups. Among Reformed martyrs only six percent were female.[57] But the martyr accounts, written to edify the next generation of believers, were mainly from the Netherlands and

Includes only three Anabaptist women from Tirol.[58] Hence, the purpose of this book is first of all, to name each of the individual women involved in this movement, including unnamed women who do not appear in Mecenseffy's index[59] and secondly, to bring to light some untold stories of women who were believers, martyrs, lay missioners and lay leaders in the Austrian Anabaptist movement.

A Word About the Sources

By August 1527, Ferdinand had issued his first general mandate or decree against all Protestants, intended to root out dissent. This led to severe persecution for all Anabaptists, including women. Women's experiences as revealed in the Anabaptist court records, or *Täuferakten* as they are called in German, are translated in this book from the archival documents collected, summarized and transcribed by Grete Mecenseffy and published in 1972 (see note 1 above). Mecenseffy's work is of great significance since Tirol was different from other German-speaking regions. In Tirol, the Reformation took shape through Anabaptism which quickly became a popular, grassroots movement.[60]

The actions taken by the government to suppress the heretical sect of Anabaptism are clearly documented in the Anabaptist court records of Tirol. They are descriptive sources which recount the actual behaviour of women and the reality of women's lives, unlike sources which prescribed how women ideally were supposed to act. In contrast to the *Martyrs' Mirror*, these records are "outsider" sources, describing the Anabaptist movement as seen by those in power. As such they provide information about many more women than the *Martyrs' Mirror* since the enemies of the Anabaptists were interested in every single person who was in any way involved in this outlawed, heretical sect. The court records do not just tell the story of the martyrs. They include information about Anabaptists who chose to recant, about those who rejoined the movement, about those who fled and those who escaped. As "transcriptions of legal proceedings and actions taken against Anabaptists,"[61] the court records are a more detailed and objective source of information than the *Martyrs' Mirror*, although they lack some of the first person confessional types of testaments from imprisoned believers.

The court records consist of reports about Anabaptist confessions, directives and letters of instruction from Ferdinand I to his officials in the central government of the territory located in Innsbruck and, from himself and his officials to the local authorities in the different districts of the territory of Tirol.[62] They give instructions on the treatment of Anabaptist women and men who had been arrested and had given statements or confessions and, about those suspected of Anabaptism who should be investigated. Mecenseffy summarized the majority of these court records in modern German writing in the past tense. In some cases she included a print version of the original, handwritten documents, written for the most part in the present tense, exactly as they would have been sent to the local officials. These original archival documents usually provide more details than Mecenseffy's summaries, even though they present their own challenges of sixteenth century sentence structure and vocabulary.

After arrest, at their first hearing, Anabaptist prisoners were required to make a statement or confession[63] to the government. Then they had to decide whether to recant and renounce their Anabaptist faith in order to save their lives and be reinstated in the traditional church.[64] The Appendix includes an example of the questions used in interrogations. Many Anabaptists, including women, chose to recant as a means of staying alive. Recantation was not held against them by fellow believers. At their first arrest most Anabaptists were treated moderately. However, if they recanted, went back to their fellow believers and were caught a second time, they could expect a trial in the criminal court with a jury, chosen from among prominent local citizens, and a death sentence.[65] The court records are a key source of information for recanters and those who "relapsed" and rejoined the movement.[66] The details of the short, private form as well as the long, public form of recantation are discussed in Chapter Two. In most cases, before being tried in the criminal court, Anabaptists were required to confirm their initial confession. At times the interrogation of Anabaptist women and men included torture, especially if it was their second arrest. Chapter Three includes an overview of this aspect of Anabaptist treatment. Moreover, Anabaptists who fled or were executed forfeited their property and possessions to the government. "Anabaptist property was heretic-property and by ancient right fell to the fisc, the royal treasury."[67] Thus, the court records of 1530 and 1531 include a number of inventories of confiscated Anabaptist properties. They provide insight into the social, family and economic status of the Anabaptists in Tirol during this time. Chapter Four includes the main discussion of these records.

Finally, although there are many similarities in the treatment of Anabaptists in the different districts throughout the territory, there are often differences as well, depending on the place where an Anabaptist lived and the will of the authorities governing there. Each case is somewhat different from the rest depending on what the Anabaptist woman decided and on the attitude of the authorities dealing with her. These attitudes also changed over time. When Ferdinand saw that the Anabaptists were not afraid of death he changed his strategy. In various proceedings during 1529, the government sought to bring them back to the traditional church through the persuasion and instruction of knowledgeable priests, in large measure to no avail. When the opportunity arose to emigrate to Moravia where the rulers were more tolerant, many Anabaptists left Tirol.

Government officials were fully aware that women were no less involved than men in the Anabaptist movement. The many arrests of women as well as the high percentage of Anabaptist women who were executed, attest to their equal involvement. In sixteenth century Austria, a woman could not legally speak in court on civil matters. A male guardian had to speak on her behalf. But in matters of criminal law and in capital crimes, including heresy, women *had* to speak for themselves.[68] A number of times, as in the mandate of April 4, 1528, local authorities were instructed to question each person individually since each one of these persons had made their own choice to be baptized. A government directive of February 1, 1528 stated that the Anabaptists were "to recant publicly each with their own mouth, confessing their mistake."[69]

Like all sources, these court records have limitations in that the stories are usually not complete. It can be assumed that when an order for execution was issued by the criminal court, which made decisions in capital crimes and had the right to issue death sentences, it would have been carried out. But, information is not always available on whether the government directives were carried out and on how each case ended. Furthermore, in these sources, male court secretaries recorded women's experiences within the patriarchal framework of the time. Considering this context, the number of women named and the information about their active involvement in Anabaptism was above the norm and indeed unusual. Whether there is only a line or two or whether there are several references to a woman's story, the court records provide valuable snapshots of women's involvement in the early Anabaptist movement of Tirol that we otherwise would not have. Conversations at the town well, "around the spinning wheel or the table of an inn do not survive as historical records." However fragmentary the stories in the court records may seem, they provide "a substantial written legacy…. (and) represent the tip of the proverbial iceberg."[70] Mecenseffy's volume of Anabaptist court records is just one of three for Austria and one of over 30 such volumes that have been published in German in recent years for different parts of Europe. The social historian Claus-Peter Clasen, who in the 1970s listed every Anabaptist in southern Europe by name, stated:

> We are better informed about the outlawed Anabaptist sect than any other religious movement of the sixteenth century…. The wealth of Anabaptist material permits us to study many problems to which the material on the Lutheran movement does not lend itself.[71]

The court records are indeed a unique source of information on the lower classes and especially on the role of women in a religious movement. They allow us to study the choices made by women in detail. These records lend themselves to an in-depth, systematic regional study such as the author undertook in the late 1980s. The translations and discussions in this book are based on that study and research done since then. The court records then illustrate the breadth as well as the depth of women's participation in the early years of the Austrian Anabaptist movement.

Format of the book

The Anabaptist court records are dated and organized chronologically, making it possible to present the history of Anabaptist women by the days of the year on which their cases were discussed. The stories of Anabaptist women are presented in this book in the form of key passages translated from the German court records word for word, with brief explanations in brackets where necessary. The translations are in italics. The information added to the translations in block letters make the stories more complete. The titles of the translated passages impart the main idea of the women's experiences. For Anabaptist women where less information is available, their stories are summarized briefly also using block letters.

In the majority of cases the date associated with a woman's name is the first time she is mentioned in these court records. For some women, their story is told under several dates. The stories are organized chronologically within each of the five years, 1527 to 1531, the documents for which are in Mecenseffy's 1972 volume of court records. This is when Anabaptism took root in Tirol and when the persecution was severe. Introductions to each of the five years provide overviews of the events in each year, highlight changes in the treatment of Anabaptists and offer a context for the experiences of the women. Discussions on various themes round out the chapters. The illustrations provide valuable historical information and assist in visualizing the life and times of Anabaptist women in sixteenth century Tirol.

The Challenge Today

Ironically, the persecution that brought difficulty and pain to Anabaptist women in the sixteenth century, is a rich source of information for us today about their choices, activities and religious faith. It is difficult for us to imagine a time without the religious toleration we enjoy at present in the western world. Recently, the Pope was given a copy of the *Martyrs' Mirror* when Mennonites from ten countries discussed Christian unity with Catholic officials in Rome during October 18-23, 2007. This invitation followed from international dialogue between Mennonite World Conference and the Pontifical Council for Promoting Christian Unity "which took place from 1998-03 and resulted in the 48-page report, 'Called Together to be Peacemakers.'"[72] After five years the dialogue ended "with mutual expressions of repentance. The Catholic representatives expressed regret for the violence that members of the Catholic Church were involved in during the time of the Reformation."[73] It is a positive sign that, "Catholic

Church leaders desire dialogue with Mennonites…."⁷⁴ and will meet together again in the near future.

In the recent past, a number of reconciliation events have taken place in which Protestants have apologized to descendants of the Anabaptists for the persecution of the sixteenth century. One such event took place in southern Germany in 2001 led by the Lutheran "Dean" (*Dekan*) of Passau, Herr Strohm.⁷⁵ A time of reconciliation took place, in Zurich, Switzerland in May 2003 at a conference attended by more than 800 people including Reformed pastors and lay persons, Amish, Mennonites and Anabaptists from many countries in Europe as well as Canada.⁷⁶ Perhaps the largest event of this nature took place in September 2007. "Site of martyrdom 450 years ago, Trachselwald welcomed 10,000 worshippers in open air as part of the Swiss government's Year of the Anabaptists." On the grounds of this castle in the Emmental Valley, leaders and members of the State Reformed Church, the Free Church and Anabaptist churches together "… celebrated forgiveness outside this symbol of state oppression."⁷⁷ Between 2001 and 2008 at least eight various reconciliation events have taken place between the Reformed Church and Mennonites. On April 13, 2008, a group of visitors from the Swiss Reformed Church made a public apology for persecution in times past to the Mennonites in Filadelfia, in the Chaco of Paraguay.⁷⁸

In 2012 Lutherans and Mennonites celebrated a reconciliation in Augsburg, Germany similar to the one which had taken place in Stuttgart, Germany in 2010. When the Mennonite World Conference executive committee met in Augsburg in February 2017 they gave incentive for many more such observances to take place by initiating a decade for remembrance and renewal worldwide, "Renewal 2027."⁷⁹

In some parts of the world, however, neither reconciliation nor toleration are on the horizon. The older story is not finished. It continues today, in every place where Christian men and women are still persecuted and in every place where the Christian underground church flourishes. Since August 2008, violence has flared up again and Christians in the state of Orissa, India and in Nepal have been under attack.⁸⁰ A Canadian newspaper reported that Christians, both Protestant and Catholic, were being persecuted in Communist China during preparations to host the

Olympic games in Beijing. Especially targeted were members of the Protestant House Church Movement "who meet in private residences so they are not subject to the rules of the government." Pictured were nuns at prayer with the caption: "In an attempt to scare ordinary Christians, China is imprisoning church leaders...."[81] The house churches in Hmong villages in Vietnam still practice night baptisms to avoid detection by the authorities as did the sixteenth century Anabaptists.[82] In discussing "our spiritual ancestors" Walter Klaassen writes, that in places like Vietnam where Mennonite Christians today are persecuted for their faith, they "know what it was like to be Anabaptists back then."[83]

The story of Austrian Anabaptist beginnings amid severe persecution is told in this book from the point of view of the women's experiences and makes women the central focus. The history of Anabaptist women calls us to view Anabaptism in a new light. It asks the question of why there were so many Anabaptist women only in the early years. Finally, it is not just a story of persecution and suffering, but about the choices which women made concerning their religious faith. The choices and actions of sixteenth century Anabaptist women signify a faith and commitment which remain a challenge for all of us today.

Notes

1. The translations in this book are taken from Grete Mecenseffy, *Quellen zur Geschichte der Täufer XIII Band Österreich II. Teil* (Gütersloh: Gerd Mohn, 1972), hereafter: TA 1972, the page number: and the line number(s) cited, or, TA 1972, the page number, and the number of the document.

    Regarding historical memory see Adriana Valerio, "Women in Church History," in *Women, Invisible in Church and Theology*, ed. Elizabeth Schüssler Fiorenza and Mary Collins, *Concilium*, 182 (Edinburgh, T. and T. Clark, 1985), 65. Valerio states here that when women have a historical memory they no longer need to create their history and identity anew in each generation.

    For the most detailed and complete account of Austrian Anabaptism as a whole in English see Werner O. Packull, *Hutterite Beginnings Communitarian Experiments during the Reformation* (Baltimore, MD: John Hopkins University Press, 1995), hereafter, *Hutterite Beginnings*. For the German edition see Werner O. Packull, trans. by Astrid von Schlachta, *Hutterer in Tirol: Frühes Täufertum in der Schweiz, Tirol und Mähren*, (Innsbruck: Universitätsverlag Wagner, 2000).

2. Packull, *Hutterite Beginnings*, 164. The administrative districts were called "Gerichte."

3. Johann Loserth, and Robert Friedmann, "Tyrol (Austria)," in *Global Anabaptist Mennonite Encyclopedia Online* (1959), at www.gameo.org, 1.

    In this book "Tirol" not "Tyrol" will be used.

4. See C. Arnold Snyder, *Anabaptist History and Theology An Introduction* (Kitchener, ON: Pandora Press, 1995), 12-13.
5. Regarding the debate on baptism and the biblical references see Snyder, *Anabaptist History and Theology An Introduction*, 54-55. "... the Anabaptists were among the first to make the (Great) Commission binding upon all church members." Franklin Hamlin Littell, *The Origins of Sectarian Protestantism, a Study of the Anabaptist View of the Church* (New York: Macmillan, 1964), 112.
6. In earlier times, Justinian's legal code had ruled re-baptism to be heretical. See Snyder, *Anabaptist History and Theology An Introduction*, 1. See also reference in TA 1972, 87:36-44 to the medieval constitution of Friedrich II.
7. The Anabaptists were executed by Protestant and Catholic rulers alike, the exception being Philipp of Hesse in central Germany.
8. Ferdinand became the first Archduke of Austria when his older brother Charles V, who became Holy Roman Emperor in 1519 "entrusted him with the government of the Habsburg hereditary lands" including Tirol in 1521. See Wikipedia contributors, "Ferdinand I, Holy Roman Emperor," *Wikipedia, The Free Encyclopedia,* 15 March 2008, 18:40 UTC, <http://en.wikipedia.org/w/index.php?title=Ferdinand_I%2C_Holy_Roman_Emperor&oldid=198455087 and also, Grete Mecenseffy, Robert Friedmann and Richard D. Thiessen, "Ferdinand I, Holy Roman Emperor (1503-1564)," *Global Anabaptist Mennonite Encyclopedia Online* (2007), at www.gameo.org /encyclopedia/contents/F467.html.
9. Mary T. Malone, *Women and Christianity* (Ottawa: Novalis, 2003), Vol. III, 35. "Religious fervor, not apathy or indifference, fueled alienation from the church...." *Hutterite Beginnings*, 168.
10. Snyder, *Anabaptist History and Theology An Introduction,* 1.
11. *Hutterite Beginnings*, 201. Zaunring used the words "zum Zeichen und Gedächtnis."
12. See "Schleitheim Confession (Anabaptist, 1527)" and there Article VII. "The Lord's Supper shall be held, as often as the brothers are together," in *Global Anabaptist Mennonite Encyclopedia Online* (1527), at www.gameo.org. In her discussion of the first Anabaptist congregations in Tirol, Astrid von Schlachta describes an Anabaptist meeting in Welsperg, in the Puster Valley in May 1529 led by Jacob Hutter. She also lists Anabaptist beliefs and on the list is, "... das Abendmahl unter beiderlei Gestalt" (the Lord's Supper in both kinds). At this meeting then, persons were baptized and participated in the Lord's Supper, partaking of both the bread and the wine. See her book, *Die Hutterer zwischen Tirol und Amerika Eine Reise durch die Jahrhunderte* (Innsbruck: Universitätsverlag Wagner, 2005), 15.
13. The phrase "honest fanatic" comes from the Austrian historian, Wolfgang Lassmann. Packull, *Hutterite Beginnings*, 188.
14. In German the passage reads, "Erging dabei von der Überzeugung aus, er sei als Landesfürst Gott für seine Untertanen verantwortlich, und zwar nicht nur für ihr leibliches Wohl,

sondern er habe, wie es in einem am 1 September 1524 erlassenen Mandat heisst, dafür zu sorgen, dass *den underthanen under verwandten seelen heil zu güt das heilig Evangelium und ander götlich schrifft* ordentlich verkündigt werde." Thomas Winkelbauer, "Die Rechtliche Stellung der Täufer im 16. und 17. Jahrhundert am Beispiel der habsburgischen Länder," in *Ein Thema—zwei Perspektiven Juden und Christen in Mittelalter und Frühneuzeit* (Innsbruck: Studienverlag, 2007), 37. I am grateful to Dr. Ellinor Forster of the Institute of History and Ethnology in Innsbruck for making me aware of this article.

15. Gerald Strauss, *Law, Resistance, and the State, The Opposition to Roman Law in Reformation Germany* (Princeton, NJ: Princeton University Press, 1986), 268.
16. Walter Klaassen, *Michael Gaismair: Revolutionary and Reformer* (Leiden: E. J. Brill, 1978), 4-5.
17. *Ibid.*, 56-70.
18. The legal basis for the sixteenth century laws against heretics on which Ferdinand based his mandate of August 1527 was the Edict of Worms, issued by Charles V against Luther and his followers after the Pope banned Luther as a heretic when he refused to recant. Imperial laws against the Anabaptists were passed in 1529 at the Diet in Speyer. See Winkelbauer, "Die Rechtliche Stellung der Täufer," 36-37.
19. Discussion of the first three years was done in Linda Huebert Hecht, "Faith and Action: The Role of Women in the Anabaptist Movement of the Tirol, 1527-1529" (unpublished Cognate Essay, Master of Arts, History, University of Waterloo, 1990), 144 p. A limited qualitative analysis was done which confirmed Max Weber's hypothesis for Anabaptist women in Tirol. The Data Base on which the Cognate Essay was based included information from the court records of 1527 to 1529 in TA 1972. The author later expanded this Data Base to include all the records from TA 1972. It now consists of over 400 profiles of Austrian Anabaptist women in: "Data Base on Anabaptist Women in Tirol, 1527-1531" hereafter, Data Base. This book completes the author's study of TA 1972. The figures and percentages mentioned above have increased now that the 1531 volume is complete.

   Some of the author's other articles not included in the notes of this book are: "Finding Connections: Reflections on the lives of 16th Century Anabaptist Women," *Sophia*, 7, 2 (Spring 1997), 12-13; "Anabaptist Women: Faith Hidden Until the Time of Harvest," *Sophia*, 9, 3 (Fall 1999), 8-9; "Helena von Freyberg Woman of Noble and Spiritual Stature," *Profiles of Mennonite Faith* church bulletin insert series, 22 (Winter 2003), Mennonite Brethren Historical Commission, available at www.mbhistory.org; "Review of the Literature on Women in the Reformation and Radical Reformation" 406-15, in C. Arnold Snyder and Linda A. Huebert Hecht, eds., *Profiles of Anabaptist Women Sixteenth-Century Reforming Pioneers* (Waterloo, ON: Wilfrid Laurier Press, 1996), 438p. Sixth impression 2002, hereafter, *Profiles of Anabaptist Women*.
20. The author calculated the forty-six percent based on data in Claus-Peter Clasen, *Anabaptism A Social History, 1525-1618 Switzerland, Austria, Moravia, South and Central Germany* (Ithaca:

Cornell University Press, 1972), 21. Clasen's Table 2 lists 455 Anabaptists for Tirol using 1529 as the cutoff point. The author found a total of 268 women named in the 1972 records between 1526 and 1529. After deducting the women categorized as indirect participants and those named by Leonard Schiemer on January 12, 1528 most of whom were not from Tirol, the number of female members in Tirol, 210, was compared to Clasen's number of Anabaptist men and women (210 divided by 455 x 100= 46). A percentage for the number of women compared to men for the five years of records in 1972 court records, 1527 to 1531, is difficult to calculate since Clasen does not take 1531 as a cutoff.

21. Linda Huebert Hecht, "Women and religious change: The significance of Anabaptist women in the Tirol, 1527-29," in *Studies in Religion*, 21, 1 (1992), 61.
22. Harold S. Bender, "Women, Status of," in *Mennonite Encyclopedia* (Scottdale, PA: Herald Press, 1959), IV, 972. See also, Marilyn G. Peters, "Women," *Mennonite Encyclopedia* (Scottdale, PA: Herald Press, 1990), V, 933.
23. *Hutterite Beginnings*, 2.
24. Weber stated that: "The religion of the disprivileged classes,...is characterized by a tendency to allot equality to women....The great receptivity of women to all religious prophecy except that which is exclusively military or political in orientation comes to a very clear expression in the completely unconstrained relationships with women maintained by practically all prophets, the Buddha as well as Christ and Pythagoras. But only in very rare cases does this practice continue beyond the first stage of a religious community's formation, when the pneumatic manifestations of charisma are valued as hallmarks of specifically religious exaltation. Thereafter, as routinization and regimentation of community relationships set in, a reaction takes place against pneumatic manifestations among women, which come to be regarded as dishonourable and morbid. In Christianity this appears already with Paul." Max Weber, *The Sociology of Religion,* trans. by Ephraim Fischoff (Boston: Beacon Press, 1922), 104, 105.
25. Some have disagreed with Bender and Weber. The social historian Claus-Peter Clasen, surveyed more Swiss and South German Anabaptist records than any historian of his generation. Clasen described the different stages of Anabaptism, with 1529 as the end of the early phase, yet stated "...the sect showed no inclination to grant women a greater role than they customarily had in sixteenth century society." See, *Anabaptism A Social History,* 207. In Joyce L. Irwin, *Womanhood in Radical Protestantism 1525-1675* (New York: E. Mellen, 1979), xvii, using prescriptive sources, Irwin concluded that the religious status of women did not change until the 17th century Quaker movement. More recently James M. Stayer discusses the different phases in: "The Passing of the Radical Moment in the Radical Reformation," in *Mennonite Quarterly Review* LXXI, 1 (January, 1997), 149, whereas Sigrun Haude argues against a preponderance of women leaders in the early years in, "Anabaptist Women—Radical Women?" in *Infinite Boundaries, Order, Disorder and Reorder in Early Modern German Culture* ed., Max Reinhart (Kirksville, MO: Sixteenth Century Journal Publishers, Inc., 1998), 9.

26. Four of these leaders were from the neighbouring territory of Styria. All the rest were from Tirol.
27. These profiles discuss over fifty women and cover all the developmental stages of Anabaptism.
28. Linda A. Huebert Hecht, "A Brief Moment in Time: Informal Leadership and Shared Authority Among Sixteenth Century Anabaptist Women," in *Journal of Mennonite Studies*, 17 (1999), 52-74.
29. Ernest W. McDonnell, *The Beguines and Beghards in Medieval Culture* (New York, NY: Octagon Books, 1969), 126, n. 81, 197.
30. Emmanuel LeRoy Ladurie, *Mountaillou, The Promised Land of Error*, trans. Barbara Bray (New York: Vintage Books, 1978); Gottfried Koch, *Frauenfrage und Ketzertum im Mittelalter: die Frauenbewegung im Rahmen des Katharismus und des Waldensertums und ihre sozialen Wurzeln* (Berlin: Akademie Verlag, 1962), 159; Shulamith Shaher, *The Fourth Estate A History of Women in the Middle Ages*, trans. by Chaya Galai (New York: Methuen, 1983), 258; Richard Kieckhefer, *Repression of Heresy in Medieval Germany* (Philadelphia: University of Pennsylvania Press, 1979), 111. Penny Shine Gold, "Male/Female Cooperation: The Example of Fontevrault," in *Distant Echoes, Medieval Religious Women Volume One*, ed., John A. Nichols and Lillian Thomas Shank (Kalamzoo, MI: Cistercian Publications Inc., 1984), 151-168; Robert E. Lerner, *The Heresy of the Free Spirit in the Later Middle Ages* (Berkeley: University of California Press, 1972), 230, n. 7.
31. The Lollards and Hussites had many female members. See Susan Stuard, "The Dominion of Gender: Women's Fortunes in the High Middle Ages," in *Becoming Visible, Women in European History*, 2nd ed., ed. by Renate Bridenthal, Claudia Koonz, Susan Stuard, (Boston: Houghton Mifflin, 1987), 168. Claire Cross, "'Great Reasoners in Scripture': the Activities of Women Lollards 1380-1530," in *Medieval Women*, ed. by Derek Baker (Oxford: Basil Blackwell, 1978).
32. Martin H. Jung, *Frauen des Pietismus, Zehn Porträts* (Gütersloh: Gütersloher Verlagshaus, 1998), 9.
33. "During the movement's first decades, Quakers urged and enacted their experience of salvation in a highly public arena – in streets, marketplaces, churches, fields, and prisons – and they did this through flamboyant public gestures: symbolic signs, charismatic preaching, and martyrdom. By the final years of the century, after decades of systematic persecution.... Their public behaviour, now subjected to the moral discipline of recognized elders and ministers, became sober and restrained." Phyllis Mack, *Visionary Women Ecstatic Prophecy in Seventeenth-Century England* (Berkeley: University of California Press, 1992), 1-2.
34. Elizabeth Gillan Muir, *Petticoats in the Pulpit The Story of Nineteenth-Century Methodist Women Preachers in Upper Canada* (Toronto, ON: The United Church Publishing House, 1991), 30; Marilyn Färdig Whiteley, "Modest, Unaffected, and Fully Consecrated: Lady Evangelists in Canadian Methodism," in Elizabeth Gillan Muir and Marilyn Färdig Whiteley, eds.

Changing Roles of Women within the Christian Church in Canada (Toronto, ON: University of Toronto Press, 1995), 195-96.

35. Marilyn Färdig Whiteley, "Deaconess Redefined: Seeking a Role for Women in the Holiness Churches of Ralph Horner," in *Historical Papers 1999 The Canadian Society of Church History,* Annual Conference Bishop's University, 3-4 June 1999, 73 ed. by Bruce L. Guenther.
36. Gillan Muir and Färdig Whiteley, *Women within the Christian Church in Canada,* 5-8.
37. Rosemary Ruether and Eleanor McLaughlin, eds., *Women of Spirit, Female Leadership in the Jewish and Christian Traditions* (New York, NY: Simon and Schuster, 1979), 20.
38. Of the Waldensians Shulamith Shahar states, "The granting of rights to women in their religious communities was not a central objective of the Waldenses. Rather, it was part of their general broadening of the rights of the laity, their narrowing of the gap between it and the priesthood, and their rejection of the Church hierarchy – all of this relying on Scriptural authority…. Such a group needs the support of all its members, and this precipitates the collapse not only of class divisions but also of divisions between the sexes." See her book, *The Fourth Estate A History of Women in the Middle Ages,* trans. by Chaya Galai (New York: Methuen, 1983), 258. This is also true for women in England. See Keith Thomas, "Women in the Civil War Sects," *Past and Present,* 13 (1958). In her article "Radical Women," 318, Sigrun Haude states that because of the persecution of Anabaptists women remained "essential and much needed."
39. See Peter Segl, *Ketzer in Oesterreich, Untersuchungen ueber Haeresie und Inquisition im Herzogtum Oesterreich im 13. und beginnenden 14. Jahrhundert* (Paderborn: Ferdinand Schoeningh, 1984), 169, 279 and Paul P. Bernard, "Heresy in Fourteenth Century Austria," *Medievalia et Humanistica* 10 (1956), 59, 60-62.
40. Shahar, *The Fourth Estate,* 256.
41. "As early as 1495 pressure arose for chaplains to read the Gospel in the vernacular. At the same time, local communities sought control over clerical appointments and demanded that the tithe be used for local services." There was a general "crisis in the lower clergy…. For a variety of reasons … the established church … seemed unable to meet the growing spiritual need and religious fervor in the generation before the Reformation." See *Hutterite Beginnings,* 168 for more details on the lack of spiritual care for the common people.
42. In discussing the Protestant women Argula von Grumbach and Katharina Zell who were concerned about reform in the church, Wiesner states, "Women challenged this division between private and public. They argued that the Spirit had indeed given them the right to address public religious matters or else that there simply was no basis for division between public and private in matters of religion." Merry E. Wiesner, "Women's Defense of Their Public Role," in *Women in the Middle Ages and the Renaissance,* ed. by Mary Beth Rose (Syracuse, NY: Syracuse University Press, 1986), 3, 21.
43. C. Arnold Snyder, "Introduction," in *Profiles of Anabaptist Women,* 3.

44. Lois Y. Barrett, "Ursula Jost and Barbara Rebstock of Strasbourg," in *Profiles of Anabaptist Women*, 273-287.
45. Haude, "Radical Women," 318-19.
46. See Robert Friedmann, "Leonard Schiemer," *Global Anabaptist Mennonite Encyclopedia Online* (1959), at www.gameo.org.
47. TA 1972, 89:26-27.
48. "As long as celibacy was regarded as the preferable state, women, by inference, occupied not only a secondary position but could easily be seen as an evil force, the temptation which threatened every man's salvation." See Miriam U. Chrisman, "Women and the Reformation in Strasbourg 1490-1530," in *Archive for Reformation History*, 63 (1972), 166.
49. Linda A. Huebert Hecht, "Speaking up and Taking Risks Anabaptist Family and Household Roles in Sixteenth-Century Tirol," in *Strangers at Home Amish and Mennonite Women in History*, ed. by Kimberly D. Schmidt, Diane Zimmerman Umble, Steven D. Reschly (Baltimore, MD: The John Hopkins University Press, 2002), 239.
50. See Paul Peachey, *Die soziale Herkunft der Schweizer Taeufer in der Reformationszeit, eine religionssoziologische Untersuchung* (Karlsruhe: Heinrich Schneider, 1954), 20-21.
51. Two Anabaptist families each had two maids who are identified by way of the wife and not the male head of the household as, the Koblin's maid and the Gasserin's maid.
52. *Hutterite Beginnings*, 241. Maids were paid two Kreuzer per day. *Ibid.*, 378, n. 16. See Appendix for money values and wages.
53. Maids "were not servants in the contemporary sense of the word, but rather children of neighboring families in the same parish. Families were in effect training each other's children." See Elise Boulding, *The Underside of History: A View of Women through Time* (Boulder, CO: Westview Press, 1976), 552.
54. John S. Oyer, ed. By John D. Roth, *"They Harry the Good People Out of the Land" Essays on the Persecution, Survival and Flourishing of Anabaptists and Mennonites* (Goshen, IN: Mennonite Historical Society, 2000), 155.
55. "The women constituted a half of the population, and had they boycotted the movement, one may be sure that would have been the end." Roland Bainton, *Women of the Reformation in Germany and Italy* (Minneapolis, MN: Augsburg Publishing House, 1971), 9. Bainton's pioneering book included a chapter on the Anabaptist deaconess in the Netherlands, Elisabeth Dirks.
56. C. Arnold Snyder, "Introduction," in *Profiles of Anabaptist Women*, 2.
57. Harry Loewen, "The Role of Women in the Mennonite Brethren Church," (unpublished sermon, Elmwood Mennonite Brethren Church, Winnipeg, Manitoba, on Mother's Day, May, 1986), 7.
58. The three women from Tirol are: Ursula Hellrigel, Dorothea (Anna) Maler and Anna (Ursula) Ochsentreiber. See Thieleman J. van Braght, *The Martyrs' Mirror 1660*, trans. by Joseph F. Sohm (Scottdale Pa.: Herald Press, eight edition 1968), 437, 466-67.

59. Mecenseffy's index of names in TA 1972 was used by the author to work through the court records chronologically and enter profiles for each Anabaptist woman into the Data Base. In cases where a woman's name was not stated, the letters n.n. meaning "no name" and the page on which she is first mentioned in the TA 1972, were used in the Data Base for her name. This was done in order to recognize every woman involved in Anabaptism in these records, even those not named in the index of TA 1972. For example, the entry of January 26, 1529 with the title "An Unnamed Woman Condemned, Disparaged the Sacrament" tells the story of an unnamed woman in Rattenberg baptized by Leonard Schiemer who spoke unseemingly and with scornful words about the sacrament and who was to be tried in the criminal court. This woman is designated as n.n.190, woman/schiemer. There are 58 unnamed women with such designations in this book. The use of "n.n." for unnamed persons was introduced by Claus-Peter Clasen.
60. "Unlike in other German-speaking territories Anabaptism in the Tyrol came to represent the major Reform orientation, and after its demise no popular alternative emerged." *Hutterite Beginnings*, 161.
61. Huebert Hecht, "Speaking Up and Taking Risks," 241.
62. Ferdinand's court was not always in Innsbruck. It was located in different places at different times. For a discussion and a list of the decrees issued in the Holy Roman Empire against Protestants and Anabaptists see Christian Hege and N. van der Zijpp, "Mandates," in *Mennonite Encyclopedia*, (Scottdale, PA: Mennonite Publishing House, 1957), III, 446-448. For an older but still useful article on Anabaptism in Tirol see, Loserth, and Friedmann, "Tyrol (Austria)," at www.gameo.org.
63. The word in the records is "Urgicht." It was a "Geständnis" meaning an avowal or confession.
64. Recantation was a traditional right, as was stated in the decree of April 1, 1528, "nach alter, cristenlichen ordnung." See TA 1972, 101:33-34.
65. In the court records the criminal court is called "Hochgericht." The word "Malefizrecht" referred to the "hohe Recht" or "Blutrecht" meaning the right to pronounce the death sentence. Only certain judges had this special authority to rule in cases of capital crime such as heresy and to administer capital punishment. *Hutterite Beginnings*, 166. By contrast, the lower courts or "Niedergerichte," authorized in tasks related to civil authority, could arrest people under suspicion of criminal acts and conduct a preliminary hearing. Then the person had to be transferred to the appropriate territorial judge. See Ellinor Forster, "Verfolgung und Vertreibung—ein Blick ins frühneuzeitliche Rechtsystem," in Astrid von Schlachta, Ellinor Forster, Giovanni Merola, eds., *Verbrannte Visionen? Erinnerungorte der Täufer in Tirol* (Innsbruck: Innsbruck University Press, 2007), 21. "Canon law has always forbidden clerics to shed human blood and therefore capital punishment has always been the work of the officials of the State and not of the Church." See the *Catholic Encyclopedia* at www.newadvent.org/cathen.12565a.htm. See also, TA 1972, 370:2-3; 27-31.

66. "In some regions, especially where capital punishment for religious error prevailed (Hapsburg lands, central Germany), recanters numbered well over 50 percent of the Anabaptists who appeared in court. In other regions, often where exile was the unofficial but ultimate form of punishment (Strasbourg, some other south German cities, Hesse), the percentage of recanters was much lower." John S. Oyer, "Recantation," in *Global Anabaptist Mennonite Encyclopedia Online* (1989), at www.gameo.org.
67. Grete Mecenseffy, "Anabaptists in Kitzbühel," in *Mennonite Quarterly Review*, XLVI, 2 (April 1972), trans. by Elizabeth Bender from German in *Stadtbuch Kitzbühel*, IV (Kitzbühel, 1971), 105.
68. Merry E. Wiesner, "Frail, Weak, and Helpless: Women's Legal Position in Theory and Reality," in *Regnum, Religio et Ratio: Essays presented to Robert M. Kingdon*, ed. by Jerome Friedman (Kirksville, MO: Sixteenth Century Publishers, 1987), 161, 162.
69. TA 1972, 118:14-15. Another example is in TA 1972, 68:6-7.
70. C. Arnold Snyder, "Introduction," in *Profiles of Anabaptist Women*, 7, 8.
71. Claus-Peter Clasen, "The Sociology of Swabian Anabaptism," *Church History*, XXXII (1963), 150. Stayer called Clasen's new, quantitative approach, "the major research achievement of twentieth-century Anabaptist Studies." See James M. Stayer, "The Anabaptists," in Steven Ozment, ed., *Reformation Europe: A Guide to Research* (St. Louis: Center for Reformation Research, 1982), 143.
72. Ferne Burkhardt, "Dialoguing with the pope," in *Canadian Mennonite*, Nov. 26, 2007, 11, 23, 16. In the same issue see, Helmut Harder, "Affirmations and concerns, A personal reflection on meetings with the pope and Catholic officials to discuss Christian unity," 17. See also, "Pope greets Mennonites: a first in church history," in *Mennonite Brethren Herald*, December 2007, 46, 12, 8 and "Mennonite-Catholic dialogues, MWC delegation receives warm welcome in Rome," in *Courier* 22, 4 (2007), 10-11.
73. This final statement in the Introduction continues: "The Mennonites confessed that they have not done all they could to overcome divisions within or to work toward unity with other brothers and sisters. Together, Catholics and Mennonites expressed regret that sixteenth century divisions occurred, and that divisions have lasted to this day. The words of the title of the final report ... present a challenge to both Mennonites and Catholics to face a new future in a spirit of mutual respect and cooperation." Willard Roth, Gerald W. Schlabach, *Called Together to be Peacemakers Report of the International Dialogue between the Catholic Church and Mennonite World Conference 1998-2003*, Abridged ed. In The Bridgefolk Series (Kitchener, ON: Pandora Press, 2005), 14-15. The Introduction also states, "The group found that studying history together often led to a 'purification of memory' whereby false perceptions and interpretations are discarded in a search for common ground." Also, "... Catholics and Mennonites share a common commitment to peace and peacemaking." *Ibid.*, 13, 14.
74. Burkhardt, "Dialoguing with the pope," 18. The article, "German Mennonites, Catholics see common ground in peace" in *Courier* 22, 4 (2007): 10 describes another response to

the 48 page report at a conference in Hamburg, Germany, "Healing of memories," September (2007): 21-22.
75. In researching the family of Helena Baroness (*Freifrau*) von Freyberg, Anabaptist noblewoman from sixteenth century Tirol, the author made contact with Dr. Pankraz Baron (*Freiherr*) von Freyberg of Passau, Germany who carries the same name as Helena's son and has relatives in common with her husband. Dr. Pankraz suggested contact with Herr Strohm, head of the Passau Deanery (*Dekanat*) a church administrative district, who was interested in Anabaptist research.
76. See *Glimpses* #201: "In Switzerland and America, A 500-Year Wound That Had to be Healed" on the website of the Christian History Institute at: <http://chi.gospelcom.net/GLIMPSEF/Glimpses2/glimpses201.shtml>
77. Dale D. Gehman with files from Brian Doerksen, "Swiss churches reconcile Brian Doerksen witness to historic forgiveness," in *Mennonite Brethren Herald*, November 2007, 46, 11, 21. Geri Keller, instrumental during the past five years in reconciliation between the Reformed Church and Anabaptists spoke, as well as Paul Veraguth, pastor in the State Reformed Church. "Canadian musician Brian Doerksen was one of the worship leaders." Dale D. Gehman, "In the shadow of Trachselwald Swiss of all denominations gather to celebrate the Year of the Anabaptists and focus on Jesus' Sermon on the Mount," in *Canadian Mennonite*, Oct. 15, 2007, 11, 20, 16.
78. See Victor Wall, "Beugungsgottesdienst in Filadelfia Hinführung aus geschichtlicher Perspektive," in *Mennoblatt*, 1 Mai, 2008, 79, 9, 3 where Wall states that eight events took place in the last seven years. This issue includes articles on this event by Theodor Unruh, Wolfgang Krauss and Korny Neufeld.
79. Wolfgang Krauss, "Die andere Reformation – Eine Veranstaltungsreihe in Augsburg," in *Mennonitische Geschichtsblätter*, 2017, 74, 164-166.
80. This information is from Brethren in Christ missionaries located there. Earlier reports stated the following. "A series of Hindu extremist attacks beginning Christmas Eve in Orissa state's Kandhamal district made 2007 the most violent on record for Christians, with more than 800 incidents reported throughout the year." "Persecution of Christians high in 2007," in *Mennonite Brethren Herald*, February 2008, 47, 2, 16. See notes on persecution in China, Eritrea, Nigeria and Laos in the same article.
81. Charles Lewis, "Christians under the gun, Olympic-focused China rounds up dissidents, new report says," in *National Post*, June 11, 2008, A3.
82. Brian McCullough, "Redefining Normal Christianity, A Glimpse Into The Persecuted Church," in *Mennonite Brethren Herald*, November 2007, 46, 11, 16-17. The article includes a photo of a woman being baptized at night.
83. Walter Klaassen, "Who can be called an Anabaptist?" in *Mennonite Weekly Review*, October 17, 2005, 6.

Chapter One

Introduction to the Records of 1527

As the curtain rises on 1527 radical Reformation and Anabaptist ideas have already come to Tirol from Germany in the north and from Switzerland in the west. Hans Hut, a book peddler from southern Germany, took the Anabaptist message eastward all the way to Vienna. "In May 1526 Kaspar Färber, a native Tyrolian, told Hans Hut in Augsburg that several brothers in the Inn Valley had been baptized and were leading a Christian life."[1] Hut's followers Leonard Schiemer and Hans Schlaffer were thus not the first Anabaptists in North Tirol but they became leaders there.[2] Other Hut followers like the Binders, baptized in 1526, were captured in Salzburg where they had been sent to preach (November 20, 1527).[3] Hans Hut's message had apocalyptic overtones and the "climate of expectation, hope, and fear of change ... gave apocalyptic ideas new potency during the Reformation."[4] Radical Reformation ideas had taken root in parts of South Tirol by 1524 and 1525. The cutler and merchant Mathias Messerschmied was one of a whole group in Klausen and Gufidaun who denied the sacraments of the church. Messerschmied was imprisoned in Brixen from September 1524 to January 1525 after which he went to Augsburg. On his return to South Tirol in late 1525 or early 1526 he was married and carrying heretical literature.[5] All during 1526 a lowly goatherd turned preacher named Wölfl, one of several local itinerant reformers, was propagating and watering the 'seeds' helping them to take root in both North and South Tirol.[6] He "carried the new movement from the upper Inn Valley into the heart of Tyrol, the area around Brixen."[7] Messerschmied, among others, supported him fully (January 9, 1527).

At the same time, other winds of change blowing in Europe affected Tirol no less. Luther's actions of 1517 which unintentionally ushered in a European Reformation resulted, among other things, in a revolt of the peasants. The lower classes took Luther's biblical message to heart and sought to put the new religious reforms into social and political practice. The rulers of the time thought otherwise and the peasants were brutally defeated in the Peasants' War. In Tirol the Peasants' War was led by Michael Gaismair in 1525 and 1526. But by "the year 1527..., Anabaptism became firmly established in the area which had been the storm centre of the peasant uprising two years earlier." To the peasants, Gaismair's failure probably meant such resistance was against God's will.[8] Anabaptism became the strongest where the peasant revolt had begun.

Anabaptism acknowledged "the rightness of peasant grievances and aims" but offered a different way to resist. "It consisted of forming a new Christian community which saw itself as the restitution of the church of the New Testament, in which the old authorities were rejected and turned over to the sure judgement of God."[9] Messerschmied, Bader, Gasser and Müllner were among those individuals who, after supporting or participating in the peasant revolt "turned their dissent against church and feudal authority into Anabaptism where the resistance to the traditional authorities was at least as strong, although it was nonviolent in nature."[10] The stories of the Mathias Messerschmieds, Gilg Bader and his wife, Hans and Anna Gasser, Ulrich and Margret Kobl and Margret's mother, the Gallpüchlerin who were all dealt with in 1528, reveal an overlap between the two movements.[11] At the same time Jörg Blaurock, the leader who participated in the first adult baptisms in Zurich, Switzerland on January 21, 1525 – actually the first one to be baptized – brought Anabaptist ideas to South Tirol. During his two visits between May and September 1527, Gaismair supporters were among his first converts (February 19, 1528).[12]

In Tirol, Anabaptism grew then in the wake of failed revolt, with one difference: Anabaptism quickly became a widespread popular, grass roots movement. "Potentially, Anabaptism threatened to become the religion of the Tirol. It was no mere sect that the government might have safely ignored. Also it was, as the result of its situation, the religion of the commoners."[13] While his brother, Charles V, head of the Holy Roman

Empire, dealt with Reformation issues on the European scene, Archduke Ferdinand took actions of his own. Ferdinand, who became king of Tirol in 1526,[14] had no intention of letting the "damnable and pernicious sect" of Anabaptism subvert the traditional Christian faith he held dear. In August 1527 he passed the first of eleven decrees, the so-called Anabaptist mandate, to rid his domain of the "poisonous, sectarian ideas" which he saw as a continuation of the peasant rebellion among his subjects. "Anyone who violated the Twelve Articles of the Christian faith and the doctrines of the seven sacraments would be punished as a heretic 'in body and life.'"[15]

By this time Wölfl, the preacher who would soon become an Anabaptist, had already been interrogated. In January 1527 the authorities in Brixen questioned Wölfl thoroughly without the use of torture and he complied with a detailed account of all his activities, revealing his widespread influence as well as the integral involvement of women. He told his inquisitors that he had been invited to preach in the homes of both peasant and upper class families. He had spent eight days with the family of Anton Wolkenstein, members of the lower nobility. Anton was arrested on the basis of the preacher's confession and chose to recant in the summer of 1527.[16] However, his wife Elizabeth (September 1531) would later be baptized, host Anabaptist meetings in their home and give shelter to Jacob Hutter. Their younger sons Paul and Sigmund also became Anabaptists.[17] Wölfl also had listened to readings of Luther's writings from a literate woman in Innsbruck's neighbouring city of Hall and she had supported him fully (see January 16, 1527). In Gufidaun the wife of the crown administrator[18] also affirmed his teachings. Her husband was one of the most important officials in the local government. Yet this woman possessed excerpts of the Gospels which she shared with the wandering preacher. Wölfl had even shared a New Testament with a judge, Jacob Hupher of Bozen. As a result Hupher later sympathized with his Anabaptist prisoners and sought to avoid punishing them.

Jacob Hutter, a hatmaker by trade, also came under Wölfl's influence in this early phase. When Hutter was arrested in December 1535 it came to light that in 1526 he had listened to Wölfl preach in the home of his employer, Caspar Hueter, in Stegen. Influenced by Wölfl, Hutter traveled all the way to Bozen to purchase a New Testament and then read from it to members of his employer's household, which the latter soon forbade.[19] Hutter went on to become a key leader of Anabaptism in South Tirol following the deaths of Michel Kürschner (June 5, 1529) and Jörg Blaurock in September 1529. Hutter established Anabaptist communities in Moravia which abolished private property and had all things in common.[20] Perhaps Hutter's sister Agnes also heard Wölfl preach. In any case, she was not arrested until the end of 1529 at which time she, like her brother later, became an Anabaptist martyr (December 8, 1529). In short, during 1526 the goatherd preacher traveled and preached in many places in both North and South Tirol. Ferdinand was fully aware that measures had to be taken against any and all members and supporters of the new religious movement which the authorities disparagingly called Anabaptism. Yet the local officials hesitated to prosecute Wölfl, which "... permitted the spread of evangelical ideas during this crucial and receptive stage."[21]

Wölfl's confession made it clear that women entered into these events at the very beginning. The young wife of the cutler and merchant, Mathias Messerschmied in Klausen, could not only read, she could also write and perpetrated a kind of rebellion of her own (January 9, 1527). As one who could read she belonged to that minority group in sixteenth century society who was literate.[22] Her fellow believer, wife of the local barber-surgeon Gilg Bader, soon paid for her participation in house church meetings with a term in prison (December 31, 1527). Her first arrest took place in December 1527. By this time imprisonment for Anabaptist women was nothing new, as several records in November of that year attest. Some women whom Wölfl had named, like the Landbergerin (January 16, 1527), were to be questioned but others, like the wife of the crown administrator of Gufidaun, were spared that (January 16, 1527 and September 26, 1531). It is quite likely that Helena von Freyberg (March 7, 1528), a noblewoman residing in Münichau near Kitzbühel, was baptized in the latter months of 1527 since by this time Anabaptist meetings were being held in her castle. It is possible that, as a literate person, she led Bible readings at these meetings. She was certainly head of the congregation. Perhaps her well-to-do friend from Rattenberg, the mining engineer and civil servant, Pilgram Marpeck, attended these meetings and was baptized here as well. The evidence for this is not clear. However, a report from Kitzbühel at the beginning of

March 1528 raised suspicions that Helena and her entire household had been baptized. It would take almost two years before the evidence needed to arrest Helena was obtained. Ferdinand indeed had reason to be concerned if a member of the lower nobility accepted the sectarian views he feared so much.

Not many women were arrested in 1527. That would soon change.

Translations from the Court Records of 1527

January 9, 1527, Messerschmied's Wife Wrote the Ultimatum*

The January 1527 testimony of Wölfl (Wolfgang), the itinerant or wandering corner preacher[23] and future Anabaptist who spearheaded the movement for religious reform in Klausen in 1526 included incriminating information about both the cutler and merchant named Mathias Messerschmied (a former canon) and his literate wife.

(Wölfl testified that) Messerschmied, Gilg Bader, Ulrich Müllner and others whom he could not name had kept him in their homes, protected and supported him when the government or the clerics wanted to expel him. He confirmed that Messerschmied posted the letter about (their priest) Herr Steffan on the church door for which Herr Steffan became extremely angry. Messerschmied could not write but his wife could.

Wölfl also said he heard from Messerschmied that members of the group wanted to post the threatening letter about the clergy. Wölfl told them that Herr Steffan warned him not to do that, which made Messerschmied and Gilg Bader very angry and ready to attack the cleric. But Wölfl said he would not be frightened by the Word of God. Messerschmied and Bader responded that they would stand by Wölfl courageously and support him.[24]

Moreover, Wölfl had read in a booklet which Messerschmied brought from Augsburg that the mass was worthless. Wölfl had discussed the new teachings in front of Messerschmied's store. He also ate meat with Messerschmied on Fridays.[25]

In addition to these involvements, Messerschmied's wife read Scripture and pamphlet literature during meetings in their home.[26] The last reference

---

*The author's translations from the court records appear in italics and ( ) enclose brief explanations. Additional information expanding on the translations and the summaries of shorter stories appear in regular lettering.

to her in these records was on September 6, 1531 when, *the government of Innsbruck informed the city officials of Brixen that from a reliable report they knew that the following persons in Klausen were "of ill-repute due to their obvious involvement with Anabaptism and other deceptive, heretical sects."* [27] Messerschmied and his wife were among the seventeen people named.

January 16, 1527, The Landbergerin Instructs the Wandering Preacher

The wandering preacher Wölfl testified that *he had been in the home of the Landbergerin in the city of Hall. She also had read many of Luther's writings to him.*

Furthermore, Wölfl testified that *the Landbergerin told him to simply preach and let nothing distract or lead him astray. And if they expelled him from one place, he should move on to another location and preach.*

Because of Wölfl's testimony, an order to arrest the Landbergerin of Hall was issued a year later, on January 4, 1528. *The crown administrator* [28] *was instructed to interrogate her in the same manner as other persons who were suspected of Anabaptism.*

January 16, 1527, Crown Administrator's Wife Affirms the Wandering Preacher

The wandering preacher Wölfl also testified that *the wife of the crown administrator in Gufidaun gave him an excerpt from some of the Gospels and told him his teachings were completely correct.*[29]

November 15, 1527

In Salzburg it was decided that wives who were deserted because their Anabaptist husbands had been expelled, like the Ochssennfurtterin and Peter Tyschler's wife, were to be banished as well and remain in exile with their husbands until such time as the men would be pardoned.[30]

November 20, 1527, Apocalyptic Influences on a Missionary Couple

Among the Anabaptists captured in Salzburg were a couple from southern Germany who had been sent there by the prominent south German, Austrian Anabaptist leader, a book binder and book seller by trade, Hans Hut.[31] They confessed as follows.

Eukarius (Binder) from Coburg (a centre northwest of Augsburg) states that Hans Hut brought him and his wife into the movement. They accepted the faith from Hut and were baptized by him. Hut sent him out from Augsburg with Joachim Mertz to preach. Ursula Nehspitzin,[32] *wife of Eukarius (Binder), states that Hans Hut, a bookseller, brought them into the movement. Hut persuaded them to join and baptized them a year ago in a village located a mile from (their home in) Coburg, (Germany).*

The above named Nehspitzin and others also say, that Hans Hut sent them to Salzburg to preach and make their teachings known. Hut had a book with seven seals, which the Lord gave (the prophet) Daniel. But this book would not be revealed until the final judgement day of the world. In Ursula's estimation, "Hut thus stood on the same level as Daniel."[33]

"Virtually all of the early Anabaptists,… were convinced that they were living at the very end of history, and that Christ was about to return." For some, like Hut "this conviction provided the interpretive framework for reading all of Scripture." As a follower of Hans Hut, Ursula Binder's confession provides "direct evidence of Hut's approach to Scripture." The book she was referring to would have been one of Hut's writings.[34]

Eukarius was a master cabinet maker and Joachim Mertz his journeyman. Mertz and the Binders "had been enthusiastic Anabaptists since 1526. They accompanied their teacher, Hut, on numerous missionary journeys and in doing so achieved great success. For this reason they participated … in the synod which convened in Augsburg on August 20, 1527." At this meeting Hut sent them out to work in the archdiocese of Salzburg.[35]

Ursula went to Salzburg with her evangelist husband indicating that she was included in the commission to proselytize and equally responsible to teach others about Anabaptism. Both she and her husband were captured in Salzburg and he was martyred there in October 1527. Ursula returned to Augsburg where she continued in Anabaptism. She was arrested along with others on April 12, 1528, Easter Sunday at a worship service led by her brother, Jörg Nehspitzer. As a foreigner to the city, her brother was expelled and likely she was also expelled from Augsburg.[36]

November 20, 1527

Martha Wynnter and her husband Wolfgang, a tailor, were persuaded to accept Anabaptism and baptized by Hans Hut in the city of Vienna. She simply stated that her confession was the same as her husband's.

December 10, 1527
This is the first reference to Jörg Vasser, a former monk, who worked in the mines of Schwaz as a water carrier and became an important Anabaptist leader. See October - November 1530 regarding the property inventory that names his wife, later an Anabaptist in Moravia.

December 31, 1527, Gilg Bader's Wife, Involved Early But Arrested Again Later
The Innsbruck government responds to Bishop Georg (III) of Brixen regarding the confession of Ulrich Müllner from Klausen ... and the Gilg Baderin, the Anabaptist woman who is also in prison. The central government suggests the prisoners be guarded well until further instructions are sent. However, if your gracious majesty, the Bishop, desires further advice, ask those who are learned and informed in your diocese of Brixen ... (how to) deal with such agitators....

The advice of the bishop's advisers at this time was to her benefit. The Gilg Baderin was pardoned despite her incriminating behaviour. The statements made by Wölfl, the wandering preacher and future Anabaptist, showed clearly that she was integrally involved in the new Anabaptist movement. In his confession of January 1527, he named three families who protected, housed and supported him, one of them being that of Gilg Bader and his wife. Wölfl stated: *he had preached in the home of Bader in St. Lorenzen, saying the holy cross was nothing more than a piece of wood, like a stick which one throws to a dog, or uses to heat an oven.* The Baderin would have been present on this occasion with others when *Wölfl preached openly in the homes of Müllner, Messerschmid, Gilg Bader and Hans Weber, where many people had come together.*[37]

Two years later, August 26, 1529, the Gilg Baderin was arrested a second time. Hans Prew, crown administrator of Gufidaun, was instructed on August 30 to put her on trial. *September 1, 1529, he was to told to present the petition of her husband Gilg Jager, Bader*[38] *on behalf of his wife to the jury and interrogate her once more.* The report of September 11, ten days later, states that, *Gilg Bader's wife has been injured in a fall. She should remain in prison until she has recovered.*

A month later, October 9, 1529 Prew was instructed *to keep her in prison longer because it is not known "whether she is not in her right mind, or rather is just confused and simple-minded."* By November 5, 1529 the Innsbruck government decided that *Gilg Bader's wife is in her right mind and she should be put on trial because she is a relapsed Anabaptist.*

The summary of the last record in which she is mentioned indicates that she was probably tried in the criminal court which would have meant a death sentence. Since Prew was a Lutheran it is possible that he let her go. On the other hand Clasen includes her in the list of martyrs for Tirol.[39]

Notes

1. C. Meyer, "Zur Geschichte der Widertäufer in Oberschwaben," *Zeitschrift des historischen Vereins fuer Schwaben und Neuberg I*, 1874, 245, cited in Klaassen, *Michael Gaismair*, 107. Klaassen tells us, "they became Anabaptists through the efforts of missionaries from Switzerland."
2. Schiemer came from Vienna in November 1527. See *Hutterite Beginnings*, 34-35. See the Introduction, n. 46 regarding a biography of Schiemer. Hut was "the most significant advocate of Anabaptism in South Germany and Austria." *Ibid.*, 4. Hut's work is discussed in C. Arnold Snyder, "The South German/Austrian Anabaptist Context," in *Profiles of Anabaptist Women*, 72-74.
3. The date in brackets refers to the translated passage for this person.
4. *Hutterite Beginnings*, 10.
5. *Ibid.*, 176, 177. Messerschmied preached in the Eisack Valley. See James M. Stayer, *The German Peasants' War and Anabaptist Community of Goods* (Kingston, ON: McGill-Queen's University Press, 1991), 87.
6. His confession given on January 9, 16 and 18, 1527 was discovered after 1972 and published in Matthias Schmelzer, "Jakob Huters Wirken im Lichte von Bekenntnissen gefangener Täufer," in *Der Schlern*, 63 (1989), 596-618. Unlike in the Swiss cities, "no dominant reformers emerged" and there was "no urban reformation." Although there were other evangelical itinerants preaching in 1526, like Hans Vischer from Ulm, "Wölfl is the best known of these pre-Anabaptist evangelicals." See *Hutterite Beginnings*, 176, 177.
7. Klaassen, *Michael Gaismair*, 107.
8. *Ibid.*, 108, 115. "Gaismair's party had moved through the Puster region as late as July 1526, accompanied in some instances by raids on parsonages." *Hutterite Beginnings*, 179.
9. Klaassen, *Michael Gaismair*, 115-16.
10. *Ibid.*, 110.
11. Of the persons named by Wölfl in his confession, like Messerschmied and Gilg Bader, "Practically all reappeared as Anabaptists in 1527." *Hutterite Beginnings*, 177.

12. Blaurock's return to Tirol in the spring of 1529 led to his martyrdom. See *Hutterite Beginnings*, 182. See also, C. Arnold Snyder, *Anabaptist History and Theology: Revised Student Edition* (Kitchener, ON: Pandora Press, copublished with Herald Press, 1997), 185f.
13. James M. Stayer, "Anabaptists and Future Anabaptists in the Peasants' War," *Mennonite Quarterly Review*, LXII, 2 (April, 1988), 131.
14. Astrid von Schlachta, "Die Geschichte der Täufer in Tirol ein Begleiter durch die Austellung," in von Schlachta, *Verbrannte Visionen?* 10.
15. Clasen, Social History, 376. Also, *Hutterite Beginnings*, 188.
16. Matthias Schmelzer, "Elisabeth von Wolkenstein of Uttenheim," trans. by Linda A. Huebert Hecht in *Profiles of Anabaptist Women*, 166.
17. *Ibid.*, 143, 164-77.
18. The crown administrator was a "Pfleger," the government official who held political and judicial authority at the local level as head of the local government. He reported directly to the king and had administrative duties such as the collection of taxes. Many of the government reports were addressed to the crown administrator. Strauss, *Law, Resistance, and the State*, 254, 268.
19. *Hutterite Beginnings*, 178, 252 and Grete Mecenseffy, ed. with Matthias Schmelzer, *Quellen zur Geschichte der Täufer XIV. Band, Österreich III. Teil* (Gütersloh: Gerd Mohn, 1983), 314. Hereafter, TA 1983, the page number: and the line number(s) cited.
20. "In fact, Anabaptist community of goods represented a pronounced radicalization of the Christian social objectives of the commoners of 1525." James M. Stayer, *The German Peasants' War and Anabaptist Community of Goods* (Kingston, ON: McGill-Queen's University Press, 1991), 3.
21. *Hutterite Beginnings*, 179.
22. See C. Arnold Snyder, "Introduction," in *Profiles of Anabaptist Women*, 6-7 regarding the theme of literacy. Other references to read are in July 24, 1529 and August 18, 1531.
23. He is called a "Winkelprediger" meaning he wandered about, preaching in many different places, by hedges, in nooks and in corners. Wölfl had been a goatherd and his preaching was unauthorized. See TA 1972, 2:4f.; 29f.
24. See his confession in Schmelzer, "Jakob Huters Wirken," 616. Packull describes the group around Wölfl as follows. "How quickly these sacramentists converted to a non-resistant position when they joined Anabaptism is difficult to ascertain, but allowance must be made for a transitional phase, including inconsistencies and ambivalences." Nonresistance was taught in South Tirol by 1530-31 at the latest, although threatening letters were still being posted on January 25, 1530 (TA 1972, 331:9-10). See *Hutterite Beginnings*, 174.
25. *Hutterite Beginnings*, 176-80, n. 118, 369 and Schmelzer, "Jakob Huters Wirken," 616, 618. The Messerschmieds are mentioned in TA 1972, 39:2, 16 in a December 23, 1527

report of meetings held by Caspar Mairhofer in the Gasser's home for which the latter were in prison February 13, 1528. There were links between Mairhofer, Wölfl and Messerschmied. Anna Gasser was Mairhofer's sister (April 23, 1529).

26. *Hutterite Beginnings,* 176.
27. The quotation is from the original text included in the summary of the record.
28. Wölfl's confession in Schmelzer, "Jakob Huters Wirken," 617, 618 and TA 1972, 49:1-4.
29. Wölfl's confession in Schmelzer, "Jakob Huters Wirken," 617.
30. TA 1972, 24:21-25.
31. "Hans Hut was by far the most significant early apostle of Anabaptism in the region extending from Thuringia to the Tyrol and from Württemberg to Moravia." See Johann Loserth, Robert Friedmann and Werner O. Packull, "Hans Hut (d. 1527)," *Global Mennonite Encyclopedia Online* (1987), at www.gameo.org.
32. Her brother, Jörg Nehspitzer, was leader of the Augsburg Anabaptist church. See Grete Mecenseffy, ed., using texts from P. Dedic, *Quellen zur Geschichte der Täufer XI. Band Österreich I. Teil* (Gütersloh: Gerd Mohn, 1964), 116:20. Hereafter, TA 1964, the page number: and the line number(s) cited.
33. The quotation is from, Walter Klaassen, *Living at the End of the Ages Apocalyptic Expectation in the Radical Reformation* (Lanham, MD: University Press of America, Inc., 1992), 81. Hut was the first Anabaptist to establish a date for the end of the world. He predicted it would happen at Pentecost 1528. *Ibid.*, 26.
34. Snyder, *Anabaptist History and Theology: Revised Student Edition,* 243.
35. Klaus Rischar, "Research Notes, The Martyrdom of the Salzburg Anabaptists in 1527," *Mennonite Quarterly Review,* XLIII, 4 (October, 1969), 324.
36. Klaus Rischar, "Der Missionar Eucharius Binder Und Sein Mitarbeiter Joachim März," *Mennonitische Geschichtsblätter,* 25, 20 (1968), 22-23.
37. Schmelzer, "Jakob Huters Wirken," 616-17: fol. 761, line 29; fol. 763, line 5; fol. 760, 21.
38. Her husband's name was "Jager" so that Bader referred to his occupation as a barber-surgeon.
39. Claus-Peter Clasen, "Executions of Anabaptists, 1525-1618 A Research Report," *Mennonite Quarterly Review,* XLVII, 2 (1973), 138.

Chapter Two

Introduction to the Records of 1528

By 1528 Ferdinand was fully aware of the strength of Anabaptist leaders and their networks. On January 12 the influential Anabaptist leader Leonard Schiemer, a former priest, was interrogated in Rattenberg. The list of close to two hundred people he had baptized during 1527 included thirty women, half of whom were from Austrian lands (January 12). Schiemer was executed two days later and his fellow leader Hans Schlaffer and the Anabaptist Leonhard Frick soon thereafter, in Schwaz on February 4.[1] Ferdinand sent an open letter to his officials in Innsbruck on January 24 informing them that Anabaptist membership had increased to one thousand, which was more than enough reason to capture their leaders.[2] The decree of November 1527 issued from Salzburg was expanded on April 18, 1528 and included the following passage regarding leaders.

> First of all, that those persons who have been re-baptized…, especially those who deny the holy sacrament of the altar etc. and in faith have accepted, acknowledged, taught and disseminated such religious ideas and especially those, who are baptizers, who most often have been progenitors and instigators, whether they are sacred or secular, natives or foreigners, who persist … in their faith are to be punished with death at the stake.[3]

In addition, anyone supporting the Anabaptists in any way should be punished as well.

> Likewise all those who allow Anabaptist preaching or meetings to take place under their roof, as well as those in charge of the money,

persons who inform others of such meetings or call people together even if they are not baptizers or preachers themselves, should not receive the death sentence if they recant, but should be punished severely; their houses are to be torn down or confiscated, or they are to pay heavy fines, with lengthy imprisonments, signs on their clothes, carry no weapon for a time and attend no meeting other than church; those whom the authorities consider to be unruly persons should be exiled, all according to the careful deliberations of the authorities.[4]

Pardon was possible then for Anabaptists who were not leaders. Though spared death, they would still be penalized, as described here, or with corporal punishment. Ferdinand gave instructions that "the decree had to be read in all the parish churches on Christmas Day 1527 and at Easter 1528. It was assumed that attendance would be highest on these most important church days."[5]

In Rattenberg in North Tirol, Pilgram Marpeck submitted his letter of resignation to the government on January 28.[6] The next day Ferdinand addressed Jacob Hupher, judge in Bozen in South Tirol. Ferdinand expressed surprise that the judge had not reported the whereabouts of the Swiss missionary Jörg Blaurock, his wife Els, and his fellow leaders in the region, the woman named Gallpüchlerin, whose record of radical action began in the Peasant War, (January 29) and her sons-in-law, Adam and Ulrich (Kobl), the latter married to her daughter Margret. By February 19 Ulrich was traveling to Berne, Switzerland and it became clear that Hans and Anna Gasser, who had participated in the Peasant War as well (February 19), were among the earliest Anabaptists in this region and part of the Anabaptist leadership network in South Tirol. By the time Margret Kobl was arrested for the first time in May, well advanced in her pregnancy, Ulrich was back in Tirol working in Rodeneck, near the entrance to the Puster Valley. Also in February, the Innsbruck government became aware of another key Anabaptist family, located in the region of Kitzbühel. It included older and younger members of the Taurer family among whom were a number of   male leaders (February 22). When the men fled, their wives were captured and questioned. The records of March 4, 17, and 30 and July 9, all in 1528, show just how deeply involved this extended family and members of their households were in the Anabaptist movement.

In the territory of Styria east of Tirol, there was also a network of leaders. The preaching of three women there – one had also read mass[7] – and the radical activities of this large group of reform minded people came to light on June 23. Two other women, from Graz, the capital of Styria (July 14), voiced their opinion about the sacrament of communion.[8]

Although the government actively sought to eliminate all Anabaptist leaders, rank and file members were not immune from arrest. Among those in prison at the same time as Schlaffer and Frick were a married couple, Hanns and Eva Schneider, and a single woman, Apollonia Niedermaier. Eva and Apollonia would become the first female martyrs in Tirol. Other Anabaptists in prison in the early months of 1528, like the miller, Leonard Spitzhamer and his maid, were fortunate to receive more lenient treatment, at least for a time.

In response to the officials in Innsbruck new decrees were issued in February and April 1528. The officials did not agree with Ferdinand that Anabaptists should be dealt with only according to the August 1527 decree without public trial as the criminal law of Tirol required. They were also against the execution of recanting Anabaptists. Moreover, they "pointed out that many Anabaptists who lived in the mountain districts had never heard of the mandate of August 20, 1527, and therefore could not very well be held responsible for failing to obey it."[9]

The law of February 24, 1528 repeated the punishments for the various groups of Anabaptists and included the death sentence but also provided an opportunity to recant and receive a pardon during a so-called period of grace, for those who reported to the authorities before Palm Sunday, April 5. On April 1 this period of grace was extended further, to the end of the month, April 26. The reprieve was open to those whose only crime was re-baptism but did not include leaders, baptizers or those promoting Anabaptism. Three of the following stories of 1528 in particular mention the period of grace: Barbara Schützinger (March 30), Dorothea Frick (April 23) and Pentzel's daughter (December 20).

Recantation had always been an option.[10] The earlier decree of February 8, 1528, described four categories of offenders: baptizers, those who had been baptized and persisted, those who chose to recant and desist, and those who rejoined after their recantation and pardon.[11] Persons who only had been baptized or who "had merely been present at a sermon or Lord's Supper or the reading of Holy Scripture" were eligible for recantation and pardon. The procedure for recantation had been issued already November 1527: Anabaptists willing to denounce their faith in order to be reinstated in the church were required to recant publicly at mass on three consecutive Sundays in front of the people, confirm their promise with an oath, not to associate with Anabaptism any longer and to remain faithful to the traditional Christian church,[12] perform the spiritual penance which their priest required of them and pay the costs of the court and of their upkeep in prison.

In the region of Kitzbühel the crown administrator was instructed to require the following spiritual penance for recanting Anabaptists.

> for one year, on every Thursday or on every Sunday, 'during the procession with the Holy Sacrament,' they were to attach themselves to the procession holding a lighted candle. Throughout the year they were not to enter a tavern, not attend a gathering, carry no weapon (this prohibition was the equivalent of a denial of their rights as citizens); and for three years they should continue to present a formal statement that they had gone to the confessional at Easter and received the sacrament.[13]

The specific requirements differed slightly in different locations of Tirol. In general, the "short form" of recantation could be spoken in private to a few government officials the way Helena von Freyberg did. The humiliating "long form," including a public statement and the penance of walking in the procession and kneeling in front of the altar during Sunday mass, was required most often. Some recantation statements were written by the Anabaptists themselves; more often they spoke "the accepted formal, courteous speech"[14] for such requests, written by a professional court secretary. The recantation texts of Lamprecht Penntz and his wife (June 5, 1528), of Hans in the Valley and his wife Ursula (January 4, 1530) as well as of Elisabeth von Wolkenstein (September 1531) are examples of the latter.

Recantation may be seen as a kind of "occasional conformity," that is, a process of "going through the motions of compliance with Catholic ritual."[15] It can also be viewed as Nicodemism. Like the biblical Nicodemus, a leading Jewish ruler who met with Jesus secretly at night in order to avoid detection, some Anabaptists kept their faith secret. David Joris, Anabaptist leader in the Netherlands in the 1530s, allowed his followers to practice Nicodemism, "conforming externally to the outward trappings of official orthodoxy while continuing secretly to cherish his more esoteric teachings."[16] Other leaders, notably Jacob Hutter, did not view Nicodemism favorably. Some Anabaptists who renounced their faith returned to their congregations and secretly retracted their public recantations.[17] It was not held against them by their fellow believers. It was a means of "buying time" and of surviving. "Anabaptist men and women were devout human beings, not automatons marching en masse to their death."[18]

The punishments and penance varied according to a person's degree of involvement in Anabaptism. Sometimes recanters were required to kneel during mass or walk barefoot in the procession, holding a burning candle. Such was the case for Elisabeth Wolfram (March 17, 1529) and Margarethe Hueberin (June 21, 1530). Hanns in the Valley and his wife Ursula were required to recant bare headed (January 4, 1530). Often it is stated that the recantation had to be spoken "from the pulpit"[19] as in the case of Bärbel from Rettenberg (May 28, 1530). In medieval churches pulpits were usually located near but above the congregation, accessible by stairs. This would have meant the recanting person had to "mount the pulpit" so that they would be seen and heard by everyone present in the church.

When the period of grace ended at the end of April, harsher punishments were the order of the day. For three women in Bregenz who were dealt with in May, the period of grace had run out. One of them was martyred while the other two were to wait until their children had been born, by which time they had chosen to recant. For two women arrested in the district of Uttenheim, the wives of Wolfgang Strael and Martin Nock (November 27), the reprieve was also no longer valid. They were to be tried in the criminal court. Three years later, in September 1531 the noblewoman Elisabeth von Wolkenstein would be discussed in the records from Uttenheim.

On May 13, several months after the first report of Helena von Freyberg's baptism, officials in Kitzbühel were investigating an unprecedented number of Anabaptists of whom 106 were willing to recant. No reference is made to the number of women in this group, only that thirty-six of them had changed their mind and rejoined the movement and now persevered.[20] Because the judge in Kitzbühel, Jörg Preger and the court secretary were openly sympathetic to the prisoners, there was a delay in carrying out punishments. When they were finally given, the punishments were very mild. No death sentences were issued.[21] Moreover, the prominent Anabaptist Helena von Freyberg (March 7, 1528) was allowed to visit the prisoners, which frustrated the central government further. Several women were in this group of prisoners (July 9, 1528).

"On September 26, 1528 the government arranged for the pardon of the remaining twenty-four Anabaptists in Kitzbühel." In addition to the usual recantations and penance, "the terms were extended to include the lifelong prohibition of ever carrying a weapon."[22] Ferdinand was not pleased and would later intervene and overrule the local authorities. In the meantime, he tried to break the strength of the Anabaptist movement in Kitzbühel in late summer with the execution of several male leaders.[23]

In general, the conditions of pardon for Anabaptists varied to some extent during 1528, depending on the severity of the crime and the attitude of the particular local judge or crown administrator. In Rattenberg the authorities themselves submitted the petition for three couples where the husbands worked in the mines (June 28), following up on one that had already been submitted for one of the wives, Barbara Pernhappel (May 20). At times corporal punishment, that is, a public flogging at the town pillory, was part of the punishment. Such was the case for Margaret Glenerin on June 4 and for Fundnetscher's wife on December 16, despite the fact that the latter was pregnant at the time. In a similar way, the amount of bail required for release from prison varied. In the case of Anna Rinnerin, discussed July 21, bail was set at one hundred Gulden, a high amount considering that a carpenter or bricklayer at that time earned around fifty Gulden annually.[24] The cost of the imprisonment was borne by the prisoners as part of their punishment. For Martha Weltzenbergerin there was specific mention that she was required to pay for her prison stay (March 26). She was to be kept in prison for eight to twelve days on a sparse diet. The latter was also required for the women and men arrested May 23, 1528 and for the three women imprisoned January 23, 1530. This was one of the requirements for their recantation.

Despite the threat of punishment to life and limb for officials and subjects alike[25] some officials maintained a sympathetic attitude toward Anabaptists and were lenient in punishing them. The judge in Bozen in South Tirol who delayed the executions of Hans and Eva Schneider and Apollonia Niedermaier for several months is a case in point. However, Hupher's policy did not always dominate, as the drowning of three women in Bozen on October 27 illustrates. On the other hand, the governor in this region, William Liechtenstein, whose authority extended to the regions south of Bozen, despite being told on October 13 to sentence a mother and daughter even if they showed remorse, was chided on November 4 for allowing a woman from Deutschnofen to simply leave. The authorities in Innsbruck insisted that if the woman from Deutschnofen was captured again, she should be tried in the criminal court, which would have meant the death sentence. A group of male and female prisoners in the neighbouring district of Völs, whose cases were discussed December 16, were supposed to be sentenced regardless of any last-minute regrets they might have.

As stated in the decrees, providing lodging for Anabaptists who had fled their homes and were on the run was also considered a crime. In the patriarchal society of the sixteenth century, women's status was defined in terms of their social and family roles as wives, mothers, daughters and sisters, and the husband or father was the head of the household. However, the government of Tirol did not consider husbands alone to be guilty in the dangerous crimes related to Anabaptism. Women too were arrested for hosting meetings and providing food and shelter to itinerant leaders and fleeing Anabaptists. This was the case for three couples, the Palpatschers, Fras and his wife and the Jacob Schäntls, discussed November 27 and 28. The wives were accused and held responsible for the same crime as their husbands, namely, aiding those who had broken the law. Fras and his wife were perhaps more guilty than the rest since they had aided a group of five Anabaptists among whom were the prominent leader Ulrich Kobl and his wife Margret, fellow leader Hanns Portz and a woman also wanted for murder, Katharina Torgglerin.

No one was exempt from arrest and interrogation as the government in Tirol attempted to root out and eradicate the growing Anabaptist movement which was becoming stronger in all the regions of this territory. The first male Anabaptist leaders had been martyred in nearby Rattenberg in North Tirol early in the year and the first "rank and file" Anabaptists, including the first female martyrs, were executed in South Tirol several months later (January 29). The situation was indeed serious.

Anabaptist Women Leaders, 1527-1531

The women in the territory of Styria in Upper Austria were not the only female Anabaptist leaders. In July 1530 the wife of the blacksmith and the local miller had been preaching daily to the people in Au with considerable success. She and the noblewoman Elisabeth von Wolkenstein are the only additional female leaders named in the published records for Tirol after 1529 and before the end of 1531. During the first three years, fifteen women acted as lay missioners and lay leaders in Tirol.[26] Just as there were a greater number of women involved in the earliest phase of the Anabaptist movement in general, there were more women in leadership at the beginning. Charismatic, self-appointed, informal, lay leadership was favored more in the early years of Anabaptism when there was less structure and more openness. In defining lay leadership Wolfgang Schäufele explains that in the Anabaptist community,

> there was no distinction between an academically educated ministerial class on the one hand and the laity on the other. Each member was potentially a preacher and a missionary, and each single member had equal opportunities for advancement according to his (or her) own competence, just as was the case in primitive Christianity. Luther's 'priesthood of all believers' became a practical reality in Anabaptism. [27]

This lay emphasis was particularly important for women to participate in leadership. The Anabaptists were "... less professional, less bookish, less hierarchical...." thus opening the door to a fuller participation by women.[28]

The Anabaptist movement gave women the opportunity to be "extra-ordinary lay witnesses of the gospel."[29] Their authority to act came from an inner spiritual call and the exercising of their spiritual gifts, not from the power of holding office, as happened in the second generation of the movement or as might be the case today.[30] The emphasis on freedom of conscience meant women had to make their own decisions regarding faith. Husbands or guardians could not decide matters of faith and discipleship for women.[31] The belief in the Holy Spirit meant each believer had the authority from within to speak for herself or himself. All of these factors, together with the openness in the early years of the movement gave women "many more possibilities of direct participation and leadership … than was the social norm in the sixteenth century, or than would become the norm in later Anabaptism."[32]

One reason that so many people joined the Anabaptist movement was that there were so many leaders in the early years of Anabaptism in Tirol. This is the view of the historian Claus-Peter Clasen, who published a list with the names of the leaders in all the Swiss, south German and Austrian Anabaptist regions. He found a total of forty-five leaders in Tirol during 1527 and 1529 with three women among them.[33] In actual fact, the published court records name fifteen women lay missioners and lay leaders, including the three which Clasen found. Thus, the total number of male and female leaders is close to sixty in Tirol in the first three years.[34] If we include the three women preachers and the missioner, the Caspar Malerin, active in Styria during 1528, the blacksmith's wife who preached in 1530 and Elisabeth von Wolkenstein, active in the Taufer Valley, the total number of women leaders over the five years reaches twenty-one. This means that women comprised one-third of the total number of male and female leaders between 1527 and 1531. Given the restrictions on women in that time period, thirty-three percent is quite significant.[35]

Women of the peasant classes were not expected to be leaders as men would have been, especially men who were craftsmen or innkeepers[36] and more likely to be literate. In a society with strict social roles, there was more at risk for women to take on leadership roles: "… the educated and socially privileged tended to rise naturally to leadership positions in Anabaptism."[37] The upper class women Helena von Freyberg and Elisabeth von Wolkenstein are the best examples of this. However, it is also true that in Tirol many Anabaptist leaders were, perhaps not poor, but illiterate peasant folk. They were women and men who felt called to speak and act for their faith in unofficial roles in the context of their everyday experiences.[38] In a society where the main means of communication was oral, "an extensive network of speakers"[39] was needed to make the movement a success, and women were an integral part of those networks.

The missionary activity of itinerant leaders was "vigorously supported by the missionary activity of the ordinary members."[40] In the decrees of 1527 and 1528, the government listed the kinds of leadership activities that they were looking for. Anabaptist women leaders were engaged in a number of these. A few of the female leaders were itinerant lay missioners and lay leaders themselves while others maintained local initiative and connections with other congregations. In the case of the latter they would "inform others of such meetings or call people together." They played a role as organizers. Women also provided food and lodging for Anabaptist leaders and those who were fleeing. They hosted meetings and held Scripture readings in their homes. They taught others and they proselytized. A few led local congregations, as did Helena von Freyberg[41] and a small number preached. Some of the Anabaptist women leaders were single and some were widowed; some married women were active as co-workers and co-teachers with their husbands or with other male Anabaptist leaders.[42]

The experience of Anna Egger raises the question at to whether she was a baptizer. Unfortunately the evidence is not clear in the records for Tirol. In the past, historians like Schäufele have assumed that only men were baptizers.[43] On the other hand, the sociologist Elise Boulding stated that Anabaptists "practiced complete equality of women and men in every respect, including preaching."[44] Women were present at baptisms and could very well have been baptizers, as the case of Anstad Kemmerer in Halle, southern Germany illustrates. He was baptized at an inn by some apostles of Hut. "Someone brought a 'little mustard pot' of pure water, and in the presence of three or more men and the same number of women (people Anstad did not know), they read from books they carried, they prayed, and then asked him to kneel. Anstad did, and recited the Creed out loud, after which they poured water on him and made the sign of the cross on his forehead."[45]

On the other hand, the three women in northern Germany "… reported to be 'apostles,' perhaps itinerant preachers.…" were viewed as "the exception rather than the usual."[46] The later pragmatic stance of Menno Simons was probably due to the harsh persecution and the fear of upsetting the social order if women undertook the same tasks as men. Therefore, "Menno did not encourage Mrs. Bouwens to join her husband as an equal in pastoral ministry."[47] The authorities in Tirol certainly did not eliminate the possibility of women baptizers as the story of the Anabaptist woman carrying the register of eight hundred names indicates (May 26, 1529). In Styria, the wife of Veit Riemer (June 23, 1528) "took some holy water from the church." Did she want to have it available for baptisms?[48] We do not know what this woman's motives were. The published records for Tirol do not specifically state that women baptized others. However, women were part of leadership networks and leadership teams where persons were being baptized.

The names of the individual Anabaptist women leaders deserve special mention and this will be done following in chronological order. In 1527 of the nine women discussed in the records of Tirol during 1527, three were missioners: the literate wife of Mathias Messerschmied (January 9), the Landbergerin who instructed Wölfl, the radical preacher (January 16) and Ursula Binder, who was commissioned with her husband by Hans Hut. Ursula felt equally responsible to preach and teach in Salzburg (November 20). Ursula, her husband and her husband's journeyman "accompanied their teacher, Hut, on numerous missionary journeys and in doing so achieved great success."[49]

During 1528, in addition to the four women in Styria, seven women were named as leaders in Tirol. Helena von Freyberg was not only the first female leader to be mentioned in 1528 (March 7), she was the first noblewoman to be baptized in Tirol. She made her castle at Münichau near Kitzbühel an Anabaptist centre for that region. Later it was discovered that her involvement was one of the reasons for the vigor and strength of that group of Anabaptists. Her story is fascinating for several reasons. First of all, it spans more than fifteen years, all phases of Anabaptist development. It begins in the unstructured Anabaptist environment of 1520s Tirol and ends in the more ordered later years of Augsburg Anabaptism in the 1540s. Secondly, the fact that a piece of her writing has been preserved is highly unusual. Very few writings by sixteenth century women in general have survived and only a few from Anabaptist women. The published booklet of the visions of the prophetess in Strasbourg, Ursula Jost, was forty pages in length.[50] The "Confession" which Helena wrote near the end of her life to her Augsburg congregation was only a few pages long but it is unique in Anabaptist History and in the history of religious women[51] not just for its rarity but for the depth of faith it revealed from an older Anabaptist leader. It also revealed that discipline and forgiveness were practiced in the Anabaptist community.[52]

It has been said that true leaders show their weaknesses as well as their strengths. However, Helena was not just discussing her weakness. Her "Confession" is one of the few places in Anabaptist writings where the central Anabaptist concept of "yieldedness" (in German "Gelassenheit") – that true Christian faith could be attained only through "self-negation, leading up to the birth of Christ within" – is expressed.[53]

> Believers were called to yield inwardly to the Spirit of God, outwardly to the community and to outward discipline, and finally, in the face of a hostile world, believers could be called upon to give way before God's greater purposes by accepting a martyr's death.[54]

Of note is that Helena's humility, yieldedness and self-denial did not lead to a loss of her personal self as might be the case for some women. At the end of her "Confession," she forgives those whom she supposes to have done things against her. Helena does not view herself as "passive or powerless."[55]

Mary T. Malone includes Helena's story in her book *Women and Christianity* and concludes that in this personal confession "… the strength of Helene's character shines through." Malone then offers another interpretation of Helena's "Confession."

> One wonders whether or not it was a case of Helene's own leadership being questioned as the Anabaptist community entered the settling down phase of its development. As in all Christian reform movements, the freedom of the gospel is never intended to change the supposedly 'natural' subordination of women.[56]

Helena's story illustrates the cycle of women's participation, which differed in the early and the later stages of the Anabaptist movement. She was more than an ordinary member, not just in her social status, but in her long, influential and continued role as an Anabaptist leader. Helena and the noblewoman Elisabeth von Wolkenstein did not die as martyrs. Their stories are nevertheless both of great significance and are the longest ones in this book.

When artisans like the baker Peter Egger became lay preachers, that was dangerous enough, but, the fact that his single sister Anna worked with him as he and another male leader preached and baptized west of Innsbruck was even more dangerous (April 4). Other women did missionary work in their own families. Hans Velcklehner's sister (May 12) convinced two other women, her sister-in-law Barbara and Barbara's sister, to become Anabaptists. On December 16, 1528 an order for the arrest of four "principal baptizers and persons who lead others astray" was given. The government did not refer to these leaders as apostles, preachers or prophets as the Anabaptists might have. The vocabulary of the government was different. Since the authorities were not entirely sure that the lower classes would rebel again as they had in 1525 and 1526, they referred to these leaders as agitators, instigators or rebels and in this case, as "persons who lead others astray." The list of leaders included the Gallpüchlerin (December 16), who, as noted above, had been named already eleven months earlier (January 29), a married couple, Mathias Waldner and his wife – the only reference to them – and the prominent male leader Michel Kürschner. The authorities suspected the two women in this group of working along with the men as leaders. These four Anabaptists escaped arrest. Five days later a report stated that the Gallpüchlerin had attended a meeting with fourteen other Anabaptists, Michel Kürschner and a woman named the Silberin (December 21), who was likely also a leader since her name was singled out.[57] The Gallpüchlerin was probably a widow[58] and clearly had a significant role as an older woman in her village. Perhaps this gave her more freedom to act as a lay leader, a role which the authorities in Völs and Bozen assumed she had when they discussed her attendance at the Anabaptist meetings of December 16 and 21.

The year 1529 was a high point in women's involvement and six women can be identified as missioners and leaders. The wife of Gilg Klein "made six new Christians in a short time" (May 10). The two unmarried sisters of Caspar Schwartz were part of a group that was distributing books in the Puster Valley (May 23). In the territory of Styria, the wife of Caspar Maler disseminated a radical view of communion. Like the Anabaptist Hutterite leader Jörg Zaunring from Rattenberg, she too believed it did not make sense to believe that the bread at communion contained the actual body of Christ (July 14).[59] In North Tirol, an unnamed woman was suspected of being a leader since she possessed a register containing the names of eight hundred Anabaptists (May 26).[60]

The final testimony of Michel Kürschner from Völs (June 5) provides a rare glimpse into how Anabaptists became leaders, not just because of the women present, but because many times, "… Anabaptists deliberately avoided ordaining leaders as a further protection against more severe punishment in the event of their capture."[61] Kürschner stated that aside from the baptizer, Jörg Zaunring, only three trusted Anabaptist members were present when he became an Anabaptist leader in 1528: Melchior Schneider's wife and Magdalena and Mathäus Wald. The two women were likely not leaders, but their presence at this very important meeting underscores their integral involvement in affirming Anabaptist leaders and participating in leadership networks where women and men supported each other.

Years later in the Netherlands when Elisabeth Dirks was arrested, her captors called her a man. They said, "We have the right man! We now have the teacher."[62] The authorities made no distinction in the persecution of Anabaptist lay leaders male or female. Their strategy was to capture and punish the leaders first and foremost in the hopes of eliminating the movement. It was just as important to capture female as male leaders and the authorities were fully aware of the initiatives taken by women. Indeed, female leaders were a greater threat to society than male leaders since their activities represented a reversal of the established order. Protestant leaders expressed such views. "Luther criticized girls and women for trying to speak eloquently in any context."[63] In Luther's view, "When women are eloquent, that is not praiseworthy; it suits them much better to stammer or to speak badly."[64] In their fear of ridicule, some Calvinists expressed similar views against women who took on leadership roles, saying, "How will the Papists and Anabaptists scoff to see us run by women!"[65] These negative attitudes toward women could work in favor of the officials in Tirol if they carefully documented the actions of women leaders. It was a means of discrediting the Anabaptist movement.

Wives of Anabaptist male leaders were always at greater risk because of their husbands. Despite that, many wives of male leaders made choices similar to those of their husbands. The group of female leaders discussed above does not include women like Hans Maurer's wife (November 20, 1529) or Katharina Streicher (December 22, 1529) who, like their husbands, were martyred. The men were local leaders and undoubtedly the wives were their co-workers.[66] The many cases where husbands and wives were both martyred indicate mutual influences and interdependent relationships between husbands and wives.[67] In the majority of cases among the 36 families for whom the authorities conducted property inventories in 1530, in 11 of the 19 families, the husbands and wives were both executed.[68] This underscores the interdependence in Anabaptist family relationships, making it hard to judge the actual number of leaders.

Martyrdom can also be viewed as a form of leadership. In martyrdom sex roles and distinctions were abolished, "embuing women with a 'manly spirit' to fight side by side with their brothers.... [In the early Christian church], the one who had suffered for Christ was believed to be endowed with sacramental powers that rivaled those of the episcopal leadership."[69] Balthasar Vest and his wife (November 24, 1529) were given .8 litre of wine on the day of their execution. Likely they used this to have the Lord's Supper together and served each other. In the face of martyrdom women too could serve in this ceremony of remembrance.

In conclusion, as Arnold Snyder explains, "While Anabaptist women usually were not 'equal' to men in terms of the 'official leadership roles' within the movement, they did experience far more freedom of choice than was the social norm, especially in the earlier more pneumatic stages of Anabaptist development."[70] Although Tirol did not have women prophets such as Ursula Jost and Barbara Rebstock of Strasbourg, many women in the Austrian regions acted on their spiritual call, thereby contributing to the strength of the Anabaptist movement.

Translations from the Court Records of 1528

January 10, 1528, Miller and His Maid Imprisoned in Rattenberg

The postscript to this document states: *We also received your request for instructions on how to deal with a miller named Leonhard Spitzhamer and his maid (of Brixlegg) whom you have imprisoned because they are Anabaptists. It is our command that you keep these two persons in prison until the trial of Leonhard Schiemer is concluded and you receive further instructions from us regarding them.*

Three weeks later, on February 1, 1528 the Innsbruck government wrote the following to Bartlme Anngst, the judge in Rattenberg. *Faithful one! Because of the petition that has been submitted to us on behalf of Leonhard Spitzhamer and his maid, we have decided that if they accept the following punishment, they can be pardoned from the severity of the law. They must both submit to a public flogging at the pillory and swear an oath not to take revenge on the local government of Rattenberg, etc. And if in spite of this punishment they again join the devious sect of Anabaptism, we will punish them to life and limb.*

Twice more, instructions were sent to keep the two in prison longer, on Februay 6th and a month later, on March 5. It is not clear if the corporal punishment was carried out. Finally, on March 26, 1528 the officials in Rattenberg were instructed regarding Spitzhamer and his maid. Their punishment was to be similar to that of Michael Hueber, the bathmaster, and two other Anabaptist women from Rattenberg, namely, Martha Weltzenberger and Springenfell's wife. See March 26, 1528 for further details about the two women. The punishment should be as follows.[71]

Their lives will be spared and they will be absolved from punishment[72] provided they: confess to their error in becoming Anabaptists, recant publicly in front of the people during the holy mass on three consecutive Sundays, give the required oath, and accept the penance required of them by their priest.

Discussion of Leonhard Spitzhamer's case occurred again more than two years later. The property inventories from the fall of 1530 include one for the miller and his wife but no mention is made at that time of their maid (see October - November 1530).

January 12, 1528, Women Baptized by Leonard Schiemer

The town council of Rattenberg met, together with various assessors and judges[73] (from different districts in Tirol), regarding the criminal proceedings against Schiemer. The confession which Schiemer had given on December 23, 1527 was read (in their presence) in order to confirm it.

On Monday after Trium Regnum in the year 1528, Leonhard Schiemer's confession was read to the officials who had been called to be present from: Bozen, Brixen, Bruneck (in the Puster Valley), Innsbruck, Hall, Freundsberg, Rattenberg, Kufstein, and Kitzbühel.

The confession noted that Leonard Schiemer was the son of Veit Schiemer of Vöcklabruck, a tailor, and was twenty-seven years old. On the Monday before Christmas in 1527, Leonard Schiemer confessed the following, both with and without torture, in the castle of Rattenberg.

Leonard Schiemer had baptized close to two hundred people in all. In the confession he gave in Rattenberg, the list of people whom he had baptized in various places in southern Germany and the Austrian territories included 30 women. The only information available for these women is their name and where they were from. Some of the women joined Anabaptism with their husbands or parents and some joined on their own. Their names are an important record of women's participation in the Anabaptist movement and all thirty are included here since they are named in the Anabaptist records for Tirol.

Of the fourteen women from southern Germany, eight were baptized in Augsburg, most of them with their husbands. The Augsburg Anabaptists included, Hanns Lautterwein, Uetz Schleiffer, Hanns Weber, the tailor Hans Leopold, the priest Herr Jacoben and all of their wives, two cooks[74] and a young woman.[75] Four women were among the Anabaptists from the region of Landsberg in Bavaria. Hanns Riedhofer and his wife were from Riedhofen, as was a maid.[76] Hanns Rueff and his wife were from Winndach and the tailor Hanns Craft and his wife were from Hausen near Geltendorf. Two couples were from Knüsslhofen, likely also in Bavaria, Liennhart Smit and his wife and a man named Lucas and his wife.

The sixteen women from the Austrian territories were as follows. Three women were from Lower Austria. In Etting, possibly near Vienna, Schiemer baptized the mayor and his wife.[77] In Gaunersdorf below the Manhartsberg, he baptized Matheus Schneyder and Jacob Ungelter and their wives.

Ten women were from places in Upper Austria. The innkeeper and his wife[78] were from Wels, and the crown administrator Hanns Wennter and his wife and daughter were from Mondsee. Those baptized in Styria included: a young woman,[79] a cook,[80] a maid,[81] the maid's mother and father,[82] the cook of the chaplain in the castle,[83] and Weissenhofer and Hanns Schneider and their wives.

In the bishopric of Salzburg, in Titmaning, Schiemer had baptized only one couple but they were people of status, the city judge and his wife.[84]

Finally, Schiemer had baptized several people in the mining town of Schwaz in Tirol, a shoemaker and his wife[85] and a couple he simply referred to as a husband and wife.[86]

The report of January 26, 1529 indicates that Schiemer also baptized an unnamed woman in Rattenberg and relates some words she spoke. See this report in Chapter Two.

January 29, 1528, The First Women Martyrs in Tirol

Ferdinand I instructed Jacob Hupher, territorial judge of Gries and Bozen, as follows. *Hanns Schneider and Apollonia Niedermaier who staunchly persevere in their Anabaptist faith and do not want to recant, are to be tried before a jury and sentenced at the next court session… (February 4). They should be informed of the edicts and mandates that have been issued as well as of… the emperor's authority to deal with rebellious action. Thus, the jury who serve under oath will be carrying out the law….*

If the court decides not to take the life of these two persons … they should still not be released. Rather, you should report back to us and await further instructions.

Both Hupher and his superior, William of Liechtenstein, governor of the territory of Bozen, were lenient toward Anabaptists and hesitated in carrying out Ferdinand's orders. On February 7 Hupher was instructed to set a trial date and not wait for the jury members who had still not returned from Schwaz. February 16 he was instructed to issue the death sentence and was reminded of this on February 29 (1528 was a leap year) and again on March 22. The postponements ended following the new mandate of April 1 and three days later, on April 4, instructions were given to execute Hans and Eva Schneider and Apollonia Niedermaier immediately.[87] By this time Eva, Hanns' wife, had also been condemned to death. The three persevered in their faith and although several key leaders had been executed recently (Leonhard Schiemer on January 14, 1528 and Hans Schlaffer and Leonhard

Frick on Feb. 4, 1528) Hans and Eva Schneider and Apollonia Niedermaier were among the first rank and file Anabaptist martyrs. These women were the first female martyrs in Tirol.[88]

January 29, 1528, The Sacrilegious Talk of an Anabaptist Woman Leader

On this date, the authorities first take notice of the Gallpüchlerin in these records. However, she is named here, not for her own activities but for those of her two sons-in-law. *The Innsbruck authorities inform Jacob Hupher, city and territorial judge of Gries and Bozen, that they are astonished that he has not informed them of the whereabouts of Jörg (Blaurock), and the sons-in-law of the Gallpüchlerin, Kobl and Adam. They should be arrested immediately.*

Ulrich Kobl, Adam and the Swiss leader, Jörg Blaurock, had been conducting Anabaptist meetings. The Gallpüchlerin's daughter Margaret was married to Ulrich and would be arrested the first time a few months later (see May 13, 1528). The Gallpüchlerin was not included in the orders given a few weeks later, on February 19, to search for other members of her family and this leadership network. However, from other sources we know that the she had displayed radical behaviour already much before 1528.

In June 1526 the Gallpüchlerin is named in documents related to the peasant uprisings as being from the Kunsterweg[89] on the Ritten plateau in the mountains above the urban centre of Bozen.[90] She was accused of speaking blasphemous words, to be exact, of *sacrilegious talk*. Consequently, orders were given to arrest her and to search her house, looking in particular for letters.[91] We do not know her exact connection to the peasant revolt but these orders provide evidence that her early radical religious behaviour was consistent with her later action of becoming an Anabaptist.

February 9, 1528,

Jörg Held and his wife from Hall were to receive the same treatment, interrogation and then a trial.

February 16, 1528, Anabaptist Artist Bartlmä Dill Riemenschneider and His Family Recanted

The Innsbruck government instructed Jacob Hupher, judge of Gries and Bozen to try Schneider and the Niedermaierin in the criminal court. The other Anabaptists including…

*the artist Bartlmä Dill, his (first) wife Katharina, his mother-in-law Margreth Wolf, and his maid,... all of whom wanted to recant, were to be well guarded.*⁹²

Their story continues on April 4, 1528 when Ferdinand informed Hupher as follows: *... the estates, consisting of prelates, lords, nobles, government and judicial officials in the Burggrave and territory of the Etsch,... recently meeting in Bozen, submitted (a petition) in writing to the upper Austrian government on behalf of the prisoners. It is our view that, in consideration of their lack of understanding and in order to hurt their pride, the prisoners should be punished severely. The prisoners should be interrogated thoroughly, one after the other, discussing the questions in ... the documents sent to the crown administrator of Kitzbühel April 2, 1528. If during the examination and discussion, nothing is found other than that they were re-baptized and, if they acknowledge the error of this and request a pardon, they can be pardoned and their lives spared on the basis of the petition from the (four) estates. Since each of these persons individually have allowed themselves to be baptized, they are each to recant publicly in the church before holy mass on three consecutive Sundays and must each provide an affidavit in writing supported with an oath....*

According to an unpublished record, Bartlmä, Katharina and Margreth recanted and swore the oath at this time so they could be reinstated in the church. However, seven months later on November 28, *the Innsbruck government informed Jacob Hupher ... that some of the Anabaptists who had been pardoned on the basis of the petition sent in by the officials from Etsch, had not performed their punishment and penance as required. This applied to nine Anabaptists including ... the artist Bartlmä Dill, his wife and his mother-in-law.... The judge should ensure that they carried out the penance as promised in their recantation.*

Two further references, December 23, 1530 and January 3, 1531, state that Bartlmä was accused of *"unseemly talk,"* suggesting that he was likely still associating with Anabaptists. He, but not his wife, was imprisoned and released without consequence. By June 1531 he had left Bozen to work for the Bishop in Trent and by 1536 his second wife, Elisabeth, had died. Bartlmä, the leading Renaissance artist of South Tirol, was the first Anabaptist artist.⁹³

February 16, 1528,
Five other Anabaptists from Gries and Bozen, Sebastian Ess, his wife and their maid and Sigmund Treibenreif and his maid appear in the same

records as the Anabaptist artist, Bartlmä Dill Riemenschneider, his wife, mother-in-law and maid. At first only the husbands are named. But in April and November of 1528 the women in these households are included. They were likewise questioned and chose to recant.

February 19, 1528,

Els, Jörg Blaurock's wife[94] from Switzerland accompanied her exiled husband to Tirol. The authorities were told to search for her and her husband as well as for the Gallpüchlerin's daughter who travelled with them. Hans and Anna Gasser, were already in prison in Wangen on February 13 due to their participation in the peasant rebellion.[95] Now it was reported that they had held meetings in their home on the Ritten plateau led by Caspar Mairhofer, Anna Gasser's brother.[96]

February 22, 1528,

Local officials were told to question Cristian Taurer's wife and daughters-in-law, all from the region of Kitzbühel, about their husbands who had fled. If these men were Anabaptists they should be imprisoned and an inventory made of their goods. If the women were Anabaptists they too should be imprisoned. See March 4, 1528 below.

February 29, 1528,

Orders were given to start criminal proceedings against the Messerschmiedin from Hall, a captured Anabaptist.[97]

February 29, 1528, The Treibenreifin Was Pregnant, Proceedings Suspended

The Innsbruck government instructed Jacob Hupher, judge of Bozen, to suspend the proceedings against the Treibenreifin until the birth of her child since she was far advanced in her pregnancy.

This is the only reference to this woman. As far as we know, she did not have to spend her pregnancy in prison nor did she have to report back to the authorities when her child was born.

March 4, 1528, Were the Women in the Taurer Family Really Simple-Minded?

The Innsbruck government addressed Hans Finsterwalder, crown administrator of Kitzbühel in response to his report of March 1 regarding Cristan and Andre Taurer, their wives, maids and labourers. They are pleased with the way he has handled things. The situation with the (Anabaptist) sect is dangerous and therefore everything must be done to capture its adherents. Because Cristan Taurer is truly a ringleader and principal Anabaptist,[98] the women should be questioned in all seriousness with the threat of torture regarding who baptized them and who else belongs to the sect. In particular, the names of those who have fled need to be determined. This report should be sent to the governor of Rattenberg, Christoff Philipp von Liechtenstein. The crown administrator will act on the basis of the (government) mandate, when the information is obtained about the treatment of the ringleader and those who have become part of the sect out of simple-mindedness and who wish to recant.[99] The views and opinion of the judge and jury regarding what each of these persons is guilty of should be recorded and sent to us.

The initial questioning of the women had failed (February 22). The women had not provided any information. Therefore, they would be treated more harshly now.[100] However, the government's assumption that the wives and the maid had not known what they were doing and had become part of Anabaptism out of ignorance and simple-mindedness is questionable. Unfortunately the records do not tell the whole story. They do not provide the women's own point of view, only what their actions were. In the coming months more members of the extended family and households of the Taurers were captured and questioned and some chose to recant.

March 7, 1528, The Baroness, Extraordinary in Status, Leadership and Influence[101]

The First Report

Just three days after dealing with the Taurer families Hans Finsterwalder, crown administrator of Kitzbühel was instructed regarding another serious matter. Again, *he was praised for the way he was dealing with the Anabaptists. If it proved to be true that the Helena Baroness von Freyberg and her servants had allowed themselves to be baptized, her property and goods should be confiscated.* This summarized report is the first reference to Helena in these records. As the following passages illustrate, there is more information available for this noblewoman than for any other Anabaptist woman we know of to date.

Helena, daughter of Gilg von Münichau and Magdalena von Hamerspach, was born at Münichau Castle, three kilometres from the urban centre of Kitzbühel in western Tirol into a family of the lower nobility of Tirol.[102] The links between Helena and the well-to-do civil servant in Rattenberg Pilgram Marpeck destined to become a prominent Anabaptist leader in southern Germany, began in her father's generation. Gilg Münichau was a university graduate employed as a crown administrator. In 1491, possibly the year of Helena's birth, he bought "mining and grazing rights" from Pilgram's father Heinrich Marpeck.[103] The Münichau castle, built in the mid fifteenth century, had been the residence of her paternal grandfather, Hanns Gilg. By 1506 Helena had married a man of equal rank, Onophrius Baron von Freyberg,[104] of Swiss-Bavarian descent from Hohenaschau in Bavaria, southwest of Chiemsee. She raised four sons at Hohenaschau, Pankraz, born in 1508, being the eldest, followed by Christoph Georg, Willhelm and Hanns Sigmund.

Sometime after 1523 when Helena inherited the castle of Münichau she returned there, possibly in her mid to late thirties.[105] By this time her sons were all knights. Legend has it that Martin Luther visited Hohensachau in 1518, indicating that Onophrius supported the Reformation.[106] Helena was influenced by the Reformation as well but made a different choice, namely to become an Anabaptist.[107] Perhaps Helena was already taking on a missionary role in convincing her household (male and female servants) at Münichau to be baptized.[108] The report of March 7, 1528 clearly incriminated them all. But definite proof was needed to arrest a member of the nobility and confiscate her property. It took the authorities almost two years to confirm this first report.[109]

The April Report

On April 2, 1528, the Innsbruck government explained the laws concerning the period of grace for Finsterwalder specifically. Those Anabaptists who reported to the government on their own before the end of April and whose only crime was baptism could receive a pardon.[110] Towards the end of this report the following details about Helena and Münichau are brought to light.

The clergyman named Paul (Rassler), former priest in Kitzbühel, who preached about Anabaptism last Fall at Münichau and his student Hanns Rat should also be captured and suppressed. When Paul went up into the mountains for a time, he left Hanns behind to continue preaching to the people. Paul also preached in the castle at Münichau and in the houses around it,…[111] *And supposedly he baptized people in the castle.*[112]

The Freybergerin of Münichau, her family and her household [113] *are suspected of being tainted with Anabaptism for the following reasons. Anabaptism has been preached at Münichau. The preacher Paul and his student worked in and around Münichau last Fall, baptizing people. Helena is said to have encouraged him to remain there for some time. She listened to his devious teaching, promoted it and provided lodging for these leaders (and other Anabaptists).*[114] *For now we will leave it at that (and not take action). If she takes the initiative to give a guaranty, this must be submitted to our upper Austrian government. You should continue to observe her and see what she will do next.*[115]

From other sources we know that the houses in which nocturnal meetings had been held and where the Lord's Supper had been observed were to be burned or dismantled as an example to the population. Münichau was on the list of such places.[116] Helena remained head of the congregation despite such potential risks.[117]

Helena, Under Suspicion, Visits Prisoners

Although the government did not feel confident in taking action against the Baroness, they did arrest many others from the region. Later that spring an exceptional number of Anabaptists were imprisoned in Kitzbühel – 106. *All of them chose to recant but 36 of their number had fallen again (that is, rejoined their fellow believers) and were in prison again on May 13. The judge was to interrogate them and determine just what the convictions of these persevering Anabaptists were.*[118] No doubt some of these prisoners were from Helena's congregation since she is mentioned in their regard some time later. Several women were part of this group (July 9, 1528).

On July 8, 1528, the Innsbruck government expressed its frustration to *Finsterwalder specifically about the Münichauerin's recent activities. He is the one who first reported her and about whom he was given orders earlier. (They remind him that) she is under no small suspicion regarding this sect and yet she was allowed to visit the Anabaptist prisoners in Kitzbühel. Moreover, a letter was discovered among the prisoners written by an Anabaptist leader named Partzner which he had sent to the prisoners.*[119]

Subsequent instructions from the Innsbruck government to Matthias Lang and Finsterwalder on July 11, three days later, made it very clear that *Helena, should not be allowed contact with Anabaptist prisoners.... She has given shelter and protection to Paul Rassler, a real and principal Anabaptist leader who leads many astray as well as to his assistant Hanns Rat. And she has never yet reported or answered to the government for her actions or submitted a guaranty…. (She) should be sent to Innsbruck to carry out this responsibility.*[120]

Likely Helena was the one who brought the letter of encouragement to the prisoners from Partzner, another leader to whom she had given protection. In any case she offered the group moral support. As a member of the upper class Helena would have been able to visit the prisoners, unlike the Anabaptist preacher for whom she acted as a mediator. Still no specific actions were taken against Helena. A whole year passed before the government had the proof it needed.

At the end of April 1529, the governor of Kufstein, *Christoff Fuchs reports that Onophrius von Freyberg (his brother-in-law) had come to him to excuse himself, (and clarify) that he did not belong to the Lutheran sect…. The government had not heard from his wife but it was said that supposedly she was Lutheran.*[121]

The Earlier Reports Confirmed

New evidence on July 6, 1529 confirmed all the earlier reports and gave the authorities the proof they needed. Therefore, the Innsbruck government instructed *Christoff Fuchs not to grant Helena safe passage to Kufstein for her to report to the crown administrator. Executed Anabaptists had confessed that she in fact was an Anabaptist and had given shelter to Anabaptists.*[122]

(The recanting Anabaptist Gabriel) Sunschwennter named the Münichauerin, Helena von Freyberg, in his confession of December 7, 1529. (He said) she was baptized two years ago either by a preacher named Paul or by Hanns Rat. (Moreover,) she supported the brothers and sisters financially by sending them 11 Gulden for their livelihood.[123] *(This evidence was enough) to give orders to arrest Helena and the two preachers and bring them into the custody of either the Archbishop of Salzburg or the bishop of Chiemsee. Sunschwennter's confession should be sent to the dukes of Bavaria, Wilhelm and Ludwig.* A second confirmation came two days later on December 9, *from the confession of the Anabaptist martyr from Kitzbühel, Peter Aschlberger, who had given information about Helena.* The word of a martyr was indeed authoritative.

Helena now fled to Hohenaschau in Bavaria. But when an armed guard came to arrest her there on January 2, 1530[124] *she left her husband and sought refuge in South Tirol near Eppan where she owned vineyards. On February 12, 1530 the Innsbruck government made it known that she was back in Tirol. An all-out effort would be made immediately to capture her, since the government was not inclined to allow this devious* sect to take root in anyone, whether of high or of low status. The decree and order for her arrest was sent to all local authorities in the region. They were to establish her whereabouts secretly and take her captive.[125] But Helena eluded them, escaping to the city of Constance.

By April 21, 1529 authorities in Tirol were dealing with Helena's property. Onophrius held her property in trust for her.[126] Several months later, on June 18, with help from friends and relatives, her sons obtained possession of all her property, vineyards and income from the latter in Tirol.[127]

Two years in Constance

Helena lived in Constance for two years before her property there was confiscated and she was expelled. The Lutheran leader Ambrosius Blaurer wrote on February 2, 1532: *Look out, that the Freybergerin does not cause problems in her house.*[128] Helena was continuing her role as a leader. Just as she had in Tirol, she was holding forbidden Anabaptist meetings in her home. Her association with her friend and fellow Anabaptist leader, Pilgram Marpeck, did not help her reputation in Constance. After her expulsion she spent time in the more tolerant city of Augsburg.

Recantation Negotiations

By December 24, 1533 Helena decided to return to her husband and to recant. Thus, a petition submitted on her behalf supported by Wolf, the Count of Montfort and Christoff Fuchs, governor of Kufstein in Tirol had been sent to the king.[129] On January 6, 1534 Ferdinand responded directly to Helena's request for a short and private recantation, instructing the Innsbruck government as follows.

Although Helena von Freyberg is a noblewoman, she cannot be excused from a public recantation because of what the common people would say and the kind of example it would be to the people.[130] *However, if she cannot be convinced to carry out a public recantation, she should recant in front of the (territorial) government promising never to adhere to the sect for the rest of her life. She will also have to promise in writing to go to confession according to the Christian order, to partake of the sacrament and to do penance. She should obtain possession of her properties again.*

On January 21, 1534 the Innsbruck officials sent copies of Ferdinand's answer to her mediators, Montfort and Fuchs, for approval adding their own reasons why Helena should recant publicly.

She has been so intensely and deeply involved in the Anabaptist sect, providing refuge and lodging for persons who have been baptized in the region of Kitzbühel, some of whom have been executed, that she has been the primary cause of so many people joining the movement. Therefore, we do not find it wise or advisable that she recant to us, but rather to as many people as possible in the church at Kitzbühel.[131]

The Innsbruck officials were now fully aware of Helena's widespread influence and also of how the recantation of a prominent leader like her could break the strength of the Anabaptist movement in Kitzbühel. Ferdinand on the other hand, thought it better that she at least recant in private rather than not at all, even if not in front of the people.

Still Helena hesitated. She too was aware of what a public recantation would mean. "Such conduct by a leader injured the Anabaptist cause more seriously than all the exertions of the government...."[132] In the meantime the Innsbruck officials were in correspondence with officials in Augsburg. On July 2, 1534 Innsbruck stated their views in no uncertain terms. *No one, also not the Freybergerin, can be excused from public recantation, especially since she has sinned more than others and forfeited the privileges of her class.*[133]

The young nobleman, Sigmund von Wolkenstein, also petitioned for release from public recantation. The Innsbruck officials wrote to the Bishop of Brixen on October 9, 1534, rejecting his request since his mother, Elisabeth, had already recanted publicly and Helena von Freyberg would be doing the same.[134] The government assumed too much.

Later that month, October 1534, Helena achieved her goal of giving the short form of the recantation. She returned to Tirol and recanted in private in Innsbruck to the viceroy, a lower order government official. Other sources relate that "with words loud and clear" Helena declared that she would desist from her erring ways.[135] She was spared from public humiliation but her life was still in danger despite her recantation. The decrees stated that leaders who recanted "could not escape execution, but would be buried in consecrated earth."[136] Helena left her homeland for the last time. She remained in exile in Augsburg for the rest of her life.

The Augsburg Interrogation

From the last years of her life we have two statements given in Helena's own words. Her interrogation in Augsburg – the only record of her spoken words – reveals her continued leadership activities. In 1535 the radical action of Anabaptists in the north who had taken over the city of Münster,[137] made Anabaptists in all of Europe highly suspect. Mass arrests followed even in the more tolerant city of Augsburg and included Helena.

Helena von Freyberg's Testimony to the Augsburg City Council, April 11, 1535

Present: Wolf Langenmantel, Ulstat, Drechsel, Schmalholz (members of the city council)

Helena, Onoffrius von Freyberg's wife of Aschau, located two miles from Kufstein, testified without torture, that she had three sons who were knights. She knew nothing about them other than that they were with their father. All the details of her situation, how and why she came here and also why she was exiled, were known to the Lord Mayor, to Dr. Wolfgang (Thalhauser), a medical doctor, to (the preachers) Bonifacius (Wolfart) and to (master) Michel (Keller). She had held no large meetings in her house, only two, three or four brothers came and went and they discussed the Word of God.

She came and went to the Kunigspergerin, to Bonifacius, (master) Michel, Dr. Thalhauser and (a man named) Regel and (also) ate with them. They also came to her and they knew how she lived.

She was baptized in the region next to Bavaria (namely Tirol).

She had not become involved with anyone and did not think she had done anything wrong since she had not allowed many people to come to her here in Augsburg. She knew of no brothers and sisters other than those who were now in prison.

Her financial support came from her husband and her sons.

If she knew of something in which she had erred, she wanted to improve and would gladly be advised of it.

No one had been baptized in her house.

On the reverse side of this testimony was written: expelled from the city.[138]

Helena had debated theology with the Protestant leaders of the city and held small meetings in her house to discuss the Word of God. Jörg Maler, another Anabaptist leader in Augsburg, told the authorities about the Anabaptist group which met in Helena's house and "in Rosenau, just outside the city gate to the east."[139] Helena refused to name other Anabaptists but the mere fact that she had been baptized incriminated her. She was treated like a common criminal, laid in chains overnight and expelled from the city the following day.[140] Her name disappears from the record until January 1539. At that time her sons Pankraz and Christoph Georg, who were supporting her with 100 Gulden per year,[141] wrote a letter to the Augsburg city council on behalf of their mother, now widowed, so that she could live in the city.

During the last years of her life in Augsburg Helena continued her leadership role in Anabaptism. In 1542 she taught her tailor, Hans Jacob Schneider who became a key leader in Augsburg in the 1550s and 1560s.[142] She corresponded with her friend and fellow leader Pilgram Marpeck when he was absent from Augsburg. Like her fellow believer Magdalena von Pappenheim, Helena acted as a mediator between Marpeck and the Silesian nobleman Caspar von Schwenckfeld who debated with the Anabaptists. In 1543 she gave Schwenckfeld's written response to Marpeck's book, *The Admonition*, to Marpeck.[143]

"Confession of Sin" to the Augsburg Congregation

In contrast to her interrogation record, the "Confession" which Helena wrote to her own congregation in Augsburg is extraordinary for different reasons. Sometime in the last years of her life, Helena was motivated to write down a confession regarding some unnamed sin, possibly her recantation in Tirol. In the process Helena provides a glimpse into her personal spiritual journey and her dependence on the Holy Spirit. She speaks of herself as an old woman in the faith since she had persevered in Anabaptism now for more than fifteen years. Her "Confession on Account of Her Sin," the text of which is in the Appendix, was preserved in the *Kunstbuch*, a book of writings from members of Marpeck's circle. It leaves no doubt about the depth and sincerity of her religious faith in the face of spiritual discipline. When she speaks of her "yieldedness" or "Gelassenheit" she is expressing a central Anabaptist belief, that of "giving place to God's will" and accepting the suffering that such yielding entailed.[144]

Helena's Influential Son

A final word must be said about the influence of her eldest son Pankraz. He was not an Anabaptist but his contributions to Protestantism in Bavaria are highly significant. After he took charge of the Hohenaschau castle in 1535,[145] he made important economic innovations in the region, establishing an iron industry[146] and a market.[147] Through Pankraz the Freybergs became a leading noble family in Bavaria.[148] In 1553 Pankraz became the most influential civil servant in Bavaria as Hofmarschall (Seneschal) to Duke Albrecht V, being second in command in the government.[149] Together with other members of the nobility, he almost succeeded in establishing the Protestant faith in Bavaria. But in 1561 Pankraz fell into disfavour, was imprisoned and lived in exile at Hohenaschau until his death in 1565. His biographer suggests he became a martyr for the Lutheran faith.

March 17, 1528,

From the region of Kitzbühel, Hans Pletzer's wife, Hans Taurer's wife and maid and another maid who also fled[150] were all to be interrogated.

March 26, 1528,

Martha Weltzenbergerin was required to stay in prison in Rattenberg another eight to twelve days on a sparse diet and to pay for her keep, in addition to the other punishments required of her (see January 10, 1528).

March 26, 1528, Bartlme Springenfell's Wife Came Back Sick

Ferdinand I's government instructed Christoff Philipp von Liechtenstein, governor of Rattenberg about a number of Anabaptist prisoners. In addition to the punishments meted out to her, Martha Weltzenberger, Leonhard Spitzhamer and the Spitzhamer's maid the following was required of her.

... *regarding the Bartlme Springenfell's wife, we have the following opinion. She herself did not request a pardon. We are aware that she is now back in Rattenberg on her own but is apparently sick. You are to imprison her again when she is well and keep her there until the government of Upper Austria sends further instructions.*

March 30, 1528,

The Schlosserin and Peter Taurer's wife were among those imprisoned in Rattenberg who requested a pardon at their arrest.

March 30, 1528, Barbara Schützinger, Left Young Children

Barbara (but not her husband Sigmund) was among the Anabaptists who requested a pardon from Bartlme Anngst, the judge in Rattenberg. The central government had given orders that those Anabaptists who turned themselves in before the upcoming Palm Sunday (April 5) could receive a pardon if their only crime was re-baptism or attending a nocturnal communion meeting and sermon.[151] But, baptizers, preachers and those spreading the teaching that all goods should be held in common were not eligible for pardon. While her husband Sigmund was not named on March 30, he was already a co-worker of Jacob Hutter in Tirol at this time.[152]

Barbara's story continues on May 20, 1528 when Anngst was told he could still accept the petitions sent in by various families, including that of Sigmund for his wife Barbara. A year later, July 31, 1529, the list of Anabaptists who fled Rattenberg and left children behind included Barbara and Sigmund (also called Simon). They left one child in Rattenberg.

On October 22, 1530 the Innsbruck government suggested to the governor of Kufstein that he write the governor of Burghausen, Bavaria instructing him, *to capture Sigmund Schützinger and his wife since Sigmund was apparently a real leader in the (Anabaptist) sect.*[153]

Sometime during October or November 1530, the following information was reported concerning the confiscated Schützinger property and their children:

Sigmund Schützinger, who also fled, left 120 Gulden with Purgl Schmid, citizen of Rattenberg, of which all but 55 Gulden has been paid to his wife, to which she is entitled.

Moreover, Anngst has confiscated half of their small hilltop property to which Schützinger's wife has a right and collected the surplus it brought in. Anngst is to settle this account with the heirs. The two young, underage children, who are between three and seven years of age, are entitled to half of the surplus if there is any.[154]

On July 11, 1531, there is a final reference to Barbara. *Ernst Pranndt, the new judge, as well as the mayor and the town council of Rattenberg, were to provide information concerning the petition submitted for Barbara Schützinger. (The Innsbruck government wanted to know) how she related to the Anabaptists, whether she gave them lodging, whether or not there was reason to suspect from her actions that she was one of them and why she was to be exiled from the territory. The petition was to be set aside (and would not be taken into account).* In the end Barbara escaped to Moravia to join her husband who became the leader of the Auspitz congregation. There her story continues.

Hutter arrived in Auspitz in August 1533. Soon after he came he began teaching a stricter practice of community of goods. Subsequently, it was discovered that a number of families had kept back property. Simon and

Barbara Schützinger had more linens and clothing than they needed and in addition had hidden forty Gulden under the roof of their dwelling. The congregation excommunicated Schützinger and on October 12, 1533 Hutter became their leader.[155]

April 3, 1528,
Lienhard Platten's wife of Volders, baptized with two young maids,[156] stayed with her sister in Telfs, the Velcklehnerin.

April 4, 1528,
Hanns Vischer of Liesfelden and his wife turned themselves in to the judge in Rattenberg and requested a pardon.

April 4, 1528, Anna Egger, Lay Leader on a Preaching Tour
The Innsbruck government instructed Erasmus Offenhauser to search for and capture the Anabaptists who had fled from the city of Hall into the nearby districts of Hertenberg, Stams and St. Petersberg including a baker named Peter Egger, his one-eyed sister (Anna) and Lorenz Aufleger. They were preaching and baptizing around the Mieminger mountain and the village of Rietz (below Stams, towards Telfs, west of Innsbruck).

April 7, 1528,
Several unnamed women believers from Stams[157] were among the seven persons baptized by Jörg Vasser who requested a pardon which, unlike their teachers and baptizers, they were eligible to receive. But first they were to be questioned individually.

April 17, 1528, Ursula Sailerin, Punishment Even For the Feeble Minded
In a communication about a number of Anabaptists, *the Innsbruck government asked the local judge in Hall, Wolfgang Waltenhofer to report whether Ursula Sailerin was in fact feeble minded.*

Later that week, on April 21, Waltenhofer was instructed further. *Ursula Sailerin was to do the penance also required of her, despite her mental condition.*[158]

April 23, 1528,
Dorothea Frick, wife of the Anabaptist martyr Leonhard Frick, received a pardon which friends had requested for her several weeks earlier on April

4. This was granted to her since it was still during the period of grace when pardons were given to those who reported to the government. The government assumed, *she may have come into the sect only because of her husband.*

May 7, 1528, Dorothea Angstwurm, Leader's Wife Requests Share of Property[159]

On April 24, 1528, the Innsbruck government informed Bartlme Anngst, judge in Rattenberg, that Martin Angstwurm from nearby Brixlegg stated in his petition that he baptized five people. Because of this, he could not be pardoned. The judge was instructed to bring him back to prison. After conducting an inventory of his possessions they were to be locked up and a report sent to Innsbruck.

Not quite three weeks later, on *May 7, 1528, a directive was sent to Wolfgang Schönmann, the mining judge in Rattenberg. He was to look after the claim of Dorothea Angstwurm for the share of her husband's property to which she was entitled.*

May 12, 1528, The Sister of Hans Velcklehner Also Proselytized

Lamprecht Haun, judge of Hertenberg, was instructed to capture an Anabaptist woman who was fleeing, namely, Hans Velcklehner's sister. She had been with her brother Hans in Telfs and with the baker, Lamprecht Penntz and had converted two women to her heretical beliefs, namely, Velcklehner's wife (Barbara) and her sister (Lienhard Platten's wife).

May 13, 1528,

Margret Kobl from the Ritten plateau was the wife of a leader and near the end of her pregnancy at her arrest. She first recanted, then rejoined and subsequently fled with her husband. Their two maids were also involved (see August 26, 1528).

May 15, 1528,

Four unnamed Anabaptist women[160] were beaten in public in Rettenberg because there was no pillory in Kolsass.

May 17, 1528, Three Women From Bregenz, Two Pregnant, One a Martyr

The authorities in the district of Bregenz (in Voraarlberg) … were informed about four Anabaptists, Anna Krätlerin (I), wife of Hans Ernst from Malas in the parish of

Steufen, Michel Huepp on the Stäbis, his wife (also named) Anna Krätlerin (II), and Cristina Artzatin.... All of them were to be put on trial.

When the Innsbruck government wrote to Bregenz again on June 3, 1528, the instructions were as follows: *Michel Huepp on the Stäbis, Cristina Artzatin of Weissach and Anna Krätlerin (I), wife of Hans Ernst from Malas should be tried in the criminal court. Even though Anna Krätlerin (I) was condemned to death, she should not be executed until after the birth of her child. If Anna Krätlerin (II) wanted to recant, she was to swear the oath, take on the penance required of her by the priest and pay for her keep, if she was able to. Also, she had to promise to report back to the authorities after the birth of her child and at that time accept corporal punishment at the pillory from the executioner.*

Two of the prisoners felt the effects of the new law of April 1, 1528 which decreed harsher punishments for Anabaptists. The instructions of July 23, 1528, sent in response to the local government's report of July 13 (the day honouring St. Margaret, the saint to whom prayers for pregnant women were offered)[161] stated that, *Michel Huepp and Cristina Artzatin had been sentenced and burned at the stake. A pardon for Anna Krätlerin (II) who was pregnant and showed remorse could not be granted from Innsbruck because the period of grace had run out. The king (who held court elsewhere at this time) would now have to decide this.*

On August 13, 1528 ... the king granted a pardon to Anna Krätlerin (II) on the condition that she would swear the oath, agree to accept a reasonable punishment and do penance for both the sacred and the secular authorities. Her promise and the oath to confirm it had to be given right away, while the penance could be done after the birth of her child.

Anna Krätlerin (I), wife of Hans Ernst, was eventually ready to recant as well. She also received a pardon in August and was released after swearing the oath. Just as for Anna Krätlerin (II), her punishments could be delayed until after her child was born.[162]

May 19, 1528,

In Rotenfels in the domain of Hohoneck, the officials of the Duke of Montfort overstepped their authority when they drowned an unnamed woman, one of four who had been arrested and tried. A second unnamed woman was released without punishment. The two others were discussed later (see August 6, 1528).[163]

May 20, 1528,
Petitions were submitted in Rattenberg for Elsbeth Taurerin and for Barbara Pernhappel. Barbara's husband was a miner.

May 23, 1528, Eight of the Fourteen Prisoners Were Women
The Innsbruck government responded to the judge in St. Petersberg, Hanns Erlpeck, who had requested advice about the persons named in the report he had sent them. On the basis of the imperial mandates, the persons (in this group) who had been baptized were to be kept in prison for fourteen days on a sparse diet. Following that, they could be released if they provided a proper oath and payment for their keep if they had the money to do so. The prisoners were: Bernhard Sneider and his wife, Cristan Muntafoner and his wife, Sebastian Ampos and his mother, Hanns Ampos and his wife, Gross Enngerle and her daughter, Ambrosy Pitzen, Äfferlin Rospuchlerin, Melchior Feyrabendt and the crown administrator's wife who was an older woman.[164]

Their punishment was not harsh given that the period of grace had just ended.

June 3, 1528,
The crown administrator of Altenburg began proceedings against Mathes Kerschpaumer's wife. Despite a petition from the priests and officials of Ritten on her behalf, she was not granted a pardon. By the spring of 1529 she and her husband were burned at the stake and left two children. The appraised value of their property was between 1400 and 1500 Gulden.[165]

June 5, 1528, The Baker and His Wife From Hertenberg Recanted
Lamprecht Penntz and his wife from the district of Hertenberg were one of several Anabaptist couples in prison. Lamprecht, a baker by trade, had been named already in a report of May 12 (see above) and possibly this is when he and his wife were baptized. The request for the pardon of the prisoners, submitted by the citizens of three villages in the region, had been rejected. The Anabaptists could not be excused from the requirements of the latest decree of May 27. When their fellow prisoners, Hans and Barbara Velcklehner escaped one week later, Lamprecht and his wife chose to remain in prison. For this action they gained their freedom but they were not spared from a humiliating recantation, penance and payment for their upkeep in prison. They both recanted in October of that year and spoke the following words in order to be re-instated in the church.[166]

On October 10, 1528, Ferdinand I sent instructions from Innsbruck to Lamprecht Haun, judge of Hertenberg, to pardon Lamprecht Penntz and his wife. The wording of the recantation was enclosed.

Faithful one! We have read your report regarding Lamprecht Penntz and his wife and respond with the order that you ensure that they recant. Both are to be present on three consecutive Sundays in front of the high altar in their parish church before the observance of mass, in order to join the usual procession and walk barefoot in front of the priest around the church. Penntz is to wear a shirt which has a cross sewn on it and his wife is to carry a cross in her hands. Following that they are to give a public recantation in the church as recorded on the enclosed papers. Then they are to remain in front of the altar on their knees for the duration of the mass and receive absolution from the priest after that. This is the mandate from his majesty, the 10th day of October, 1528.

1. I confess, that through damnable unchristian teaching and instruction, I fell away from the Christian baptism, and no longer adhered to it.

2. In addition, I confess that I did not believe in the holy mass and the most worthy sacrament and did not believe that the bread and the wine truly contained the body and blood of Jesus Christ our Saviour.

3. I confess that I did not place my faith in the mediation of Mary, the Mother of God and the saints or in many other articles of the Christian faith. I have erred and did not believe and have gone against the practice of the Christian Church and have instructed others in my erroneous faith.

All this I recant voluntarily and with proper understanding. I contradict all of (my previous belief) and praise God the almighty in front of those assembled in this church, promising to desist from such error, never again to associate with it, and also to believe all that which the united Christian church has estabalished and ordained. I also want to attend confession with my priest and partake of the holy sacrament when he deems it appropriate.[167]

June 6, 1528,

A woman named Maurfoglin was to be tried in Rattenberg, despite her simple-mindedness. Then she was to be pardoned like Margaret Glenerin.

June 16, 1528, Women Pardoned But Could Not Escape Corporal Punishment

Margaret Glenerin of Rattenberg has been named initially on June 4 along with four other Anabaptists including Hans Letzelter and his wife. A pardon request had been submitted for all of them. The report of June 16 dealt with her case further, stating, *Margaret Glenerin should be pardoned, despite the fact that she neglected to report during the period of grace, which was now 14 days past. Nevertheless, she reported to the authorities on her own, seeking their mercy. She could not be released until the executioner had given her a flogging at the pillory.*[168] She was also required to do penance. The Maurfoglin was to be given the same treatment.

The petition submitted on behalf of the two women was rejected. On June 29 the judge in Rattenberg was instructed that, *The Glenerin and the Maurfoglin cannot be excused from their punishment at the pillory despite the petition.*

June 16, 1528,

A petition was submitted by the judge himself, officials from the mining smelters, and the society of Rattenberg, for three couples: Hans Letzelter, Hans Greiner, and Cristan Pernhappel and their wives. Hans Letzelter and his wife later fled (see October – November 1530).

June 23, 1528, Women in Styria Preached and Did Radical Things

Excerpts from the visitation and inquisition register for the territory of Styria, in the year 1528.

Viet Mössner stated (the following in his confession.) Jörg Fleischacker's portly wife preaches in homes... The (woman named) Gallin also preaches publicly in her house, ever since Hans Has, (their leader) was taken away and several times following that. She does not want to admit that many people came to hear her....

Weinprenner and Riemer still preach in their homes. Jörg Fleischacker and his wife do not believe or see any worth in the mass, the mother of God or the saints. They believe only in the one God and also see no value in infant baptism....

Peter Kramer's wife said she is as good as our lady, the Mother of God.... It was said that Veit Riemer's wife took some holy water from the church. Her maid brought it home for her.[169]

The Kreutzerin ... apparently also preached, but (Mössner) had not heard anything about this....

Fleischacker's wife is supposed to have read mass with Riemer's wife and Weinprenner present.

Weinprenner read mass (in the home of) Caspar Riemer's wife and the women sang. Fleischackher's wife was present there with her daughters. Pangratz Riemer's wife organized it all, the sacrament and the mass.[170]

June 23, 1528,
If the Waltsamin of Wattens is an Anabaptist she is to be imprisoned. Cristina, daughter of the farmer from Scheyern, should receive the same treatment as others if she wishes to recant and do penance. No exceptions are to be made for young people.

July 9, 1528, Three Women Benefit from the Hesitancy of Kitzbühel Officials
The discussions with the crown administrator of Kitzbühel named at least eight prisoners among whom were three women, *Helene Schesserin, Cristan Taurer's maid and Wilhem from Tuna's wife Ottilia for whom a trial date was to be set.*[171] *On the basis of the confessions which they have given, they should be asked how they became part of the forbidden sect of Anabaptism and what they think about the holy sacrament. In spite of their neglect of the imperial mandate which granted pardons to those who had joined before March 26, they should be asked if they want to persevere or leave the sect. (If they choose to persevere in their faith), the authorities are to deal with them according to the mandate and let the law be carried out.*

Ottilia's husband was one of four male Anabaptists who escaped prison. The elder Taurer (Cristan) had by now carried out the penance required of him and was willing to swear the oath promising to desist from Anabaptism. But his son Andre remained at large as did Jacob Partzner, the leader aided by Helena von Freyberg.

On August 10, 1528 we learn that two of the women, Helene Schesserin and Cristan Taurer's maid were among those who had been pardoned on the basis of petitions submitted for them. Their sentences had been postponed but they had not performed their penance. The Innsbruck officials had not found the judge of Kitzbühel, Jörg Perger, to be reliable and sought to have Bartlme Anngst of Rattenberg take over. But Anngst hesitated as well. Several of the prisoners, including the women, benefited in that their sentences were very mild and no death sentences were given. Others were not so fortunate. By the end of August several men were executed in Kitzbühel, Thomas Hermann and Hans Schwaigkhofer, who were leaders and Hans Pletzer, also called Aschlberger, from the group discussed on July 9.[172] Aschlberger's widow would be questioned much later. See May 12, 1530.

July 14, 1528, Explanation of the Sacrament (Communion), Passed on by a Woman

Excerpts from the visitation and inquisition register in Graz, in the territory of Styria, 1528. Caspar Maler was an important Anabaptist in Graz.

Procopius Huschimley was the Reformer in Graz who preached in the castle like Herr Jörg, a priest and friend of Procopius who was Lutheran.

In the village of Strassgang, Achacius Khelner, the chaplain, says that Procopius Huschimley and Herr Jörg preached against the intercession of the saints. They also said that the mass was useless.

... Caspar Maler's house is called the synagogue, (that is, the house where Anabaptist meetings take place). The woman innkeeper, Steffan's wife, said she heard the following from Maler's wife, who in turn had heard it from her husband. Caspar Maler's wife said she is amazed that people take the sacrament (communion), that they think God would have allowed himself to be baked in an oven.[173]

July 21, 1528,

In June Anna Rinnerin escaped from prison in Hertenberg but was recaptured in July. The bail for her release was set very high at one hundred Gulden. If she could not pay this she would have to recant publicly on three consecutive Sundays and return to prison after giving birth. But the judge was to confirm that she was actually pregnant.

July 23, 1528,

Hans Viltzurner's wife, well advanced in her pregnancy and leaving many children behind, fled with her husband who was accused of evil talk. Hans asked the crown administrator of Gufidaun, Hans Prew, to write a petition on his behalf so they could return home.

August 6, 1528,

A petition for clemency was submitted for Elsbeth Gesslerin and her daughter, Katharina from Hoheneck who had been arrested May 19, 1528.

August 26, 1528, One of Margret Koblin's Maids Helped Her Husband Escape

The Innsbruck government instructed Jörg Sunnstainer, judge of Sarnthein, to investigate the former maid of Margret Koblin named Els. She had brought things into the prison for (Ulrich) Kobl which had helped him to escape and to flee.[174]

This was a serious accusation as Ulrich Kobl was a major Anabaptist leader. Ulrich and his wife Margret had two maids indicating they had a larger farm. Their second maid, Bärbl as well as Lienhard, their labourer, were on the list of those named by Margret on August 27, 1528 who were to be arrested.

August 27, 1528, Anabaptist Woman Suspected of Murder

... on the basis of their confessions as Anabaptists, Katharina Torgglerin and Margret Kobl, who have fallen again (rejoining their fellow believers) after their recantation are to be tried with the law of capital punishment. The sentence is to be carried out immediately.

The two women were not executed. As reported in the previous record of August 26, Margret's husband Ulrich had escaped prison with the help of their maid Els. Margret and the Torgglerin managed to escape as well and are not mentioned again until two months later. On October 27, 1528 orders to search for Ulrich Kobl, his wife Margret, the Anabaptist leader Hanns Portz and the Torgglerin were issued from the Ritten to all the surrounding authorities as far south as Trent. Two wanted posters giving physical descriptions of the men were attached. And the Torgglerin was wanted for murder. No details are given in this summarized record, only this statement is included.

Shortly thereafter, on November 6 it is reported that the group, joined now by the servant of Hanns Portz, is fleeing south towards Venice. An innkeeper in the bishopric of Trent had warned the fleeing Anabaptists of the government search party. Also, *Wilhelm von Liechtenstein is advised to obtain information from Wilhelm Schuster from the district of Steinegger. Schuster brought flour and other food provisions to the escapees.* Schuster was captured by the end of November and named the persons among whom were a man named Fras and his wife, who had given the fugitives food and drink. The final references to Ulrich, Margret and Hanns refer to the sale of their property, indicating that they did not return to their homes. The Kobl's property on the Ritten was sold for 1300 Gulden – no small amount.[175]

The Torgglerin also managed to elude the officials. On June 14, 1530 Christoff Fuchs, the governor of Kufstein, *was instructed to capture her. The king granted her safe passage to come to Kufstein for a hearing in front of a jury. If the jury determined that she was not an Anabaptist she should be imprisoned in any case and tried under the law of capital punishment for the murder she had committed.*[176]

September 11, 1528,
Michel Oberhofer's wife, in prison with her husband in Schwaz, was to testify about him and their intentions. A fatal disease in that town prevented the jury from meeting so they were pardoned.

October 5, 1528,
The king granted a pardon to Lorenz Vitzthum from the region of Hall based on the petition of the local government and his wife, who was recovering from childbirth. They had eight under-age children. Lorenz was a simple-minded, God-fearing man. Part of his penance was to remain in prison 14 days on a meagre diet.

October 13, 1528,
A mother and her daughter, captured in Karneid south of Bozen, had been baptized by Michel Kürschner, a former court secretary and key Anabaptist leader. The women were to be interrogated, tried and sentenced even if they showed remorse.[177]

October 27, 1528,
Three women[178] first mentioned on this date were executed by drowning, despite the leniency of the governor of Bozen. One of the women left seven children, the oldest of whom was ten years. She also left a house, some moveable property and some cows. The cost of executing these women was 54 Gulden and 36 Kreuzer.[179] See November 24, 1529 for another case where execution costs are mentioned.

November 4, 1528,
The Innsbruck government was astonished that Wilhelm von Liechtenstein, crown administrator of Kurtatsch, had allowed the Anabaptist woman from Deutschnofen,[180] who had promised to report back to the authorities, to simply leave. If she was captured again she would have to be tried in the criminal court as the laws and mandates require.

November 27, 1528,
Florian Palpatscher's wife from the district of Bozen was accused with her

husband of providing lodging for Anabaptists. For this they were to be punished.

November 27, 1528, Pregnancy Did Not Preclude Martyrdom

The crown administrator of the Neuhaus Castle, located near Gais in the district of Uttenheim in the Taufer Valley, was instructed as follows regarding three Anabaptists.

Wolfgang Strael and his wife, (who were baptized by Michel Kürschner), and the wife of Martin Nock were all Anabaptists and were in prison. They were partly under his jurisdiction and partly under the authority of the neighbouring district of Deutschnofen. They were to be tried in the criminal court and dealt with in the same manner as Wilhelm of Liechtenstein had dealt with the three women in Bozen (see October 27 above). *All three had joined the heretical sect of Anabaptism after the period of grace had run out and therefore they had to be dealt with according to the latest (more severe) decree of April 1, 1528. They could not be pardoned.*[181] But Nock's wife should be spared until she had given birth to her child. It is likely that both of these women were martyred.

November 28, 1528,

The crimes of Fras' wife and Jacob Schäntl's wife from the district of Völs were, giving food and drink to the leader Ulrich Kobl and the Anabaptists fleeing with him. For this they were to be captured and interrogated.

December 16, 1528, Persistent Anabaptists, Male and Female Leaders

The Innsbruck government addressed Lienhard von Völs as follows. From the confessions of the following prisoners which he sent in earlier, of Haintz Bair's wife Magdalena, Elisabeth the sister of Wolfram, Lienhard Fundnetscher the younger and Hans Kölls from the Ritten plateau, one can see that they remain steadfast in their deceptive (faith) and sect and do not want to recant. They should be brought before the judge, Lienhard Friedrich, and the jury, who should swear an oath to uphold the mandates, particularly the (more severe) one issued April 1, 1528. The sentence should be carried out even if the prisoners declare themselves ready to recant at the last moment.

Fundnetscher's wife, who is pregnant, Christof Mesner from Umbas, and Melchior Schneider from Völs, who want to recant, are to be pardoned on the usual conditions, after a flogging at the pillory. The brother of Melchior Schneider from Völs, who is a trustworthy person, has offered that if his brother is pardoned, he will see to it that the principal Anabaptists and persons who lead others astray, namely, Michel Kürschner, Mathis Waldner and his wife and the Gallpüchlerin,[182] *are brought to prison. Jacob Schäntl and his wife should be released on bail and a written promise as the territorial governor suggests.*

Despite these instructions for severe treatment, we do not know if Magdalena Bair was actually executed. It is the only reference to her. Elisabeth Wolfram was treated leniently and allowed to recant in the spring of 1529. As for the female leaders named here, Mathis Waldner's wife is mentioned only in this record.[183] On the other hand, the Gallpüchlerin was named already at the beginning of 1528 (January 29) and was reported to have attended an Anabaptist meeting on December 21, 1528, five days after this report was issued (see below).

December 20, 1528,

The Pentzel's daughter from Wangen above Bozen was released because she had reported to the authorities during the period of grace before Palm Sunday and had done the required penance. Two pregnant women, also from Wangen, were arrested on the same day and named again the next day, December 21.[184] They were to be brought to Bozen for interrogation and punishment, but not until they had given birth.

December 20, 1528,

Dorothea Gärber and her husband from the Ritten plateau were interrogated both with and without torture. Despite petitions submitted by themselves and the sacred and secular authorities in Sarnthein, a directive of April 11, 1529 ordered their trial in the criminal court.

December 21, 1528,

The summary of this document names three persons whom the judge in Bozen, Jacob Hupher, should search for, namely, the prominent leader Michel Kürschner, and the two women, the Gallpüchlerin and the Silberin. These three had been together with fourteen others on the mountain of Breitenberg near Leifers south of Bozen. These Anabaptists had held the Lord's Supper.[185] This is the only time the Silberin is mentioned.

Notes

1. Regarding Schlaffer and Frick see TA 1972, 64:34-35 and 73:2.
2. TA 1972, 65:25f.
3. TA 1972, 21:5-11.
4. TA 1972, 23:3-11.
5. *Hutterite Beginnings*, 191.
6. TA 1972, 66, document 61.
7. Katharina Kreuter held mass in Mühlhausen, Germany in 1526. Marion Kobelt-Groch, *Aufsässig Töchter Gottes Frauen im Bauerkrieg und in den Täuferbewegungen* (Frankfurt/Main: Campus Verlag, 1993), 150.
8. See TA 1964, 33:8-9; 34:9f. and TA 1972, 25. See also, Grete Mecenseffy and Robert Friedman, "Styria (Austria)," in *Global Anabaptist Mennonite Encyclopedia Online* (1959), at www.gameo.org.
9. Clasen, *Social History*, 377.
10. Linda A. Huebert Hecht, "Anabaptist Women in Tirol who Recanted," in *Profiles of Anabaptist Women*, 156-63, gives an overview and specific details for the case of Lamprecht Penntz and his wife.
11. TA 1972, 75:31-34.
12. The written statement or promise (affidavit) to desist from Anabaptism and/or the oath sworn to confirm that promise was called an "Urfehde." "It became a very prominent instrument during the Reformation in the persecution of 'heretics,' particularly the Anabaptists. Breaking the *Urfehde* became a key cause of prosecution ... The *Common Urfehde* was a simple oath usually rendered after an imprisonment or legal custody in which the prisoner acknowledged his guilt, accepted his sentence and punishment, and promised by oath not to seek vengeance, thereby renouncing all claims to wrongful or unjust treatment and absolving his captors of all responsibility. It was an oath of truce to keep the peace and respect the due process of law." Edmund Pries, "Anabaptist Oath Refusal: Basel, Bern and Strasbourg, 1525-1538" (unpublished PhD dissertation, University of Waterloo, 1995), 37-38.
13. Mecenseffy, "Anabaptists in Kitzbühel," 101-2. Some of these humiliating requirements are also discussed in *Hutterite Beginnings*, 191.
14. Oyer, *"They Harry the Good People Out of the Land,"* 312.
15. Kieckhefer describes such means of avoiding detection in regard to the 14th century Waldensians. See his book, *Repression of Heresy*, 53.
16. Gary Waite, "Women Supporters of David Joris," in *Profiles of Anabaptist Women*, 330-31.
17. Oyer, *"They Harry the Good People Out of the Land,"* 42, 244.
18. Brad S. Gregory, *Salvation at Stake Christian Martyrdom in Early Modern Europe* (Cambridge, MA: Harvard University Press, 1999), 208.
19. In TA 1972, 366:21 it states she is to recant "von der Kanzel."
20. TA 1972, 134, document 152.

21. TA 1972, 149, document 185. See also, Grete Mecenseffy, "Anabaptists in Kitzbühel," 102-3.
22. Mecenseffy, "Anabaptists in Kitzbühel," 104. Also, TA 1972, 170-71.
23. TA 1972, 150, 156, 158, 160-163, 169, 177. *Hutterite Beginnings*, 192.
24. Sixteenth century wages are discussed in Matthias Schmelzer, "Geschichte der Preise und Löhne in Rattenberg vom Ende des 15. bis in die 2. Hälfte des 19. Jahrhunderts" (unpublished Doctoral dissertation, Leopold-Franzens University, Innsbruck, 1972). Regarding wages see the Appendix.
25. TA 1972, 104:1.
26. For a discussion of this early time period see Huebert Hecht, "A Brief Moment in Time, 52-74.
27. Wolfgang Schaeufele, "The Missionary Vision and Activity of the Anabaptist Laity," *Mennonite Quarterly Review* XXXVI, 2 (April, 1962), 100.
28. Natalie Zemon Davis, "City Women and Religious Change," *Society and Culture in Early Modern France, Eight Essays* (Stanford, California: Stanford University Press, 1975), 84.
29. Keith L. Sprunger, "God's Powerful Army of the Weak: Anabaptist Women of the Radical Reformation," in *Triumph Over Silence, Women in Protestant History*, ed., Richard L. Greaves, (Westport, CT: Greenwood Press, 1985), 54.
30. Max Weber, *Max Weber on Charisma and Institution Building, Selected Papers*, ed. by S. N. Eisenstadt, (Chicago, IL: University of Chicago Press, 1968), 20; "It is characteristic of the leadership roles in Christianity claimed by women that they derive their authority from personal charisma rather than from office." Ruether and McLaughlin, *Women of Spirit*, 19, 21-22; Phyllis Mack states in her book: "… yet it was precisely *because* women had no formal authority as ordained ministers or magistrates that their activities were so effective in shaping and sustaining the Quakers' charismatic movement in its formative years." See, *Visionary Women Ecstatic Prophecy in Seventeenth Century England*, 4; C. Arnold Snyder, "Introduction," *Profiles of Anabaptist Women,* 8-12.
31. C. Arnold Snyder, "Introduction," in *Profiles of Anabaptist Women*, 11.
32. *Ibid.*
33. The female leaders Clasen names for Tirol up to 1529 are the Gallpüchlerin, Anna Egger and the wife of Mathis Waldner, the latter two being qualified with the phrase "maybe leader." He includes the Blacksmith's wife from Au for 1530. Clasen identified 45 male and female leaders in Tirol between 1525 and 1529 and another 45 over the next 20 years between 1530 and 1549. Claus-Peter Clasen, "The Anabaptist Leaders: Their Numbers and Background, Switzerland, Austria, South and Central Germany 1525-1618," *Mennonite Quarterly Review*, XLIX, 2 (April, 1975), 122, 123, 126, 144-46.
34. The evidence for Dorothea Maler and Melchior Schneider's wife who were described as leaders in Huebert Hecht, "Faith and Action," 57, 63, is less clear, although they were part of important Anabaptist networks. See Huebert Hecht, "A Brief Moment in Time," for a discussion of the 15 women leaders, 62f.

35. Many Anabaptist prisoners who were questioned about their preaching activities, "ingeneously denied that they 'preached' at all: they had merely 'read the Gospel' to people who requested it." C. Arnold Snyder, "Word and Power in Reformation Zurich," *Archive for Reformation History*, 81 (1990), 280-81. Thus, there may have been many more lay missioners and lay leaders than indicated by these numbers.
36. There are quite a few innkeepers mentioned in the Anabaptist records. Inns were needed about every 25 kilometres since that is the distance that horses could travel in a day.
37. *Hutterite Beginnings*, 167.
38. The leadership activities of men were also unofficial and informal. Wölfl's preaching was "unauthorized." See *Hutterite Beginnings*, 178.
39. Snyder, "Word and Power," 265. Sixteenth century communication is discussed in Snyder, "Introduction," *Profiles of Anabaptist Women*, 6.
40. Schäufele, "Anabaptist Laity," 99.
41. Mecenseffy, "Anabaptists in Kitzbühel," 100. Helena's case is not unlike Beatrice de Planissoles of Montaillou or the noblewomen who were patrons of the Hussites. See Susan Stuard, "The Dominion of Gender: Women's Fortunes in the High Middle Ages," in *Becoming Visible, Women in European History*, 2nd ed., ed. by Renate Bridenthal, Claudia Koonz, Susan Stuard, (Boston: Houghton Mifflin, 1987), 168. In the Cathar movement, "Women, therefore, no less than men, were admitted to the superior caste of the Perfect and could perform priestly rites. This circumstance helps to explain the great appeal of the Cathar religion to spiritually minded women, especially among the noble families of Languedoc." Williston Walker et. al., *A History of the Christian Church, Fourth Edition*, (New York, NY: Charles Scribner's Sons, 1985), 304.
42. Elizabeth Gillan Muir refers to Methodist husband and wife teams as clergy couples. See her book *Petticoats in the Pulpit*, 23. Haude refers to women co-teachers in, "Radical Women," 318, n. 13.
43. Wolfgang Schäufele believed that women were fully emancipated in Anabaptism through their missionary activity yet stated in his book that women were forbidden to preach, baptize or take part in the election of leaders. See *Das Missionarische Bewusstsein und Wirken der Taeufer, Dargestellt nach oberdeutschen Quellen* (Lemgo: Neukirchener Verlag des Erziehungsvereins, 1966), 298.
44. Unfortunately she did not give a source for this. See Elise Boulding, *The Underside of History: A View of Women through Time* (Colorado: Westview Press, 1976), 548.
45. Paul Wappler, *Die Täuferbewegung in Thüringen von 1526-1584* (Jena: Fischer, 1913), 259, discussed in Snyder, *Anabaptist History and Theology: Revised Student Edition*, 168.
46. Sprunger, "God's Powerful Army of the Weak," 51-52, 54.
47. M. Lucille Marr, "Anabaptist Women of the North: Peers in the Faith, Subordinates in Marriage," *Mennonite Quarterly Review* LXI, 4 (October 1987), 355, n. 39.
48. The Austrian custom was to keep a special vessel, a "Weihbrunnkessel," with holy water in the home hanging below a devotional picture so that people could cross themselves,

say their prayers, or touch the sick or women who were pregnant. This information is from conversations with Prof. Ilse Friesen.
49. Rischar, "The Martyrdom of the Salzburg Anabaptists," 324.
50. Barrett, "Ursula Jost and Barbara Rebstock," in *Profiles of Anabaptist Women*, 273.
51. "… the earliest extant full autobiography written in English rather than dictated in English by a woman." Retha M. Warnicke, "Lady Mildmay's Journal: A Study of Autobiography and Meditation in Reformation England," *The Sixteenth Century Journal*, XX, 1 (Spring 1989), 68, 56.
52. Walter Klaassen and William Klassen, *Marpeck: A Life of Dissent and Conformity* (Lancaster, PA: Herald Press, 2008), 254.
53. C. Arnold Snyder, "Introduction," in C. Arnold Snyder, ed., *Sources of South German/ Austrian Anabaptism*, trans. by Walter Klaassen, Frank Friesen, Werner O. Packull (Kitchener, ON: Pandora Press, co-published with Herald Press, 2001), xx-xxi. "Gelassenheit" was rooted in medieval mysticism and piety.
54. Snyder, *Anabaptist History and Theology An Introduction*, 89.
55. Linda Huebert Hecht, "An Extraordinary Lay Leader: The Life and Work of Helene of Freyberg, Sixteenth Century Noblewoman and Anabaptist from the Tirol," *Mennonite Quarterly Review*, LXVI, 3 (July, 1992), 336, n. 87. See Virginia Wiles Holsey, "Philippians 2:5-11: A Paeon to Submission or a Call for Confidence?" in *Mennonite Central Committee Women's Concerns Report*, Report 89, March-April 1990, 10.
56. Malone, *Women & Christianity Volume III*, 50.
57. The authorities always singled out the names of the leaders and the Silberin is named here with two others whom we know were leaders.
58. If women did not die in childbirth for which the risks in the sixteenth century were very high, they likely outlived their husbands since they married at a younger age. Thus there were likely many widows in that society. See Edith Ennen, *Frauen im Mittelalter* (München: C.H.Beck, 1985), 228.
59. Zaunring's treatise is discussed in the Introduction 19 n. 11.
60. Linda A. Huebert Hecht, "Wives, Female Leaders and Two Female Martyrs from Hall," in *Profiles of Anabaptist Women*, 187-94.
61. Oyer, *"They Harry the Good People Out of the Land,"* 40.
62. Elisabeth is "the first known Anabaptist deaconess." She was drowned in 1549. See Cornelius J. Dyck, "Elisabeth and Hadewijk of Friesland," in *Profiles of Anabaptist Women*, 360, 363.
63. Bonnie S. Anderson and Judith P. Zinsser, *A History of Their Own, Women in Europe from Prehistory to the Present*, Vol. I (New York: Harper and Row, 1988), 246.
64. Hanelore Sachs, *The Renaissance Woman*, trans. by Marianne Hertzfeld (New York: McGraw-Hill Book Company, 1971), 48.
65. Bainton, *Women of the Reformation in Germany and Italy*, 247 and Anderson and Zinsser, *A History of Their Own*, 246.

66. Not all leaders' wives were members. The wife of Jörg Vasser, a former monk, is one such case. See December 10, 1527 and October-November 1530. The wives in the Taurer family were to be questioned under threat of torture because of their husbands.
67. If, as some have argued, wives had an ability for moral persuasion and were expected to convince their husbands in matters of religious faith as "preachers to their husbands," the number of missioners could increase. Some medieval writers placed a high value on the ability of the wife "to exercise her influence by means of oral communication.... [and] the value of communication within marriage." Sharon Farmer, "Persuasive Voices: Clerical Images of Medieval Wives," *Speculum, A Journal of Medieval Studies*, 61, 3 (July, 1986), 517, 532, 531.
68. Linda A. Huebert Hecht, "Anabaptist Women and Their Families in Tirol, 1527-1531: Dispelling the Myth of Poverty" 63-87, in Mirjam van Veen, et al., eds., *Sisters: Myth and Reality of Anabaptist, Mennonite, and Doopsgezind Women, ca. 1525-1900* (Brill: Leiden, 2014).
69. Ruether and McLaughlin, *Women of Spirit*, 20.
70. Snyder, "Introduction," *Profiles of Anabaptist Women*, 9. In the most recent survey of the research done on women in Anabaptist and Spiritualist groups, Haude finds that several scholars agree that, "women joined the Anabaptists because they offered greater opportunities for women." Sigrun Haude, "Gender Roles and Perspectives Among Anabaptist and Spiritualist Groups," in *A Companion To Anabaptism and Spiritualism, 1521-1700*, ed. by John D. Roth & James M. Stayer (Leiden: Brill, 2007), 446-47.
71. See February and March references in TA 1972, 68, document 65; 69:10; 94:5f. and 98, document 106.
72. The wording in the court record is, "des lebens frisstest, auch des freyen manns straff erlassest." TA 1972, 99:3.
73. These officials were "Beisitzer." See TA 1972, 53:15.
74. They are designated in the index as n.n.56c and d, two cooks.
75. She is designated in the index as n.n.56e, a young woman.
76. She is designated in the index as n.n.56f, a maid.
77. She is designated in the index as n.n.56b, mayor, wife.
78. She is designated in the index as n.n.55f, innkeeper, wife.
79. She is designated in the index as n.n.55a, young woman.
80. She is designated in the index as n.n.55b, a cook.
81. She is designated in the index as n.n.55c, a maid.
82. She is designated in the index as n.n.55d, mother of maid.
83. She is designated in the index as n.n.55e, chaplain's cook.
84. She is designated in the index as n.n.56a, city judge, wife.
85. She is designated in the index as n.n.57a, shoemaker, wife.
86. She is designated in the index as n.n.57b, wife.
87. TA 1972, 117:20.
88. See also February 16, 1528 Bartlmä Dill Riemenschneider family, which includes a

reference to these martyrs. Little is known about Leonhard Frick and it is not clear if he was an Anabaptist leader. He may have been an ordinary Anabaptist member making him the first rank and file male martyr.

89. The Kunsterweg was a fifteen kilometre toll route built in the fourteenth century through the valley between Trostburg and Bozen, through the Eisack gorge. It was part of the Brenner trade route that led over the Ritten and shortened the route considerably. See Eduard Widmoser, *Tirol A Bis Z* (Innbruck: Südtirol-Verlag, 1970), 432.

90. The Ritten has been described in *Hutterite Beginnings*, 183 as: "a rather wild, inaccessible terrain" and as "an inaccessible high plateau between the Sarn and Eisack rivers" in Stayer, *The German Peasants' War,* 87. Wangen was another district on this plateau, separate from the district called Ritten. This plateau is located to the northeast of Bozen in the mountains above this urban centre.

91. Tiroler Landesarchiv Innsbruck, Empörung der Bauern in Tirol, Kopialbuch, Hs 1874, Bl. (pages) 477r -477v; 567v-568r; 579v cited in Kobelt-Groch, *Aufsässig Töchter*, 191, n. 14. This document speaks of the Gallpüchlerin's "freventlich Reden."

92. Dill was the son of Tilman Riemenschneider, famous south German sculptor who had been involved in Peasant War. After he recanted Bartlmä saw himself as Nicodemus in the Bible who had to practice his faith in secret. Margreth Wolf was martyred in 1531.

93. See references to Elizabeth's will in Leo Andergassen, "Die Altarwerke Bartlmä Dill Riemenschneiders," in *Renaissancealtäre und Epitaphien in Tirol Schlern-Schriften 325* (Innsbruck: Universitätsverlag Wagner, 2007), 62. See Hanns-Paul Ties, "Bartlmä Dill—der Maler und Wiedertäufer, Neues zum Leben und zum Werk des wichtigsten Südtiroler Renaissancekünstlers," in *Dolomiten,* 25/26, 2 (2006), 45; Linda A. Huebert Hecht in collaboration with Hanns-Paul Ties, "Research Note: The Tirolean Anabaptist Artist Bartlme Dill Riemenschneider and the Anabaptist Women in His Household, 1526-1549, in *Mennonite Quarterly Review* 92 (July 2018), 439-461, especially note 60. See page 95 note 186 for more information on Bartlmä Dill.

94. After her husband's execution in the fall of 1529 Els returned to Switzerland remaining in her home region into the 1560s. See Heinold Fast, ed., *Ostschweiz* (Zurich: Theologischer Verlag, 1973), 248.

95. TA 1972, 78-79. Hans Gasser earlier had been imprisoned in Gufidaun for his involvement with Gaismair in the peasant rebellions in which he and Ulrich Kobl were local leaders. See *Hutterite Beginnings*, 366, n. 63; 183, also TA 1972, 39.

96. See April 23, 1529 for Anna Gasser's story. In TA 1972, 325:23 Anna is named as Mayrhofer's sister.

97. 1528 was a leap year. See TA 1972, 543.

98. In this summarized record Cristan Taurer is called "ein rechter Rädelsführer und Principal."

99. In TA 1972, 92:21 the word "Einfalt" is used to indicate simple-mindedness.

100. Mecenseffy, "Anabaptists in Kitzbühel," 100.

101. Earlier accounts by the author were: "An Extraordinary Lay Leader: The Life and

Work of Helene of Freyberg, Sixteenth Century Noblewoman and Anabaptist from the Tirol," 312-41; "Helena von Freyberg of Münichau," in *Profiles of Anabaptist Women*, 124-39; "Response to Heinold Fast on the Confession of Helena von Freyberg, Staunch Leader With a Contrite Heart," Paper presented to the Anabaptist Colloquium, Waterloo, Ontario, April 9, 2005. This response was done using the copy of Helena's Confession from Prof. Heinold Fast's transcriptions of the *Kunstbuch* collection of writings from the Marpeck circle which Prof. William Klassen and Prof. Walter Klaassen kindly provided. Some new information was obtained from the archives in München in September 2005: see note 129.

102. Regarding Helena's family see: Kaspar Schwarz, *Tirolische Schlösser, Heft I, Unterinntal, I Teil* (Innsbruck: Verlag der Wagner'schen Universitäts Buchhandlung, 1907), 66-68 and Klaus Kogler, *Stadtbuch Kitzbühel, Bd. III, Baugeschichte, Kunstgeschichte, Theatergeschichte, Schlösser* (Kitzbühel: E. der Stadt Kitzbühel, 1970), 355, Tafel III.

103. Regarding Heinrich Marpeck see Stephen B. Boyd, *Pilgram Marpeck His Life and Social Theology* (Durham: Duke University Press, 1992), 5, n. 3; 6, n. 4.

104. Baron is the translation for "Freiherr," a title indicating that Onophrius had the highest rank of the lower nobility. "Frau" already indicated upper class status and when she married Helena became a "Freifrau" or Baroness. Her social status gave her a certain authority in that society, and made her a 'natural leader,' that is, one expected to lead others. "Neither the Protestant nor the Catholic reformers differentiated between noblewomen and commoners in their public advice to women; noblewomen, too, were to be 'chaste, silent, and obedient.' Privately, however, they recognized that such women often held a great deal of power and made special attempts to win them over.... Noblewomen, both married and unmarried, religious and lay, had the most opportunity to express their religious convictions, and the consequences of their actions were more far-reaching than those of most women." Merry E. Wiesner, "Nuns, Wives, and Mothers: Women and the Reformation in Germany," in *Women in Reformation and Counter-Reformation Europe, Public and Private Worlds*, ed. by Sherrin Marshall (Bloomington: Indiana University Press, 1989), 21.

105. For upper class women in early modern Italy the average age at marriage was 15. Merry E. Wiesner, *Women and Gender in Early Modern Europe* (Cambridge, England: Cambridge University Press, 1993), 57. If Helena was married by 1506 she may have been born in 1490 or 1491. For early modern Europe in general the average age of marriage was 15 to 18 for girls and 25 for men. See also, Ennen, *Frauen im Mittelalter*, 228.

106. Friedrich Roth, *Augsburgs Reformationsgeschichte, 1531-1537 bezw. 1540, Bd. II*, (München: Theodor Ackermann, 1904), 410.

107. It is of note that the husbands of both Helena von Freyberg and Elisabeth von Wolkenstein were Lutheran while the wives became Anabaptists.

108. The word "Gesinde," in Mecenseffy's summary and "Hauszvolk," in the original text of March 7, 1528 See in the Index, 3 maids listed as n.n.95a, b and c, Freyberg maid. be, 63.

109. Ten days later, on March 17, the territorial judge of Kitzbühel, instructed to investigate a long list of Anabaptists, was told "also to inquire about Helena and her two sons." See TA 1972, 96:17-18.
110. This record includes a reference to Onophrius and Helena who were among those who had written to the government. It is not clear whether they had sent in a report in their own defense or not. See TA 1972, 108:9-10.
111. The phrase in this passage "in das reut gethan" may refer to the village of Reith which is located near the castle, meaning the preacher worked there too. See Widmoser, *Tirol A Bis Z*, 722. TA 1972, 110:4-11.
112. This passage is from TA 1972, 110:21-22.
113. The phrase used in the original text is "die iren" which could refer to her family or the members of the castle household. See also TA 1972, 110:21; 355:5-9.
114. The phrase "platz geben haben" could well mean she promoted it and provided lodging for Anabaptists.
115. This passage is from TA 1972, 110:16-25. The word for guaranty is "Burgschaft." The word used in this original passage is "purgiern."
116. See *Causa Domini II*, 206, 207, cited in Johann Loserth, "Der Anabaptismus in Tirol Von Seinen Anfängen Bis Zum Tode Jakob Huters (1526-1536), Aus den Hinterlassenen Papieren Des Hofrathes Dr. Josef R. von Beck," *Archiv für Osterreichische Geschichte*, 78, 1 (1892), 466.
117. In her article, "Anabaptists in Kitzbühel," 100, Grete Mecenseffy interprets these reports to mean that Helena's role was head of the congregation based in her castle. But Clasen did not include Helena either on his list of leaders or members. See his article, "The Anabaptist Leaders," 122-64 and Claus-Peter Clasen, *The Anabaptists in South and Central Germany, Switzerland, and Austria their names, occupations, places of residence and dates of conversion: 1525-1618* (Michigan: *Mennonite Quarterly Review*, 1978), 1-224.
118. TA 1972, 134, document 152. See Chapter 2 Introduction regarding this group.
119. TA 1972, 150:21-26. Partzner, mentioned here for the first time, was the former chaplain in Kitzbühel. He had worked there, in Rattenberg and in Kufstein. See Mecenseffy, "Anabaptists in Kitzbühel," 106.
120. TA 1972, 153:11-14; 9. Rassler is a "verfuerer," one who leads others astray.
121. TA 1972, 223:18-21. Anabaptism is referred to here as a Lutheran sect. For the orthodox rulers of Tirol all deviations in religion were viewed as sects.
122. TA 1972, 258:12-16.
123. TA 1972, 311:1-8. The value of eleven Gulden would have been equal to one month of the annual salary of a civil servant like Pilgram Marpeck. As a mining engineer in Rattenberg Marpeck earned 65 marks per annum with an additional three guilders

for his professional gown. A mark equalled 2 guilders or 2 Gulden. Later, in Augsburg Marpeck earned 150 guilders per annum. Klaassen and Klassen, Marpeck, 63, 289.

124. Roth, *Augsburgs Reformationsgeschichte* (1904), 410-11.
125. TA 1972, 338, documents 495 and 496.
126. He was referred to as the "Lehentrager."
127. TA 1972, 354-55, document 520 and 371:25-27; 401:27-29.
128. Traugott Schiess, *Briefwechsel der Brüder Ambrosius und Thomas Blaurer, 1509-1548* (Freiburg i. Br.: Friedrich Ernst Fehsenfeld, 1908), 321.
129. TA 1983, 194:23-28 refers to the petition or "Bittschrift" a copy of which is included in the Hft. Hohenaschau A 22 in the Staatsarchiv München, Germany. This document has been transcribed by Prof. William Klassen and Nikolai Penner.
130. TA 1983, 197:1-9. The phrase "des gemainen mans nachrede" is taken from the original document. The mention of being an example to the people is included in the TA 1983, 200:28 but had been in the king's communiqué as well.
131. TA 1983, 200:30-201:3, especially lines 30-31 which state, "der widertauffer sect so hoch angehangen."
132. Mecenseffy, "Anabaptists in Kitzbühel," 107.
133. TA 1983, 260:12-17.
134. TA 1983, 264:8-13. This is the last reference to Helena in these records.
135. The Austrian historian Johann Loserth probably saw this document which has been lost. See, Loserth, "Anabaptismus in Tirol," 490.
136. Mecenseffy, "Anabaptists in Kitzbühel," 101. Erhardt Urscher stated in his confession: "Wenn einer stirbt und zu einer Gantmauer (Geröllhalde) oder zu einem Zaun gelegt wird, liegt er eben so wohl als im Friedhof." (If someone dies and is buried near a wall or a fence, that is as good as being buried in the cemetery.) TA 1983, 92:35-37.
137. See C. Arnold Snyder, "The North German/Dutch Anabaptist Context," in *Profiles of Anabaptist Women*, 249-51 and two articles on women in Münster, Marion Kobelt-Groch, "Hille Feicken of Sneek," trans. by Linda A. Huebert Hecht in *Profiles of Anabaptist Women*, 288-297 and Marion Kobelt-Groch, "Divara of Haarlem," trans. by Walter Klaassen in *Profiles of Anabaptist Women*, 298-304.
138. Translated from Roth, *Augsburg Reformationsgeschichte* (1904), 426-27.
139. "The members included Pauls Weckerlin (weaver), Philip Schlosser and Bernhart Schmidt (wool carder)." Stephen Blake Boyd, "Pilgram Marpeck and the Justice of Christ," (unpublished Doctor of Theology, Harvard University, Cambridge, MA, 1984, 302. Roth estimated approximately 1000 Anabaptists were in Augsburg.
140. Roth, *Augsburg Reformationsgeschichte* (1904), 411 and 422, n. 55.
141. Helena's income in Augsburg is documented in Hft. Hohenaschau A 22 in the Staatsarchiv München, Germany.
142. Schneider testified in Augsburg in 1562. See Boyd, "Pilgram Marpeck and the Justice of Christ," 303-4, 320.

143. *Ibid.*, 76, 241. C. Arnold Snyder, "Magdalena, Walpurga and Sophia Marschalk von Pappenheim," in *Profiles of Anabaptist Women*, 113.
144. Snyder, *Anabaptist History and Theology: Revised Student Edition*, 129. See 9, Holy Spirit.
145. The three living sons inherited the castle and its domains on April 6, 1535 but Pankraz was in charge. Pankraz married in 1538 at 30 years of age. See his biography written by Dieter Schäfer, *Aufstieg, Fall und Ruhm des Pankraz von Freyberg* (Prien am Chiemsee: Ecora-Verlag, 1996), 33.
146. *Ibid.*, 46.
147. Stefan Breit, *450 Jahre Aschauer Markt, 1555-2005* (Prien: Gemeinde Aschau i. Chiemgau, 2005), 1-30.
148. Schäfer, *Pankraz von Freyberg*, 34.
149. *Ibid.*, 39.
150. This unnamed maid who fled is designated in the index as n.n.96a maid.
151. TA 1972, 107:32-108:4.
152. Robert Friedmann, "Schützinger," in *Mennonite Encyclopedia*, (Scottdale, PA: Mennonite Publishing House, 1959), IV, 485.
153. This report referred to Sigmund as "ein rechter Vorsteher" or a real leader. TA 1972, 414:28.
154. TA 1972, 140:13f.; 266:11-12; 422:25-423:3. The children were described as "unerzogen" meaning they were young or "underage." Children often began to work at seven years of age. They were not considered adults until 16 years of age. "… baptism was reserved for adults from the age of sixteen on." *Hutterite Beginnings*, p. 196.
155. Schützinger's excommunication led to separation of the Auspitz group from the other groups in Moravia, the Gabrielites and the Philipites. *Hutterite Beginnings*, 229. 235 and 224-235 for a discussion of "The Great Schism of 1533." See also Hutterian Brethren, ed. *The Chronicle of the Hutterian Brethren*, Vol. I, trans. by the Hutterian Brethren (Rifton, NY: Plough Publishing House, 1987), 103-4.
156. These women are designated in the index as n.n.113a maid and n.n.113b maid.
157. They are designated in the index as n.n.120a and n.n.120b several women.
158. TA 1972, 127:12-13. Here her condition is described as "Irrsinnigkeit."
159. The highest number of arrests took place in the month of May, before the alpine farmers moved up to higher meadows from where it was harder to capture them.
160. They are designated in the index as n.n.137 a, b, c and d four women.
161. *New Catholic Encyclopedia* (New York: McGraw-Hill, 1967-96), 9, 200.
162. See additional sources for Anna Krätlerin I in Hildegund Gisman-Fiel, *Das Täufertum in Vorarlberg* (Dornbirn: Vorarlberger Verlagsanstalt, 1982), 178, n. 141, 142.
163. The unnamed woman who was drowned is designated in the index as n.n.138b, 1 of 3 women and the unnamed woman who was released is designated in the index as n.n.138a, one woman. Hoheneck may have been located near Feldkirch in Voraarlberg bordering on Swiss territory. See TA 442: 8-9.

164. See TA 1972, 142:15 where she is called the "alt Pflegerin." She was the wife of a "Pfleger" or crown administrator, one of several wives of crown administrators in these court records.
165. Further references to her are in: TA 1972, 148:24; 221:40; 466:33; 467:29.
166. TA 1972, 146, document 174.
167. The text of their recantation is in TA 1972, 173, document 220. It was translated in Huebert Hecht, "Anabaptist Women who Recanted," in *Profiles of Anabaptist Women*, 162 and is presented here with one minor change: the phrase "Penntz is to bring up the rear" has been replaced with "Penntz is to wear a shirt which has a cross sewn on it." The penance procedures sent out November 1527 by the bishopric of Salzburg stipulated that penitent men and women should wear plain clothing onto which a cross was sewn. TA, 1972, 18:10-14.
168. One of the duties of the "Scharfrichter" or executioner was to administer corporal punishment. See Heinz Moser, *Die Scharfrichter von Tirol, Ein Beitrag zur Geschichte des Strafvollzuges in Tirol von 1497-1787* (Innsbruck: Steigerverlag, 1982), 69.
169. The exact words are: "dy Veit Riemerin hab in den weichprunn thann, ir diernl habs darein tragen." TA 1964, 155:25-26.
170. TA 1964, 149:32-33; 154: 6-16; 155:23-29; 155:38-156:6. Later some of these people recanted and a group of 28 men and 27 women requested absolution. *Ibid.*, 156, n. 32. See July 14 for another entry on this group.
171. TA 1972, 151:34-152:1; 152:15-19.
172. Mecenseffy gives the details of these politics in "Anabaptists in Kitzbühel," 103-04. Regarding the male leaders see TA 1975, 149:9; 161:5-6; 169:10.
173. TA 1964, 150:4-10. See the Introduction, notes 11 and 12 regarding the Lord's Supper or communion.
174. Els "smuggled tools into prison." See *Hutterite Beginnings* 369, n. 115.
175. TA 1972, 176:27, 29-30; 177:25; 178:10; 180:1-4; 221:43-222:22. The wanted posted described Kobl as a tall man with a clubfoot.
176. TA 1972, 370:7-8, 21-25.
177. They are designated in the index as n.n.174a mother and n.n.174b daughter.
178. They are designated in the index as n.n.175a, band c, 3 women exec.
179. In TA 1972, 175:26; 179:3-8; 181:25-31 the woman with the seven children, designated in the index as n.n.175c, 3 women executed, is discussed. See TA 1972, 179:8-10 regarding the execution costs.
180. She is designated in the index as n.n.177a, woman.
181. This information is from the second reference to them in TA 1972, 182, document 241.
182. These four leaders are called "Prinzipaltäufer und Verführer." See TA 1972, 183:28.
183. It is not clear if the woman present when Michel Kürschner became a leader, named Magdalena Wald, was the same person. See June 5, 1529.

184. They are designated in the index as n.n.184 a and b, two pregnant women. The second reference to them is TA 1972, 185:22-23.
185. Reference to the Lord's Supper held here is stated in Kobelt-Groch, *Aufsässige Töchter*,
186. This information is a continuation from page 89, note 93. The Austrian Anabaptist court records of 1972 document the arrest of Bartlmä Dill Riemenschneider and his family and maid on February 16, 1528. Beside his name is the word "Maler" meaning artist. Until now Anabaptist historians have considered David Joris, an Anabaptist leader in the Netherlands, to be the first Anabaptist artist. David Joris was born around the same time as Bartlmä Dill Riemenschneider but he was not baptized until 1535 or 1536 and did not create Anabaptist art until 1542 when his *Wonder Book* was published. On the other hand, Bartlmä Dill was already an Anabaptist in 1528 and a widely recognized artist by 1533 when he painted "The Crucifixion." More specifically, in 1540 Bartlmä Dill painted frescoes at Castle Rubein which was owned by Hans Wangga, an Anabaptist patron. These frescoes represent Anabaptist beliefs, namely, the Lord's Supper in the way Anabaptists celebrated it, in a home not in a church (inscribed with Bible verses "central to Anabaptist faith and practice"); wall frescos of five New Testament table scenes; and "the occasion when Jesus announced the end of the world and his Second Coming." For these reasons I agree with Dr. Leo Andergassen, of Brixen, Italy and Hanns-Paul Ties of Bozen, Italy who have suggested in their research and publications that Bartlmä Dill Riemenschneider was the first Anabaptist artist and not David Joris of the Netherlands. See Hecht and Ties, "Research Note:" 456-458, especially n. 68.

Chapter Three

Introduction to the Records of 1529

Ferdinand I's persecution of Anabaptist women and men reached a high point in 1529. As in the other years, the highest number of arrests took place in May, more likely due to the practice of transhumance of the alpine farmers in Tirol than due to any variation in government action. The peasant farmers took their herds of grazing animals up to the higher meadows for the summer months and brought them down again in September. It was harder for government officials to make arrests when the Anabaptists resided on the higher mountain elevations.[1]

Not just the number of arrests, but in particular the number of executions rose to the highest level so far in 1529. The total number of women martyred in all five years in Tirol was 77. Whereas in 1527 there was only one probable female martyr, there were 13 (known and probable) executions of Anabaptist women in 1528. But the number more than tripled in 1529 when 41 of the 110 Anabaptists martyred were women.[2] One quarter of these 41 women, ten in all, lost their lives on one day in Rattenberg at the beginning of May. The number of martyrs for the last two years considered in this book was less than in the previous three years with 22 (known and probable) executions of women, 19 in 1530 and only three in 1531.

The Innsbruck officials informed Ferdinand in February 1530 that up to that time at least 200 Anabaptist men and women had been executed.[3] They did not differentiate between the numbers of men and women who were martyred. But we know that there are 55 (1+13+41) known and probable executions of Anabaptist women documented in the published court records of 1972 between 1527 and 1529. The estimate of the officials was probably correct and comes close to the numbers quoted by the Austrian historian Heinz Moser for only North Tirol. He states that during 1528 and 1529 the total number of Anabaptist men and women executed was 193, with 71 martyrs in Rattenberg, 68 in Kitzbühel, 22 in Kufstein, 20 in Schwaz, eight in the city of Innsbruck, two in the city of Hall and two in Rotholz.[4] Estimates for longer time periods range from 600 martyrs in Tirol up to 1539 and 1000 martyrs in all the Austrian territories for all of the sixteenth century, with one-third or approximately 300 of the latter estimated to be women, the same proportion as in the *Martyrs' Mirror*.[5] As already mentioned, compared to the proportion of Reformed female martyrs, which was only six percent, the one-third proportion for Anabaptist women is high.[6]

With the increased number of arrests and executions, a change in policy was necessary. The government saw that it was losing too many subjects to the movement and thus began to make more concentrated attempts to re-educate Anabaptist prisoners. The authorities sought to use biblical instruction to convince Anabaptist men and women of the error of their ways. These educational measures underscore not just the perseverance of the Anabaptists but also the sound teaching they received from their leaders. The advice from Innsbruck that local authorities should send only "competent" (July 24), "learned" (September 25) and "knowledgable" (August 11) priests to instruct the prisoners is evidence of this. Each of the Anabaptist believers knew what they believed, the women no less than the men. As in the other regions of Europe where Anabaptism flourished, the inquisitors were often "… astounded by the 'biblical knowledge' of the 'simple' Anabaptists, including the illiterate women, and peasants."[7]

At the beginning of 1529, the Innsbruck authorities wasted no time in discussing Anabaptist prisoners, sending out their first instructions on January 1. They were not pleased that local authorities seemed to sympathize with the prisoners, by giving such mild sentences, especially to the woman named Passerin. These Anabaptists got away with only a public flogging at the town pillory. Corporal punishment was one of the less severe forms of punishment.[8] On the other hand, orders were given to put the maid of Jacob Koler on trial, since granting pardons and giving warnings had not deterred her and others from joining the Anabaptists in the rural region of Ritten, the plateau located above the urban centre of Bozen.

Despite the new law of February 5 that intensified the punishments for Anabaptists, some mercy was shown to Cristina Egger, the baker's wife from the city of Hall whose case was discussed that same day. She was allowed to return from her exile to care for her many children. The baker himself, Peter Egger, and his single sister Anna, were probably away at this time since later records inform us that they went on preaching tours in neighbouring regions. Child care was a problem when Anabaptist mothers were exiled.

For the wife of Michel in the Hülbn of south Tirol, whose martyrdom was reported February 8, there was no mercy. She left her seven children four hundred Gulden, a sizeable inheritance considering that carpenters and bricklayers in that time period earned around fifty Gulden per year. The money would be used to raise her children but would not make up for the lack of her presence in their lives. A similar fate awaited the children of Ursula Kuen, wealthy wife of the silversmith in Rattenberg who was reported in April and whose property was discussed in September. She joined her husband in martyrdom.

Toward the end of April the so-called Anabaptist mandate was passed by the Imperial Diet meeting in Speyer which supported Ferdinand's efforts to eradicate Anabaptism.[9] However, he followed up with a law of his own for his territories on May 18 that was more severe than those passed in Speyer; Ferdinand decreed death by fire for all Anabaptists.[10] The severe persecution in Tirol reached a climax in the mass trial which took place in Rattenberg on May 12 when seventeen Anabaptists were executed. Ten of the martyrs were women. The town councillors themselves observed that never before had so many persons been executed at one time in the town of Rattenberg.[11] Moser places this mass trial in the broader context of the territory as a whole when he states that never before that day and never since then have so many people been executed at once in all of Tirol.[12] Moreover, the May 23 report of these executions made it clear that these Anabaptists had no intention of rebelling against authority. They were only concerned about their sins and living peaceably. Their motives were not political, although their disobedience of imperial orders was interpreted as seditious. But what truly amazed the authorities about the women and men who were martyred in Kitzbühel and Rattenberg was their attitude. They had no fear of the most severe punishment.[13] In Kitzbühel there had also been a mass execution of Anabaptists but of a smaller number. Nine were executed with sword, fire and water. Only one person in this group is named, a woman named Katharina Schwaiglin (June 6). She was spared because she was sick. After she was back in prison she chose to recant but then was arrested again in December. Aside from Katharina we do not know how many women were in the group.

To the south in the Puster Valley, arrests took place in the region of Welsperg on May 23 where the two single sisters of Caspar Schwartz were among a group who had been doing mission work and distributing books. It was not unusual for women to be involved in such activities. Earlier, on May 10, it had been reported that Gilg Klein's wife had "made six new Christians." These three women were missioners.

The issue of "simple-mindedness" appears a number of times in the court records including in May 1529. As noted below in the discussion of the use of torture, the law considered women to be mentally weak and simple-minded and therefore not fully responsible for their actions. This was reflected in the laws of Tirol in the decree of February 8, 1528 which discussed young persons, women, those who found it hard to understand and those who were simple-minded, of whom there were many in these mountains. These people, said the mandate, do not have much reason or good sense and make little use of what reason they do have. If such persons persist in their beliefs and do not want to be re-converted, they must be kept in prison longer and given instruction.[14] The decree of March 26, 1528 stated that punishments were to be meted out "according to the intelligence, criminal offence and persistence of the offenders" regardless of sex.[15] On August 4, 1529, Ferdinand's officials were discussing how the laws for the Holy Roman Empire recently passed in Speyer should apply to Tirol. They reported to Ferdinand that there were juries who refused to condemn every Anabaptist to death if they had not baptized others and were not rebels or relapsi. This was making the situation worse. Ferdinand's officials also referred to "the many women as well as young and simple-minded persons" who were being led astray and re-baptized by the rabble rousers who wandered the countryside – the government referred to Anabaptist leaders as rabble rousers – but who later regretted their actions and came back to the church.[16] Clearly, women were making choices about their religious faith despite the negative attitudes toward them under the law. The case of Dorothea Maler (September 7, 1529) is a case in point. She must have claimed that she did not understand her interrogators since they stated that she was "not as innocent or as simple-minded as she claims to be."

Within the Anabaptist community simple-mindedness was not looked on negatively, in fact the attitude toward it was almost the opposite. The uneducated faith was highly valued. Luther had said, the laity "had the right to interpret Scripture for themselves."[17] In the Anabaptist community the unlearned peasant, with the help of the Holy Spirit, offered a more genuine interpretation of the Bible than a highly educated person.[18] "The whole Anabaptist movement believed itself to be under the immediate inspiration of God." True authority did not reside in scholarship but came from God.[19]

It is not clear if Waldburga Ameiser (May 16) truly did not understand what her re-baptism meant or if she sought to take advantage of the legal attitude toward women. In the case of Agatha, who was Anna Gasser's maid (April 3), the young men she was imprisoned with were excused for their lack of understanding, whereas for her, the assumption that she was simple-minded together with the fact that she was young spared her from death. Earlier, in 1528, when the wives and maid in the Taurer family were arrested after the men in these families fled, the government wanted to know if the women had joined Anabaptism out of simple-mindedness (March 4, 1528).

In another case which began in May the degree of fear which the government had about women's involvements in Anabaptism becomes evident. They acted on the assumption that an unnamed woman leader had baptized the eight hundred people listed in the register she was carrying. This was hardly possible. It was known that male leaders such as Michel Kürschner (see June 5, 1529) and Leonhard Schiemer had each baptized around two hundred people.[20] The mining towns of Rattenberg and Schwaz in particular, with their surrounding regions where this woman was supposed to be staying, were of special concern for the government due to their large immigrant population of miners, many of whom were Anabaptists. In some cases Innsbruck's jurisdiction was limited over these miners as was the case in Sterzing (March 6, 1529). But the fears of the government were not unfounded.

The woman carrying the register eluded arrest. No mention is made of her family. Perhaps her single or widowed status allowed her to flee successfully. For other women, family obligations did not prevent them from fleeing their homes. On July 31 it was reported that the miller and his wife from Brixlegg had fled, leaving their infant behind unattended in a cradle. To the south in Klausen, on August 2, the wife of Wolfgang Schneider left when their child was just three days old. Her husband was arrested for not baptizing their child.

The perseverance of Anabaptist women evident in the records of September 7 and 12 and December 7 and 22 illustrates the use of different measures in dealing with prisoners. The shift in government policy to attempt a re-education of Anabaptist men and women was evident already on July 24 as well as August 11 and was pursued again on September 25 and October 9. But the new approach had limited success for the government. Many Anabaptists, including the women persisted in their faith.

The contribution of two women from the September records is of particular note. There is a hymn commemorating the persecution and martyrdom of Dorothea Maler and Anna Ochsentreiber entitled, "A Song about (or by) Anna Malerin and Ursula Ochsentreiber, Who Were Drowned at Hall in the Inn Valley." We do not know when this hymn was written but the use of the word "by" in the title indicates that possibly the women themselves wrote it (September 7). They were sentenced in the city of Hall and drowned in the Inn River bordering the city. The *Chronicle of the Hutterian Brethren* says of them, "Thus they witnessed to the truth in life and in death." The title given in the chronicle for their hymn is, "An unsrer Frauentag das geschah" (It happened on Our Lady's Day). It is the only known hymn which tells their story.[21] Of the several sources where it is included, the women's names were mixed up in the Hutterite songbook and the *Martyrs' Mirror*.[22] However, "the close similarity between the events recorded in Anabaptist sources and the court records lead to the conclusion that Anna Maler and Ursula Ochsentreiber, and Dorothea Maler and Anna Ochsentreiber refer to the same women."[23] The text of their hymn is in the Appendix.

On September 14, the same day that the judge in Hall was instructed to set a trial date for Dorothea, the Innsbruck authorities instructed the mayor in Hall to imprison the Anabaptists separately. When they were kept together they sang hymns, as was the practice in their sect. Their singing angered the citizens of the city when they heard it and served to reinforce the Anabaptists in their heretical beliefs. Hymns played an important role then in the Anabaptist community, by telling the martyrs' stories and building the believers up in the faith.

In the last months of 1529, perseverance led to martyrdom for a number of Anabaptist women. The leader's wife Katharina Streicher, as mentioned above, is of particular note. The case of the bookseller, Balthasar Vest and his wife from November and December is unique for its detailed information about the expenses of their trial and execution – everything is listed from the expenses of the judge for his horse, to the payment of the jury members and the wine purchased for the couple on the day of their execution. As for most other Anabaptist martyrs, there are far fewer details available for the trial and death of Agnes Hutter. Although her brother, Jacob, a prominent Anabaptist leader, influenced many people, Agnes is the only one in his immediate family who is discussed in the court records. She was arrested a second time and interrogated with torture to confirm her earlier confession (December 8). The authorities were not inclined to be lenient when a person was arrested a second time. Her story is significant not just for the fact that Jacob was her brother but because she too had to face martydom.

Jacob Hutter's work in the Puster Valley came to the attention of the authorities in mid summer 1529 when four women and five men whom he had baptized were arrested and were to receive instruction from a priest (July 24). A few months later when a woman and several men from the congregation in Welsberg were imprisoned, Hutter was among them (August 27). Fortunately he managed to escape and, having heard that the lords who ruled Moravia did not persecute the Anabaptists, he made his way there. For a time he lived with Jörg Zaunring and his followers in Auspitz.[24]

We know that he was back in Tirol in 1530 from the report about two older women in Steinach where he and Zaunring were two of the baptizers (May 25, 1530). In December 1531 he was at the extended Anabaptist meetings in Hörschwang with other leaders like Cristan Gschäll (October - November 1530). Between 1531 and 1533 Hutter travelled four times between Moravia and Tirol. During some of his time in Tirol he received protection from Elisabeth von Wolkenstein at Uttenheim (September 1531).[25]

At Anabaptist meetings near Sterzing in 1533, Katharina Purst, a young woman, probably in her early twenties, working as a maid in the home of Anabaptists Paul and Justina Gall,[26] was among those baptized by Jacob Hutter. Katharina, like a number of others, was arrested, chose to recant and after a second arrest, fled to Moravia in 1534. A year later, in a simple wedding ceremony conducted by Hans Amon, Katharina married Jacob Hutter on May 16, 1535.[27] She too was an ardent Anabaptist. When persecution broke out in Moravia the couple returned to Tirol. After managing to evade arrest for six years, Hutter was now captured along with his wife. He was matryed in 1536 and Katharina two years later.

Hutter had filled a gap left by the martyrdom of the leaders Michel Kürschner and Jörg Blaurock. "A charismatic leader with 'abundant gifts from God,' Hutter proved to be a fine organizer and very persuasive New Testament exegete and preacher." As Werner Packull explains further,

> Despite Ferdinand's oppressive measures and the scattered nature of Anabaptist existence in South Tyrol, Hutter and his associates unfolded an amazing congregational life supported by a network of committed converts, dedicated supporters, and sympathizers. Although these were not drawn exclusively from the Puster Valley, the inner core was; and before they became collectively known as Hutterites, they carried the designation Pusterers, with the connotation that they were particularly tough and dedicated. At least since 1529 these Pusterers belonged to the staff-bearing (nonresistant) Anabaptists....

The Pusterers followed the model already established in Austerlitz, Moravia. "This meant that Hutter also taught the ideal of community of goods as the proper New Testament norm...."[28] While they were still in Tirol, the

Anabaptists established a rudimentary form of this type of congregational life by keeping a common treasury. The money in this treasury was used to support widows and children, buy provisions for meetings, aid those in prison or in hiding and, after 1530, "to finance the exodus to Moravia."[29]

Emigration to the "New Tirol" seemed to be the only means of survival.[30] Anabaptist refugees left Tirol by land or water. The most open and frequently used trade route led from the south over the Brenner Pass, down the Wipp Valley to the Inn and Danube rivers. Choosing a route by land meant going over the mountains, taking the smaller, less used roads of the trade routes. For the route by water Anabaptists embarked at Hall or Rattenberg hoping to avoid the notice of transportation crews as they travelled downstream first on the Inn River and then on the Danube to Moravia.[31] The journey was long and dangerous. "Hundreds of miles of mountain terrain lay between" Tirol and Moravia.[32] But as the persecution in Tirol continued, many believers risked the journey to find safety in the nominally Habsburg land to the east.

Use of Torture in Interrogating Anabaptist Women, 1527-1531

Also notable in 1529 are the increased number of references to the use of torture during the interrogation of women. They occur eleven times during 1529 whereas in 1528 there are only two references to the use of torture, in 1530 one and in 1531 five. In the context of the total number of arrests of women in 1529, which was 116, the eleven references to the use of torture in interrogating women is not a large number. However, that torture was used at all in questioning women is surprising. Sixteenth century law did not make gender distinctions in criminal proceedings.

> … both sexes were required to confess in capital crimes, which led to judicial torture…. Roman law stressed women's alleged physical and mental weakness,… and held women, along with peasants and the simple-minded, as not fully responsible for their own actions…. Academic jurisprudence … made clear distinctions between men and women, and further subdivided women according to their relationship to a man; a woman's legal status was determined by her marital status as maiden/wife/widow, and occasionally also by her

physiological status as virgin/pregnant/nursing mother/mother.³³

The punishments outlined in the decrees issued in Tirol reflect this view of women. Anabaptism was an outlawed heresy and therefore Anabaptist women were guilty of committing a capital crime and treated according to criminal law.

The treatment of Anabaptist prisoners in Tirol depended to some degree on the attitude and will of the local authorities. At their first hearing, the prisoners were to give a confession or statement about their beliefs, particularly about the sacraments of baptism and the mass. Torture was sometimes used to confirm a confession as well as to obtain further information. Secondly, the authorities wanted to know who had baptized them, the names of fellow believers and where they were meeting so that further arrests could be made. Examples of the questioning procedures are given in the Appendix from May 12, 1530 and in Elisabeth von Wolkenstein's story of September 1531. The increased use of torture during 1529 demonstrates both the increasing severity of the persecution and the high degree to which women were involved and active in the Anabaptist movement. Those women involved to a greater degree were treated more severely. Thus, the treatment is an indirect measure of women's participation. Those Anabaptists accused only of being baptized, as a rule, were not punished as severely as those who acted as missionaries and leaders. This was true for women as well as for men. However, Anabaptists, including women, who had recanted and been pardoned and then rejoined the movement were made to endure torture more often.

In the published court records for Tirol used here, there is no specific mention of the type of torture used. Often just seeing the instruments of torture such as thumb screws or arm and leg irons was enough for a person to give a confession. We know that during Elisabeth Dirks' second interrogation, thumb screws were applied to her thumbs and forefingers because she would not confess voluntarily. When screws were applied to her shins she fainted and they were removed. Elisabeth would neither reveal the name of her baptizer nor change her mind about her beliefs and she became a martyr.³⁴

Some Anabaptist women in Tirol were to be interrogated merely under the threat of torture. This was the case for the wives, maids and the labourer of the Taurer households. The husbands, Andre and Cristan had both fled and the latter was an Anabaptist leader (March 4, 1528). Three Anabaptist women in Bozen were also threatened with torture but in their case the judge and the jury did not want to see torture used (November 30, 1530). Most often the instructions were simply to interrogate "with and without the use of torture." Such instructions were given for three young people, Agatha, maid of the Gasser family and the two herdsmen of the Sackman family with whom she was in prison (April 3, 1529). They were also given for Dorothea Gärber (December 20, 1528), and the Anabaptist women being discussed on September 12 and 25 of 1529. A number of times, the authorities were told specifically that the torture should be orderly and appropriate for a woman. This was the case for Dorothea Maler (September 7), for the women being interrogated December 7, 1529 and for Agnes Hutter (December 8, 1529) at her second arrest.[35]

By 1531 the government was more determined than ever to root out Anabaptism and instructed the judge in Freundsberg to use torture in the questioning procedures for all five of the prisoners including the two women, Barbara Maler and the wife of Briccius Räss (July 3, 1531). The judge had questioned whether he should do so, indicating that the local authorities did not necessarily want to use such severe methods. The judge who interrogated Michel Oberholler in Sarnthein also seemed to hesitate in using torture. He simply encouraged Oberholler (March 2, 1531) to tell the truth and his method seemed to work. Oberholler spoke in detail about what the Anabaptists had been taught. But in a follow up interrogation of his fellow believer, Peter Schneider, torture was used at least for part of the interrogation. Schneider named the Lenntz Urstetterin (March 17, 1531) and other women and likewise discussed the sermons they had heard at Anabaptist meetings in Sarnthein. It is hard to know if Schneider would have given all this information under normal questioning.

A few of the cases where torture was used are of particular note. Barbara Gasteiger (September 25 and November 16, 1529) may have been younger in age but was nonetheless very staunch. She had been pardoned once already but now was in prison again, along with her brother Hans. The interrogations of the prisoners had included the use of torture. Still, Barbara persevered and in November she was condemned to death.

As a rule, the treatment of Anabaptist leaders was harsher. At times the wives of male leaders shared the same fate as their husbands, especially if they were working together with them. Such was the case for Katharina Streicher (December 22, 1529) who was a relapsi. Despite the severe torture that she and two male prisoners endured, she stated along with them, that she would rather die than give her captors any information.[36] Katharina's case is proof that "women were quite able to express their religious beliefs and remain true to them in the face of death."[37] The wife of Balthasar Vest also shared the same fate as her husband. He was a different kind of leader, an Anabaptist bookseller, and he and his wife were both martyred (November 24, 1529). As previously mentioned, their case is unusual in that we have the financial record of all the costs involved in their trial and execution. The judge related: "I interrogated the bookseller using torture, in the presence of the court secretary and five jury members, that is, seven persons each receiving 6 Kr, amounting to 3 Pd 6 Kr." The total cost for this part of the trial, 3 Pounds and 48 Kreuzer, would have amounted then to less than 2 Gulden.[38]

Whereas corporal punishment was administered more often for women than for men, the court records of Tirol provide evidence that Anabaptist women were not spared torture.[39] Leona Stucky Abbott's study of Anabaptist women was limited to women in the *Martyrs' Mirror* but her discussion of women and the use of torture is not demeaning to women and does not compromise the stand which they took in enduring such procedures. Abbott states, "Shame was the expectation and the creation of the male-dominated culture.... The failure of the effort to 'break' women witnesses through shame can be credited to the single-mindedness of their theological position."[40]

Translations from the Court Records of 1529

January 1, 1529, The Passerin of Kurtatsch, Corporal Punishment, Banishment

The Innsbruck government responded to a report of December 28, 1528 from the local official, the crown administrator of Kurtatsch, Wilhelm von Liechtenstein, expressing surprise that such mild sentences were given to the prisoners, especially to the woman named Passerin. However, the Innsbruck authorities would leave it at that. The prisoners could be released after the executioner had given them a public flogging at the pillory and after they had sworn an oath to leave their homeland, the territory of Tirol, and never to return 'for all eternity.'

On January 13, 1529 this exile order was revised. The pardoned captives were banned from ever again entering their neighbouring districts, Gries and Bozen, which were also under Liechtenstein's jurisdiction.

January 5, 1529,

One of the confessions sent in was from Lucia, who worked as a maid for Hans and Anna Gasser who lived on the Ritten plateau above the urban centre of Bozen and held Anabaptist meetings in their home.

January 22, 1529,

Anna, Jacob Koler's maid from the Ritten plateau[41] was to be put on trial since pardons and warnings didn't seem to deter people from becoming Anabaptists.

January 26, 1529, An Unnamed Woman Condemned, Disparaged the Sacrament

The woman in Rattenberg baptized by Leonard Schiemer who spoke unseemingly and with scornful words about the sacrament was to be tried in the criminal court. This meant she would be condemned to death.[42]

February 5, 1529, Cristina Egger, Leader's Wife and Mother of a Large Family

The Innsbruck government instructed Erhard Hall, judge in the city of Hall as follows. In recognition of the many intercessions that had been submitted for her and because of the many children she had, Cristina, wife of Peter Egger (the baker), who had been exiled, would be allowed to return home under the following conditions. She had to recant publicly on three Sundays during mass and perform the penance which the local priest required of her. Moreover, an affidavit should be drawn up in which she would swear to desist from being an Anabaptist and promise not to leave the city of Hall.

Cristina's husband and sister-in-law were lay leaders, proselytizing in neighbouring districts already in April 1528.[43]

February 8, 1529, Michel in the Hülbn's Wife, Martyr, Left Seven Children

The Innsbruck government wrote to William von Liechtenstein, the crown administrator of Kurtatsch. The possessions of Michel in the Hülbn's wife,[44] *who was executed as an Anabaptist, were estimated to be worth approximately 400 Gulden (of quite some value). Her relatives and other notable people had made repeated requests that what was left of this money after the court costs had been deducted should be used in raising the seven children whom she left behind.*[45]

The only reference to this woman is in this summarized document. By this time 12 of the 77 women who became martyrs in Tirol between 1527 and 1531 had been executed. Most often martyred women were drowned.

February 9, 1529,

In Sterzing, two unnamed women were arrested with three men. The woman who was not pregnant was to be tried with the men and, according to the new decree, all were to be condemned to death. The trial of the pregnant unnamed woman should be postponed until she had given birth.[46] Elisabeth Mair, also from Sterzing, was a single woman who named Anabaptists from Bavaria in her confession.

February 20, 1529,

Juliane Gärn, fled with her husband. They were captured a second time in the city of Hall.

March 6, 1529,

Jörg Schweitzer was a miner and his wife was pregnant at her first arrest. The petition submitted for her was turned down because the government of Innsbruck did not have jurisdiction over the miners in Sterzing in this matter. In any case, she would only be tried after giving birth. Finally, on September 1, the authorities in Sterzing were authorized to grant her a pardon.

March 9, 1529, Barbara Velcklehner Stated Her Beliefs During Interrogation

Barbara and her husband Hans had both escaped prison on June 10, 1528.[47]

*The Innsbruck government instructed Erasmus Offenhauser to get in touch with Lamprecht Haun, the judge of Hertenberg (who was less experienced in these matters) and together, in the presence of the judge and the jury, they should interrogate the imprisoned (Barbara) Velcklehner. (She had recently returned to prison of her own free will when she was well advanced in her pregnancy).*⁴⁸ *They were to find out if she had been baptized, if so by whom, if she had fallen away from the Christian faith and "if she believed the body and blood of Christ our Saviour are in the sacrament of the altar."*⁴⁹

Nine days later, on March 18, 1529, a second report discussed her case further.

*The judge of Hertenberg, Lamprecht Haun and Erasmus Offenhauser report that they questioned Barbara Velcklehner in the presence of four jury members. She does not want to admit that her faith in the holy sacrament and in the mass is false. She denies having been re-baptized or baptizing others. She also denies having accepted the Lutheran or any other sectarian faith or having aided in spreading such a faith. Because she is not aware of having done anything to merit the favour or disfavour of the king and, based on the petition made on her behalf from several districts in the upper Inn Valley, Offenhauser and Haun are to release her from prison on a written promise and oath after she has paid the costs for her imprisonment. She will be allowed to return to her household and her children after paying a proper amount of money as security. If the government were to ask her to appear before them again, whether sooner or later, she has to promise to report obediently to provide them with further information and await further instructions. Also, her affidavit is to be sent to us (in Innsbruck).*⁵⁰

March 17, 1529, Elisabeth Wolfram's Oath of Recantation

At the castle of Prösels near the town of Völs on the Schlern mountain, Elisabeth, ... daughter of ... Michael Wolfram and his wife Magdalena, gave her oath and promise.

Her recantation was essentially the same as that of Cristoff Mesner. By becoming an Anabaptist Elisabeth Wolfram had forfeited life and limb and her goods. But, she was pardoned by the king and allowed to accept a milder punishment. She was even excused from this milder punishment on the basis of her own and her brother's request and the intercession of her friends and the whole district of Völs. However, the condition was that she would recant, swear an oath, perform penance and pay her court costs. For her penance, she was to kneel holding a burning candle and recant publicly following the blessing, on three consecutive Sundays during mass in the church in Völs. In her affidavit she also promised to return to prison if the district governor requested her to do so.

March 19, 1529,

The two young herdsmen and the maid, Agatha, of Hans and Anna Gasser from the Ritten above Bozen, all had given a confession. Mathes Moser and his wife, also from the region of Bozen, had escaped from prison. The judge, Jacob Hupher, was reprimanded for his carelessness which made their escape possible.

April 1, 1529,

The son of Elspeth Zägeler, a citizen of Hall, made trouble in church during Lent. On August 12, 1530 Elspeth admitted to have attended communion and the breaking of bread in a house in Wattens. She was to describe the house to them.[51]

April 3, 1529, Anna Weltzenberger, Pregnant and Persistent

The instructions of the Innsbruck government to Bartlme Anngst, judge in Rattenberg were summarized (as follows). Anna Weltzenberger is tainted with Anabaptism and persists in her damnable, sectarian thinking despite serious discussions with the territorial judge, her father and her husband. She cannot be released from prison on bail under any circumstances and should be kept in prison in a manner befitting a pregnant woman. If she continues in her erring ways after the birth of her child she is to be tried in the criminal court.

April 3, 1529, Agatha, the Gasserin's Maid, Young, Spared Death

The summary which introduces this document refers to the objections of the jury to try these three young people. The jury said they were too young to be tried in the criminal court.

The Innsbruck government instructed Jacob Hupher, judge of Bozen (as follows).

O faithful one! We understand from your report of March 27 that your jury registered a complaint regarding the three Anabaptists, Agatha, (Anna) Gasser's maid and the two young herdsmen of (Benedict and Anna Sackmann, Paul, the oxen herdsman and Viet, the other herdsman).[52] (The prisoners)... have given confessions, with and without the use of torture, concerning their involvement with Anabaptism. Therefore they should be condemned to death despite their youth and simple-mindedness. But, considering the youth and lack of understanding of the two boys and the simple-mindedness of the maid, (the jury) was persuaded at this time, to spare their lives. However, in order to make an example of them and to protect and prevent the young people themselves from further involvements with the damnable, deceptive, false teachings and sects, they are not to be spared punishment....

Also, if you have not already done so, you (Hupher) should inquire if and where Agatha, who admits to having believed falsely, actually carried out the required confession and whether she took the holy sacrament last Christmas, the latter being part of Christian practice. If she has not done this, then you and the jury are to punish her more severely than the two herdsmen.

April 6, 1529,

Blasius Gengl's wife from the district of Sterzing fled with her husband.

April 15, 1529,

Bartlme Has's wife is to stay in prison in Landeck with Hans Scheuring's wife until she has given birth, at which time both women are to be interrogated. This is the only reference to the wife of Bartlme Has. Hans Scheuring's wife was captured again May 13, 1531 and executed.

April 16, 1529,

Ulrich Lindner's wife from Schwaz was critiqued by her husband, who spoke with slander when she took the sacrament. He said he had not been re-baptized and was not Lutheran.

April 23, 1529, After Losing Her Husband Anna Gasser Lost Her Unborn Child

The Innsbruck government wrote to Jacob Hupher, judge of Bozen... in response to his report of March 3 following the execution of Hans Gasser. Hupher informed Innsbruck that Anna Gasser, Benedikt Sackmann and his wife, (Christoff) Stoffl Mair from Egg and his wife and Lucia, the Gassers' maid would be allowed to live. With the exception of Anna Gasser and Stoffl Mair's wife, the prisoners should all be released on bail. However, the government asked specifically why Anna Gasser had been kept in prison so long after her miscarriage. Had Anna given her confession to the judge and jury with or without torture? It was necessary to report on this.

Earlier that year, on January 5, orders had been given to punish Anna (from Lüsen) and the other prisoners with a flogging. Anna and Mair's wife were pregnant at the time. Also on January 5, the order for her husband's execution had been issued. All this was less than a year after the first mention of Hans and Anna Gasser in the court records on February 13, 1528. As described above, on April 23 Anna was granted a second pardon. Later that year, October 13, 1529, Anna's request for permission to travel outside of her district was discussed. The authorities in Ritten rejected her request, thinking it would only encourage her to leave altogether. She proved them right and had left Tirol by January 12, 1530, when we read about her for the last time in these records.

In the final reference to Anna she is identified as the sister of Mairhofer from Gufidaun. He was the leader who held meetings in their home in February 1528. Anna then was not the only one in her extended family to be deeply involved in Anabaptism. However, in her immediate family, Anna's daughter Barbara made a different choice than her parents. On May 24, 1533 she testified that she had left home, going to Sterzing on her own, because her parents were Anabaptists and she did not want to have any part of this superstitious faith. Barbara told her inquisitors that: *Recently, on Palm Sunday, she had taken the sacrament and gone to confession in her native Ritten. She believed in the Christian church, in honouring God and in the Virgin Mary*.[53]

April 29, 1529, Two Poor Women, Drowned by a Harsh Ruler

The Innsbruck government sent Christoff Fuchs, governor of Kufstein, instructions on how to deal with two imprisoned, unnamed Anabaptist women. In the summary preceding this document it is stated that: *The simple-mindedness and poverty of the two women would justify giving them a pardon. However, since nothing good would result from such action, they should be executed.*

The original document included the government's justification as follows: *Until now, from day to day, almost all of those who are pardoned for their adherence to the Anabaptist and Lutheran sects, do not obey the imperial mandates of his majesty. Therefore, in the name of the king, (his Innsbruck advisers) command, that the two women should each be dealt with according to the imperial mandates and that the law should be carried out against them, based on what they have confessed.*[54]

May 10, 1529, A Boy Gives Information on the Mission Work of Gilg Klein's Wife

Orders were sent from Innsbruck to Sigmund Capeller, territorial judge of Freundsberg, regarding Gilg Klein's wife. She had been imprisoned by the judge on the basis of information given to him by a boy who said he heard her say, that she had made six new Christians in a short time. If nothing crucial was revealed at her interrogation in front of the jury she should be released from prison on bail.

May 15, 1529, The Young Daughter Could Not Be Excused Easily

The crown administrator of Ehrenberg was directed to *cease proceedings against the young daughter of Hans Reck from Tannheim because her father had submitted a petition for her.* She was in prison for Anabaptist involvements.

A few weeks later, on June 26, 1529, the crown administrator was instructed again about the young girl. *If she had recanted, gone to confession and taken the sacrament before she came to prison, then she should be released on the promise that she would pay her prison costs and swear an oath. The recantation on three consecutive Sundays would have to be included in this promise. (But,) if she was sorry for her actions only after her imprisonment, a report should be sent in about her.*

May 16, 1529,

Waldpurga Ameiser of Rattenberg was pregnant and requested mercy because she was sorry about her re-baptism, which she said she had accepted out of ignorance and simple-mindedness. See also September 1, 1529 regarding her.

May 22, 1529,

A woman named Rotvelderin from Rattenberg was pregnant and not willing to desist from her faith. However, she would not be condemned to death until after her child was born.

May 23, 1529, An Unprecedented Number of Women Executed on One Day

On May 9, 1529 the town council met in Rattenberg and made an extraordinary decision. They decided that 18 Anabaptists should be executed on the coming Wednesday, May 12. Just the day before, on May 8, three women in this group of 21 prisoners had chosen to recant.[55] The council was fully aware of the magnitude of their actions when they stated that, *without a doubt, in the history of Rattenberg there had never been executions of so many persons at once.*[56] They feared reaction from the citizens and thus requested that six knights be present to avert potential danger. Bartlme Anngst, the judge of Rattenberg reported on the executions the next day, May 13 and the report was in the hands of the officials in Innsbruck only three days later, on May 16. (It usually took five days to send reports to the capital.)

Ten days later, on May 23 the events in Rattenberg were discussed again in the correspondence between Ferdinand and his officials in Innsbruck. The latter stated that since the imperial mandate against Anabaptists recently passed at the Diet in Speyer was more lenient than Ferdinand's own law, it should not be published in Tirol. They went on to say: *we have spared no diligence, work and effort in our attempts to eradicate the sect. As we have already informed your imperial majesty, recently in Rattenberg, we allowed the full power of the law to be carried out against 17 persons, among whom 10 were women. In no way did these prisoners want to recant. (They were all Anabaptists,) being either those who baptized or those who had joined the movement ... Now we have imprisoned a true Anabaptist leader, Michel Kürschner, who has baptized over 200 people (see June 5, 1529). In questioning him with and without torture we have found no evidence that this man or any of the other prisoners had any motives of rebelling against the authorities.... On the contrary, (these Anabaptists) confessed that their purpose is that people should refrain from sin and irresponsibility and live together in a quiet and peaceable manner....*

In fact then 17, not 18 persons were executed as the town council had originally ordered. And over half of the martyrs – 10 in all – were women.[57] The executions in Rattenberg were unprecedented and not repeated ever again.[58] Moreover, the authorities finally saw that the motives of the Anabaptists were solely religious and not political.

May 23, 1529,

The two single sisters of Caspar Schwartz, a tailor from Welsberg, were missionaries. The women lived in the nearby hillside village of Alen and were arrested with five other Anabaptists from the Puster Valley, all of whom were accused of promoting the sect, participating in meetings and peddling books. The destruction of a wayside image of the Virgin Mary near Welsberg was also reported in the discussion of these Anabaptists.

May 26, 1529, Woman Leader With a Register of 800 Names
Ferdinand I wrote from Linz to his Innsbruck advisers informing them that four major Anabaptist leaders were currently in the Ziller Valley and baptizing there, namely, Hans Streicher, Adam Stainer, Paul von Zillerprugg and Wolf Mayr. There was also said to be a woman among the Anabaptists who had in her possession a register of 800 names.[59] She was staying with Crispin Maler. Leonhard Lackner's wife and the miner Jörg Obermayr apparently know her. Information should be obtained from all of these people.

The judge in Rattenberg, Bartlme Anngst, was given the task of investigating this matter. On May 29, 1529 he was also told to obtain the occupations of the persons listed in the book. *He wrote back to Innsbruck on June 3 that despite a diligent search, he was not able to obtain any information about the book with the 800 names.*

On June 5, the Innsbruck government followed up with instructions to *Cristan Noel, who was the crown administrator as well as the mining and territorial judge in Schwaz. He was commanded again to search for the unnamed woman, who was supposed to be a leader and might have baptized the 800 people (whose names were in the book she was carrying). He was to make inquiries of Leonhard Lackner's widow and Jörg Obermayr as to where she was at the present time.* But nothing came of these inquiries as the documents from June 5 and a subsequent one from June 6 indicate.

There are no other references to this woman's activities. It is highly unlikely she baptized 800 people as the government suspected. However, of great interest is that she was the person reportedly carrying the Anabaptist register. Documents from May 28 and 29, 1529 reveal the government's fear that Anabaptism was gaining the upper hand. The population of the mining town of Schwaz was 1200 and two thirds of its inhabitants, 800 persons, were reported to be Anabaptists. And death did not frighten them (*kein Entsetzen*). The fears of the government were justified.[60]

May 31, 1529, Five of the Fifteen Prisoners Were Women
The Innsbruck government addressed Georg, the Bishop of Brixen as follows. They were aware that the Bishop recently captured several Anabaptists in the district of

Michelsburg and imprisoned them in Brixen. Apparently there was a real leader as well as Anabaptist members among them. The government had no doubt the bishop would interrogate them in orderly fashion; they were interested in the name of the leader, whether he had baptized other persons in Schwaz, and who else belonged to the sect. Following interrogation the prisoners were to be sentenced in Michelsburg. Thus, the judicial rights of the district of Michelsburg would not be infringed upon.

The district of Michelsburg, not the bishopric of Brixen had the authority to hold court and pass sentence. Because of the many arrests in May, the prisons were full and this group of prisoners, although arrested in Michelsburg, was transferred to the prison in Brixen. This directive was intended to make sure they came back to Michelsburg to ensure the proper execution of justice. On June 11, it was repeated emphatically.

The names of the fifteen Anabaptists in this latter group come from a financial report of 1529. Five of the prisoners were women, namely, Lienhard Kofler's widow from Reischach, Agnes, a widow from Erspan, a woman named Raderin from St. Lorenzen, (Margreth), called the old Wiserin and Dorothea, Margreth's daughter.[61]

The story of Margreth and Dorothea Wiser continues on August 11. From this report we know that Lienhard Kofler's widow from Reischach chose to recant, whereas Margareth Wiser and her daughter did not. The woman named Raderin from St. Lorenzen was baptized by a man named Luckhner, who in turn had been baptized by Jacob Hutter. The Raderin may have gone to Moravia. Erspan was in the village of St. Lorenzen so that possibly Agnes the widow from Erspan and the Raderin may have known each other.

May 31, 1529,

A document of 1532 names the following Anabaptists from the district of Sonnenburg who were active between 1529 and 1531: Hanns Letta and his wife, Caspar Müller and his wife Dorothea and Agnes Kassian, all of whom had fled. Katharina Kassian, the mother of Agnes, had been executed.

June 5, 1529, Two Women and Two Men Witnessed the Appointment of a Leader

The Innsbruck government informed Lienhard Friedrich, judge of Völs on the mountain of Schlern, that in his confession Michel Kürschner, executed three days earlier on June 2, spoke of his baptism and becoming an Anabaptist leader in the presence of several trusted members, two of whom were women.

This was described in the original document as follows: *Faithful one! Last Wednesday, on June 2, 1529, an Anabaptist leader was burned at the stake here. Kürschner confessed that he was baptized, made an Anabaptist leader and registered in the Anabaptist brotherhood by Jörg Zaunring, who is also a leader in the sect. This took place on the Tuesday before Corpus Christi, June 9, 1528, in the presence of three people from Völs: Melchior Schneider's wife*[62] *and Magdalena and Mathäus Wald.*

June 5, 1529,

The trial of Magdalena, Valtin Schneider's daughter and Dorothea, Hans Ortner's wife, took place in Rattenberg behind locked doors. With all that was going on in Rattenberg, the government did not want the proceedings to influence others in favour of Anabaptism.[63]

June 6, 1529,

Katharina Schwaiglin from the district of Kitzbühel was to have been executed along with nine other Anabaptists. It was a mass execution but on a smaller scale than had taken place in Rattenberg and reported May 23 (see above). Because Katharina was sick, she was taken back to prison from the place of execution. When she recovered she chose to recant but then rejoined the Anabaptists. By the end of the year she was captured again and put on trial (see December 7, 1529).[64] Because Katharina was sick we have her name. None of the other male or female martyrs in this group are named.

June 17, 1529,

Thomas Stainperger from Rattenberg submitted a petition for his wife, who confessed to having erred and having made a mistake in becoming an Anabaptist. The matter was to be investigated.

July 3, 1529,

Benedikt Tischler and his wife from Brixlegg were poor Anabaptist martyrs owning less than twelve Gulden, which should be given to their four children.

July 5, 1529, The Punishment of Two Anabaptist Women Was Gradually Reduced

The Innsbruck government wrote the following to Augustin Heirling, crown administrator for the Ritten. On the basis of their petition, Benedikt Sackmann and Stoffl Mair should be allowed the freedom to do business and come and go as they chose in and around the urban centre of Bozen, but the same freedom was not extended to their wives.[65]

This was the ending to the story which began January 5, 1529 after Jacob Hupher, judge of Bozen, sent in the confessions of these four Anabaptists along with those of their fellow believers from the Ritten plateau, Hans and Anna Gasser and their maid Lucia. *Because the prisoners had not reported to the government within the period of grace (the previous year) and, in part, had become involved in Anabaptism after that, they deserved more severe punishment. But considering their remorse and their circumstances, that they had been led astray, they should be pardoned under the following conditions: corporal punishment at the pillory "with all due modesty toward the women"; the promise to do penance and a guaranty for the latter; and their sworn promise. Finally, they were to leave the territory of Tirol and never return. Those who did not accept this penance, except for the pregnant women (Stoffl Mair's wife and Anna Gasser), were to be tried and Hans Gasser was to be executed.*

In February 13, 1529, the king expressed astonishment that nothing had been done concerning these prisoners.... (Moreover), a report that the prisoners had received permission from the judge to attend a dance and that the judge was promoting their release in every way he could, elicited the king's greatest displeasure.

Further dealings of the central government with these prisoners were undertaken with other officials. By March 3, 1529 Hans Gasser had been executed.

On April 21, 1529, Innsbruck instructed Georg Freiherr von Firmian that on the basis of his intercession and that of other noblemen, Stoffl Mair and his wife and Benedikt and Anna Sackmann, could remain in the territory but had to swear not to leave the district of Wangen or they would lose their lives. April 23, they were released on bail.

The next and last reference to them was in July, described above, and ordered different treatment for the women. It is not revealed why the women got different treatment than their husbands.

July 8, 1529,
Margareth (Frönerin) Mayrl was the wife of an Anabaptist leader in St. Petersberg. She was arrested before her husband but no information is available about how she was treated.

July 24, 1529, Pregnant Woman Arrested, Her Execution Ordered
Anna Gasteiger may not have been pregnant for very long when she was arrested. The judge in Rattenberg was directed to call in another woman, likely a midwife, to determine if she was pregnant. Moreover, he was to see to it that the child was born under the proper conditions, be given a Christian baptism and be cared for by a wet nurse so that it would not be in need. Anna herself was to be executed, following the birth of her child.

July 24, 1529, Women Baptized by Jacob Hutter in the Puster Valley
This original document discussed fourteen Anabaptists from the region of Toblach of whom nine, four of them women, had been baptized by Jacob Hutter, namely, Gregori Erler's wife, the Caspar Schneiderin, Ursula, the daughter of Tillen from Lüenz, and Ursula, the old woman named Müllerin from Pflaurenz. They had given their confessions in June. *Now, in the presence of the governor (of Toblach), a competent priest was to instruct them thoroughly on two articles of faith (in particluar), namely, the holy sacrament and baptism.* The women were genuinely sorry and chose to desist and be pardoned.

Andre Planer and Balthasar Hutter had not been baptized but were guilty none the less. *Balthasar had provided lodging for Anabaptists, such as Gregori Weber (a martyr) ... and Jacob Hutter, a real leader.... Communion, the breaking of bread as they call it, was held in the downstairs rooms of Andre Planer's house and Ursula, Tillen's daughter... and others listened to Andre read from a book of the Gospel (there).... Through this Tillen's daughter had fallen into this heresy....*

Moreover, *the baptized wives of Andre Planer and Balthasar Hutter had been allowed to return home without interrogation because they were nursing infants. They were to be arrested again when their children were no longer nursing to see if they persisted in their beliefs.*

July 31, 1529, Miller's Wife Leaves Her Four-Week-Old Infant
This report from Innsbruck to Ferdinand I concerning the properties and children of executed and fugitive Anabaptists in Rattenberg included a reference to the child the Dänckls left behind. The families named were not poor, as the following passages attest.

On December 20, 1529, Bartlme Anngst, judge in Rattenberg, sent the following report to the regents and advisers of the treasury in Innsbruck.

Benevolent Lord, I received the instructions of your grace regarding Wilhelm (Dänckl) Stablmüller the Anabaptist executed in Rattenberg. The property he left consisted of a mill with two working stones and a house, (both) located in Brixlegg,...

This miller, together with his wife, joined the heretics and fled, leaving a four week old infant lying in a cradle alone and forsaken. When I discovered the child, I took custody of it so that it would not perish, confiscated all of their property and informed my gracious lord of this matter. Then you instructed me to take charge of the house and the mill and to support the child from it, which I have done. At the same time I instructed a labourer to work in the mill and boarded up certain rooms in the house where it was necessary. On the basis of a petition from Herr Murnauer, the crown administrator here and other lords I have asked a man named Palgmacher to manage the house and the mill.... And I have asked his wife to care for the child but I have not made any further agreement with them.[66]

The final accounting of their property took place in October or November 1530 and stated that their child was to be raised from the income of the house and mill.

August 2, 1529, Wolfgang Schneider's Wife Left Three Days After the Birth

The judge of Klausen wrote to the advisor and governor of Brixen concerning Wolfgang Schneider, an Anabaptist who had recanted. *Apparently, on July 29 at the birth of his child he had allowed the wet nurse to baptize the child even though there was no threat of death. As a consequence Schneider was captured and brought to Säben, (the monastery on the mountain above the town of Klausen). When the judge asked him why he had not baptized the child in the proper manner, Schneider answered, "The child did not need it. I believe the child has been baptized by God."*

During the time that the judge was in Säben and three days after the child was born, Schneider's wife packed her things and left. It is not known where she went. She left the child behind. The judge took over the care of the child and boarded up the house.

Within a week, on August 6, an order was issued to try Wolfgang Schneider in the criminal court. More jury members were to be chosen so that he could be tried properly. Since there were only nine jury members in the district of Klausen, each of whom was named, the local officials should add three more men to the list.

August 11, 1529, Family Involvements, Re-education and a Burning Crucifix

Several of the fifteen Anabaptists arrested in Brixen May 31, 1529 were still in prison August 11, more than two months later. After reading their confessions, the authorities concluded that several of them, including Oswald Wiser and his three sons and Lienhard Kofler's widow, had joined Anabaptism out of ignorance and simple-mindedness, being persuaded by others. Therefore their punishments would be: *to recant publicly on three consecutive Sundays in their parish church in front of the people during the holy mass; to give a sworn oath promising to abstain from (Anabaptism) totally and from this time on not to have anything to do with it for the rest of their lives; to accept and to carry out the penance required of them by their priest.... If they break their promise they... are to be condemned to death. (On these conditions) these persons may be pardoned and released. In addition, they are to pay for their keep if they are able to, and if not, promise to pay it later.*

But Margreth, Oswald Wiser's wife and Dorothea, their daughter, *whose confessions confirmed that they were obstinate and not willing to recant, should be treated differently. Knowledgeable and intelligent priests were to speak with them and instruct them so they would be ready to desist. If they chose not to do this, they should be dealt with according to the imperial mandates and laws and be made aware that they would endure punishments to life and limb. Or, if they agreed to desist, they could be pardoned (like the others) according to the procedures outlined heretofore.*

One thing was different about Margreth's case. *She reported in her confession, that she and several others witnessed the desecration and burning of a crucifix. Not only did she not do anything to stop this action, she remained silent and had not reported it. Whether or not the others involved chose to desist and recant right away, as had been ordered, Margreth's negligence and secrecy, since it is a grievous crime akin to blasphemy, deserves more severe punishment. The jury should be made aware of her actions which require penance. This is the judgement of his imperial majesty....*

This was the last reference to Margreth. Her final choice remains unknown.

August 20, 1529, Anabaptist Meetings in the Forest

The Innsbruck government informed ... the judge of Rettenberg they had been told about a meeting of about twenty men and women in the forest near Mils on August 15, the Ascension Day of Mary.... The leader at this meeting was "a straight-standing man with a long red beard...." whom they later found out was Peter Egger the baker.[67]

On August 29 two unnamed women from the city of Hall[68] were to be questioned under torture about this meeting. The local officials were informed as follows: *Because this meeting was held in such a suspicious and secret location, undoubtedly there must be something more involved than what the two women have revealed so far. It is hard to believe that they cannot at least identify the persons at the meeting that were sitting next to them. Thus, in the name of his majesty... the judge ... is solemnly commanded to imprison these two women immediately and ask them earnestly who was with them at this meeting. If they will not report any names, then they are to be interrogated using torture to find out what took place at this meeting (called a synagogue) ... what the names and residences were of those present, as well as those who had all things in common.... There should be more diligence and courage shown (by local officials) in the eradication of this deceptive sect....*

August 26, 1529, Cristina Paneyder, Ordered to Remain in Her District For a Year

A report from the Innsbruck government to Hans Prew, crown administrator of Gufidaun, included the following instructions.... Lienhard Paneyder and his wife Cristina should to be well guarded. Because the judge does not have the authority to deliver the death sentence we are writing to the judge of (nearby) Rodeneck to preside.

Two weeks later, October 9, the Innsbruck government instructed Prew (further). Paneyder and his wife should be released under the usual conditions of recanting three times and swearing the oath with a guaranteed promise which included the stipulation that if they broke their promise they forfeited life and limb. Moreover, for one year they could not leave their judicial district and they could not leave the territory of Tirol for the rest of their lives. Also, they had to pay the costs for their imprisonment.

August 27, 1529,

Following the report of July 24, 1529 from Toblach in the Puster Valley which named men and women whom Jacob Hutter had baptized there (see above), several of the men in the group were questioned with torture in front of a jury. On August 27 the crown administrator reported on these proceedings. The men had not revealed any new information except for the following. When Jacob Hutter, referred to now as a principal leader, and a local leader named Schilling, were captured in Toblach, an unnamed woman was captured with them. The three escaped before any proceedings could be undertaken against them. It is not clear if she was the wife of Schilling or someone else. However, it is of note that she is named as having been captured with the two men.[69]

August 31, 1529, Susanna Köberl, Back in Prison of Her Own Free Will

The Innsbruck government wrote the following to Ulrich Rungger, crown administrator of St. Petersberg. Jörg Köberl's wife (Susanna) escaped from prison but now has reported back to the authorities of her own free will in order to recant. She can be pardoned under the usual conditions (of recanting publicly at mass on three consecutive Sundays, giving an affidavit and doing penance). But before she recants she should be interrogated once more to find out where she went when she escaped prison with the others, who assisted them and how, and where and why she separated herself from the others to return home. On September 7, 1529 the Innsbruck government addressed Rungger, (again).

Susanna Köberl who came back to prison of her own free will, should go free on the basis of the petition submitted by her relatives on her behalf. Her brothers Andre and Hans Gabel from Reppen who had fled could likewise be pardoned if they presented themselves to the court and showed true remorse.

September 1, 1529, Ursula Kuen, Silversmith's Wife, Had Considerable Property

The Innsbruck government gave instructions to Bartlme Anngst, judge of Rattenberg, regarding Anabaptist properties including that of Ursula Kuen, the silversmith's wife. These properties were to be expropriated and the money from the harvested fields accounted for carefully. Ursula was an Anabaptist already in April 1529, explicitly denying having had her two young daughters baptized and refusing to give up her faith, even if it meant sacrificing her citizenship.[70]

On November 20, 1529 Bartlme Anngst, wrote directly to Ferdinand I concerning Anabaptist properties.... Ursula Kuen, widow of Caspar the silversmith, who was tainted with Anabaptism and fled, left a house in the town and other things belonging to this property, as well as several day labourers and two children. The guardians of the children and Sebastian Anndorffer, the royal silversmith in Schwaz, have registered a complaint against her. They want to have 600 rheinisch Gulden and the property which has been confiscated, that is, her house. This money is to be paid to the guardians of the children and Sebastian Anndorffer.

On June 23, 1530 Ferdinand I informed... the governor of Rattenberg that, on the basis of a petition from the guardians of the executed Caspar Khuen's children, the mother's inheritance was to be given to the children, if they could prove their claim to it. (In the Anabaptist inventories of October and November 1530 recorded in Rattenberg), the property left by the old silversmith's wife, who fled (and was executed), included a house and yard, a bath (for washing clothes) and stables, together with a plot of land outside the town, located on the road toward Radfeld. This property was appraised at 400 Gulden.

September 1, 1529,

The wives of Jörg Ameiser (Waldburga), Cristan Gschäll (Anna) and Lienhard Vischer, all from Rattenberg, could be pardoned but they also had to promise in writing, confirmed with their own oath and that of some citizens, that for one year they would not leave their district and not leave the territory of Tirol for the rest of their lives.

September 7, 1529,

Magdalena Futterreith of Rattenberg, daughter of the court accountant was arrested, along with an adviser to the king and another man. Their confessions were to be confirmed and then they were to be tried in the criminal court.

September 7, 1529, Dorothea Maler Was Influenced to Rejoin by Other Women

The Innsbruck government wrote to Erhard Haller, judge of Hall. They had received... the confessions sent in for Dorothea Maler, Anna Ochsentreiber and Katharina Praun who were in prison in Hall. Dorothea Maler had sworn the oath promising to leave the Anabaptist sect but had broken her promise, which had not been guaranteed on her release. Two women convinced her to go with them to the forest near Mils to meet Scherer (Hans Amon, the clothmaker), who was on the run, Peter Egger (the baker), the son of Scherer, a man whom they did not know wearing a dark jacket, as well as several women from Wattens and other places. From this it can safely be assumed that Dorothea is not as innocent or as simple-minded as she claims to be. She likely is acquainted with and could name the two women who persuaded her to rejoin, as well as the women from Wattens. The government's solemn command is that they question her, with and without torture, as appropriate for a woman, in the presence of the jury and others who had been at her first hearing. They should find out the names of the other women and their husbands and what she had heard from the women as well as from Scherer and Peter Egger and what their plans are. In particular, Dorothea should be asked if she was not sorry to have recanted the Anabaptist faith she had accepted earlier. The information obtained from her is to be reported to the upper Austrian government. Dorothea and the other two women, Anna Ochsentreiber and Katharina Praun are to be kept (in prison) with all diligence until further instructions were sent.

Dorothea stood firm. On September 14, 1529 the order was given to put her on trial.[71] Both she and Anna were martyred. Katharina Praun chose to recant and a month later, on October 16, was pardoned and released on the usual conditions.

September 11, 1529, Two Wives and a Daughter, Questioned About Their Beliefs

Peter Müllner's daughter from Stubai had been baptized and her brother, a blacksmith, knew about this.

Part A: The Innsbruck government addressed Bartlme Anngst, judge in Rattenberg, about a report from Hans Floser, judge in Stubai, who had captured an Anabaptist named, Hans Weissenflecker. The latter testified about a miner... named Hans Gruener, about 40 years old, who wore a red garment, was quite tall and somewhat bald on the front of his head, who had baptized him and had brought others into the sect.

Part B: The (central) government wrote (the following) to the crown administrator, Wilhelm Schupfer. Weissenflecker, the Anabaptist imprisoned in Stubai, also testified about the daughter of Peter Müllner from Ellenbogen in the region of Ambras. Her brother, the blacksmith in Erlach, could give information about her. Information was to be obtained about her and she was to be captured since she also had allowed herself to be baptized.

Peter Müllner's daughter was not arrested in 1529. A report of May 25, 1530 stated she was baptized in a pasture and repeated the order for her arrest.

The third part of the report discussed two other women.

Part C: The (central) government wrote to Hans Floser, judge in Stubai, concerning his report of September 9 about what Weissenflecker had confessed without the use of torture. On the basis of that confession Floser had taken the wives of Christoff Gärber and the blacksmith from Enngendeiner captive.[72] The two women were to be interrogated separately and asked the following questions: who brought them into the sect and what were their names; where did they live; what did they have against the traditional Christian order and against the "worthy sacrament of the altar"; what other secretive things they knew of related to the Anabaptist sect; and whether they had participated in a nocturnal communion or the breaking of bread as they called it. This information was to be sent to the territorial judge of Sonnenburg.

September 12, 1529, Persevering Women

The Innsbruck government wrote to Bartlme Anngst, judge of Rattenberg ... concerning the capture of three Anabaptists: Anna, the widow, and Ursula, the mother of Walthauser Heuberger from Radfeld,[73] and a woman who had been baptized by the former priest Virgil Plattner in the former house of Hans Maurer.[74] The three women were determined to persevere in their heretical opinions, in the same way as the labourers and the Schueler's maid (who were also in prison). They should be interrogated in front of the jury both with and without torture, especially concerning the Lord's Supper and the meeting held at night which a neighbour in Bruck am Ziller had seen recently. Ten or twelve people had been together there, but he had not been able to get close enough to see who they were. This same neighbour also had pointed out the houses in which Anabaptists were currently staying. Of these, the two free standing houses should be burned to the ground but the third one should not be taken down at this time. The plan of Bartlme Anngst to carry out a raid together with the crown administrator of Kropfsberg against the Anabaptists and those who harboured them, was approved.

September 14, 1529, Singing Strengthens the Prisoners

The Innsbruck government wrote to the mayor and council in the city of Hall.

The mayor should prevent the Anabaptist prisoners from being kept together as a group, for then they sing hymns as is the practice in their sect. When the common people hear this it makes them angry and it strengthens and encourages the prisoners to persist in their erroneous, heretical beliefs. There should be enough prisons in Hall to keep the prisoners in solitary confinement.

September 17, 1529,

Barbara Frewoltin and Anna Riederin, captured in Kufstein, chose to desist from their erring ways and were to be pardoned on the usual conditions, like Susanna Köberl (See August 31, 1529).

September 25, 1529, Seven Anabaptist Women in Rattenberg, Widowed or Single

The Innsbruck government wrote to Bartlme Anngst, judge of Rattenberg concerning 13 Anabaptists (seven of whom were female) whose confessions, given with and without torture, had been sent to them. On September 12 only three of these women were mentioned, namely, Magdalena Futterreith, Anna, the widow and Ursula, the mother of the executed Waldhauser Heuberger, but now there were four additional women, namely, Cristan Gasteiger's daughter Barbara, the Weltzenberger's daughter Magdalena, the Gschälen family maid, and Kunz Schuster's widow Katharina from the Puster Valley.

With the exception of... (two of the men) all of these people were to receive instruction from learned priests so that they would give up their erring ways and come back to the traditional Christian faith. The government wanted to be informed of the priest's success. Those who remained impenitent should be brought to trial and sentenced to death....

It is certain that Magdalena Weltzenberger was executed. She had lived with her father and owned property valued at 60 Gulden, of which 39 Gulden had been collected from her brother and guardian, leaving 21 Gulden owing to the government by the fall of 1530.[75] On November 16, 1529 the only woman still in the Rattenberg prison from this group was Barbara Gasteiger. Since Barbara was a relapsed Anabaptist no mercy was shown and she was condemned to death. Katharina Schuster from the Puster Valley south of Rattenberg may have been trying to escape to Moravia when she was captured. Nothing more is known about the other women in this group. Likely they were all condemned to death.[76]

October 9, 1529, Anabaptist Women in Gries and Bozen Are to be Re-educated

Ferdinand I wrote to Jacob Hupher, territorial judge of (the district of) Gries and Bozen concerning the people imprisoned due to his diligence and that of his administrators, namely: Simon Kob and his wife from the hillsides of the Breitenberg, Margreth, the Kobin's sister; Rosina, Benedict Gamper's sister; Margreth, sister of the wife of Adam Manngl from the Aw (pasture) and Jorgen Dollingen from Kärnten.[77] These people held (Anabaptist meetings) in places such as Leifers on the Breitenberg, in the Au below Bozen and many of them at a place called the Gauppenhof. Some of them were baptized by Michel Kürschner from Völs (on the mountain of Schlern), formerly active in this region, and some by Georg von Chur (Jörg Blaurock), who also worked here. Any further information received from the prisoners and whether the prisoners persist in their deceptive Anabaptist intentions, is to be confirmed with oaths.

And we command you (Hupher) to pass this information on to the Guardian of the Order of Barefoot Monks in Bozen (the Franciscans). We want him or someone in his order who is learned and intelligent to be available to the prisoners, to discuss (matters of doctrine) with each of them individually, in such a way that fellow prisoners will not be aware of it. The discussions with the prisoners should be grounded in and make frequent use of the Holy Scriptures in order to convince them that their belief in re-baptism and their wish to negate the holy sacrament is wrong and goes against the Christian order....

And if these men and women in prison choose to remain in their impenitent Anabaptist ways... they are to be tried on the basis of their confessions in the criminal court with a jury. Let nothing hinder you (the judge) in this process. Before passing sentence, the jury members should be made aware of their responsibility and swear to it...

The Guardian reported on October 19 that the imprisoned Anabaptists remained obdurate. Thus, an execution order was given October 25, 1529.

We know from references in 1530 and May 1531 that Simon Kob and his wife were executed. For the others we only know that they were condemned to death.

October 29, 1529, Margarethe Gschäll Requests Her Inheritance[78]

Jakob Braunbeck (territorial judge in Rattenberg) wrote to Ferdinand I as the representative of Margarethe, wife of the Anabaptist Jörg Gschäll. Braunbeck appealed to the King in regard to the October 29 decision of the lawyer, Dr. Basilius Precht. According to that decision, Margarethe, who was not an Anabaptist, was to receive only half of the property rights (to the fief called Schöfferlehen)[79] which she had inherited from her parents. The letters related to this were located in the (Dominican) Convent Mariatal. Braunbeck's request for a revision of the decision was made in the name of the friends and relatives of Margarethe Gschäll. In a note of November 10 Jakob Braunbeck ... stated his intention to resubmit the petition.

Bartlme Anngst's report of November 20 to Innsbruck brings more detail to light. *After the death of Frohner, Margarethe Gschäll's father, she and her husband Jörg, who were innkeepers, were given the tenure for their property by the prioress of Mariatal in exchange for an annual rent. Since Jörg fled as an Anabaptist, the judge confiscated the half of the property to which the king had a right and promised the other half to Margarethe. In the discussion of Anabaptist properties on October 29, this decision was confirmed by Dr. J. Frankfurter*[80] *who officiated in the place of Dr. Basilius Precht. The note attached to this report indicated the imperial treasury was satisfied with this decision.* But for Margarethe it was still an issue.

The matter was resolved in the November 20 proceedings as follows…. The wife of Jörg Gschäll whose husband fled as an Anabaptist, because of which half of the property went to the king, now submits a petition being of the opinion that the letter created by the deceased prioress from Mariatal was not written up properly and was prepared without Margarethe's knowledge. The king had been informed already about these details…. Margarethe would gladly pay the 30 or 40 Gulden needed to obtain (the other half) of the property so that it remained undivided. Many friends gave Margarethe their support in this matter… requesting that it be given (to her) out of mercy. It is likely that Margarethe's request was granted.

November 16, 1529, An Unnamed Woman Was Pardoned by the King's Children

Bartlme Annst, judge of Rattenberg received the following instructions from the Innsbruck government. Of the two women who were still in prison in Rattenberg, Cristan Gasteiger's daughter Barbara (see September 25, 1529) was a relapsed Anabaptist and should be tried in the criminal court. The other woman,[81] *for whom a petition had been submitted to the children of the king, should be pardoned under the usual conditions.*

Mecenseffy adds a note to this report that at this time Ferdinand was holding court in Innsbruck and this pardon might have been submitted to his two oldest children, Elisabeth, born in 1526 and Maximilian II, born in 1527.

November 17, 1529, Barbara Weylmesserin, Also Pardoned by the King's Children

The Innsbruck government instructed Erhard Haller, judge of Hall, to pardon Barbara Weylmesserin from Wattens on the basis of her confession and the petition submitted for her. This petition (also) had been sent to the son and daughter of the king.

November 20, 1529,

Hanns Maurer and his wife from Rattenberg, a somewhat older couple, had allowed baptisms to take place in their home. Their son was suspected of re-baptism as well. By November they had been executed and their property was being discussed. Their land was worth 80 or 90 Gulden.

November 24, 1529, Balthasar Vest, the Bookseller, and His Wife, Both Martyred

The Innsbruck government asks... priests in Innsbruck and Hall to seek to convert the imprisoned Anabaptist bookseller Balthasar Vest and his wife. But the couple refused to be converted. They were executed December 10, 1529. An inventory of their house and goods was called for eight days later.

On March 16, 1530,... In an act of grace, the king commands the treasury to grant their inheritance, which had become the property of the king, to the family.

Part B:... Because they fear not much will be left, since the Vests were poor people, (the heirs and relatives) humbly appeal once more to the grace of the king, on behalf of the young children, to pay the inheritance without deducting government costs.

Part C:.... 3. The financial administrator, Dr. Frankfurter,[82] notes:... What is left is not of much value, approximately 24 to 26 Gulden....

Part D: The judge in Sonnenburg, Peter Praunegger, reported the following for his costs in the proceedings against Balthasar Vest (and his wife).

First of all, I received an order from the government that I should accept the two persons with their confessions from the judge in the city of Innsbruck and carry out the execution order. Thereupon, I rode to Innsbruck and according to the command, took these persons. On this day, the Saturday before St. Nicolas Day (December 4, 1529) my horse and I used, 1 Pd 6 Kr.[83]

In addition, on the Monday after St. Nicolas Day (December 6, 1529), according to the above command, I interrogated the bookseller using torture, in the presence of the court secretary and five jury members, that is, 7 persons each receiving 6 Kr, amounting to 3 Pd 6 Kr. My horse used 4 Kr.

On the following Thursday, I rode to Innsbruck to see the prisoners and to ask the mayor if the judicial procedures could be carried out in the city hall. On that day my horse used 1 Pd 3 Kr.

On Friday, December 10, 1529, when the execution took place, 13 jury members, 13 village mayors, two labourers, myself and the court secretary used 4 G. On that Friday the prisoners were given .8 litre of wine which cost 2 Kr 4 Vr. The court secretary and I each received 2 G for being present, amounting to 4 G. To execute the two persons, the executioner was paid 1 G 4 Pd. To bury the bodies, the grave digger was paid 2 Pd 6 Kr. The total sum of the expenses was 11 G, 3 Pd, 3 Kr, 4 Vr.[84]

November 24, 1529,
The Häselerin of Innsbruck who was innocent of Anabaptist involvements, was released from prison due to the petition submitted by her sister, Margarethe Werd, whose husband was a court carpenter who recanted (January 4, 1530).

December 3, 1529,
Katharina Wagner of Innsbruck joined Anabaptism without her husband and then was pardoned.

December 7, 1529, Of Twenty Anabaptist Prisoners, Eleven Were Women
The central government writes to Matthias Lang, crown administrator of Kitzbühel,... regarding the confessions of 20 Anabaptists he had captured.... Seven of these persons ... (including three women), Agnes Frawnholtz, Katharina Schwaiglin and Cristina Luntzbegkerin,[85] *had been pardoned previously, but had fallen again... and (now) stubbornly persist. The solemn command of the central government is to question these seven people again using torture, in an orderly manner, as is fitting, to confirm their earlier confessions. Encourage those who want to die, to do so as good Christians. And if they show remorse and regret for their erring ways, they should go to confession and take the holy sacrament. Whether they choose to do this or not,... they are to be brought before the jury and tried in the criminal court and the law is to be carried out according to the previously issued mandates. Those who pass sentence are to swear beforehand to judge according to these mandates.*

As for the other thirteen prisoners (which included eight women), Barbara Reschl, Katharina Widmauer, Ursula Egger, Gabriel Sunschwennter's wife Cristina, Dorothea Steiner, Margreth Katt, Steffan Veytstetter in the Weissach's daughter Barbara[86] *and Kunigund Katzingerin, send three priests ... to them.... With the use of the Holy Scripture and with all true diligence, the priests are to try to persuade them to leave the seductive*[87] *Anabaptist sect... and return to the true, traditional Christian faith, the practice of infant baptism and the holy sacrament.*

... But if these thirteen people ignore the instruction of the three priests and remain true to their earlier confessions ... treat them in the same manner as the seven persons named earlier, confirming their confessions with the use of torture ... and put them on trial in the criminal court.... For the three pregnant women, Katherina Widmauer, Ursula Egger and Gabriel Sunschwennter's wife, judicial procedures are to be postponed until they have given birth.[88]

December 8, 1529, Agnes Hutter Precedes Her Brother in Martyrdom

The report which discusses Agnes' second arrest reads as follows.

The Innsbruck government instructed Christoff Herbst, crown administrator in Toblach, as follows concerning his action in the treatment of the Anabaptist woman Agnes Hutter whom he captured and imprisoned. She comes from (the hamlet of) Moos in the district of St. Michelsburg and has 'fallen again' into the 'erring ways' (of Anabaptism). She will not return (to the traditional faith) despite instruction from him and other religious and secular persons. Herbst should interrogate her again both with and without the use of torture, following proper procedure, in order to confirm her confession. Following that, he should carry out the law according to the mandates that have been issued and try her in the criminal court. Before sitting to pass sentence, the jury must first give their oath and declare their responsibility in regard to the mandates so that they pass judgement in a proper, orderly fashion.

There is only one other reference to Agnes in the Austrian court records. In July 1532 her name is included in the discussion of the properties of the Anabaptists who were taken to Brixen from St. Michelburg for questioning.[89] Here she is identified as Agnes Hutter from Saln, a village located further up the mountain from her native Moos. Likely she was working in Saln when she was captured. There is no mention of her leaving any possessions. Agnes persisted in the Anabaptist faith and was martyred, preceding her brother Jacob who was martyred a few years later in 1536. Because Jacob was a prominent Anabaptist and Hutterite leader, he was burned at the stake at Innsbruck, the administrative and judicial centre for Tirol, on the main square in front of the Golden Roof. The execution of Agnes took place either late in 1529 or early in 1530 closer to her home.[90]

December 14, 1529,

The widow of Jörg Tollinger from the district of Kurtatsch was the only woman among eight prisoners and the only one who chose to recant.

December 22, 1529, The Leader's Wife, Katharina Streicher, Condemned to Death

Christoff Philipp von Liechtenstein, governor of Rattenberg, reported the following to the government of Innsbruck. (He addressed his superior as): Dear noble, strong, highly learned, kind and favourable friend of noble birth! I serve you gladly. When I returned here, I carried out your command and immediately gave orders to my judge to call in the executioner to hold the trial (of the criminal court) today. Accordingly, the men and women, especially those who have relapsed, were interrogated again to confirm (their confessions) and were tortured severely. However, the prisoners revealed nothing beyond what your lords already know. They want to die rather than become informers (about their fellow believers). Thus, the sentences for Hanns Nickinger, Hanns Ober, a stone mason, and Katherina, wife of Kunz Streicher (an Anabaptist leader), were handed down and carried out in every detail, in the presence of a small number of people. I will report later specifically why one of the men was not burned at the stake.[91]

The other persons were, Leonhard Kaspacher, Hanns Höl's wife Margreth and Walburg, the daughter of Caspar Kirchmair from Puech. These three had, by the grace of God, requested pardon, which was granted to them as I am commanded to do in your name. Now, on St. Thomas Day (December 21), they have publicly recanted from the pulpit, gone to confession and taken the holy sacrament during mass. They have also given an oath for themselves, as is required. Their penance is still to be done and will be carried out according to the proper procedures.

See also June 30, 1530 and regarding Katharina Streicher.

December 24, 1529, Magdalena of Rattenberg, Shoemaker's Maid

The Innsbruck government sent Ferdinand I the confession of Christoff Schauer from Munich (in Germany). This man named the leader who baptized him, a school master named Wolfgang in Linz, Upper Austria.[92] *(In addition to giving information about Jacob Hutter and other leaders, Schauer) named a maid from Rattenberg, Magdalena, who lived in the Hofgasse in Linz. (More specifically, he said she lived) in a little white house, the third house on the right, and worked in the household of a shoemaker. (He thought) she would be able to name more Anabaptist brothers and sisters in Linz.*

Notes

1. The Cathars, condemned as heretics in the Middle Ages, had the practice of retreating to higher alpine meadows with herds of grazing animals. This is depicted in map form in Ladurie, *Mountaillou*, x.
2. The Baderin was actually condemned to death in 1529 but because her case was first discussed in 1527 she is counted as a martyr for that year. Clasen lists 110 martyrs in

total for Tirol in 1529 and 13 for 1528. Claus-Peter Clasen, "Executions of Anabaptists, 1525-1618 A Research Report," *Mennonite Quarterly Review*, XLVII, 2 (1973), 125. The author's figure for 1528 is higher at 13 for the number of women alone. Triple that number would be 39 (13x3).

3. "... ob 200 manns- und weybsperonen in diser graffschaft Tirol an mer ortten zum todt gericht,..." TA 1972, 343:1.

4. Moser, *Die Scharfrichter,* 24. Moser uses numbers from Eduard Widmoser's research of the 1950s. These numbers are much higher than Clasen's who found evidence for only 123 male and female martyrs up to the end of 1529. Clasen's number was used by the author earlier to calculate the proportion of women martyred as compared to men (49/123 x 100) which resulted in a percentage of 40. See Clasen, "Executions of Anabaptists," 125.

5. The number 600 is in, Loserth and Friedmann, "Tyrol (Austria)," at www.gameo.org. The estimate of 1000 with, "ein gutes Drittel" (at least one third) being women, is stated in Winkelbauer, "Die Rechtliche Stellung der Täufer," 39.

6. Martyrdom was not unique to Anabaptists. "... many Protestants and Roman Catholic martyrs expressed the same idea and demonstrated perseverance by their actions in the sixteenth century." Brad Gergory, "Soetken van den Houte of Oudenaarde," in *Profiles of Anabaptist Women*, 370. Although he does not analyze female martyrs separately, Gregory states that in general, Anabaptist martyrs "far outnumbered their Protestant and Catholic counterparts." Brad S. Gregory, *Salvation at Stake*, 198.

7. The words used are "geschickten Priester" on July 24 and August 11 and "gelehrte Priester" on September 25. See TA 1972, 264:2; 273:2; 289:21. Regarding the astonishment of inquisitors, see Snyder, *Anabaptist History and Theology An Introduction*, 107.

8. Most towns had a "Pranger" or pillory. It consisted of a pillar the height of a man to which the delinquent's hands were bound by a metal chain. Moser, *Die Scharfrichter*, 68.

9. Mecenseffy, "Anabaptists in Kitzbühel," 104.

10. "Mandates," in *Mennonite Encyclopedia*, III, 447.

11. The council of Rattenberg met on May 9, 1529 to discuss the executions which were to take place on the following Wednesday, May 12. See TA 1972, 228, document 328.

12. Moser, *Die Scharfrichter,* 23.

13. "dass sy auch ab der strengen straff khain entzetzen haben." TA 1972, 240:15; 242:7-8.

14. The mandate reads: "Doch so wierdt mit den gar jungen personen, auch waibspildern und slecht verstendigen, ainfeltigen menschen, dero in disen gepirgen vasst vil sind, so des gebrauchs irer vernunfft wenig oder gar nichts haben, nit zu eylen sein, ob die gleich etwo lang auf irem synn verharren und sich nit bekeren wollten, sonder man muesst sy lenger enthalten [und] underweysen." TA 1972, 73:29-34. See also TA 1972, 21:26-29; 74:1-4 and 270:25-27.

15. "... nach gestalt ires verstands, verprechens und verharrung...." TA 1972, 101:25.

16. TA 1972, 267:5-7; 270:25-27.

17. Snyder, *Anabaptist History and Theology: An Introduction*, 20.
18. *Ibid.*, 3.
19. Klaassen, *Living at the End of the Ages*, 101, 103.
20. Schiemer is discussed in the "Introduction To The Records Of 1527." Regarding Kürschner see TA 1972, 237:21
21. *Chronicle of the Hutterian Brethren*, 73.
22. This hymn is in: *Die Lieder der Hutterischen Brüder* (Cayley, AB: Macmillan Colony, 1974), 46; Rudolf Wolkan, *Die Lieder der Wiedertäufer, Ein Beitrag zur deutschen und niederländischen Literatur-und Kirchengeschichte* (Nieuwkoop, B. De Graaf, 1965 [1903]), 16-17; the Pressburg Codex, 236, 24; *Martyrs' Mirror*, 437.
23. Linda A. Huebert Hecht, "Wives, Female Leaders and Two Female Martyrs from Hall," in *Profiles of Anabaptist Women*, 188-89.
24. TA 1972, VIII and *Chronicle of the Hutterian Brethren*, 83-85.
25. *Chronicle of the Hutterian Brethren*, 83, n.1 As an interesting aside, this note also cites the March 10, 1532 warrant for Hutter's arrest which described him as, "a person with a black beard, who wears a black woolen military coat, a blue doublet, white trousers, and a black hat…." See the original for the latter in TA 1983, 37, document 26.
26. Justina Gall later had a sizeable inheritance, 2,500 Gulden and a house at the gate of Brixen which was confiscated by the bishop of Brixen and later obtained by her brother-in-law. Elfriede Lichdi, "Katharina Purst Hutter of Sterzing," trans. by Linda A. Huebert Hecht in *Profiles of Anabaptist Women*, 179.
27. *Hutterite Beginnings*, 240, 241 and Lichdi, "Katharina Purst Hutter," in *Profiles of Anabaptist Women*, 178-180, 183, 184-85. Lichdi cites a source that states Katharina was pregnant at her arrest in Gufidaun in 1536. But there is no record of her giving birth.
28. *Hutterite Beginnings*, 203-4. "Staff-bearers" or "Stäbler did not carry weapons as did "Schwertler."
29. A record of December 24, 1529 notes that Jörg Zaunring, the treasurer or "Säckelmeister," gave Cristoff Schaur 12 Kreuzer. See TA 1972, 319:19-20. Regarding the common fund see *Hutterite Beginnings*, 204.
30. Stayer speaks of "Jakob Hutter's "New Tyrol" in, *The German Peasants' War and Anabaptist Community of Goods*, 92.
31. The two routes, by land and by water are described in detail in, Renate Waldhof and Julia Walleczek, "Alle Wege führen nach Mähren—welchen wählt man?" in von Schlachta, *Verbrannte Visionen?* 155-159.
32. Jacob Hutter, d. 1536, *Brotherly Faithfulness Epistles From a Time of Persecution*, trans. by the Hutterian Society of Brothers (Rifton, NY: Plough Publishing House, 1979), 5.
33. Wiesner, "Frail, Weak, and Helpless: Women's Legal Position in Theory and Reality," 161, 162.
34. Dyck, "Elisabeth and Hadewijk," in *Profiles of Anabaptist Women,* 362-63.
35. Other cases that included torture were: n.n.193a and b, two women; n.n.280 a and b, 2 women of Hall; n.n.449 women in Gschäll house; n.n.394, three women.

36. TA 1972, 317:12-19.
37. Huebert Hecht, "Faith and Action,"48.
38. See the Appendix for money values.
39. Gretl Köfler, Michael Forcher, *Die Frau in der Geschichte Tirols* (Innsbruck: Haymon-Verlag, 1986), 76. Harold S. Bender concurred with Köfler, stating, "... the women were often given milder penalties than the men." See his article "Women" in *Mennonite Encyclopedia*, 972.
40. Leona Stucky Abbott, "Anabaptist Women of the Sixteenth Century," (unpublished Masters Thesis, Eden Theological Seminary, 1979, 112, 114.
41. Anna was from Suffa on the Ritten. See TA 1972, 189:20-22; 28-32.
42. In the index she is designated n.n.190, woman/Schiemer.
43. See April 4, 1528 for their story.
44. Hülbn was the name of their property, located near the town of Kurtatsch.
45. See Appendix for money values.
46. They are designated in the index as n.n.193a and b twowomen.
47. TA 1972, 145, document 173.
48. This was reported February 27, 1529. TA 1972, 196:18f.
49. This quotation is from the original document. TA 1972, 197:22-30.
50. TA 1972, 201:31-202:11.
51. TA 1972, 212:14; 395:9-11.
52. Their names are in a previous document of March 19, 1529. TA 1972, 203:10-11.
53. For the reference to Anna's brother see TA 1972, 325:23. See also Linda A. Huebert Hecht, "Anna Gasser of Lüsen," in *Profiles of Anabaptist Women*, 140-155 and the stories of Anna Gasserin's maids, Lucia and Agatha in 1529: January 5, March 19, April 3 and July 5, 1529. For Barbara's testimony see TA 1983, 116:16, 22f. Barbara may have had a married sister as well.
54. They are designated in the index as n.n.223a and b, 2 poorwomen.
55. They are designated in the index as n.n.227a, b and c threewomen.
56. "... das ungezweifflt, dieweil die stat gestanden, sovil personen auf ain mal miteinander nie gericht ..." TA 1972, 228:20-21.
57. See TA 1972, 235:28-39; 237:14-25.
58. The female martyrs discussed here are designated in the index as n.n.237 a-j 10 women executed.
59. She is designated in the index as n.n.239, womanleader.
60. See also TA 1972, 243:36 which states a monk heard about the book during a confession; 249:19-29; 250:4; 251:17-18 and 252:20-23 in which authorities are instructed to speak to all the persons presently in prison regarding this book of 800 names. Regarding the government's fears see TA 1972, 240, document 343; 243, document 345.
61. See the footnote to the May 31, 1529 report, TA 1972, 244:23-43.
62. Her husband may have been baptized later which is why he was not present here. He

chose to recant and was punished with a flogging. Melchior's brother was the one who agreed that if Melchior was pardoned, he would help bring the four leaders named December 16, 1528 to prison. See TA 1972, 182:7; 183:23f.; 201:22 and TA 1972, 186, document 249 which is Melchior's recantation statement or "Urfehde."

63. The second and last reference to these two women is in TA 1972, 254:29-30.
64. Additional references to her are in TA 1972, 252, 254, 255, 283.
65. The phrase in the record is "Handel und Wandel" meaning doing business, going to market or conducting one's affairs. TA 1972, 258:4. See the related story of Anna Gasser, April 23, 1529 and April 3, 1529 regarding the Sackmann's herdsmen. These two couples may have been Peasant War participants. See *Hutterite Beginnings*, 370, n. 124.
66. A number of Anabaptist families had to leave without their children when they fled. Some children joined their parents later after the family was established in Moravia or elsewhere.
67. See TA 1972, 275:36-276:1-9. See TA 1972, 282:5-9 for descriptions of others present.
68. These women are designated in the index as n.n.280a and b, 2 women of Hall. See TA 1972, 281:6 and Dorothea Maler, September 7, 1529, who was also from Hall.
69. She is designated in the index as n.n.278, a woman. She is named in TA 1972, 278:8. See the story of May 31, 1529 for other female Hutter followers. Schilling was baptized by Andre and Sebastion Taurer in 1528, conducted a communion service with Paul Taurer and was still at large at the end of 1529. See TA 1972, 96:19; 110:2; 111:14, 319:32.
70. See TA 1972, 299:35-39 which states: "... Ihre bürgerliche Freiheit aufgesagt worden sei...."
71. See August 20, 1529 for more information on the meeting in the forest of Mils.
72. The name of the wife of the blacksmith from Enngendeiner was Schmied
73. See September 25 regarding the re-education of Anna and Ursula.
74. She is designated in the index as n.n.287, woman baptized by Plattner. This leader from Rattenberg was martyred in 1529. *Chronicle of the Hutterian Brethren*, 59.
75. TA 1972, 426:9-15.
76. All except Katharina Schuster are listed as martyrs in Rattenberg. See Clasen, "Executions of Anabaptits," 145. The Gschälen's maid is referred to as, "des Gelln dirn."
77. Benedict Gamper was not arrested at this time but from a record of January 5, 1530 we know he was an Anabaptist leader in Breitenberg. See also *Hutterite Beginnings*, 370, n.127 and *Chronicle of the Hutterian Brethren*, 53, 69-73 for testimonies of others from Breitenberg, baptized by Blaurock and Gamper.
78. Actually it is between October 29 and November 10. See also TA 1972, 300:17-25.
79. The word used for the land tenure of this property is "Schöfferlehn" in TA 1972, 294:2. It is also referred to as a "Gut" in TA 1972, 294:15. In the Middle Ages "Lehn" referred to land owned or rented under the feudal system. A fief was a feudal estate. Persons could inherit the right to use land even if they did not own it.
80. He was an influential and well known financial lawyer of the time. See Mecenseffy, "Anabaptists in Kitzbühel," 107. He is also mentioned in November 24, 1529.

81. She is designated in the index as n.n.297, woman pardoned.
82. See October 29, 1529 above regarding this lawyer.
83. See the Appendix regarding the abbreviations for money values. In this list of expenses and in the property inventories and discussions of them in Chapter Four, "G" is used for "Gulden" and numbers under 10 are not written out.
84. For another case where execution costs are given see October 27, 1528. See Oyer, "'They Harry the Good People Out of the Land,'" 155, for a case in the Netherlands in 1567 where costs for Anabaptist procedures are discussed.
85. The names of the male prisoners and the women's husbands are not included here.
86. Barbara later paid ten Gulden to the government for expenses. TA 1972, 404:38
87. The word in this original document is "verführerisch" which infers people were being led astray.
88. These passages are from an original document in TA 1972, 309:11-310:9; 310:21-30.
89. See their story May 31. See also TA 1983, 68:25.
90. *Hutterite Beginnings*, 373, n. 71.
91. This may have been Hanns Nickinger who was younger and had joined in May 1529.
92. Possibly this man was Wolfgang Brandhuber, Anabaptist leader in Linz.

Chapter Four

Introduction to the Records of 1530

On February 8 early in 1530, Ferdinand wrote to his officials in Innsbruck regarding his deep concern that the Anabaptist sect was not being rooted out and in fact in some places was being secretly supported. He repeated his view that the unchristian teachings of the Anabaptists would only lead to "evil, rebellion and bloodshed."[1] The teachings of the recently arrested Anabaptists in Linz were a case in point. These prisoners believed themselves to be pure and without sin, as had the heretical Cathars of times past. Moreover, they held that no one should own their own property, that all things should be held in common. Such dangerous beliefs needed strong measures and Ferdinand suggested two approaches. First, the Innsbruck government should send search parties in groups of two or three into all suspicious places in the mountains and valleys, towns and outlying farms, to make surprise attacks by day or night on all persons suspected of Anabaptist involvements.[2] Secondly, two respected persons should visit all the local districts, calling the people together to explain the dangers of the sect to them and the suffering that would come to them as well as to their ruler through this heretical sect that led people astray. Ferdinand wanted these measures to be undertaken without delay before the beginning of the summer.

Not long after, on February 19, the officials of Innsbruck rejected Ferdinand's commands outright since they did not consider them practical for the territory of Tirol. They chose instead to continue persecuting Anabaptists with the methods they had followed heretofore. They informed their superior that "In the last two years seldom has a day passed that

Anabaptist related issues have not come before our council, which is why up until now 200 men and women in our territory of Tirol have been executed, many have been exiled and even more have fled, leaving behind their property and their orphaned children."[3] The dramatic increase in the number of inventories conducted for Anabaptist properties in the fall of 1530 is proof of what the Innsbruck officials were saying on February 19.

The details of the Innsbruck officials' defence of their actions provide a glimpse into the status of Anabaptism in Tirol at this time: "If the people were not so unyielding, the punishments meted out every week to the old and the young, to men and women – some of the young women not even mature yet – would cause them to be terrified and afraid."[4] However, these unreasonable, seemingly irrational attitudes were to be found among the people everywhere. The Anabaptists seemingly had no fear of punishment. When they were pursued, they willingly admitted to their faith even without torture. They did not listen to any teaching or instruction and seldom were any of them persuaded to give up their faith. They wanted only to die. And if by chance one of them did recant, good instruction or severe punishment could not be expected to deter them. Offers of monetary rewards for the capture of Anabaptist leaders had also been issued. Wanting to remain in the King's good graces, the Innsbruck officials told the king they had done all they could to deal with this difficult situation.[5] They were doing their part in trying to avoid these problems by sending the king's decrees out to all the local authorities. They went so far as to suggest that every crown administrator and judge should personally mount the pulpit of every church in their jurisdiction, warning the people against the wicked sect of Anabaptism so that they could avoid punishment.[6]

Ferdinand's response to Innsbruck was to issue more and harsher decrees in March and July of 1530. Ferdinand's complaints about decreased church attendance further attest to the popularity of Anabaptism as a grassroots movement and the widespread sympathy it had from people everywhere.[7] The decree of July 30, 1530 discussed the negative attitude of the common people toward worship in the church. They were not attending the sermon and mass on holy Sundays and neglecting their duty to go to confession and take the sacrament annually during Lent. All this was in addition to the fact that men and women were not baptizing their infants or going to confession on a regular basis. The lack of diligence by the local authorities to make the government decrees known was thought to be the cause. The command from Innsbruck to carry out the quarterly publication of the decree from the local pulpits was accompanied by the threat of a fine for neglecting to do so.[8] The common people were not doing good works as was their Christian duty. Instead they were attending secret conventicles, hedgepreachings and meetings. The local authorities were authorized to offer rewards of 20, 30 and up to 40 Gulden in those places where persons were suspected of Anabaptism and where secret meetings were taking place in homes or in forests.[9]

In the discussions at the beginning of August with the advisers of the Archbishop of Salzburg it was emphasized that these directives were not the will of the king himself, but had been decreed at the Imperial Diet of Speyer as well.[10] Also in these discussions, the clergy was admonished to read the decrees to the people and to obey and hold to the beliefs and practices of the holy, Christian church.[11] Orders for local officials and clergy to conduct house visitations in order to speak to every "housefather" and "housemother" individually had already been given in the decree of July 30. Now, the clergy were reminded that they should speak to all members of the household including the children and the servants, admonishing them to keep the traditional beliefs and practices.[12] The report of October 20, 1530 regarding a priest in Rattenberg who announced from the pulpit that no heretic should be executed for "going astray" indicated that not all priests followed these orders.[13]

The July decree also gave orders that executions should now be carried out in secret. Perhaps this was why on September 27, 1530 the judge of Rattenberg was instructed not to publicize the hearing date for two Anabaptist women since this practice had only served to attract others to the movement rather than deter them. Indeed, instructions to maintain secrecy in dealing with Anabaptists were given a number of times in 1530, on August 9 and 12 as well as on November 14.

Another issue was "whether they should allow the Anabaptists to continue to leave the country in large numbers in order to be rid of the whole matter, or question all those who embarked on the Inn River in Hall or Rattenberg as to whether they belonged to the sect." The government wavered at first but then decided on the latter course of action. "But the measure was not very successful, for boatman and customs officials, in spite of all the orders to the contrary, refused to betray the departing Anabaptists, whose death sentences they could not understand."[14]

Regardless of the decrees issued by Ferdinand, the involvement of Anabaptist women continued through the summer months of 1530. In June in two different cases the issue was heavy fines. A couple from Reischach who had provided lodging for fleeing Anabaptists was fined 50 Gulden (June 11). A woman from Gufidaun who had been pardoned was threatened with a fine four times that amount – two hundred Gulden – if she broke her oath (June 23). Margreth Hueben related on June 21, 1530 that she had been baptized in a forest close to her home. In July some unusual events were taking place in Feldkirch bordering on Swiss territory. The central government was greatly distressed by this, despite the fact that the disturbances were taking place far to the west of Innsbruck. In the district of Feldkirch, the local miller and the wife of a blacksmith were preaching daily to the people with great success. The Innsbruck authorities viewed their influence as dangerous and threatened to punish the life and property not just of the preachers but of the local authorities themselves.

By the end of June the government called for the first extensive inventory of confiscated Anabaptist property, namely, that belonging to the former innkeepers of Rattenberg, Konrad and Katharina Streicher. Both husband and wife had been martyred leaving four children between three and seven years of age. The appraisal took place later, in the fall of 1530 when the properties of over thirty Anabaptist families from Kufstein and Rattenberg were dealt with by the government. The investigation revealed that the Streichers had owned property worth 160 Gulden, not a small sum. However, as illustrated in the following pages, there were other Anabaptists who had owned as much and more.

Because of the new communities being established in the more tolerant region of Moravia, by the fall of 1530 many Anabaptists had either fled or had been martyred in the process of trying to leave their homeland. Among the 36 families for whom the 1972 records include either specific financial information or an inventory, in the majority of cases the husbands and wives were both executed or both fled.[15] Loss of property had been listed already in the first decree of August 1527 as one of the punishments for Anabaptists. It was repeated in subsequent decrees such as the one issued in April 1528.[16] Such a policy allowed the government's expenses in dealing with Anabaptists to be paid from the sale of their confiscated property and possessions. In other words, "the financial costs were borne largely by the victims."[17] In cases where children were left behind in Tirol until they could be re-united with their families, money from the family's property was needed to provide for them. Already in June 1529 in Kitzbühel, it had been reported that again, in the last few months, many Anabaptist men had fled, leaving behind their wives, children and servants. The government was concerned about the 40 or 50 children, mostly underage dependents who had been orphaned or abandoned. They instructed the crown administrator to appoint guardians for the abandoned families so that they could be supported financially from the income of the confiscated properties.[18]

When both parents became fugitives of the law, whenever possible, they arranged for the care of their children with friends or relatives and left funds behind for that purpose. They also "made every attempt to retrieve abandoned children.... Physically strong brethren were chosen to gather the children and lead them across the mountains to the community in Moravia.... Before his arrest (in 1533), one sturdy blacksmith carried fifteen children across the mountains."[19] In 1533 the persecution was intense. *The Chronicle of the Hutterian Brethren* records that, following Pentecost of that year, it was debated in the district of Gufidaun how the believers could get to Moravia, "for in the whole country they no longer have a place of refuge anywhere." However, in July a group of men and women and twenty-five children left for Moravia and "managed to reach their goal, even though the officials at Schwaz and Rattenberg had every path watched."[20] At times, however, abandoned children had no choice but to beg. Others were placed in poorhouses, with the stewards who looked after confiscated properties or with foster parents who were then reimbursed from the confiscated property. "Older children (ages ten to sixteen) who shared the point of view of their parents could be interned and subjected to daily discipline – floggings – to correct their outlook." Baptism was only for adults and adulthood began at age sixteen.[21]

In general, the king kept half the value of a confiscated Anabaptist property and the other half went to the heirs. In some cases, if the heirs wanted the property that was left after the government's costs had been deducted, they had to buy it back from the government. It was necessary then to appraise and itemize in detail the monetary value of all Anabaptist possessions. As a result, the records of October and November 1530 include some fascinating inventories which illustrate how Anabaptist merchants, innkeepers, craftsmen, peasant farmers and their wives had lived.

These financial records attest not only to the personal sacrifices made by the Anabaptist fugitives and martyrs but also to the fact that the majority of them were fairly well off. If 50 Gulden, the approximate annual income of a bricklayer or carpenter of that time period, is used as a dividing line between Anabaptists who were better off and those who were poorer, then seventy-two percent or more than two-thirds of those families for whom we have records in 1530 were better off financially. Stories of women in a number of these families are presented in the following pages.

Some of the Anabaptists whose properties were appraised in 1530 were less well off. Regina, widow of an Anabaptist martyr, received only two or three Gulden of her husband's possessions (October 27). Two craftsmen from Radfeld who were poor each had to pay the government six Gulden for the execution expenses of their wives in order to regain the women's possessions (October 31). Heinrich Crenseisen's wife fled with her husband leaving a house appraised at 24 Gulden (November 29). The wife of the Anabaptist leader Jörg Vasser appealed to the government for the 32 Gulden worth of possessions which they had owned. The total value of the Taurer family's possessions was not much greater at 50 Gulden, but they had owned a stone house below the castle in Rattenberg (October - November). The Valtein Schmid family's house was not of stone but together with their garden was also worth 50 Gulden (October - November).

On the other hand, the property and possessions of Leonhardt of Viltz were appraised at only 43 Gulden. Since he had debts and his sick wife was left to support their three underage children, aged nine, seven and four, out of mercy, the government took nothing from them (September 19). We do not have figures for all areas of the territory, but the poverty of rural areas in Tirol is illustrated in the Anabaptist centre of Michelsburg in the Puster

Valley of South Tirol, "which had an average peasant indebtedness of fifty-nine percent."[22] This would indicate that almost two-thirds of the peasant population had debts. However, Anabaptists in other parts of the valley must have had fewer debts. Those who emigrated to Auspitz in Moravia from the Puster Valley had a significant influence in that community. For one thing so many of them came there, but also, they had "financial resources" which they had brought with them. As firm supporters of Jacob Hutter, who himself originated from the Puster Valley, their influence was an important factor in establishing him as the leader of Auspitz and of the Hutterites as an identifiable group.[23]

Although the inventory of the former judge, Hanns Obinger and his wife Ursula, is one of the most detailed, their property was expected to bring in only 100 Gulden (October 31). According to the 1530 appraisals, the value of the property which Simon Schützinger left in Rattenberg when he fled to Moravia was somewhat higher, namely, 120 Gulden. His wife Barbara (March 30, 1528) was entitled to half of this money. However, she too fled, joining her husband in Moravia, where the value of their property and possessions was further revealed in 1533.

By 1533 Simon Schützinger had become the leader of the congregation in Auspitz. When Jacob Hutter arrived there in August 1533 and began to teach a stricter practice of the community of goods, a crisis ensued. A certain Georg Fasser, not the same man as the Jörg Vasser who gave up the priesthood to become a leader among the miners of Schwaz,[24] was among those who followed up on Hutter's admonition. Fasser "lost no time in bringing his bed and chests into the communal storeroom."[25] He was donating one of the most important things he owned; the storage chest was the most important mobile piece of furniture in the early modern household.[26] Storage chests were on the list of Hanns and Ursula Obinger's inventory as well. However, perhaps Fasser's wife valued money more than their chest. She had agreed with her husband that they should place their earthly possessions at the disposal of the community but then she hesitated in giving up her own property, what may have been her dowry. Unknown to her husband, she had hidden money belonging to her and the children. For this she was disciplined and "placed under the ban, meaning that until her reinstatement she had to eat her meals in isolation."[27]

Hutter now became suspicious that Barbara Schützinger might also be a "Sapphira" (as in the New Testament book of Acts 5: 1-11) and brought his concerns to the elders. As *The Chronicle of the Hutterian Brethren* relates, the elders believed that "God had given Jacob the gift of discernment."[28] Thus, they followed up on his concerns and soon found them to be true. "As they were looking through a chest, they found a too-plentiful supply of bed linen and shirts and four pounds in Bernese money, all in small coins." The coins would have been equivalent to eight Kreuzer,[29] not that large an amount, but that was not all. Simon said he had known that his wife had these possessions. "So saying, he reached under the roof and brought out forty gulden."[30] These Gulden were only one third as much as the 120 Gulden which Simon had left in Rattenberg, but the fact that Simon had hidden them, deceiving his fellow believers, was enough to cast doubt on his commitment to the community's beliefs and values. At baptism, "converts were expected to surrender their surplus cash to the common treasury."[31] Obviously, neither Barbara nor Simon had done this. A crisis followed during which Simon was excommunicated and Hutter took over the leadership. After the schism of 1533, a stricter community of goods was practiced among the Anabaptists who would become known as Hutterites.

No monetary value was given for the abundant supply of linens and clothing which the Schützingers brought to Moravia. According to what Simon left in Rattenberg and what they brought to Moravia, the Schützingers had owned – at least before Simon fled to Moravia – no less than 160 (120+40) Gulden and eight Kreuzer. This was less than the possessions of another family, who likely also fled, Paul and Agnes Frawnholtz (September 19). The total for their appraisal was 177 Gulden. For that time period, this family was not poor since anyone owning six or eight cows, as they did, was better off.[32] Listed separately in the Frawnholtz inventory was the dowry of 24 Gulden which Agnes had brought into the marriage. This too was no small amount. The dowry of Barbara, wife of Wolfgang in the Ried (September 19), who came from the same village as Agnes, was considerably less, at six Gulden. The total value of Barbara and her husband's property, 67 Gulden, was less than that of Paul and Agnes. The dowry of Lindterspacher's wife did not have a monetary value but was equal to one-quarter of the value of the property. She was a stepmother to the two young men who had fled.

The family's total assets amounted to 56 Gulden (September 19). On the other hand, the property of the young couple, Margarete and Adam Stainer was worth more than twice that amount at 130 Gulden (August 5).

The Nickingers were one of the wealthier farm families and noteworthy for several reasons. First of all, eight members of their extended family were Anabaptists. Two of the three brothers were martyred and, three of the sisters as well as two of the wives left their homes and fled. Balthasar, one of the older brothers, was fortunate to get away. When he and his wife fled, they left their infant which was between 18 and 24 months old, in the care of his one hundred year old mother. The Nickinger farm was appraised at 250 Gulden and the livestock and hay, household items and foodstuffs added another 50 Gulden to its value making the total around 300 (August 5 and October 27).

The total worth of the property owned by the Spitzhamers who were millers, was a bit more than that of the Nickingers – 317 Gulden. When Leonhard Spitzhamer and his wife fled, they left not just a house, a mill, land and their possessions, but also their child. The property of another family of millers, Cristan and Anna Gschäll, was also of high value – 225 Gulden. By 1529 orders were given to board up their house because an Anabaptist meeting had taken place there. Cristan likely was already active as an Anabaptist leader, a role he assumed in Moravia that same year. Anna also fled, possibly at a later date but before the fall of 1530. She had owned the mill, which for some reason was not included in the appraisal. Half the value of the mill fell to the king and the other half to the family, to be divided equally between Cristan's brother and their three children.

Last but not least were several Anabaptist families who were quite well off. Anton Mair and his wife were able to sell their property before they fled. In the end they could not escape. After they were executed, Anton's father bought their property for 1200 Gulden. In the case of Anabaptist leader Ulrich Kobl and his wife Margret, their property was sold for somewhat more, namely, 1300 Gulden (August 26, 1528). Mathes Kerschpaumer and his wife were martyrs and left two children. Their property was worth between 1400 and 1500 Gulden (June 3, 1528).[33] The wealthiest Anabaptist woman was Helena von Freyberg. Ferdinand I was eager to obtain possession of her castle property in Münichau near Kitzbühel when she fled to Augsburg in 1534. However, with the help of others, Helena managed to ensure that her sons, who lived with their father at his castle, Hohenaschau, in Bavaria, inherited the Münichau property. Later her sons sold it for 7,500 Gulden (March 7, 1528).[34] Although some Anabaptists were quite wealthy, none gave up as much financially as this noblewoman who left her native Tirol to live in exile away from her family, because of her Anabaptist faith.

Pregnant Women and Nursing Mothers, 1527-1531

Pregnancy and childbirth in the early sixteenth century was a frequent experience for women and carried very high risks. Every expectant mother faced the possibility of death in childbirth and infant mortality rates were high.

> In the medieval church there was a female saint who interceded only for pregnant women, St. Margaret and prayers were constantly being said for women in this condition. In other words, pregnant women were in particular need of strong spiritual support at this time in their lives. Perhaps the fact that in pregnancy, women were facing a spiritual crisis already,… was part of the reason why women who were pregnant became involved in Anabaptism.[35]

The married medieval Englishwoman, Margery Kempe, experienced a spiritual crisis after childbirth "which led her to lead a devout life and to live the life of a virgin."[36]

The celibate life was the primary spiritual model for medieval women. As a lay movement – sometimes referred to as laicized monasticism – Anabaptism gave all women the opportunity for a devout spiritual life outside of the monastery, not dependent on prayers to the saints.

The issue of pregnant women had been addressed early on in a decree from Ferdinand I on December 13, 1527. It ruled that "Mothers who were nursing infants and pregnant women who converted to the Christian faith should be released from prison on payment of a guaranty." More specifically, the local authorities were told, "they should be allowed to return to their households but be prepared to appear before you again if you require them to do so."[37] During 1528 and 1529, in the cases of pregnant Anabaptist women who were guilty only of baptism or who were less active in the movement, recantations and penance were usually postponed until they had given birth. However, those pregnant Anabaptist women who remained steadfast and chose not to recant had to spend the months prior to giving birth in prison. The decree of July 1530 – the only one after 1527 which mentioned pregnant women – gave specific instructions to local authorities on the treatment of pregnant Anabaptist women who chose not to recant.

> They should be kept in prison, in orderly fashion, as appropriate, until they have given birth and for several days after the birth. If they cannot pay for these costs, the same method should be used as for the expenses involved in scouting for suspicious Anabaptists and bringing them to prison. The expenses should be paid from the income of the confiscated property of Anabaptists who have been executed. The central treasury in Innsbruck will handle these financial matters.[38]

Among the 32 Anabaptist pregnant women and nursing mothers mentioned in the five years of records discussed in the 1972 volume, a number spent their pregnancies in prison. But, as with Anabaptist women in general, all pregnant women did not make the same choice, as these cases illustrate.

The pregnant Anabaptist women for whom proceedings were postponed until after they had given birth include Martin Nock's wife (November 27, 1528), an unnamed woman (February 9, 1529),[39] three women discussed December 7, 1529, namely, Katharina Widmauer, Ursula Egger and Cristina Sunschwennter, as well as Hans Scheuring's wife (April 15, 1529), although she also had to remain in prison until the birth of her child. Among the pregnant women who chose to recant were Anna Rinnerin (July 21, 1528), Waldpurga Ameiser (May 16, 1529), Anna Krätlerin I and Anna Krätlerin II, two women with the same name (May 17, 1528), Jörg Schweitzer's wife (March 6, 1529) and Margreth Hueben (June 21, 1530). Some pregnant Anabaptist women were martyred after they had given birth. This was the case for Anna Gasteiger (July 24, 1529). She was probably in the early stages of pregnancy at her arrest. If it proved to be true that she was pregnant, the judge of Rattenberg was to see that the child was to be baptized properly at birth and be taken care of by a wet nurse.

Two women were linked to Anabaptism just after they had given birth.

Wolfgang Schneider's wife left her home and her newborn child just three days after giving birth (August 2, 1529). The wet nurse had baptized the child, about which the father was specifically questioned. His reply was that a "proper" baptism was not needed. He believed the child had been "baptized by God." For this action he was to be tried in the criminal court. It is not clear why his wife left. Perhaps she was not an Anabaptist as was her husband. The wife of Lorenz Vitzthum (October 5, 1528) was likewise probably not an Anabaptist. She was recovering from childbirth when she requested a pardon for her husband. They had eight underage children and he was "a simple-minded man who had lived a pious life."[40] Before his release he was required to do penance by remaining in prison for fourteen days on a sparse diet. Two mothers among the Anabaptists baptized by Jacob Hutter (July 24, 1529) were given a reprieve because they were nursing their infants. They were allowed to return home without even being questioned.

A milder form of punishment, a public flogging, was ordered for three pregnant Anabaptist women. Two of the women were from the Anabaptist families living on the Ritten plateau above Bozen. The instructions of January 5, 1529 stated that Anna Gasser (April 23, 1529) and the wife of Christoff Mair (July 5, 1529) were supposed to receive corporal punishment like the others in the group. However, their punishments were to be more moderate since they were pregnant. When the case of Christoff Mair's wife was discussed again in July of that year, no mention was made of her pregnancy. Perhaps her child had been born by then. However, when Anna Gasser's case continued on April 23, the question was raised as to why she had been kept in prison so long after her miscarriage. Did the corporal punishment cause Anna's miscarriage? The records do not give us an answer.

The wife of Lienhard Fundnetscher was part of a group of Anabaptists arrested December 16, 1528. Along with a number of others in the group she chose to recant. However, the group could not be pardoned without a flogging at the town pillory. Unlike the two women from the Ritten, it seems that no allowance was made for her because she was pregnant.

A few Anabaptist women were arrested in the last stages of their pregnancies. The Treibenreifin (February 29, 1528) was "well advanced in her pregnancy"[41] as was Margret Kobl (May 13, 1528)[42] at her first arrest. Her husband Ulrich and her mother are named as participants in peasant uprisings before they became Anabaptists. Margret recanted at her first arrest and escaped her second arrest to flee with her husband (August 27, 1528). The wife of Hans Viltzurner (July 23, 1528) was also nearing the end of her pregnancy when she fled with her husband, who was accused of "evil talk." The local authorities were directed to appoint a supervisor for their property and someone to care for their children. It is not clear if the crown administrator submitted a petition on their behalf because of their large family and her condition or because they had not been baptized.

Some Anabaptists experienced such guilt that they rejoined their fellow believers after recanting. Barbara Velcklehner (March 9, 1529), on the other hand, must have experienced much guilt after she and her husband escaped prison. She came back to prison of her own free will shortly before she was to give birth. She confessed that her beliefs regarding the sacrament of communion did not deviate from the traditional church. The authorities believed her and Barbara was released and rejoined her husband and children.

A number of Anabaptist women spent part of their pregnancy in prison. We do not know how far along Anna Weltzenberger (April 3, 1529) was in her pregnancy but her case is one of the most unusual for the persistence she displayed. Neither the territorial judge, nor her father nor her husband could persuade her to give up her Anabaptist faith. The local authorities were instructed not to release her from prison under any circumstances. If after the birth of her child she still held to her beliefs she was to be tried and sentenced.

The conditions under which Anna Weltzenberger awaited the birth of her child in prison were likely not very pleasant. The prospects for two women arrested in the high mountains of Ellmau in the summer of the following year seemed to be better. When it became clear that these two unnamed, pregnant women (July 21, 1530)[43] could be spending the winter in prison, Christoff Fuchs, the governor of Kufstein asked the Innsbruck authorities if he could build a heated room for them. His request was granted. Shortly before Christmas in 1528 (December 20) a group of Anabaptists were arrested in the district of Wangen, in the mountains above Bozen. The names of these Anabaptists are not given but mention is made of another two unnamed pregnant women[44] who also were to be kept in prison until they had given birth. The wife of Lucas Wagensail (August 22, 1531) from Freundsberg near Schwaz was likewise required to spend her pregnancy in prison. At this time the government was trying to re-educate Anabaptist prisoners and she was to receive instruction from a priest during her prison stay. If she still held to her faith after her child was born she was to be tried in the criminal court.

Pregnant women were often cared for by other women and in several cases by women also linked to Anabaptism. When Ernst Pranndt was conducting his inventory for the government on the Nickinger family property he reported that he had to interrupt his work in order to escort the five Anabaptists he found living in the vacated house to Rattenberg. He also discovered the Nickingers' mother (October 27, 1530), an old woman – said to be one hundred years old – caring for two women recovering from childbirth. The unnamed women are not named as Anabaptists but their caregiver was certainly "tainted with Anabaptism."[45] The situation of the young mothers was not unlike that of the Anabaptist woman whom Elisabeth von Wolkenstein took into her residence "so that she could give birth to her child in a secure environment."[46] The Nickinger grandmother was not the only woman affected by the actions of her extended family. The young wife whose husband fled with four other members of the extended Weissach family near Rattenberg (September 19, 1530) was also mentioned in the fall of 1530. The older father stayed back to care for the young children left behind and perhaps this young woman did not join the fugitives because she was pregnant.

All Anabaptist women made choices which were of great consequence. Their choices were of consequence not just for themselves but for the future generation. The decision as to whether to become involved in the outlawed sect of Anabaptism may not have come at the most opportune time in their lives. But that did not prevent pregnant women from taking the same kinds of actions as those who were not pregnant. For them religious faith took priority over concerns for family and children.

Translations From The Court Records Of 1530

January 4, 1530, The Recantation Text For an Anabaptist Couple

Bartlme Anngst, judge of Rattenberg, was directed to pardon Hanns in the Valley and his wife Ursula. The format of their recantation would be the same as the one for Jörg von Werd on November 26, 1529. They should speak and do the following.

I. Recantation of Jörg of Werd,

I, Jörg of Werd, a carpenter, confess that I have done wrong to be persuaded to join the seductive sect of Anabaptism and all that is involved with it. Of this I am sorry from the bottom of my heart. I herewith forswear and recant publicly of this seductive Anabaptist sect. I commit myself from this moment on and for the rest of my life, to remain in the unity of the Christian church and not to separate myself from it under any circumstances.

II. Form of Penance for Pardoned Anabaptists

First of all, they should go to confession and request absolution from their priest.

In addition, on a Sunday, prior to the procession and the mass, they should recant publicly from the pulpit of the re-baptism which they received, as well as of their evil unbelief in regard to the Christian order, how their actions went against it and destroyed it. They should promise with an oath and oblige themselves to now adhere to the unity of the Christian church and state that they do not want to separate themselves from it in the future. And on this same Sunday and on the next two Sundays following that, they must walk in the procession around the church in front of the priest, bareheaded and barefoot and remain in front of the altar kneeling, for the duration of the mass.[47]

January 6, 1530, Anabaptists Found Hiding in a Cave Under a House

The judge of Sonnenburg had captured an Anabaptist named Hanns Impach ... in the house of Gregor Weber in Pflaurenz. Weber had been executed in Brixen. The judge had not known that there were six other Anabaptists hiding in an underground cave below Weber's house. These six persons got away. Impach immediately wanted to recant and to disassociate himself from the other six. The group likely included only men.[48] By January 10, these six had been captured and local authorities were instructed on how their penance should be carried out.[49]

January 23, 1530, Three Women Held in Prison Fourteen Days on a Sparse Diet

Bartlme Anngst, judge in Rattenberg had sent in a report and the confessions of the following Anabaptists, *Bernhard Lanntringer, his wife and his mother as well as his labourer, Sebastian Peuger. If these prisoners were genuine in wanting to desist from their Anabaptist faith, they should be kept in prison for fourteen days on a sparse diet.*

Then they should be interrogated again regarding who baptized the labourer, where this took place and who had been present, since it is not likely this happened without their knowledge. They should be pardoned under the usual conditions.... (which included public recantation during mass on three consecutive Sundays, penance as prescribed by the parish priest and an oath). Peuger, who persisted in his erring ways, was to be tried in the criminal court. The (woman named) Platzfassin could be released after she swore the oath.

February 11, 1530,
The wife of Marx in the pasture, from the district of St. Michelsburg, feared arrest. She submitted a petition with her father, on behalf of her husband.

March 23, 1530,
Oberwiser's wife was from the Ziller Valley which was in the district of Rottenburg. For some time now she had not believed in the holy sacrament, the crucifix and other pictures, or the intercession of the saints. The judge and jury were instructed to question her more diligently than they had until now. Since she denied being re-baptized, on March 29 the order was given to release her on the condition that she go to confession and take the holy sacrament on the coming Sunday, give a written promise confirmed with an oath and pay the costs for her stay in prison.

April 2, 1530,
Magdalene Tonauerin from the district of Kitzbühel, sister of a monk, was martyred for her Anabaptist faith. Peter Kollis's daughter, from Roppen in the district of St. Petersberg, came back to prison, but still persisted in her faith.

April 22, 1530,
Vogellehner's wife of Rottenburg had been captured and had to promise to report back to the authorities and to pay the costs of her prison stay.

April 29, 1530,
Orders were given from Kufstein for the arrest of the woman named Prewin, who had been reported by the male leader, Grünwald.

May 12, 1530,
Four of seven Anabaptists in Kitzbühel were women: Magdalena of Hallerndorf, Barbara Widinger, Barbara's daughter Cristina and Martha

Obermauer. The Aschelpergerin's name had been reported as well in Kitzbühel. She was the widow of an Anabaptist martyr and now information was to be obtained about her.

See the Appendix for the questioning procedure for Jörg Schmid, his wife, daughter and labourer in the district of Sonnenburg on this date.

May 17, 1530,
Jacob Schuester's wife travelled around with her husband in the regions neighbouring Innsbruck. He was a master who wore a black tunic with an emblem on it.

May 18, 1530,
It was the king's wish that the cutler Hanns Laittner and his wife Elisabeth of Innsbruck, who showed remorse, should be released.

May 19, 1530,
Wilhelm Schneider and his wife of Sterzing, reported by Jörg Schmid, were to be captured.

May 25, 1530,
Valtin Mügin and Scholastica Nüssler from the district of Steinach were two older women. Two of the three leaders who had been at their baptism were Jörg Zaunring and Jacob Hutter.

May 28, 1530,
Bärbel from Rettenberg chose to recant; she was to do this from the pulpit in the local church.

May 31, 1530,
The miner's wife in Schwaz was to be asked if she had not baptized her four week old infant out of fear for her husband who was an Anabaptist.

June 11, 1530, Forchner Couple Fined For Sheltering Anabaptists
The Innsbruck government wrote the following to Balthasar Gerhardt, crown administrator of St. Michelsburg. Dear faithful one! We have received a report that you took it upon yourself to punish Niclas Mair from Luns and Florian Forchner and his wife Elspeth from Reischach, all three residing in the district of Michelsburg, with a (heavy) fine of 50 Gulden. They provided lodging for two fleeing Anabaptists, namely

for their cousin and their son-in-law.... Sheltering members of this forbidden, deceptive sect is not allowed. However, it was not in your power to mete out such punishment. Such matters come under our jurisdiction and we recommend that you bid the persons (who have committed this crime) to appear before our upper Austrian treasury and let them deal with this matter.

June 21, 1530, Ursula Pinzgauer Released, Not Margreth Hueben

Peter Praunegger, the judge of Sonnenburg was instructed to care for the many young children of Andre in the Hueben (his wife Margarethe) and Ursula Pinzgauer, to take an inventory of their property and harvest their fields. A week later Margarethe and Ursula were released under the usual conditions. Margarethe's story continues two days later with Innsbruck's report to the crown administrator of Ehrenberg.

... The wife of Andre in the Hueben, an Anabaptist in prison with her husband, confessed..., that approximately two years ago her brother, Martin Reckh from Tauheim, came to see her with an Anabaptist leader, (likely) Jörg Vasser from Schwaz. Vasser told her so much that she was persuaded to let him baptize her in the small forest called Hueben, near their home. Therefore, we suggest you secretly search for and imprison her brother and question him thoroughly ... to find out whether he is a leader and baptizer in the sect, who else is involved and who baptized him and then report back to us....

Two months later, on August 6, the Innsbruck government told Praunegger they knew *that Margareth had been released on oath but had not performed her penance. She should be imprisoned again....* On the same day, the governor of Kufstein was instructed to find out where she was staying.

On September 1, 1530 the Innsbruck government discussed Margreth's case with yet another local official, *Hans Gräfinger of Rettenberg. Margreth, widow of the executed Anabaptist Andre in the Hueben,... was in prison again. Now she was well advanced in her pregnancy and repeated her request for a pardon. This would be granted her. But, on the very next Sunday, she had to recant publicly from the pulpit in Kolsass (a parish in the district of Rettenberg).* They should not wait until her child was born.

Moreover, on each of the two Sundays she was to walk "barefoot, with burning candles in her hands" ahead of the parish priest in Kolsass, in the procession around the church and then kneel in front of the altar in sincere worship until the end of the mass. (Finally), she had to accept and carry out the penance which the priest required of her. Gräfinger was to instruct the priest to read, and have her repeat word for word, the recantation as it was written out on the enclosed note. Moreover, Gräfinger was to be present in the church on the next three Sundays....

June 23, 1530, A New Requirement For Those Pardoned
Magdalene Klinglerin from the district of Gufidaun could be pardoned if the priest instructing her found her to be remorseful. However, if she broke her oath, those speaking for her would have to pay a very heavy fine of 200 Gulden.

June 24, 1530,
Balthasar Scheffelmacher's wife and Gret, a maid working for Cristan Dauxerin in Wattens, have been named as Anabaptists and are to be captured. Another maid, also named Greth, from the district of Thaur is to be investigated.

June 28, 1530,
Melchior Mayr and his wife of Lotten in the district of Brixen have been martyred, leaving behind a young son. Discussions about their property, left to the son, continued into September 1530.

June 30, 1530, The Family and Property of Kunz and Katharina Streicher, Martyrs
Kunz Streicher had been an Anabaptist for some time. He was mentioned the first time on March 30, 1528. His petition for a pardon was denied on August 26 of that year, but another year passed before he was mentioned again. On July 31, 1529 his name was included with other Anabaptists who had either been executed or fled Rattenberg, noting that he had left three children behind. His wife Katharina was not mentioned at this time but must have fled with him since she was tried and executed in December, 1529 as one who had rejoined. In January 1530 Kunz was arrested again as well but would not admit to having been a leader. However, by May of that year he had been executed since the property and goods of the Streichers were being discussed on June 30.

Ferdinand I instructed Christoff Philipp von Liechtenstein, governor of Rattenberg, regarding a petition from ... the guardians of the children of the executed Kunz (Konrad) Streicher and his wife, former innkeepers in Rattenberg. Liechtenstein was to appraise their property and goods, in so far as they still existed, and report back.

The June 30 directive was carried out in October or November 1530. Katharina's case had been discussed earlier (December 22, 1529). Now the government wanted to know what money would be left after their expenses for the trials and executions had been deducted. The Streichers had lived in Bruck am Ziller and had owned the following:

... a demolished house together with the field in which the remains of it stood appraised at 50 G.[50] *From this amount, the basic rent for the field..., 13 Pd Berner, was to be deducted. Also, (they had) a small wooden house valued at 14 G. Of the 14 G, the woman named Walburg Mayrin paid the king the 4 G that she owed to Streicher, which (Michel Rauch)*[51] *had received. However, out of mercy, the remainder was given to support the Mayrin and her children. She was the mother of Wolfgang Mayr (a key leader) who also had fled. In addition, a rent of 6 G 2 Kr had to be paid to Erllacher annually for this small house.*

Moreover, Streicher had loaned 30 G to Wolfgang Pruner (for which he had used a portion of Pruner's land in return.) Streicher also had owned five quarters with the mining works in Wiltnkirchn which brought him profits of 80 G 5 Kr and 3 Vr during 1528, 1529 and 1530. Anngst (the former judge who had since died) was to have given this money to the heirs.

Anngst had given the Streicher children 8 G, 39 Kr, 4 Vr of this sum. It was not known if the judge had kept the rest of the money and whether he had accounted for it to the king.... At this time the mining works were only breaking even and not making a profit. Out of mercy, these rights were returned to the children,....

The young man named Empacher (also) had a legal right to the above named properties and therefore received 35 G.

There were still four young, underage children (between three and seven years of age) whom the Streichers had left. His majesty had been paid 10 G in expenses for them which (Rauch) had received.

July 21, 1530, Two Unnamed Pregnant Women Captured in the High Mountains

The government had received the report of Christoff Fuchs, governor of Kufstein from the 15th of July stating that he had captured an (unnamed) Anabaptist man and two (unnamed) pregnant women[52] *in the high mountains near Ellmau (in the district of Kufstein). Fuchs was instructed to bring the printed books and writings they had in their possession (with him when he came to Innsbruck for the upcoming discussions at the end of the month, on how to eradicate the Anabaptist sect).*

A subsequent report showed that the pregnant women were to receive humane treatment. One of the issues in Fuchs' report of August 19, 1530 was *whether he should build a room for the two captured pregnant women that could be heated in winter. On August 23 the permission for this was granted.*

The second part of the September 23, 1530 report sent to Christoff Fuchs in Kufstein from Innsbruck dealt with two pregnant women – likely the same ones as captured in August – *who wanted to recant. If they would persevere in this intention, they could be freed on their recantation, oath and security.*

July 26, 1530, The Blacksmith's Wife Preaches With the Local Miller

The Innsbruck government wrote the following to the local governor in Feldkirch. *Dear faithful one. Although, repeatedly, we have sent out stern and solemn commands to all the districts and regions in the territory (of Tirol) ordering all judicial and local officials in the strongest manner, not only to prevent the Lutheran and other new sects from taking hold among the people, but also, according the commands we have issued, to seek to eradicate these sects. Despite that, we now have a credible report that in the village of Au (in the forest of Bregenz), in our domain of Feldkirch, under your administration, a miller and the wife of a blacksmith preach (the Word of God) daily to the people, in order to convince them to leave our traditional, holy and true Christian faith and adhere to the new sectarian faith. They have indoctrinated the local inhabitants with the poison of the new sects to such an extent that the people no longer observe the holy mass, their service to God or the worship of God. Therefore, we want to admonish you earnestly, to pay closer attention to the above mentioned laws and commands that were issued than you have until now, as you are obligated to do.*

Because we in no way tolerate such falling away from the ancient, true, Christian faith, finding it more important to strengthen the faith, it is our earnest command that you and your local officials diligently undertake everything in your power to bring the aforementioned miller and the blacksmith's wife to prison and punish them according to the commands that were issued, without delay, sparing no cost, work or effort in this endeavour. In addition, you should write immediately to all our overseers and government officials concerning the above named village of Au, instructing them similarly to give all diligence and do everything in their power to capture, imprison and punish the miller and the blacksmith's wife wherever they appear in our domain. You should carry out these *commands obediently so that we (in Innsbruck) have no reason to punish you bodily or in regard to your property. It is our solemn command that you carry out these orders.*⁵³

August 5, 1530, Six of Nine Arrested Anabaptists Are Women

The Innsbruck government responded to the governor of Rattenberg regarding the confessions he had sent in for nine Anabaptists, six of whom were women: *Lienhard Nickinger, his wife Katharina and his sister Katharina, Oswald Sauerwein, Ludwig Feinpeckh, Margarete Stainer, Sigmund Körner's wife Barbara from Bruck (am Ziller), Caspar Wiser's daughter Margarete of Kirchdorf and Ursula Weissenpurgerin. Of these nine, two choose to desist, Ludwig and Ursula. All means should be used to convert the others. For this purpose you should write to the Guardian of the Franciscan monastery in Schwaz. The prisoners who remain stubborn are to be tried in the criminal court. Margarete Stainer's one year old child, still not baptized, should be baptized. The other women should be asked if they also have children at home who have not been baptized.*

Four days later, on August 9, the judge of Rattenberg was instructed to arrange a trial for the seven prisoners who would not desist. Margarete Stainer was martyred with her husband in the following months, since an inventory of their property was done in October or November of 1530. By September 7, 1530 the death sentence was carried out for Lienhard Nickinger, while his other brother, Balthasar, and his wife, both had fled. Lienhard's wife Katharina also must have fled since nothing more is said of her. Katharina, Lienhard's sister escaped too, but was arrested again September 27 and at that time was to receive a pardon. The inventories of October and November included one for the Nickinger family's property, at which time two additional fleeing Nickinger sisters were mentioned. The story of their one hundred year old mother also comes to light. See October 27, 1530 and n. 64.

August 6, 1530,

Three women from the district of Kufstein had given confessions: Elisabeth Furtnerin, Maria from the Nons and Lienhard Mittenmair's daughter. Now they should be convinced to recant through good instruction from a priest.

August 9, 1530,

Three women[54] were among the five Anabaptists captured in the vacated house of the Nickingers in Bruck am Ziller. The full authority of the law was to be used against them in the same way as for the other seven arrested four days earlier, August 5, with members of the Nickinger family.

August 12, 1530,
An order was given to investigate three young people who lived on the Sunnberg in the district of Kitzbühel, Elspeth and Margreth Ganntzler and their brother. Elspeth Zägeler admitted attending the breaking of bread, the Lord's Supper, in a house in Wattens (see April 1, 1529). The judge wanted her to be more specific in indicating the house in which this had taken place.

September 19, 1530,
The dowry of Wolfgang in the Ried's wife Barbara was six Gulden and a cow. Elisabeth Miterspacher fled with her husband despite her illness, leaving her child with the maid and property worth 130 G. Margreth Weissach fled with her married daughter Anna Schaider, whereas her pregnant daughter-in-law was left with two children when her husband fled. The Weissach family was better off owning property worth 200 G. All of these families lived in the district of Kufstein.[55]

September 19, 1530, The Property and Children of Two Anabaptist Families
The following statements on (confiscated) Anabaptist properties and their monetary value were compiled by the city and territorial judge of Kufstein ... and his judicial assistants.

(Two guardians, one of whom was from Ellmau) ... had been appointed by the territorial government for the four children of Paul and Agnes Frawnholtz.

The farm named Frawenbeltn served the (monastery of) St. George, with about 80 G.

The guardians were to pay his majesty expenses amounting to 20 G which Rauch, had received and accounted for.

Present on the Frawenbeltn farm were 8 cows, each appraised at 3 G, amounting to 24 G and 15 sheep, large and small, altogether appraised at 3 G.

Also, two poor feather beds, kettles and pans, grain and other vessels to measure liquids, appraised at 20 G.

Also, four bulls, each worth 3 G 45 Kr amounting to 15 G.

Also, four calves, each worth 1 G amounting to 4 G.

Cristan Schwabegger owed Paul Frawnholtz an amount of 9 G.

Also part of the account, Agnes brought to the marriage a dowry of 24 G.

She also reported that Andre Metzger of Rattenberg had lent her 2 G.

Lienhard Meylinger and Hanns Schaider had been assigned as guardians to the four children of Paul and Agnes Frawnholtz. The oldest child, a daughter, was 12 years old, the boy was nine and two girls were eight and six years old. All four were cross-eyed (with eyes turned upward). They paid ... the king 20 G.

(Another family) Peter and Dorothea Veytstetter (left) their four children, (ages five, four, three, and two) and a blind old man on their property. The guardians assigned ... were both from the village of Ellmau. The money to raise the children was to come from the moveable goods[56] and the blind man was to be supported from one third of the property. The outstanding debt of 45 G was forgiven since it could not be paid from the value of the moveable goods and the children needed this money to live on. The total value of their property and possessions was 87 G.[57]

Paul and Agnes Frawnholtz fled and likely Peter and Dorothea also became fugitives of the law.[58] However, Peter's unmarried sister, Barbara Veytstetter, who was arrested at the same time as Paul and Agnes on December 7, 1529 (see above), was executed in Kitzbühel. The ten Gulden owed to the government in expenses on her behalf were collected by Michel Rauch from the property of Peter and Dorothea since Barbara had inheritance rights from their parents on her brother's property.[59]

September 19, 1530,
The Anabaptist Leonhardt of Viltz fled with his son, leaving his wife, sick with syphilis, and three underage children aged nine, seven and four. The government appraised their property at thirty Gulden but it did not have much income. What they owned was not of great value, three cows worth nine Gulden and kettles, pans, bed linens and other household goods worth only four Gulden. There were debts on the property and the little money there was had to be used to raise the children. The mother was allowed to remain on the property with them. Out of mercy the property was not confiscated.[60]

September 19, 1530,
The (older) sons of Georg Lindterspacher, Peter and Martin, are fugitive Anabaptists. Georg's property is worth 40 Gulden and the moveable goods another 16 Gulden. His present wife, step-mother to his sons, wants to keep the dowry which she brought into the marriage. It amounts to one-quarter of their fief. Her three or four children that live with them are still

dependents. Georg is sick, very poor and in great need. He does not have the money to pay the government their expenses in regard to his sons.[61]

September 24, 1530,

The Anabaptist movement was spreading in the Ötz Valley west of Innsbruck. Marx Porst was one who had left his home in the district of St. Petersberg. His wife visited him twice while he was with the Anabaptist group. But by June 9, 1531 both he and his wife had been captured.

September 27, 1530, The Hearing of Two Anabaptist Widows Should Not Be Public

The central government informed Ernst Pranndt, judge of Rattenberg, that they had received the three Anabaptist confessions he had sent them, for Kunz Speckher, Margreth, widow (of the Anabaptist martyr) Hanns Ober (see December 22, 1529) and Regine, widow of Peter Schuster from Stubai. If the prisoners have not changed their minds about their confessions, they should confirm them now and then be put on trial in the criminal court. (However,) the judge should not publicize the day of the judicial hearing, as has been the practice up to this time.

This is the only reference to these two widows in these court records. Their trial in the criminal court meant they would be condemned to death. Likely they were martyred. The reason for holding the hearing in secret was to prevent others from being attracted to Anabaptism. The government was concerned that the movement was spreading.

September 27, 1530,

Margreth, Michel Lehner's wife from Radfeld and the sister of Lienhard Nickinger desisted and should be pardoned. Their oath would be accepted even if they could not pay the bail. But their sworn promise must include the condition that they will be punished if they rejoin the Anabaptists.

October 3, 1530, Anton Mair and His Wife Sold Property But Were Recaptured

Part A: The government wrote to Augustin Heirling, crown administrator for the district of the Ritten plateau. On the basis of his report of September 11 that (the Anabaptist) named Anton Mair of the village, his wife, his sister and one of his labourers had all fled, the government instructed Jacob Trapp and Victor from Montani to search for them. Heirling was applauded for the way he handled the sale of the Mair property in letting the family keep only 100 Gulden. Heirling had collected the rest of the money (an additional 300 Gulden) and kept it for the government. He was to find out from ... the judge and the neighbours present at the sale if the people who negotiated the sale knew that Mair wanted to flee.

Part B: The government sent instructions to Jacob Trapp, crown administrator of Glurns and Mals and Victor from Montani. They were to search for Anton (and his family) who took a route over the Vinschgau (mountains to the west) when they fled. He was a "short person, with a small body, lean and tanned in his face and had a visible mark on his left eye where it could be seen that he had been hit by a bull." Anton and those with him should be brought to prison.

A document of 1555 dealing with Anabaptist properties stated that Anton and his wife were re-captured and burned at the stake in Kaltern. Likely they had been executed by November 24, 1530 when their confiscated property was being discussed. A date was to be set when all should be present who thought they had a right to the property. In the end Anton's father paid 1200 Gulden for it and half the money went to their children.[62]

October 27, 1530,

A report was issued on executed Anabaptists that were caught trying to escape by ship in Kufstein. Some women from Bavaria[63] in this group chose to recant. Regina, widow of one of the executed men, was allowed to leave and was to receive two or three Gulden from her husband's possessions.

October 27, 1530, The Farm Property of the Nickinger Family

Ernst Pranndt, judge in Rattenberg, informed the imperial treasury that, *he had sold most of the property of the executed Anabaptists Hanns and Lienhard Nickinger.... Details from the original document of this report were as follows: ... (Regarding) a property, named "Vorberg" located on the mountain of Bruck am Ziller ... Pranndt sold some of the moveable goods, such as the horses, cows and grain.... Now ... there was still a good farm left, which paid rent to St. George and included items such as wagons, ploughs and other tools. Some hardworking and efficient farmer in the region should be capable of working it so that it would not fall into ruin but produce an income. There is a need to leave some of the possessions and equipment there yet for several more years. Both Balthasar Nickinger and his wife have fled as Anabaptists. But his old mother of approximately 100 years who can not see or hear and their young child, barely 24 weeks old, whom Pranndt recently had baptized, still live on the property. The old mother and the young child need financial support. In my (Pranndt's) view whoever takes over this farming property, should support the mother and raise the child....*

October - November 1530, The Value of the Nickinger Property
... (There is) a property named Vorberg located in the district of Rattenberg and the parish of Bruck am Ziller on which the Nickinger family lived. Two of the brothers, Hanns and Lienhard, (were) executed and (another brother), Balthasar and two of his sisters fled.... Balthasar (and his wife) left a young child,... and an older person,... on this property, who should be supported from the proceeds of half the property.

Based on two legal letters, this property with all its heirs, their rights, its potential and all that belonged to it, if it was worked for six days, is worth approximately 250 G. A rent of approximately 14 Pd has to be paid on this property to the monastery on St. George mountain.... Michel Rauch sold the property for 150 G.... (See the Appendix for more details.)[64]

October 31, 1530,
Cristina Lanntringer, one of the martyrs in Kufstein who was caught trying to escape by ship, left nothing of her own behind except three underage children. Leonhard Staindl's wife was also martyred in Kufstein. Later her husband said, "When she left she took along the best of what he owned." He was left to support three young children and a poor sister. Both women were from Radfeld, the village near Rattenberg. Both of their husbands had to pay six Gulden to the government for the expenses of their wives' executions in order to obtain the women's possessions.[65]

October 31, 1530, The Possessions of the Former Judge and His Wife
Ernst Pranndt in Rattenberg made recommendations to the Innsbruck government concerning various Anabaptist properties and included a lengthy inventory of what had belonged to the Obinger family.

... Hanns Obinger, residing in the valley below Breitenbach (in the district of Rattenberg) was an Anabaptist and about a year ago he was imprisoned here in Rattenberg. However, he recanted and did penance. During the night of Saturday before All Saints Day, October 29, Hanns, his wife Ursula and their two children, left Rattenberg going down the Inn River (travelling eastward). They took with them some household goods, two horses and three cows (but also) left things behind in their house, as listed in the inventory enclosed with this report. Hanns had inheritance rights to his

property. From the information I (Pranndt) have so far, I suggest that the property could be sold for 100 Gulden. In my opinion it would be in the best interests of (the king) ...to sell all the possessions of the former judge, including the three cows that are left and the entire contents of his household.

The inventory of the Obinger family's possessions is one of the most interesting in these financial records for its phenomenal detail. Virtually every item and piece of furniture in this household, from the basement to the storage room, was itemized. Reading it is like walking through a museum. It includes everything from horse harnesses to frying pans to bundles of flax not spun, storage chests, honey pots and two large wooden vats, one still full of cabbage and a box of letters, nine of which had seals. The inventory was carried out October 31, by the chaplain of Breitenbach and the four men assisting him. See the complete inventory in the Appendix.

October - November 1530, The Miner and His Wife Sold Their Property and Fled*

Hans Letzelter and his wife were among a group of miners pardoned June 16, 1528. Two years later the couple fled after selling their house, leaving their children.

Hans Letzelter's house located up in upper part of the town (of Rattenberg), near the customs house, is worth more than the 21 G and 18 K which it was previously appraised at. Letzelter sold it for aproximately 27 G so that the interest derived from it will now not be available.

Moreover, the interest he owed and the outstanding debt he had, amount to 72 G.

Also, there is a young child left who is mentally challenged. This child has a right to whatever money is left after the interest and the debts are paid. Then there are three children from his first wife, for whom the legal matters have not been resolved yet. Therefore, his majesty will not receive any income form this property.[66]

---

*A long, original document, 620, dated October - November 1530, includes inventories of confiscated properties of Anabaptists from in and around Rattenberg on the Inn River. With one exception, that for the Nickinger family (see above), these inventories and discussions of them are placed here in the same order in which they appear in the original document. This is the first of these inventories.

October - November 1530, Paul Taurer and His Wife, Shopkeepers

Paul Taurer who fled and his wife, an executed Anabaptist (left) a stone house below the castle (in Rattenberg), appraised at 50 G.

It was sold to Murnauer (the crown administrator) by Michel Rauch for 22 G and the money entered into the account books.

From this amount the basic annual rent and interest for the property of 1 G should be deducted. Moreover, Anngst, the previous judge, allowed Ulrich Tischler to buy all the goods which Taurer and his wife had in their shop located in the Mairhofer's house. For these goods, Tischler paid a total of 13 G.

From this Tischler had to pay the interest the Taurers' owed Mairhofer of 9 G.

Also, a butcher whom Taurer had dealt with was paid 2 G and a shopkeeper in Munich from whom Taurer's wife had purchased goods was paid 1 G 12 Kr.

The remaining amount which Tischler owed the king was 48 Kr. Tischler did not pay this but registered a complaint that the territorial judge had taken advantage of him.

Also at hand are some old household goods, a table, an old storage chest, three poor bedsteads, a cream container, an old box, two straw mattresses, two blankets and two small straw cushions, altogether appraised at 1 G 24 Kr.

The small amount of moveable property, out of mercy, has been left to the sister of Paul Dutzzin.

And the (Taurers) left their one child, a young, underage son.

October - November 1530, Former Monk's Wife to Receive His Possessions

Jörg Vasser was an Anabaptist leader involved already in 1527 (see December 10, 1527). His property was dealt with three years later as follows.

Jörg Vasser from the town (of Rattenberg), also fled and left nothing behind but a small number of moveable goods.[67]

Vasser's wife has a right to these goods which are valued at 32 G.

Thus, there is no income for his majesty from this property.

October - November 1530, An Inventory of Cows, Hens and Feather Beds

Hanns Tegerseer and his wife, of   Radfeld, were both executed as Anabaptists. The property they left consisted of one and a half fiefs (or "lehen" in feudal tenure). The first one, named the Herndl Lehen, owes an annual rent of 17 Pd, 2 (Stift) Kr, 4 hens and 30 eggs to the prior of the Augustinian monastery in Rattenberg. The half fief, called the Preem Lehen, also serves the prior, paying 13 Pd, 1, Kr, 2 hens and 15 eggs annually. The total value of the farmer's right to work the land and the one and a half fiefs, is appraised at 150 G.

Also on the property are: 4 cows and a beef cow (one not giving milk) which together are worth 17G, 2 old horses appraised at 5 G and 4 feather beds, 2 wagons, 2 kettles and several pans, altogether worth 15 G. In addition, all the containers for measuring liquids and the household utensils, listed in the legal inventory which was done earlier, are worth 2 G. The (total) value of the above mentioned two properties and all the possessions is 189 G.

In addition, Hanns from Stain and Sigmundt Hueber from the Schönau, appointed as guardians to their two foster children, Michel and Barbara, have been given half of all the property and goods which, according to the law, is rightfully theirs.

The other half, which rightfully belongs to the king as a confiscated property, was sold by Michel Rauch for 80 G and the money entered into the account books.

In addition there are still four underage children present. The previous territorial judge, (Bartlme Anngst), had commanded the above mentioned guardians to sell the livestock. This they did and gave Anngst 6 G from the sale. Those taking over from Anngst (who had died) were to account for this money.

October - November 1530, The Mother Had Owned Half of the Mill

When Anna Gschäll of Rattenberg was first arrested on May 22, 1529 she chose to recant. Later that month, on May 29, instructions were given to dismantle the house of Cristan and Anna and burn the remains of it, because an Anabaptist meeting had been held there. By June 17 this order was revised. The house should be boarded up so that no one would take the lumber but the roof should be removed, as a warning to others. Some time after the family fled, four Anabaptist women occupied the Gschäll house (February 22, 1531). The June 17 report also referred to the conversion of Anna and the other prisoners, Jörg Ameiser and his wife and Lienhard Vischer. But the authorities were not ready to release them and they remained in prison.

By fall the wives from all three of these families were released. They duly promised to remain in their district for a year and never to leave the territory (September 1, 1529). Anna's husband Cristan fled to Moravia, possibly in late summer, where he was one of the leaders of the refugee

Anabaptists in Austerlitz.⁶⁸ At Christmas 1531 Cristan was back in Tirol attending a major Anabaptist gathering along with Jacob Hutter, Hans Amon and other leaders, in Hörschwang, on a mountain top in the Puster Valley.⁶⁹ Anna's whereabouts at this time are not known but sometime before the fall of 1530 she also fled. The inventory of their confiscated property is as follows.

The Gschäll property, located in the Vochen Valley,⁷⁰ includes an old house in which Cristan Gschäll and his wife lived before they both fled as Anabaptists, leaving two young children behind. This property, together with the old house and the piece of land with it,⁷¹ as well as the barn located on it, are estimated to be worth 225 G.

The aforementioned Georg Gschäll, who also fled (as an Anabaptist), has a right to 34 G of this property. This amount has become the king's possession and should not be deducted from the appraised sum of 225 G.

The amount which the wife of Cristan Gschäll has a right to is 75 G, which has also become the king's possession since she fled. This amount should likewise not to be deducted from the appraised sum.

Three children have a right to 180 G worth of the property.

The surplus earned from the property has been sold to the children's guardians for 20 G and has been entered into the accounts.

And the inheritance from the mother consists of half of the mill which was not included in the property appraisal. Half of this amount belongs to Cristan's brother and the other half to the two children, who are not involved in Anabaptism.

October - November 1530,

The inventory entry for the Schmid family stated that Valtein and his wife, who had been executed as Anabaptists, left a house and yard valued at 50G, for which the heirs of Pilgram Marpeck were paid 2 G 20 Kr annually. This was sold to their three children, two of whom were underage.

October - November 1530, The Miller and His Wife Fled

Leonhard Spitzhamer of Brixlegg and their maid were in prison for almost three months at the beginning of 1528 (see January 10, 1528). In the end they were allowed to recant. Leonhard's wife was not arrested at that time. However, from the inventory of their property in 1530, it is clear that Leonhard's wife had also chosen to become an Anabaptist. The inventory reads as follows.

(The property, called Spitzhaim, includes) a dwelling and a mill together with the land belonging to it, as well as the money, five Pds Berner, for the land leased to the owner of the grinding mill which is paid annually to the mill at Spitzhaim. All of this was left behind by Leonhard Spitzhamer and his wife, who both fled as Anabaptists. (Also,) they left their child, to be cared for by a man named Jacob, both of whom are to be supported from this property which has been appraised at 300 G.

For the above mentioned dwelling, mill and land, an annual rent of seven Pd is paid to the Abbey of St. George in the Stallen Valley (near Stans in the vicinity of Schwaz) and 18 Kr to the church or parish of Reith (near Brixlegg). These amounts should be deducted from the appraised value.

The obligatory rents were deducted from the surplus of 86 G, which was the difference between the appraised value and the selling price of the mill. This amount is designated for the financial support of the child and its caregiver. I (Rauch) sold the proceeds from the mill to the child for 180 G and entered this into the account books.

Moreover, some of their possessions, the moveable goods, still at Spitzhaim, which were listed in a judicial inventory done earlier, are worth 17 G. I (Rauch) have accounted for these 17 G by adding them to the appraised value. The total estimated value (then) amounts to 317 G.[72]

This miller and his family had been well off.

October - November 1530,

Paul Pölt, a key Anabaptist leader and his wife were from Bruck am Ziller but were executed in Kufstein. They may have been in the group caught trying to escape by ship, whose cases were discussed October 27 and 31. The Pölts left a young child to be cared for by guardians and property valued at 160 G.

October - November 1530,

Leonhardt Wilthueter, also from Bruck am Ziller, fled as an Anabaptist. In the inventory of his property there is no mention of his wife, only that he left two young children.

November 14, 1530,

Three women from the district of Gufidaun were treated as follows. A young woman, Walpurga, Hans Dörrer's daughter, was to be released on the usual conditions after presenting bail. However, Barbara Lercher and

Ursula, the daughter of Jörg Schmid (see Number 1 in the Appendix), who both had been pardoned previously, were not as fortunate. If they persevered they would have to be put on trial. See November 16, 1531 regarding Barbara's family.

November 21, 1530,
Three members of one family, Anna Hellrigel, her husband Georg and his mother Else were all arrested in the district of St. Petersberg. They were to be re-educated by a local priest and could be pardoned if they showed true remorse.

November 23, 1530,
Anna, Marx Schneider's daughter who was working in the Luckhner household on the Ritten plateau, was arrested with a woman named Naterin. Neither of them would divulge any information to the authorities. Attempts should be made to convert them so that they could be buried in sacred ground after their execution.

November 29, 1530,
Heinrich Crenseisen's wife had been baptized and was brought to prison. She chose to recant but was present for only the first of the three Sundays. Then she fled, taking their four children with her, one of whom was blind. She joined her husband in exile. They left behind a house in Radfeld owned by them both valued at 24 G, a cow and some hay.

November 30, 1530, Three Anabaptist Women in Bozen
The Innsbruck government asked Wilhem von Liechtenstein, governor of Gries and Bozen again for information on the Anabaptist house in Bozen. Now Jacob Hupher, territorial judge of Gries and Bozen, reports on three captured Anabaptist women from Bozen, Cristan Wolf's wife Margreth, citizen of Bozen and Katharina Kramerin, shopkeeper in Bozen,[73] who would not recant and Hanns Pünnter's wife Anna who would. They should be brought before a jury and interrogated thoroughly. Also, the Barefoot monks who talked about the Anabaptist house should be questioned. Perhaps a meeting was held in Anna Pünnter's house.

The government informed Jacob Hupher that…. Margreth had been pardoned…. She and Katharina should not be tried for now….. But all three women should be questioned about the house in Bozen in which leaders had met for a nocturnal communion.

Their story continues December 23, 1530. Pünnter's wife, who is new to the sect, should be pardoned. Innsbruck is disappointed that more intense questioning of the Wolfin and the Kramerin did not provide the information they wanted.... Liechtenstein was instructed as follows.... If (Margreth) Wolf, a relapsed Anabaptist, and (Katharina) Kramerin, held to their erring ways they should both be put on trial.

The next day, December 24, Ferdinand I writes to Liechtenstein that (because) Hupher ... did not use torture,... he should be replaced with a courageous person who understands the situation and is not associated with the sect. Then they both should interrogate the women using torture.... (The government suspected that) Hupher did not carry out the orders because he appeared to be "somewhat Lutheran."[74]

The women remained in prison over Christmas and on January 3 of the new year the communications continued. Hupher explained that he had not used torture... because the jury did not want to be part of these proceedings anymore.... The Innsbruck government is disappointed and repeats its command to use torture in front of a jury since earlier the women were only threatened with torture. The names of the jury members who did not want to see torture used ... should be reported. In any case, whether they were questioned again or not, the women should be tried in the criminal court.

Following more instructions on January 11, 1531 to carry out their command, ten days later, on January 21, based on Hupher's report of January 15, the government sent an execution order. It is likely then that Katharina Kramerin and Margreth Wolf, mother to Katharina Riemenschneider, were martyred.

Notes

1. TA 1972, 335, document 491. The quotation is from 335:15.
2. It was referred to as a "streifenden Rotte." TA 1972, 335:31.
3. TA 1972, 342:33-343:4.
4. TA 1972, 343:19-22.
5. These points are mentioned in TA 1972, 343:15-16; 25-36.
6. See TA 1972, 344:9-17. The court secretary should read the decrees to the people.
7. *Hutterite Beginnings*, 161.
8. TA 1972, 382:2-11; 23-29.
9. TA 1972, 386:24-39.
10. TA 1972, 388, document 580, in particular there, 389:15-16.

11. TA 1972, 391:1-10.
12. TA 1972, 385:1-5; 391:14-17.
13. TA 1972, 414, document 613.
14. Mecenseffy, "Anabaptists in Kitzbühel," 110.
15. See "Overview of All Four Categories" in Huebert Hecht, "Anabaptist Women and Their Families in Tirol, 1527-1531," in *Sisters: Myth and Reality of Anabaptist, Mennonite, and Doopsgezind Women*, 79-82, 86-87.
16. TA 1972, 101:35; 105:10-14.
17. *Hutterite Beginnings*, 195.
18. TA 1972, 257, document 366.
19. *Hutterite Beginnings*, 195-96, 372, n. 49. Hans Maurer had also accompanied children to Moravia. The blacksmith's story is in TA 1983, 183.
20. *The Chronicle of the Hutterian Brethren*, 98, n. 2.
21. *Hutterite Beginnings*, 195-96. The poorhouses were called "Spitalpflege."
22. This information is from Wolfgang Lassmann's research, related in Stayer, "Anabaptists and Future Anabaptists in the Peasants' War," 131.
23. Packull views the strength of the Pusterers as a key factor in the schism of 1533 in addition to the personality clashes and leadership rivalries that led up to it. *Hutterite Beginnings*, 203, 235.
24. Mecenseffy, "Anabaptists in Kitzbühel," 111.
25. *The Chronicle of the Hutterian Brethren*, 103.
26. The storage chest was „the quintessential mobile piece of furniture in every man's home." Robert Juette, *Poverty and Deviance in Early Modern Europe* (New York, NY: Cambridge University Press, 1994), 71.
27. *Hutterite Beginnings*, 228.
28. *The Chronicle of the Hutterian Brethren*, 103.
29. *Hutterite Beginnings*, 383, n. 85 notes the monetary values for converting pounds to Kreuzer.
30. *The Chronicle of the Hutterian Brethren*, 104.
31. *Hutterite Beginnings*, 204. Erhardt Urscher (September 4, 1531) gave 200 Gulden at his baptism.
32. Peasant farmers who owned six or more cows were wealthier. Otto Stolz, *Rechtsgeschichte des Bauernstandes und der Landwirtschaft in Tirol und Vorarlberg* (Bozen: Verlag Ferrari - Auer A. G., 1949), 153.
33. The case of Justina Gall who was already mentioned in Chapter Three indicates that some Anabaptists were quite wealthy. Justina inherited 2,500 Gulden and a house. Lichdi, "Katharina Purst Hutter," 179.
34. Regarding the price of her property see Kogler, *Stadtbuch Kitzbuehel, Bd. III,* 355.
35. Huebert Hecht, "Faith and Action," 100, n. 153.
36. *Ibid.* See Margery's autobiography, the first one in English dictated by a woman in Louise Collis, *Memoirs of a Medieval Woman, The Life and Times of Margery Kempe* (New York, NY: Harper and Row, 1964).

37. TA 1964, 54:18-20; 29-30. The word for guaranty is "Burgschaft."
38. TA 1972, 387:24-32.
39. She was one of two women arrested and is designated in the index as n.n.193b, two women.
40. TA 1972, 172:33-34. "…seine Frau liege im Kindbett,…"
41. The word in the records is "hochschwanger." See TA 1972, 90:30-31.
42. TA 1972, 136:5.
43. They are designated in the index as n.n.380a and b, pregnant woman.
44. They are designated in the index as n.n.184a and b, two pregnant women.
45. TA 1972, 436:20, 25-26.
46. Schmelzer, "Elisabeth von Wolkenstein," *Profiles of Anabaptist Women*, 167-68.
47. TA 1972, 303:27-304:11.
48. TA 1972, 323:25-30.
49. TA 1972, 325, document 472.
50. See the Appendix regarding money values and salaries.
51. TA 1972, 395:23-32. Michel Rauch was the official appointed by the king to conduct inventories of all Anabaptist properties.
52. They are designated in the index as n.n.380a and b pregnant woman.
53. This record is summarized in TA 1972, document 577. The original document is in the Tiroler Landesarchiv Innsbruck, *Buch Walgau, Bd. 1*, fol. 84v-85r. It was transcribed into modern German for the author by Dr. Matthias Schmelzer.
54. They are designated in the index as n.n.394, three women. Only one entry was made in the Data Base for these women not three, since it is not clear if these women and the two men they were arrested with were part of the Nickinger network and were later referred to by name. It is a conservative estimate.
55. The stories of these women are in TA 1972, 403-407. The daughter-in-law whose husband fled is designated in the index as Weissach, wife of.
56. The phrase "moveable goods" refers to "Fahrende Hab" that is, whatever possessions could be moved and carried.
57. Regarding the Frawnholtz family see TA 1972, 402:14-16; 403:17-37; 407:13-17. Regarding the Veystetters see TA 1972, 407:28-36.
58. Following the Frawnholtz inventory, the case of Wolfgang in the Ried and his wife Barbara are discussed and it is said of him, that he also fled ("der auch vom landt ist gelauffn"). TA 1972, 404:1-2. This infers that Peter and Agnes Frawnholtz had left their home and fled.
59. TA 1972, 404:28; 407:37-40.
60. TA 1972, 405:19-31; 408:7-12.
61. TA 1972, 406:5-14; 408:17-23. "Fief" refers to a "Lehn" that is, property held in trust in the feudal system.

62. TA 1972, 222:23-26; 434:25-31; 481:25-27.
63. They are designated in the index as n.n.415 Bavarian women. See TA 1972, 415, document 616.
64. Regarding the Nickinger family see TA 1972, 416:3-24 and 428:36-429:13. In the October-November document 620, page 429, the mother is described as 110 years old and the child as 18 weeks old.
65. TA 1972, 417:15-23; 429:37-430:2 and 10-12.
66. TA 1972, 147:2; 421:6-18.
67. The word used is "varnus" meaning "bewegliche Habe" or moveable goods. TA 1972, 423:6. Vasser's wife joined him in Moravia. See Packull, *Hutterite Beginnings*, 228.
68. *The Chronicle of the Hutterian Brethren*, 85, 161, 197; *Hutterite Beginnings*, 62, 216, 266, 280. In the 1530s and 1540s Cristan was sent from Moravia as a missionary to Carinthia and Styria.
69. *Hutterite Beginnings*, 242.
70. It was referred to as a "Gut" located in the Kramsach region in the district of Rattenberg. See TA 1972, 424:27-425:17 for this family's inventory.
71. This land was named "Wört in der Schönwissen."
72. TA 1972, 425:24-426:6.
73. This woman is called "Kramerin" meaning she was a shopkeeper. Regarding Margreth Wolf, see the discussion of the Anabaptist artist Bartlm Dill Riemenschneider and his family, February 16, 1528, 59-60.
74. The radical preacher, Wölfl, spent two weeks with Hupher in 1526 "and sold him a New Testament." See *Hutterite Beginnings,* 177.

Chapter Five

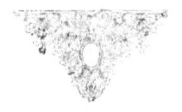

Introduction to the Records of 1531

The new year had barely begun before reports were circulating that Anabaptism was on the rise again. The orders of January 2, 1531 sent to Feldkirch, state that despite the "serious and solemn decrees" the government had issued, the Anabaptist sect was increasing in numbers in both town and country.[1] The government was more determined than ever to eradicate the sect. But it was harder to capture the heretics in winter and, as had been the case in 1530, there was little government action against Anabaptist women until the spring of 1531. This lack of records also indicates that the king was continuing to lose subjects as more and more Anabaptists migrated to Moravia. In northeastern Tirol the emigration to Moravia was one reason for a marked decrease in the number of Anabaptist trials and a decline in the movement during 1531.[2] Those who were caught while attempting to flee received harsher treatment. The directives from Innsbruck often included instructions to include torture when questioning the prisoners. To the king's dismay, some authorities refused to carry out such orders. The central government's policy was not completely successful.

Of great interest in the records of 1531 are those from March 2 and 17 where Anabaptist men from the region of Sarnthein in south Tirol relate not just the names of the persons present at several Anabaptist meetings but the content of the sermons which they heard. These records are indeed unique in that they preserve an outline of what Anabaptists actually preached. Significantly, a number of women were present at these nocturnal meetings. The wife of Lenntz even brought her two children to one of them. Whereas at one of these gatherings only six Anabaptists were together, including the leader, at other times as many as 12 and 18 people attended. Along with expounding on the Apostles' Creed, the preachers taught certain priorities, for example, that the true Christian should be willing to leave family and property for the sake of the faith. Erhardt Urscher who hosted these meetings did not desert his wife and family, but, had given the Anabaptist leaders a substantial amount at his baptism, two hundred Gulden (September 4). The many inventory records in 1530, of properties and goods which the Anabaptists left, is proof that this teaching was taken seriously.[3]

A few other cases stand out in the records of 1531 for the different kind of information they provide. Erhardt Vischer and his wife (May 4) sold some of their property and goods and gave their leaders the two hundred Gulden. Again, this was no small sum. It illustrates how the Anabaptists supported the leaders and each other financially. Also, the excuse which this couple gave the authorities, namely that they had been led astray, is a different kind of survival tactic. They were telling the government what it wanted to hear. The government decrees had stated repeatedly that people were being led astray by Anabaptist itinerant leaders so they simply confirmed this to their interrogators. It worked for a while, until the authorities heard that this couple had hosted a meeting. Then they were required to pay a heavy fine of fifty Gulden.

In North Tirol, west of Innsbruck in the district of St. Petersberg, the local authorities were told that the Anabaptist woman, Magdalena Weiss (June 9) who was to be executed, could only be buried in sacred ground if she recanted and took the holy sacrament before her death. She and her husband had been arrested in April 1530 and pardoned. However, they rejoined the Anabaptists and Magdalena was one of the four women in a group of 16 Anabaptists captured June 9, 1531. Two of the other women, Hanns Frischmann's daughter and Anna Hellrigel (also June 9) are mentioned here for the first time whereas Marx Porst's wife had been discussed already September 24, 1530. However, now in June 1531, all of those captured were to be interrogated "with and without the use of torture." Magdalena seems to have been the only martyr in this group of women.

The report of Wilhelm von Liechtenstein, crown administrator and governor of Bozen and nearby Kurtatsch, discussed on June 11, 1531, stated that around forty Anabaptists were present in his districts. He was to enlist the help of authorities in the neighbouring districts in order to capture these people.[4] There was some success when on June 21 four men and three women were captured in a night raid. Two of these unnamed women (July 19) were still in prison several weeks later. During these months the government's expenses in dealing with the Anabaptists had been adding up and one way to reduce costs was to release some of the prisoners. Thus, these two women were released with no further requirements, whereas Katharina Mair and her husband (June 27) who had also been arrested, had to recant in order to be released.

In Freundsberg – the castle for this district was located on the hill above the town of Schwaz – Sigmund Capeller, the territorial judge for the district, wasted no time in carrying out the sentence for a group of six Anabaptists (June 9). Although there are few details about their case, the method by which they were executed is clearly stated. The men died by the sword and the women were drowned, the latter being the method most often used for women.

On July 3 Capeller of Freundsberg was finally getting more information, or so he thought, about the woman carrying a register with the names of eight hundred Anabaptists. In the first discussions about this unnamed woman leader two years earlier (May 26, 1529) Barbara Maler's name had not been mentioned in regard to giving her lodging; only her husband, Crispin, had been named. Now seven persons were in prison: Barbara, her husband and their son, a miner and another couple, Briccius Räss and his wife and their landlord. The May 1529 report is the only earlier reference to Crispin. And since Crispin and their son were now released on the basis of an "old oath" it could be that they had recanted after their first arrest, although the son was also not named in 1529. In any case, the two men now claimed not to be associated with Anabaptism. All the others were to be examined more harshly, that is, with the use of torture, as had been ordered in the instructions just sent out from Innsbruck in June. The judge was not sure, however, that he should use torture for the two women, Barbara and the wife of Briccius Räss. The women had chosen to recant and give up their faith and they were not relapsi. The Innsbruck government responded four days later that all of the prisoners should be questioned under torture and those who were ready to recant should be pardoned. There are no further references to this group in these records. However, the fact that their interrogation was to include torture indicates how much more severe the treatment of all Anabaptists had become by 1531.

The judge of Freundsberg was not the only one who questioned the directives of his superior. On July 7, 1531 Jacob Hupher, judge in Bozen was reprimanded again for his lenient attitudes toward the Anabaptists.[5] Near the end of July, just after the meeting of the Imperial Diet of Augsburg, Ferdinand decided on a different approach. Out of concern that not enough was being done to eradicate the sect, on July 28 he informed the authorities in several centres of South Tirol that he was sending out his court preacher, a Franciscan named Brother Methardus. The Franciscan would preach in Matrei, Sterzing and as far away as Bruneck in the Puster Valley. He would teach the Word of God according to the common Christian understanding and the teachings of the holy fathers who confirmed the Gospel with their own blood.[6] There is no indication of how successful Brother Methardus was. In various parts of the territory, Anabaptists continued to be arrested.

In Rettenberg in the north, a mother and the wet nurse in the household were arrested with her son, Schwaykofer (August 18). There was concern about the books and the New Testament that were discovered in this farmer's home. Perhaps this family had hosted meetings where these had been used for readings. In another case, also in the north, a woman with a different kind of occupation – she worked in the mint in Hall – was arrested. The city of Hall, located just ten kilometres east of Innsbruck was important in the sixteenth century for its salt mines, its markets and for its mint where coins had been struck since 1477.

During the fall of 1531, the upper class woman, Elisabeth von Wolkenstein, became deeply involved in Anabaptism. Her husband Anton had invited the radical preacher named Wölfl into their home already in 1526. After Anton recanted in 1527 no mention is made of any of the Wolkensteins until September 1531. Elisabeth was baptized, taught her cook about her new faith and aided many Anabaptists in the surrounding region including Jacob Hutter. Elisabeth's two younger sons made the same commitment of faith as their mother. Anabaptism was "very strong and widespread in the Taufer Valley" due to the leadership of members of the Wolkenstein family. The principal Anabaptist meeting places were the Wolkenstein residence at Uttenheim and the castle of Neuhaus.[7]

Elisabeth managed to escape arrest for several years and eventually recanted as did her husband a second time. Elisabeth and Anton were allowed to live together in Brixen with their daughter and son-in-law but were not allowed to return to their home in Uttenheim following their recantations. Her biographer, Dr. Matthias Schmelzer, ends her story by saying that although the authorities of the church and of the state managed to silence Elisabeth "with their cunning and their threats.... they could not erase the evidence of her work." Her actions "surely encouraged many others in the Taufer Valley to risk taking the path to renewal."[8]

Toward the end of 1531 things seem to come full circle, with events taking place not unlike those recorded in early 1527. The first part of the record of September 26, 1531 in fact instructs the authorities in the bishopric of Brixen to look again at the confession of Wölfl, the radical preacher who was interrogated in January 1527 (see Messerschmied's wife January 9, 1527). Two of the believers he had named at that time, from the early Anabaptist network in Klausen and Gufidaun, were currently being investigated (September 6, 1531), namely, Ulrich Müllner and Mairhofer from Vintl.[9] Now, five years later, even larger gatherings were taking place in the district of Gufidaun. Around 150 Anabaptist men and women had met in a cave to hold the Lord's Supper. This was reminiscent of the beginning years of 1526 and 1527 when people flocked to hear the radical preacher and met in substantial numbers in Anabaptist homes.

The last document in the 1972 volume of court records, sent to authorities in Sterzing on December 22, confirms the king's worst fears. He had been told that in the valleys of this district crowds of Anabaptists had been meeting together.[10] The king was not pleased that nothing was being done to root out and eradicate Anabaptism. The local officials were told they should be avidly hunting down Anabaptists because now during the winter months they could not escape over the mountains.

It seems as if nothing had changed. According to the court records known to us, over 400 women had been arrested in the previous five years, because of their Anabaptist involvements. Most likely there would have been as many arrests of men if not more; there were possibly 1000 people involved in Anabaptism in Tirol alone. Many had been martyred, including 77 women, and many more Anabaptists had recanted. This much the government had achieved. On the other hand many had also fled and many had emigrated to Moravia. The de-population of Tirol continued and the government was losing its citizens. Yet the Anabaptist movement remained strong in Tirol and the underground movement continued. In this sense all of Ferdinand's decrees had accomplished little. Local officials continued to resist carrying out the orders sent from Innsbruck against the outlawed heretics. Anabaptists were still meeting together, in some places in large numbers.

The events of 1531 further illustrate what had been happening all along. In these five years, between 1527 and 1531, the Austrian Anabaptist movement had grown in numbers and in strength. This could not have taken place without the participation of women. The choices women made based on their faith experience were crucial to the establishment of the Anabaptist movement in Tirol.

Translations from the Court Records of 1531

February 8, 1531,
Katharina Stocker from Kitzbühel was to learn from the priest, recant, do penance and then leave the territory.

February 22, 1531, Four Women Captured in House of Anabaptists Who Fled

The Innsbruck government confirms that they received the report of Ernst Pranndt, judge in Rattenberg, that he captured four Anabaptist women in the empty house of Cristan (and Anna) Gschäll (in Kramsach).[11] *In their first interrogation, two of the women would not reveal the names of the men who were in the house with them and who fled. The women should now be interrogated using torture to find out by whom and when they were baptized, who was present and if they were acquainted with the leader named Vasser. If they persist in believing that their re-baptism is true and valid, the judge knows how to deal with them on the basis of the imperial mandates. The same applies to relapsed Anabaptists (who rejoin the movement). Those who show remorse and are ready to repent can be pardoned.*

Cristan Gschäll and his wife had owned a house and a mill, all of which they left, along with their two children, when they fled as Anabaptists. The inventory for their property was carried out in the fall of 1530 (see October-November 1530). Their house must have been standing empty since these Anabaptists were making use of it.

March 2, 1531, Michel Oberhöller and His Wife Attended Anabaptist Meetings

The introductory summary reads as follows. *On Thursday, March 2, after the first Sunday of the month, Michel Oberhöller gave the following confession in the presence of the crown administrator, Hanns from Sarnthein, the chief judicial authority in the district of Sarnthein, Jörg Sunnstainer, the judge, and the jury... because it had been reported that he had been with the Anabaptists (in the home of) Urscher (and his wife). The judge encouraged him to tell the truth.*

Oberhöller stated the following in his confession. *It happened that eight days ago, on the day of Pentecost, he was on his way down to fetch some wine for his wife. On the way he met Erhardt Urscher who told him there were two teachers in his house who were teaching the word of God. He was persuaded to go with Urscher to his house. Twelve people were present there and two teachers who were strangers. The teachers preached all night and taught the Gospel. Among other things, they spoke about the seed, how the Lord Himself cast it abroad and sowed it, interpreting these things admirably well. They also spoke of how the Lord said, every Christian should leave his property and goods together with his wife and child and follow Him alone. Moreover, faith and baptism should go together. They taught other things as well, but he did not find them acceptable and he did not pay particular attention to them.*

The case of Oberhöller was handled in the following way. Because he confessed to having been with the Anabaptists this was reason enough for the authorities to put him in prison. But, because so few jury members were present, out of mercy he was to be exempted from prison this time on the condition that he return on the coming Sunday at 12 o'clock and obediently present himself to the authorities.... If he did not appear he could be punished in his person and his property. He agreed to present himself and confirmed it with an oath.

He does not name his wife here but they were both in attendance at another meeting.[12]

March 17, 1531, The Lenntz Urstetterin Attended Three Meetings in Sarnthein

...Peter Schneider confessed under oath, with and without torture, that twice recently he and his servant went up to the home of (Erhardt) Urscher (and his wife). The first time he was there those present were: a stranger named Cristel from Völs who was a leader, also the (woman named) Lenntz Urstetterin, (and) Ul and Mathis Rueb. The second time those present were: Cristel, the leader from Völs, Herr Michel, the local priest, Andre from the Wiss, a miner's wife and her daughter, Breidl, the cook of Michel Schuester (an innkeeper), Anna, the Goldschmidt's maid, Michel Oberhöller, Ziperl, the son of the Matheis Schuesterin and around midnight Michel Schuester and Jörg Khramer also came.

But on these two nights, Peter Schneider saw nothing else in the Urscher home. The leader preached the Word of God and the Gospel, taught them how they should live, improve their lives and abstain from sin. He told them not to go to church because it was the house of the Babylonian whore. Whoever wanted to be a true Christian should leave his wife and child and follow this faith and teaching. (The leader) recited and taught them the Creed and how they needed it. First of all, they should believe in the invisible God, creator of heaven and earth, also in His only-begotten son, Jesus, (who was) brought to life in the virgin Mary without male seed, crucified by Pontius Pilate, who died and was raised from the dead and ascended into heaven. In the future, He would judge the living and the dead. In the same manner they were to believe in the Holy Spirit and not in the "houses of idols" but (instead in) the fellowship of the saints, in leaving sin behind and in the eternal life which followed this life. But he, Schneider, did not give one word of agreement to such teaching and knew nothing more to confess.

These are the teachings the Urstetterin would have heard and the people she would have met at the meetings she attended in the district of Sarnthein. In the confession of another man, Valtein Schuster, recorded on the same day, the Urstetterin is named twice more among those present at the Anabaptist meetings in Urscher's home. Moreover, Schuester stated that she attended one of these meetings with two children.[13]

March 18, 1531,

Gilg Marpeck of Rattenberg (no relation to the prominent leader Pilgram Marpeck), pardoned already in 1528, would not leave his wife who was in that town.

March 21, 1531,

Before their release Andre Ghreuter and his wife were to be asked about the leaders and who provided lodging for them. The Ghreuters lived in the district of Scheena near Rattenberg.

March 27, 1531,

A pardon could be granted to Ruprecht Kaiser's wife and Cristan Lentz's mother if the priest found them genuinely remorseful. These Anabaptists were from Altrasen in the Puster Valley.

March 27, 1531, Jörg Weber's Wife Fled With Him

Ferdinand I confirmed receiving a copy of the report which Balthasar Remich, crown administrator of Altrasen, had sent to the vice-governor, Oswald Freiherr von Wolkenstein. The directives from Innsbruck included instructions for Jörg Weber's wife.

If Jörg Weber's wife was not re-baptized and only fled with her husband out of concern for him, the judge should allow her to come back to her home. On the other hand, if she presents herself to the court, she can be pardoned.

April 14, 1531,

Wolfgang Schmid's widow, from the region of St. Lorenzen, bought their property back for six Gulden. Also on this date, a petition was submitted for Anna Kellen, another widow. Eleven days later her brother and another man swore the affidavit for Anna at the castle of Prösels in Völs.

May 4, 1531, Couple Sells Property and Gives Money to the Leaders

Jacob Hupher, judge of Bozen had sent in the confessions of Erhardt Vischer and his wife from Sarnthein. The two denied being baptized and insisted they had been led astray by their leaders. Now Hupher was instructed *to question them seriously in the presence of a jury as to whether they had accepted the (beliefs of) the sect or, whether they were only lying out of fear. If the latter was the case, they were to be pardoned after recanting, swearing the oath and paying for their keep. They maintain that they gave the money derived from the sale of their livestock, some provisions and some wood – 200 Gulden –* to the Anabaptist leaders, one of whom, Cristel, had led a meeting in the home of Erhardt Urscher (see March 17). *They should be questioned further on this matter.... If Vischer and his wife go free, their right to use their property should be restored to them.*[14] It had been *given over to a man named Salomon, with whom they had to come to an agreement about the use of the land for this year.*

The order of June 16 to restore their property to them following their pardon was rescinded on June 21 after it was discovered that this couple had given lodging to Anabaptists and had allowed unauthorized preaching in their home. For this they were fined fifty Gulden.[15]

June 9, 1531,

If the six Anabaptists whom Sigmund Capeller, territorial judge of Freundsberg, had reported, persisted in their faith, they were to be tried in the criminal court and their sentence carried out immediately. By June 14 this had been done. The men were executed with the sword and the women were drowned.[16]

In the northern district of St. Petersberg, Hanns Hellrigel's wife Anna and Marx Porst and his wife were among sixteen imprisoned Anabaptists. These Anabaptists were all to be interrogated with and without the use of torture. Magdalena Weiss (see below) was probably the only martyr in this group.

June 9, 1531, Magdalena Weiss Arrested a Second Time

Ferdinand I wrote to Sigmund Freiberger, judge of St. Petersberg,... regarding (Magdalena), Hanns Weiss' wife, who had confessed to having fallen again into the sect of Anabaptism despite her earlier pardon and oath. It is our command that you (Freiberger) question her, following proper order, in the presence of a jury in order to confirm her statements about rejoining the Anabaptists. Because she has violated the imperial edicts and the mandates that have been issued, she is to be put on trial again in order to be condemned to death. But before her execution she is to be instructed by a spiritual and knowledgeable priest who can dissuade her of the falseness of her belief, so that she admits she has erred and will take the holy sacrament. If she does this of her own free will then, after her execution, her body may be buried in sacred ground.

June 9, 1531, Did Hanns Frischmann's Daughter Go To Confession at Easter?

Ferdinand I also wrote to Sigmund Freiberger, judge of St. Petersberg, about Hanns Frischmann's daughter. *She has (confessed) that her beliefs are the same as those of any other Christian, and that this past Easter she went to confession and took the holy sacrament. (The judge) should find out from her priest if this is true. If it is, because she has been re-baptized, she will have to recant publicly, do penance and swear the oath. Only then can she be released from prison. If the priest states the opposite and she only wants to protect herself…, then (the judge) should continue the procedure with (more) severe questioning.*

June 14, 1531,
In Sterzing several farmers, their wives and their servants had fled, leaving their children and all their goods behind.[17]

June 20, 1531,
Helena Weiss's case was unusual in that she was given a second pardon. This was granted to her because she had come back to the church again during the previous Easter and had not joined her husband in fleeing. It was suggested that her friends keep her in their homes to protect her against the leaders and persons in the region who lead others astray. Helena was from Sautens in the Ötz Valley west of Innsbruck.

June 27, 1531,
Katharina Mair and her husband from the Ritten plateau were arrested with five others but the judge in Kaltern was allowed to release them on the usual conditions since they were not leaders or relapsed Anabaptists. They would have to recant publicly at mass on three Sundays, swear an oath and do penance.

July 3, 1531, Torture To Be Used in Questioning the Women
Barbara Maler and her husband Crispin of Freundsberg had provided lodging for the woman leader with the register of eight hundred names in 1529. Now they were both arrested along with their son. The two men denied any association with Anabaptism but Barbara and the miner imprisoned with them named the couple Briccius Räss and his wife as Anabaptist members. The judge then arrested these two and their landlord. Crispin Maler and the Maler's son were released on the basis of an oath they had sworn some time ago. However, according to the decree just issued in June 1531, the questioning of the other five was to include torture, or harsh questioning. There is only one other reference to these Anabaptists, in a report four days later.

On July 7, 1531 Innsbruck government wrote the following to Sigmund Capeller, district judge of Freundsberg. The answer to your question about the use of torture in questioning the women is as follows. The women want to desist from their erring ways and recant. Furthermore, they are not relapsi. They should be interrogated using the list of questions sent out recently (in June) and the interrogation should include torture. Then you should deal with them according to the directives in the decrees. Those who are willing to recant should be pardoned.

July 19, 1531,
A month after their arrest in a night raid in Deutschnofen (with about 40 Anabaptists), two unnamed women[18] were still in prison in Bozen. The jury had refused to try them because their own judge had not arrested them. Now the command came to sentence them immediately because of the cost of keeping them in prison.[19]

July 24, 1531,
Margarethe Schröffl and Wolfgang Huber's wife of St. Michelsburg both submitted a petition for Margarethe's husband and were to be interrogated. They could be pardoned if their only crime was re-baptism.

August 2, 1531,
Katharina at the Kolbenthurn chose to desist at her arrest. She was to recant publicly in the place where she lived, namely in the Volderwald forest in the district of Sonnenburg. Margreth Neschgartin, also from Sonnenburg, could be pardoned but had to pay the costs for her prison stay. Peter Egger's daughter fled from her home in Hall as did an unnamed carpenter's wife. Orders were given to search for and arrest the Reichlerin and Gärberin, who were both from Rettenberg.

August 7, 1531,
Petitions had been submitted for two women from Hall: Ursula Zehentnerin and the baker's wife, Margreth Pästler. Ursula was to be brought to prison whereas Margreth and her husband were in prison and could be released on the basis of an old oath and payment for their keep.

August 8, 1531,
Margarethe Tückhls, a miner's wife, and the wife of brick layer Gilg Obinger were both from the district of Freundsberg. Both women had been arrested

and now were to be questioned and convinced to recant. The case of a third woman named in this report, Lucas Wagensail's wife, was discussed further on August 22 (see below).

August 13, 1531,
The Ragermachers' maid fled with other Anabaptists from Hall. Like Ursula Zehentnerin, from that group, she was to be released on her recantation.

August 18, 1531, Women Arrested Had Books and New Testament in Their Home
The crown administrator of Rettenberg was notified that a farmer on the Volderberg (mountain), named Schwaykofer, his mother and his wet nurse had become Anabaptists. They should be arrested and interrogated by a jury....

The August 23 report stated that Schwaykofer's mother and wet nurse should be released without paying anything. Schwaykofer himself should be released on a written and sworn oath and a promise to present himself to the authorities if requested to do so. The two books in his possession, the New Testament and a book entitled "The Creation" should be confiscated and sent to Innsbruck. Moreover, the judge is to inquire from the priest whom he had named, whether Schwaykofer had gone to confession and taken the sacrament this year.

The presence of books in this household indicated that this farmer likely could read or, if he could not read himself, readings took place in his home at which these women would have been present.

August 18, 1531,
It was rumoured that Martin Praun of Hall and his wife were in the process of selling their house in the Vassergasse and moving away. If this was true they were to be arrested. The same applied to Sigmund and Cristina Ziegler of Thaur. Ten days later it was noted that Cristina Ziegler regretted her action and could be pardoned on the basis of petitions submitted for her. Nothing more is said of the others.

August 22, 1531, Pregnant Wife to be Instructed in Prison
Lucas Wagensail's wife from Rattenberg was reported already on August 8 but she would not give up her faith. Thus, on August 22, the following instructions were sent to the territorial judge of Freundsberg regarding her.

The wife of Lucas Wagensail is to be kept in prison for the rest of her pregnancy, During this time she is to be instructed by a priest. If she remains obdurate, she is to be tried in the criminal court after the birth of her child.

We do not know whether or not she was condemned to death. A note about a report sent to the territorial judge at the end of August stated that two Anabaptists, who are not named, had been executed in the nearby town of Schwaz. Perhaps Wagensail's wife and another man discussed in the same report were the ones referred to.

September 1531, A Noblewoman Leads the Anabaptists in the Taufer Valley

Elisabeth von Wolkenstein was a member of an important Tirolean noble family whose family tree reached back to the second half of the thirteenth century.[20] Her husband Anton, had been imprisoned already in 1527 after the radical preacher Wölfl, who spent eight days in the Wolkenstein home, named him in his confession to the authorities. Anton Wolkenstein recanted on June 26, 1527, promising in future not to allow "Lutheran preachers or teachers of other sects into his house or allow them to preach there." He also promised he would not use "any books that contained dissenting beliefs, but would read only the true Christian Bible."[21]

During 1529 when Jacob Hutter took over leadership of the Anabaptists following the executions of Michel Kürschner and Jörg Blaurock, Elisabeth von Wolkenstein was among his first followers. "She remained with the community of faith led by Jacob Hutter when he made numerous trips through the region and came to the Taufer Valley on missionary journeys from Moravia to Tirol." Between September 1531 and March 1532 when Hutter was in Tirol, Elisabeth met with him a number of times. "She attended his meetings, baptisms, and celebrations of the Lord's Supper, held either in the Neuhaus Castle at Gais or in the forest behind the castle."[22]

As Hutter won more and more followers in the Taufer and Puster Valleys, his activities caught the attention of the authorities. Then he sought refuge in the forests above St. George where he had free access to the Neuhaus Castle. The owner of the castle was Elisabeth's son-in-law, Michael von Teutenhofen. He permitted this and his administrator for the castle, Erhard Zimmerman, supported the Anabaptists. The previous administrator of the castle had not been friendly to Anabaptists, as the earlier arrest of two women in Uttenheim (Novmember 27, 1528) had shown.

Elisabeth also gave Hutter protection at her residence in Uttenheim where he spent much time.[23] Anabaptist meetings, discussions, Bible readings and celebrations of the Lord's Supper took place in her residence. Elisabeth allowed her two younger sons, Paul, 19 or 20 years old and Sigmund, 17 years old, to attend these meetings.[24] Moreover, she forbade her cook to attend mass, choosing instead to read to her from the Bible and instruct her in Anabaptist beliefs. The date for Elisabeth's baptism is not known. However, later Anabaptists testified that Elisabeth had not attended mass or gone to confession for several years prior to 1532. She gave food, lodging and protection to many fellow believers. The Anabaptist leader Hans Amon Tuchmacher, Hans Mair Paulle and his wife, Valthin Luckhner from Sand in Taufers and his wife, and, Paul Rumer, Veronika Grembs and Anna Stainer, all from St. George, were among the many Anabaptists who spent time in Elisabeth's home. When Hans Mair Paulle's wife was close to giving birth, Elisabeth took her in and allowed her to be cared for at Uttenheim following the birth.[25]

For a number of years, Elisabeth continued her activities.[26] Finally on January 28, 1534, orders were given to arrest Elisabeth, her sons Paul and Sigmund, her husband Anton and the family's cook. "The vice marshal made his way with two single team wagons to Fridrich Fueger (the crown administrator) in Taufers who made several soldiers available to him."[27] Thus, the vice marshal and his men surprised the Wolkensteins at their residence and took them captive. Anton was imprisoned at Innsbruck; Elisabeth and her cook were brought to the Taufers Castle.[28]

During their first interrogations the cook was threatened with torture if she would not provide information but no torture was used for Elisabeth in respect of her noble birth.[29] Elisabeth and her cook were asked the following questions.

  — *Why have you not gone to confession and Holy Communion for the past several years?*
  — *Why have you not gone to church like other good Christians?*
  — *Have you been re-baptized? If so, by whom and when were you re-baptized? Who witnessed the re-baptism?*

— *Have your husband Anton and your son Paul also been re-baptized?*

— *What are your views concerning the seven sacraments: confirmation, the sacrament of the altar, the sacrament of penance, the anointing of the sick, the ordination of priests, the sacrament of marriage, and infant baptism?*

— *Do you know the names of Anabaptists and where are they staying?*

— *Did you participate in Anabaptist meetings and celebrations of the Lord's Supper? Where did these take place?*

— *Who brought you into the Anabaptist faith? Who persuaded you to join the sect?*

— *Do you believe in the virginity of Mary? Do you believe that God the Father hears the prayers of believers through the intercession of Mary and the saints?*

— *Do you choose to stay in Anabaptism or are you ready to leave the sect and repent?* [30]

The report with Elisabeth's answers is no longer available but the crown administrator reported on February 15, 1534 that she admitted belonging to the sect and having been baptized. Also, "the judge had ascertained that Elisabeth's faith included some very grave errors. Moreover, she was determined not to change her mind and held firmly to her false convictions."[31] The cook was released since she was not an Anabaptist but Anton and Elisabeth remained in prison. Their property was confiscated and their eldest son Hans, who was also not an Anabaptist, was assigned to manage it. On February 22 two learned priests were sent by the bishop of Brixen to instruct Elisabeth in "the true Christian faith."[32] As a result, by March, Elisabeth had admitted the error of her ways on many points of her faith except two, the sacrament of the altar and infant baptism. She requested a year's time to re-consider her views on these doctrines.[33]

A request from her eldest son and her son-in-law to speak with her did not seem to bring results. "… Elisabeth was not ready to make a full recantation."[34] The king now sent an order, on April 15, 1534, to conduct a third hearing, this time with "serious" interrogation meaning that torture should be used. The records do not reveal if she was tortured or only threatened with torture. This interrogation took place in mid-April in front of a number of officials. The king was disturbed by the events occurring in Münster, northern Germany where, a month earlier, in February,

Anabaptists had taken over the city. Thus, he wanted "detailed information from Elisabeth about her own activities as well as the goals and plans of the Anabaptist movement."[35] But neither the proceedings nor the discussions with her relatives convinced her to recant fully.

On April 28, 1534, the Innsbruck government tried a different approach, requesting "the bishop of Brixen to send a priest well-versed in theology to Elisabeth."[36] Perhaps these discussions had some effect.

On May 8, 1534, the court met a fourth time with two very learned theologians and members of the clergy as well as officials of the court in attendance.[37] At this hearing Elisabeth finally relented. She declared her adherence to all points of doctrine in regard to all of the sacraments of the church, acknowledging that *"infant baptism is justified and good.... confirmation is a sacrament, as established by the Christian Church,* that she would do penance and attend confession and take the sacrament of the altar. Regarding the latter she said, *I believe, that in the Holy Mass, by the consecration of the priest, bread and wine are transformed into the body and blood of Christ, and that Christ is fully present in the sacrament of the altar in the form of body and blood. I will receive the sacrament of the altar at the prescribed times like other believing Christians and no longer, as I did until now, as the symbol of body and blood of Jesus Christ in both kinds (bread and wine). Finally,* she stated, *I believe that the holy Christian Church did not err by instituting the sacraments and by proclaiming these doctrines.*[38]

Following this full confession, Elisabeth was required to swear an oath and recant publicly. She knew her fate if she broke this oath and rejoined the Anabaptists and the government made it very clear that in that case she would be treated like anyone else. No mercy would be shown and a death sentence would await her. She repeated the following words before the judges as they were written out for her.

— *I will not take revenge on anyone, neither the government nor the others who put me in prison.*

— *I am prepared to recant publicly from the pulpit in front of the people in my parish church at Taufers, as is appropriate, on three consecutive Sundays during the Holy Mass.*

— *I am willing to accept and carry out the penance imposed on me by my parish priest.*

— *On three Sundays in succession I will follow the priest in the procession in the church holding a burning candle and, after the procession stand, for as long as the mass continues, in the anteroom (Atrium or Paradise) of the church holding the burning candle and doing penance.*

— I promise that following the recantation and the oath I will have nothing more to do with the (Anabaptist) sect for the rest of my life.

— I promise that for the next year I will not leave the district of Uttenheim, to which I belong.

— I commit myself not to leave the princely territory of Tirol for the rest of my life.

—I am prepared to pay the costs for my imprisonment and court proceedings.[39]

After swearing this oath Elisabeth asked to be released from the humiliating experience of a public recantation in front of the people in her church. However, on June 3, 1534 the Innsbruck officials wrote back making it clear, that *because the king had commanded that all those who choose to leave the sect of Anabaptism must recant publicly, this is commanded for the noblewoman von Wolkenstein as well. On three consecutive Sundays she must repeat from the pulpit in Taufers what the priest reads to her. Only then will it be possible for her live with her son-in-law, Teutenhofen, in Brixen, in order to prevent the Anabaptist leaders from coming to see her now and then.*[40] They were making an exception for her by allowing her to leave the district of Uttenheim.

The instruction that Elisabeth was to repeat what the priest read to her indicates she may have claimed she could not read. By October 9, 1534[41] Elisabeth had recanted in her parish church in Taufers with the following words.

I, Elisabeth, wife of Anton von Wolkenstein, confess that I erred when I became a member of the devious and seductive sect of the Anabaptists. Because I regret this from the bottom of my heart, I recant and forswear publicly, give my assent, and commit myself to live from this moment onward for my whole life, according to the principles of the true Christian church and in no way to deviate from it.[42]

Following this recantation Elisabeth was pardoned and allowed to live with her daughter Anna and son-in-law, Michael von Teutenhofen in Brixen. Her husband had already relocated to Brixen on the request of their son-in-law in June of that year.

September 4, 1531,
Ziprian Sallman's wife of Sarnthein was to receive the first compensation payment which Erhardt Urscher and his wife had to pay in the re-possession of their property after being pardoned. At his second arrest in January 8, 1533, Erhardt stated that he gave 200 Gulden to the leaders at his baptism.[43] See the Epilogue for more details of their story.

September 6, 1531,
Anabaptists in Klausen, Hans Sumerer (miner) and his wife, Hans Feichtner and his wife as well as Balthasar Mairhofer of Niedervintl, his wife and their household servants were all named as guilty to the authorities in Brixen. By September 26, 1531 only one of the labourers of the Mairhofer household was found guilty. The Mairhofer maid then was an indirect participant.[44] Mairhofer and his wife had belonged to same early group of Anabaptists as Ulrich Müllner and the Messerschmieds (see January 9 and December 31, 1527). Müllner who refused to recant was now to be interrogated using torture.[45]

September 26, 1531, Caves, Meeting and Hiding Places and the Official's Wife
Five years earlier, Wölfl, the radical preacher, had received an excerpt from the Gospels from the wife of the crown administrator of Gufidaun (January 16, 1527). The preacher did not give her name in his confession of January 1527 but likely she was the wife of Prew, the older man discussed in this report. Her affirmation of what the preacher taught indicates that indeed, the Reformation took hold in Gufidaun early on.

The government wrote to Georg, Baron of Firmian. We have made you aware a number of times in the past, that the older man, Prew, who has died in the meantime, belonged to the Lutheran sect and was of no use as the crown administrator of Gufidaun. His son is also not suited for this office. Forbidden tracts and books have been found in the possession of the son-in-law of the elder Prew. The results of all this have now come to light.... namely, we have been informed by the bishop's officials in Brixen that just a few days ago in the above named district of Gufidaun, at Theis or in Villnöss, up to 150 Anabaptists, both men and women,[46] were together in the hidden part of a cave and held the Lord's Supper there.

A month later, on October 30, 1531, it was reported that 40 to 50 persons had been together in a pit.[47] Again, the report did not come from the crown administrator, but from others. The king was not pleased with the state of affairs in Gufidaun.

Earlier, on August 25, 1531, the judge, Jacob Hupher, in South Tirol, was directed to arrest five Anabaptists who had been discovered meeting in a cave in the district of Leifers south of Bozen.[48] And the year before, (see January 6, 1530) Anabaptists were found hiding in a cave under a house.

October 18, 1531, Anabaptist Woman Minted Coins in Hall

The government in Innsbruck informed the judge in the city of Hall, east of Innsbruck, as follows.

They have heard that a woman coinmaker (employed at the mint in Hall), named the Waltzenpergerin is tainted with Anabaptism. She accepted it in the home of (the Anabaptist martyr) Andre Moser who was burned at the stake. The judge should summon her to court. If it is true that she was re-baptized, she should be arrested. If she denies this, she should still be asked if she went to confession and took the sacrament during the Easter season. Her confession is to be confirmed by the priest responsible for her. If she is not telling the truth she should be imprisoned.

November 16, 1531, Father Petitions On Behalf of Martyred Daughter's Children

In the district of Völs, Barbara Lercher and another young woman, Ursula Schmid (see the Appendix) had been condemned to death a year earlier, on November 14, 1530. Ursula was not married but Barbara was and had children.

Now, in 1531, *Hans Lercher submitted a petition to the (barons who ruled Völs) for the children of his daughter who was martyred as an Anabaptist. Up until now he has taken care of these poor orphans. But he does not know how he will continue caring for them. Barbara's property, as has happened in many other cases where Anabaptists were executed, was taken by the authorities. In this particular case, out of mercy, the territorial ruler wants to make Barbara's property available for the support of the orphans. Therefore, Barbara's property,[49] which the father of the baron of Völs confiscated, shall be given to Lercher, after the costs for her execution have been deducted.*

December 22, 1531, Anabaptism Was Not Being Eradicated
Ferdinand I wrote from Innsbruck to Hans Gräfinger, the territorial judge of Sterzing. *It has been reported to the king that in the valleys of the district and especially in Ridnaun, crowds of Anabaptists are coming together, listening to sermons and meeting so openly that surely the judge must know about this. The king expresses his disapproval that the judge is doing nothing to eradicate the Anabaptists. The king commands the judge to hunt them down, since now during the winter they cannot escape over the mountains. They should be captured and punished in accordance with the decrees. The expenses of the court will be paid for by the royal treasury whereas the Anabaptists' properties and goods become the possession of the king.*

This is the final document in these court records. Indications are that women would have been present at these meetings as well as men.[50] In the middle of winter the focus of activity for people in Tirol was in the valleys. The sympathetic attitude of this judge negated any advantage there might have been in capturing Anabaptist peasant farmers during the winter when travel over the snow-covered mountains made an escape to Moravia very difficult if not impossible.

Notes
1. TA 1972, 442, document 638.
2. Mecenseffy, "Anabaptists in Kitzbühel," 109, 110.
3. This teaching, "we must leave wife and children," was also mentioned in verse 6 of the hymn by Anna (Dorothea) Malerin and Ursula (Anna) Ochsentreiberin. See Huebert Hecht, "Wives, Female Leaders and Two Female Martyrs from Hall," in *Profiles of Anabaptist Women*, 192.
4. TA 1972, 471, document 688.
5. TA 1972, 478, document 700.
6. TA 1972, 483, document 711.
7. Schmelzer, "Elisabeth von Wolkenstein," in *Profiles of Anabaptist Women*, 168. See n. 20.
8. Schmelzer, "Elisabeth von Wolkenstein," in *Profiles of Anabaptist Women*, 175.
9. TA 1972, 497:13-23 and *Hutterite Beginnings*, 183.
10. The record states: "haufenweis zusammenliefen." TA 1972, 502:5.
11. These women are designated in the index as n.n.449 women in Gschäll house. TA 1972, 449:25f.

12. TA 1972, 455:14-15.
13. For Peter Schneider and Valtein Schuster see also TA 1972, 453:24-454:17; 455:7f.
14. The right to use their property was called "Baurecht." TA 1972, 464:33.
15. TA 1972, 472:27-473:5.
16. They are designated in the index as n.n.472a and b, women drowned. TA 1972, 471:6; 472:16. There may have been more than two women in this group, the evidence is not clear.
17. They are designated in the index as n.n.472a and b, wives who fled.
18. They are designated in the index as n.n.474 a and b.
19. See TA 1972, 474:9; 475:30-33; 476:1-2; 481:12, 19.
20. This account of her Anabaptist involvements is based on Matthias Schmelzer, "Elisabeth von Wolkenstein of Uttenheim," trans. by Linda A. Huebert Hecht in *Profiles of Anabaptist Women*, 164-177. See there 164 and 165 for references to her family. For his detailed discussion of Elisabeth's life, Dr. Schmelzer used original, archival documents, many of which are only summarized in TA 1972. As in the case of Helena von Freyberg, the prefix "von" indicates Elisabeth's noble status.
21. Schmelzer, "Elisabeth von Wolkenstein," in *Profiles of Anabaptist Women*, 166 and TA 1972, 4-6, document 6.
22. Schmelzer, "Elisabeth von Wolkenstein," in *Profiles of Anabaptist Women*, 166.
23. *Ibid.*, 167. Elisabeth's cook testified about these meetings. In her fourth statement she said, "Zum vierten hab der Jacob Hutter vil zeit sein von- und zugang by irer frauwen gehabt." TA 1983, 219:30-31.
24. Schmelzer, "Elisabeth von Wolkenstein," in *Profiles of Anabaptist Women*, 167.
25. *Ibid.*, 167-68.
26. It is Schmelzer's view that she was active in Anabaptism for seven years. *Ibid.*, 168.
27. *Ibid.*, 169.
28. *Ibid.* and TA 1983, 231, document 268.
29. TA 1983, 205:20-25.
30. Translated in Schmelzer, "Elisabeth von Wolkenstein," in *Profiles of Anabaptist Women*, 169-70 from TA 1983, 205:30-206:13.
31. Schmelzer, "Elisabeth von Wolkenstein," in *Profiles of Anabaptist Women*, 170; TA 1983, 220:23-31.
32. *Ibid.*
33. *Ibid.*, 171; TA 1983, 224, document 261.
34. Schmelzer, "Elisabeth von Wolkenstein," in *Profiles of Anabaptist Women*, 171.
35. *Ibid.*
36. Schmelzer, "Elisabeth von Wolkenstein," in *Profiles of Anabaptist Women*, 172; TA 1983, 249:10-14.
37. Schmelzer, "Elisabeth von Wolkenstein," in *Profiles of Anabaptist Women*, 172.
38. Translated in Schmelzer, "Elisabeth von Wolkenstein," in *Profiles of Anabaptist Women*, 172-73 from TA 1983, 250:23-25, 31-34; 251:10-11.

39. Transcribed form the original document by Schmelzer and translated in Schmelzer, "Elisabeth von Wolkenstein," in *Profiles of Anabaptist Women*, 173.
40. TA 1983, 258:3-9.
41. In TA 1983, 264, document 324 the request of her son Sigmund is rejected on the basis that his mother had already recanted and that Helena von Freyberg would be recanting.
42. Translated in Schmelzer, "Elisabeth von Wolkenstein," in *Profiles of Anabaptist Women*, 174 from TA 1983, 255:19-24.
43. TA 1983, 93:3-6.
44. TA 1972, 497:13-14.
45. TA 1972, 81:1; 39-40; 42 regarding Mairhofer and Müllner. For more information about these two men see *Hutterite Beginnings*, 177, 181, 183, 206-208.
46. One entry represents these women. They are designated in the index as n.n.498, women at cave meeting. TA 1972, 498:8-18.
47. The Anabaptists had gathered in "einem Loch." TA 1972, 500:15-16.
48. TA 1972, 492:25-26.
49. Her property is called a "Gut" which could indicate it was a larger piece of land.
50. The women are represented by n.n.502, women in Sterzing, and designated as such in the index.

Epilogue

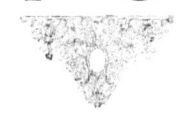

"In Matthew ten it is declared
Home and child we must forsake
When God's honour is at stake"

So wrote the Lutheran noblewoman Argula von Grumbach in Ingolstadt, Germany in 1523 responding to a critique of her defense of Lutheranism.[1] Her words express the sentiments and actions of Anabaptist women in the Austrian territory of Tirol between 1527 and 1531. We have always known that women were present in the Reformation and in the Anabaptist movement, but how many there were and what they actually said and did has been left out in our discussions. What religious choices did women make? And why were so many women involved in Anabaptism in the beginning? These are the questions this book has attempted to answer, for those interested in their own religious history, for those interested in the history of religious women and for those studying the Reformation. Through the eyes of Grete Mecenseffy, the Austrian historian who carefully summarized so many court records from the archives of Tirol in her 1972 volume, the stories of women who made crucial decisions have come to light. Their numbers are astounding – over four hundred are mentioned in the 1972 records alone – and their stories are moving. We can learn much by focusing on the experiences of women in this time period. Their stories provide another building block in the history of Christian women.

Women's Activities and Treatment in Anabaptist Tirol

Acting alone or together with other family and household members, women chose to be baptized as adults on the confession of their faith, knowing full well that in this public expression of their Christian experience they were breaking the law. The first "Anabaptist mandate" of August 1527 condemned members of both sexes for such action. The following paragraphs highlight aspects of Anabaptist beginnings in Tirol.

During the first five years of its development in Tirol, women played a major role in Anabaptism in their social positions as wives, mothers, daughters, sisters, widows and single women. While the majority of the women who became Anabaptist members were believers, a small number acted as lay missionaries and lay leaders in the informal environment of the developing movement. The women formed the backbone of the movement comprising forty-six percent or nearly half of the total Anabaptist membership in its first three years (1527 to 1529) with a total of 77 women martyrs in the five year period, 1527 to 1531. In 1528, Anabaptist women were among the first rank and file Anabaptist martyrs in Tirol. In her recent survey of the research on women in Anabaptist and Spiritualist groups, Sigrun Haude states regarding the proportion of women, "… the trend in scholarship is moving toward a substantial increase in our estimates of women's numerical share in the movements."[2] The number of Anabaptist women in the 1972 court records supports her conclusion.

From the beginning, the goal of Archduke Ferdinand I, ruler of the Habsburg territory of Tirol, was to root out and eradicate this new sect called Anabaptism which he viewed as heretical and a threat to the traditional, established Christian church. Between August 1527 and April 1534 he passed eleven decrees to that end. When he realized in 1528 that the initial decrees were not deterring people from becoming Anabaptists, he offered those guilty only of baptism an opportunity to recant and receive a pardon. This period of grace lasted until the end of April of that year. Anabaptist numbers reached a peak in 1529 with 116 arrests of women in that one year alone[3] and 41 female martyrs, the highest number since 1527 and the most in any one of the five years between 1527 and 1531. Ten of these women were martyred in one day in the mass execution of 17 Anabaptists that took place in the town of Rattenberg in May 1529.

The years 1528 and 1529 were also a high point in women's leadership activities. While one woman proudly "made six new Christians in a short time" other women proselytized in their extended family and others joined their family members as itinerant leaders. The evidence is not clear as to whether women were baptizers, but statements regarding women's preaching are documented in the Austrian court records. Overall, 21 women were active as lay missionaries and lay leaders between 1527 and 1531, including two women from the upper classes. These female leaders strengthened the growing Anabaptist movement.

The high number of arrests and executions during 1528 and 1529 called for a change in the way Anabaptists were treated. More often now, the local officials were instructed to focus on re-educating the Anabaptist prisoners so that they would leave their "devious ways" and come back to the traditional church. The local officials were told to send only "knowledgeable" and "competent" priests to instruct them. These Anabaptist peasant and artisan men and women may have been largely illiterate, but, they could ably defend their faith. In some cases the instruction brought success for the government, in other cases it did not. Pregnant women, in most cases, were allowed to go free until they had given birth.

By 1529 then, the peak year of arrests and executions, Anabaptism was rooted and growing in Tirol. However, if they were to survive individually and as a group some means would have to be found for the Anabaptists to do so. Jacob Hutter found one answer for them. He began leading them out of Tirol to the neighbouring territory of Moravia where the rulers were more tolerant. When Anabaptists were martyred or fled, their properties were confiscated by the government, appraised and where necessary, sold. These financial records reveal that, contrary to traditional assumptions, the majority of the peasant farmers living in Tirol were not poor. Indeed, more than two-thirds of them or seventy-two percent had owned property and goods valued at more than 50 Gulden. Some of their farms sold for over 1000 Gulden.

As the persecution continued into 1531, more and more Anabaptist women and their families sought refuge in Moravia. The government succeeded in eliminating some Anabaptists, but not all. The women and men who chose the communal life of the Anabaptist colonies in Moravia formed a core of believers whose descendants maintain the Hutterite way of life in North America to this day. The Hutterian Brethren are "the only communal Anabaptist group in all of Europe that was able to survive as an identifiable group, and the only identifiable group to survive the sixteenth century from the original South German/Austrian Anabaptist movement."[4]

What motivated Women's Actions, Why did they do it

When her interrogators told her she spoke with "a proud spirit" Elisabeth Dirks of Friesland responded, "No, my lords, I speak with free courage."[5] Elisabeth expressed what many Anabaptist women probably felt but did not say. The Anabaptist court records of Austria are silent about women's motives for their participation in Anabaptism as believers, leaders or martyrs. The authorities were interested mainly in the names of the fellow believers and the religious beliefs of their captives. There is no record in Austria that includes an assertion like that which Elisabeth Dirks made to her captors when she said, "… I have not been re-baptized. I have been baptized once upon my faith, for it is written that baptism belongs to believers," (Mark 16:15-16).[6] From this early time period in Tirol there is good evidence that women proselytized but, due to the nature of the sources that have survived, there is "very little evidence that sheds light on their spiritual calling."[7]

Despite the lack of specific references to their motives, a number of factors likely affected women in their thinking, their choices and their actions in Tirol. As mentioned earlier, a number of historians have expressed the view that in the unstructured and open beginning years of a new religious movement everyone is needed in order for it to survive and succeed. The Anabaptist focus on the New Testament which emphasized the spiritual equality of all Christians and the fact that Anabaptism was a persecuted community in which all members were needed regardless of gender or class, affected the participation of women.[8] Also, in the first phase, the opportunity for personal initiative and charismatic leadership attracted many followers, especially women. In 1922 Max Weber discussed this classic hypothesis, that women are more visible in the early phase of a religious movement. His wife Marianne Weber, however, provides a clue about women's motives.

In 1914 Marianne Weber wrote an essay discussing the modern marriage ideal and the legal position of women. The age-old Christian command to women, "Your will shall be subordinate to your husband's and he shall be your lord" had a religious basis and was affirmed by the Apostles. She explained how this became the moral and legal obligation which regulated the lives of married women both in and outside the home and restricted their independent thinking. "But," says Marianne, "we cannot emphasize enough, that the modern ideal of marriage is likewise deeply rooted in religion. The oldest sanction of it is in the illustrious Christian message of the religious equality of men and women and 'the glorious freedom of the children of God.'" The imperative to "obey God more than human beings," originating in the Reformation, affirmed the freedom of conscience as the right of each individual. This gave religious legitimacy to the moral and legal responsibility of women to answer for themselves.[9] It is notable that Marianne Weber's affirmation of religious decision making for married women stems from the Reformation. As science was substituted for religion as the key authority for seventeenth and eighteenth century educated Europeans, "those advocating greater opportunities for women had to find a new basis for their arguments, because spiritual equality based on Christian teachings was no longer seen as a strong enough foundation."[10] For Marianne Weber, however, the Christian foundation still held fast in 1914. Her views on women and religion are substantiated in the Anabaptist Reformation of Austria in the experiences of women, where the decision for adult baptism on confession of one's faith was an individual choice.

Several historians writing in the 1980s add other dimensions to the possible motivations of sixteenth century Anabaptist women. Retha Warnicke concludes in her discussion of the journal of a woman in Reformation England, Lady Mildmay, that, "she was able to use her religion to assert control over her life, even while accepting the subordinate gender role society deemed proper."[11] The same was true for Anabaptist women who, whether married or single, of high or low status, took control of their own religious lives and made personal choices of great consequence for themselves and their congregations. Jane Rendall, in discussing the evangelical religion of the nineteenth century states, "Undoubtedly, the individualistic act of conversion, the constant watchfulness which women, like men, had to keep over their own souls reasserted in a fundamental way the principle of religious equality, yet that was joined by a definition of the sphere of woman within religion."[12]

Words like "conversion" may not have been part of sixteenth century Anabaptist vocabulary. They spoke about yieldedness, the idea of "dying to self and rising in Christ" as well as about "rebirth."[13] But the idea of Christian freedom was certainly part of the thinking of the time. It is mentioned twice in the decree of April 1528 which sought to clarify and expand on Ferdinand's first decree of August 1527. The April decree discussed those who have been re-baptized, those who negate the holy sacrament and those who have joined the sect in which they think they have Christian freedom. If baptism is their only crime, the Anabaptists can be pardoned if they recant. However, this is not the case for leaders who have preached Christian freedom, leading the people astray. On the basis of this freedom which they assume to have, they have baptized others, destroying the sacrament of infant baptism as well as the holy sacrament by holding the Lord's Supper, as they call it, read the forbidden books and teachings to others and preached about having all things in common. Such persons should be burned at the stake and their property confiscated.[14] Clearly, Anabaptist women and men were making personal and individual decisions about their spiritual lives and their souls regarding baptism and the sacrament. Their actions show that they "exercised their freedom of religious choice."[15]

One other factor is important in the actions of Anabaptist women. Merry Wiesner states, "It is only in the religious sense that the word 'free' is applied to women in the Renaissance." And we could add, in the Reformation. For women of this time period says Wiesner, freedom meant "the ability to participate in public life." The general trend in the sixteenth century was to restrict the activities of women. However, some women ignored the limitations between public and private spheres as they had been defined by men. Wiesner emphasizes that divine inspiration is what gave women the freedom to speak out on religious matters and to act in the public sphere.[16] Her explanation is fundamental in explaining the actions of women in the Anabaptist movement. Believers in Tirol greeted each other with the words, "The Holy Spirit live in you!" The Holy Spirit lived in the heart and soul of each believer, whether woman or man, literate or illiterate. Anabaptism then, was radical in giving women new freedom and a widened horizon of personal choice.[17] It allowed women to speak and act, in the words of Elisabeth Dirks, with "free courage."

How Anabaptism Continued

The Austrian territory of Tirol was different from other regions in that it was "one of the strongest centres of Anabaptism during the sixteenth century…."[18] Anabaptists continued to be pursued in Tirol throughout the sixteenth century. The persecution was very severe until 1533 and after 1539 only a few Anabaptists were martyred.[19] But, "Even after ten years of vicious official suppression, many commoners refused to cooperate with the authorities in hunting the heretics."[20] On October 17, 1539 officials of the prince bishop in Brixen reported that the people were still supporting the Anabaptists,

> giving them food and drink, permitting them to come and go from their houses and not notifying the authorities of their whereabouts. When the authorities learn of an Anabaptist meeting, they cannot count on the help or support of the subjects to raid the meeting and imprison them. Even if some do go along, they will not lay a hand on them. People permit the Anabaptists to run to and fro in the forests near (where they live), claiming not to have seen any. They even warn them of possible raids.[21]

Furthermore, "those who are executed are happy and willing to die. They die for (the sake of) justice and righteousness and for the Word of God.[22] The last known execution of Anabaptists in Tirol, took place in 1618 in Au, in the same location as where the local blacksmith's wife had preached in July 1530. In 1618, a wealthy farmer and a widow, who had decided to emigrate to Moravia, were put to death by the sword in Au.[23]

Although the number of executions decreased over time, the number of persons joining the Anabaptist movement did not. While numerical strength does not tell the whole story, the findings of Claus-Peter Clasen, who surveyed so many Anabaptist records, are noteworthy. He found that between 1525 and 1529 the number of persons baptized in Tirol was 455. Anabaptist membership doubled in the next twenty years, between 1530 and 1549, when the total number of women and men who joined was

1,178. Following that, between 1550 and 1618, Clasen found only 379 Anabaptist members. Mecenseffy's third volume of court records for Tirol published in 1983 includes documents for a thirty-two year time period, 1532 to 1564. During these years the proportion of women who became members dropped to twenty-nine percent, a much lower percentage than were involved in the first years.[24] These figures confirm that there were more women involved in Anabaptism in the beginning years.

Many Anabaptists chose to become refugees and risk the journey to Moravia where their religion was tolerated, at least for a time. From 1530 until the early 1600s, an average of one hundred Anabaptists, men, women and children, came to Moravia annually from middle and southern Germany, Switzerland and the Austrian territories.[25] Several Anabaptist groups established settlements in Moravia. The Gabrielites were from Silesia, the Philipites from the Palatinate, Rhine and Neckar Valleys of Germany and the Austerlitz Brethren from Tirol. In January 1531 the group from Austerlitz, people mostly originating from North Tirol, moved to Auspitz and Schützinger became their leader. They were joined by many newcomers from the Puster Valley of South Tirol. Known as Pusterers, they "formed the backbone of these newcomers, and their undisputed leader was Jacob Hutter."[26]

"After almost yearly visits since 1529 and after sending numerous converts to Moravia, (Jacob) Hutter arrived in Auspitz on Monday, August 11, 1533."[27] A crisis developed when Hutter began teaching that true community involved totally giving over one's possessions to the community.[28] Simon and Barabara Schützinger were among those in Auspitz who kept back some of their property. The discovery that the Schützingers had hidden 40 Gulden led to the establishment of Jacob Hutter as the leader and to "a strict and legislated community of goods in the Auspitz community under Hutter, which has characterized the Hutterian fellowship ever since."[29] Werner Packull provides a full account of these events. Among other things, he describes the newly forming communities in Moravia clearly as a "human enterprise ... susceptible to human weaknesses...." At the same time, says Packull, the crisis reveals "the intensity of commitment that motivated participants" in this first generation.[30] Hutter's followers, the Hutterites eventually became the largest group of Anabaptists in Moravia.[31]

In 1535, the same year that Jacob Hutter married Katharina Purst, the rulers of Moravia expelled the Anabaptists for a time. This intolerance resulted from the events in northern Germany in the city of Münster. Jacob and Katharina returned to Tirol only to be captured. Hutter was burned at the stake in Innsbruck in 1536 and his young wife was martyred two years later. Hans Amon took over the leadership and began a time of proselytizing, sending out missioners in pairs to various parts of Europe, among them Peter Riedemann a future Hutterite leader. In Moravia the Hutterites enjoyed a "Good Period" from 1554 to 1565 and even a "Golden Age" from 1565 to 1578.[32]

The observations of a Roman Catholic traveller visiting the Hutterites in the mid-seventeenth century, give a glimpse into the life of women in this later time period.

> Nowhere did I see men and women together but everywhere each sex was performing its own work apart from the others. I found rooms in which there were only nursing mothers, who, without the supervision of men, were abundantly supplied, together with their infant children, with the necessary attention by their sisters. The duty of caring for the nursing mothers and children was committed to the widows alone. Elsewhere I saw over a hundred women with distaffs. One was a washerwoman, another a bed-maker, a third a stable-maid, a fourth a dish-washer, a fifth a linen maid, and so all the others had a particular work to do. And just as the duties were systematically assigned to the women, so each one of the men and youths knew his business....[33]

One important area of work open to women was education.

The children were raised apart from their parents. "In the little school the younger children (two years and over) were taught and looked after by certain sisters…. In the big school the older children were brought up more strictly … by the schoolmasters." The brothers responsible for the school worked together with the sisters to look after the children "and their needs in all areas."[34] The Hutterite leader Peter Walpot suggested, however, that schoolmasters be present to aid and advise the sisters.[35] The curriculum was basic, consisting primarily of learning the three Rs and for the boys, a trade. Songs were a key part of their learning. "…Hutterites had universal education in the sixteenth century when a large part of the rest of the world remained illiterate."[36]

Between 1578 and 1619 there followed a time characterized by ambivalence, when individualism and the personal good threatened the communitarian ideal.[37] This period was cut off when the long period of tolerance ended in 1622 during the Thirty Years' War and the Hutterites were forced to leave Moravia. At that time the majority of the remaining 25,000 Hutterites reconverted to Catholicism but 10,000 resettled to Oberungarn, today eastern Slovakia, and Siebenbürgen in Transylvania. They were invited to Siebenbürgen by the Calvinist ruler who sought them out as good workers. By 1756 this group had declined to 30 or 40 people when a group of Protestants exiled there, converted to the Hutterite faith and community of goods was reinstated. The Hutterites had been forbidden to do mission work and the Jesuits sent out by Maria Theresa brought many back to the Catholic faith. In 1767 the Hutterites moved eastward once more, across the Carpathian Mountains to the region of Walachei in Romania.

As the result of another Turkish war the Hutterites were uprooted in 1770 and found refuge near Kiev, Ukraine on the estate of a Russian general where they lived until 1802. When their privileges there were in doubt the group moved 10 miles north onto Czarist land in Radichev. In 1842, after internal conflicts, about 50 Hutterite families moved to the Molochna settlement of the southern Ukraine, aided by the Mennonites, Anabaptists originating in the Netherlands, who lived there. The Mennonites had been invited to settle in the Ukraine by Catharine the Great in the eighteenth century. When the government policies of the 1870s threatened their privileges such as exemption from military service, the Mennonites and Hutterites sought new opportunities in North America.

The Bon Homme colony, near Yankton, South Dakota, USA, established in 1874, is the oldest Hutterite settlement in North America and still exists today. These Hutterites were named the "Schmiedeleut" after their leader who was a blacksmith ("Schmied") and a second group, followers of Darius Walter and known as "Dariusleut," established a second colony. A third group arrived in 1877 led by a teacher ("Lehrer") and were known as

"Lehrerleut." The "Prairieleut," a fourth group that came to South Dakota, did not practice community of goods and eventually gave up their Hutterite identity. The doctrines of all these groups were the same but they differed somewhat in practice. During World War I when their German background and belief in nonresistance made them suspicious and caused hardships, the Hutterites established the first colonies in southern Alberta and south, central Manitoba. Today over 40,000 Hutterites live in approximately 470 colonies in western Canada and the midwestern United States.[38] Despite all their crises and migrations, the Hutterites have survived to the present as the only group to retain and institutionalize the Jerusalem model of the church, "laying claim to the original communitarian vision."[39]

Identifying with the Anabaptist Experience

What was it like to flee one's home in the sixteenth century, to live as a refugee or to be a fugitive of the law? It would not have been easy, to say the least, to live in the forest or camp on an open field, dependent on one's neighbours for food and drink. Jacob Hutter and a group of his followers lived for a time in the open fields around the Neuhaus Castle at Gais, near Uttenheim, the residence of the Wolkensteins. This became their meeting place.[40] What was it like to start a new life far from one's home? What was it like to live this new life having all things in common with no private property? The example of Simon and Barabara Schützinger is a case in point. Not all the Anabaptists in Tirol had been poor before they left their homeland.

What other difficulties might there have been? What would it have been like for women who were pregnant at their arrest in Tirol or when they decided to flee? What was it like to have a baby while "on the run" or in a strange place. Erhardt Urscher's wife gave birth in the tavern to which the family had fled. In January 1533 Erhardt described these circumstances in his confession to the authorities of Sarnthein, in South Tirol. When his wife was in the last stages of her pregnancy and the authorities from Bozen came to their home to arrest two Anabaptist men who were staying with them, she was overcome with shock. She had not really known who these people were. Fearing the worst, she tried to persuade her husband to flee; his response was that they were safest at home. Where should they go? She appealed to her husband a second time and finally they both fled. When she could go no further Erhardt asked for help and a fellow believer recommended a tavern to them, one mile from Brixen, where Anabaptists were welcome. The child was born but not baptized and the family remained at the tavern for eight days. Following that, Erhardt found shelter for his wife and children in the mountains in an alm hut. Later they returned to the tavern and lived there for a time.[41] Their story goes on. Suffice it to say, those who cared for Erhardt's wife at the tavern would have been strangers to her but they came to her aid nevertheless.

Other Anabaptist birth mothers also received care in unusual ways. When the wife of Hans Mair Paulle was about to give birth, Elisabeth von Wolkenstein invited her into her home at Uttenheim. It was a more secure environment than the nearby forests where this pregnant woman had been living with fellow Anabaptists. In 1530 in the district of Rattenberg, the 100 year old mother in the Nickinger family had remained behind to care for her son and daughter-in-law's child, not yet 24 months old. Now she was attending two women who had just given birth.

The women and men who chose to renounce their faith in order to be reinstated in the church had to deal with other issues. What was it like to recant your new faith in front of family and friends from the church pulpit? Mecenseffy empathized with their situation.

> Concerning the relapse to Anabaptism, it should be said that their conduct can be understood when one considers that the decision to accept the sign (baptism) meant a radical inner change – it can be called conversion – and that membership in the brotherhood meant unreserved submission to the Lord Jesus Christ. If the authorities succeeded – by prison, rack, trials, and efforts at conversion – in breaking a person's will and making them recant, he was soon seized by severe qualms of conscience for having betrayed his Lord and Master. Anabaptists were unable to withstand these tortures of conscience, and they returned to their brethren and sisters in spite of the certainty of death if they were caught.[42]

It would not have been easy to confess one thing in public and believe another in private.

The words of Elizabeth Kampner, baptized by Jörg Blaurock in 1529 at Breitenberg, are recorded in *The Chronicle of the Hutterian Brethren*. She talked to her interrogators about suffering. They wanted to know what she believed about Mary, the Mother of Jesus. She gave the following answer. "… Mary was a virgin and bore Christ our Savior. Mary and the saints had to suffer just as much as she and many others were suffering now, but she did not believe that Mary was a mediator, because all power in heaven and on earth is given to Christ alone."[43] Elizabeth Kampner remained steadfast and was martyred.

The Legacy of Anabaptist Women
In the generations following the sixteenth century persecution, the *Martyrs' Mirror*, the *Ausbund* of Anabaptist hymns and *The Chronicle of the Hutterian Brethren* among other texts, were written to remind those who followed of the suffering and the difficult times the believers had. Anabaptist martyrs "far outnumbered their Protestant and Catholic counterparts."[44] The rich written legacy of Anabaptist court records portrays the choices and actions of women who lived in their own time and place. What do the stories of Anabaptist women mean for us today? They speak of faith, courage and commitment. The faith of these women carried them through imprisonment and interrogation, for some through recantation and rejoining the movement and for some through martyrdom. Sixteenth century women and men were committed Christians making choices and acting, sometimes alone, sometimes together, interdependently, on a faith they had experienced. Their actions were above and beyond what was expected of women in that time period. The accounts of women in the Anabaptist court records of Austria illustrate that women were not just participants but active members in the establishment of the Christian church in the beginning years of Anabaptism.

In a sense, each of the Anabaptist women discussed in this book was a leader. As one writer wrote recently, "Even if we don't identify ourselves as leaders, there is an element of leadership in whatever we do in life." Whatever our position in family or society, "… we all have the ability to influence other people." This means that leadership is "often part of our reality and responsibility."⁴⁵ This broader definition of leadership was true for each of the Anabaptist women portrayed in the court records of Tirol during the Reformation. It is true also for their descendants in the faith living today in many different parts of the world and it will be true for the Anabaptist women of the future. It certainly describes the experience of Ursula Hellrigel from the Ötz Valley in Tirol. At seventeen years of age, in 1538, she was imprisoned in the St. Petersberg castle. She spent five years in prison and, following her release, lived out her life among the Hutterite Anabaptists in Moravia.⁴⁶ A verse from the hymn she wrote illustrates her faith and leadership.

> I do not doubt God's power.
> His judgements all are true.
> He will not abandon anyone
> Who stands firm in the faith,
> And stays on the true paths.⁴⁷

Notes

1. Translated in Bainton, *Women of the Reformation in Germany and Italy*, 104, cited in Wiesner, "Women's Defense of Their Public Role," 18-19. Argula was in prison twice for her outspoken anti-Catholic stance. Anderson and Zinsser, *A History of Their Own*, 246. The Anabaptist leader Balthasar Hubmair ranks Argula, a woman of his time with female prophets in the Bible, "But where the men are afraid and have become women, then the women should speak up and become manly, like Deborah, Hulda, Anna the prophetess, the four daughters of the evangelist Philip, and in our times Argula." H. Wayne Pipkin and John H. Yoder, eds. and trans., *Balthasar Hubmaier Theologian of Anabaptism* (Scottdale, PA: Herald Press, 1989), 56.
2. Haude, "Gender Roles and Perspectives," 444.
3. Huebert Hecht, "Faith and Action," 32.
4. C. Arnold Snyder, "Introduction," in Snyder, ed., *Sources of South German/Austrian Anabaptism, l.*
5. *Martyrs' Mirror*, 481-82 in Dyck, "Elisabeth and Hadewijk," in *Profiles of Anabaptist Women*, 361.
6. *Ibid.*
7. C. Arnold Snyder, "South German/Austrian Anabaptist Women," in *Profiles of Anabaptist Women*, 76.

8. These factors which Shahar discusses in relation to the Waldensians of Austria apply to the Anabaptists as well. See her book, *The Fourth Estate*, 256 and 258.
9. The passage in German reads as follows: "Wir können deshalb nicht oft genug klarstellen, dass das moderne Eheideal mit seinen tiefsten Wurzeln ebenfalls in das Religiöse hineingesenkt ist. Die erhabene christliche Botschaft religiöse Ebenbürtigkeit von Mann und Weib und die 'herrlichen Freiheit der Kinder Gottes' ist seine älteste Sanktion." Marianne Weber, "Eheideal und Eherecht," in *Frauenfragen und Frauengedanken Gesammelte Aufsätze* (Tübingen: Verlag von J. C. B. Mohr (Paul Siebeck), 1919), 144-145.
10. Merry E. Wiesner, *Women and Gender in Early Modern Europe* (New York, NY: Cambridge University Press, 1993), 29.
11. See Warnicke, "Lady Mildmay's Journal," 56, 68.
12. Jane Rendall, *The Origins of Modern Feminism: Women in Britain, France and the United States 1780-1860* (London: Macmillan Education, 1985), 74.
13. In Snyder, *Anabaptist History and Theology An Introduction*, 204, yieldedness or "Gelassenheit" is defined in this way by Melchior Hoffman and Hans Hut. See also, Helena von Freyberg and yieldedness in Chapter Two. References to, "individual spiritual rebirth" and "spiritual regeneration" are in C. Arnold Snyder, "Introduction," in Snyder, ed., *Sources of South German/Austrian Anabaptism* 1. Anabaptist use of the word "rebirth" is also in Snyder, *Anabaptist History and Theology An Introduction*, 87, 89, 218.
14. The record of April 1, 1528 includes the words, "der sect vermainter cristenlicher freyhait." TA 1972, 101:7-8, 38. See also April 2, 1528, TA 1972, 108: 29-36.
15. C. Arnold Snyder, "Introduction," in *Profiles of Anabaptist Women*, 8.
16. Wiesner, "Women's Defense of Their Public Role," 3, 21.
17. C. Arnold Snyder, "Introduction," in *Profiles of Anabaptist Women*, 12.
18. This was the view of 19th century Austrian historian Johann Loserth. See *Hutterite Beginnings*, 364, n. 8.
19. Heinz Moser, *Die Scharfrichter*, 23. This is confirmed in the list of names of all the male and female martyrs for each location in Tirol in Clasen, "Executions of Anabaptists, 136-151. Clasen states: "From 1529 through 1533, not fewer than 228 Anabaptists lost their lives in the Tirol according to precise evidence." His table of statistics gives the total number of martyrs for Tirol as 257 so that there were only 29 martyrs (257-228) in Tirol after 1533. *Ibid.*, 125
20. *Hutterite Beginnings*, 161.
21. TA 1983, 420:24-32.
22. TA 1983, 421:11-13.
23. Winkelbauer, "Die rechtliche Stellung der Täufer," 38-39. The last known execution of an Anabaptist in Europe was in 1626 on the upper Rhein. Hanspeter Jecker, "Die Hinrichtung einer Täuferin in Rheinfelden—die letzte im frühneuzeitlichen Europa?" in *Mennonitische Geschichtsblätter* 54 (1997), 76-88.

24. In the index for these records of January 11, 1532 to October 25, 1564, 177 women and 607 men are identified as Anabaptists, giving a percentage of 29.
25. Winkelbauer, "Die rechtliche Stellung der Täufer," 36.
26. *Hutterite Beginnings*, 235. Werner Packull suggests that the money and support which the Pusterers brought to Auspitz was one more reason for the schism of 1533.
27. *Hutterite Beginnings*, 225.
28. Snyder, *Anabaptist History and Theology An Introduction*, 241.
29. *Ibid.*, See the story of the Schützingers in March 30, 1528 and in "Introduction To The Records Of 1530."
30. *Hutterite Beginnings*, 234-35 in the chapter on the schisms of 1531 and 1533.
31. Astrid von Schlachta, "Die Geschichte der Täufer in Tirol ein Begleiter durch die Austellung," in von Schlachta, *Verbrannte Visionen?* 40.
32. See Leonard Gross, *The Golden Years of the Hutterites The Witness and Thought of the Communal Moravian Anabaptists during the Walpot Era 1565-1578*, Revised ed. (Kitchener, ON: Pandora Press, 1998); Werner O. Packull, Peter Riedemann: Shaper of the Hutterite Tradition (Kitchener, ON: Pandora Press, 2007).
33. These observations are from a novel by Hans Jakob Christoph Grimmelshausen, *Der Abenteuerliche Simplicissimus* published in 1669, cited in John Horsch, *The Hutterian Brethren A Story of Martyrdom and Loyalty 1528-1931* (republished: Cayley, Alberta: Macmillan Colony, 1985), 67. See also, Marlene Epp and H. Julia Roberts, "Women in the *Chronicle of the Hutterian Brethren,*" in *Profiles of Anabaptist Women*, 202-221.
34. *Chronicle of the Hutterian Brethren*, 405, 562, n. See also, Bodo Hildebrand, *Erziehung zur Gemeinschaft Geschichte und Gegenwart des Erziehungswesens der Hutterer* (Bamberg: Centaurus-Verlagsgesellschaft Pfaffenweiler, 1993), 33, 43 regarding duties of the "Schulmütter" (school mothers).
35. Snyder, *Anabaptist History and Theology An Introduction*, 261.
36. Helen Martens, "Women in the Hutterite Song Book (*Die Lieder der Hutterischen Brüder*)," in *Profiles of Anabaptist Women*, 236.
37. "Eigennutz und grundlegende Zweifel an der Gütergemeinschaft waren nicht zu unterdrücken. Drei allgemeine Prozesse, die den Wandel und die Veränderungen in der Struktur und Organization bedingten, sind innerhalb der Gemeinde zu beobacthen: Die Konfessionsbildung, die Institutionalisierung, und die Entstehung des spezifischen Norm- und Regelsystems." Astrid von Schlachta, *Hutterische Konfession und Tradition (1578-1619) Etabliertes Leben Zwischen Ordnung und Ambivalenz* (Mainz: Verlag Philipp Von Zabern, 2003), 395-96 as well as 117-121.
38. Astrid von Schlachta discusses the Hutterite migrations in, "Die Wanderungen," in von Schlachta, *Verbrannte Visionen?* 40-45. See also the map in Robert Friedmann, "Hutterite Brethren," in *Mennonite Encyclopedia* (Scottdale, PA: Herald Press, 1956), 858 and a newer discussion in Astrid von Schlachta, *Die Hutterer zwischen Tirol und Amerika Eine Reise durch*

die Jahrhunderte (Innsbruck: Universitätsverlag Wagner, 2006). Articles on the Hutterites are available on the website, *Global Anabaptist Mennonite Encyclopedia,* www.gameo.org.

39. *Hutterite Beginnings*, 11.
40. They had free access to the castle, owned by Elisabeth's son-in-law, Michael von Teutenhofen and his administrator at the castle, Erhard Zimmerman, supported the Anabaptists. Schmelzer, "Elisabeth von Wolkenstein," in *Profiles of Anabaptist Women*, 167 and TA 1983, 216.
41. TA 1983, 90. See March 2 and 17 and September 4, 1531 for the earlier part of their story.
42. Mecenseffy, "Anabaptists in Kitzbühel," 109. Brad Gregory mentions the "difficulty of enactment" and how for the Anabaptists, "fear often got the upper hand on faith," *Salvation at Stake*, 208.
43. *Chronicle of the Hutterian Brethren*, 73.
44. Gregory, *Salvation at Stake*, 198.
45. April Yamasaki, "Trust God's Leadership," in *Rejoice! Daily Devotional Readings, June, July, August 2008* (Winnipeg, MB: Kindred Productions, 2008), (Monday, June 16) 25. April Yamasaki is the pastor of the Emmanuel Mennonite Church in Abbotsford, British Columbia.
46. C. Arnold Snyder and Linda A. Huebert Hecht, "Ursula Hellrigel of the Ötz Valley and Annelein of Freiburg" in *Profiles of Anabaptist Women*, 195, 197-98.
47. *Ibid.*, 199-201. This hymn was translated in *Profiles of Anabaptist Women* by Pamela Klassen. For some reason that remains unknown, Ursula's hymn from the *Ausbund* was attributed to Annelein of Freiburg and accompanies the account of Annelein's martyr death in the *Martyrs' Mirror*. Both women were Anabaptist prisoners but one, Ursula, was eventually released. See the Appendix for the complete hymn.

Illustrations

1. Women in Swiss costume in the 1531 *Froschauer Bible*, printed in Zurich.

2. Martyrdom of Jephthah, Judges XI.
A ceramic tile from a richly illustrated stove of 1532 by the leading Renaissance artist in South Tirol, and first Anabaptist artist, Bartlmä Dill Riemenschneider.

3. Bartlmä Dill Riemenschneider, leading Renaissance artist in South Tirol was the first Anabaptist artist. This painting, "Kreuzigungstafel" of 1533 (191 x 170 cm.), included many women and a self-portrait. Dill, the bearded man at right wearing a green velvet hat, thinks he is Nicodemus and points out his monogram to the Roman soldier who is seated.

4. Rattenberg Castle, fresco by Matthäus Günther, 1737.

5. Rattenberg town and castle, adapted from sixteenth century sources.

6. Place of execution in Bozen, painted by the mayor, Martin Hörtmayr, 1541.

7. Late Gothic sandstone pulpit in the Bozen cathedral, 1514, by Hans Lutz von Schussenried. Anabaptists had to recant from the church pulpit.

8. The Freyberg family tree includes
Helena von Freyberg's Münichau crest, a monk.

9. Hohenaschau, the Freyberg Castle in Bavaria,
sketched by Philipp Apian, 1550.

10. A woman baking bread in the fifteenth century.

11. Pregnant woman on a birthing stool,
the midwife and assistant, in the midwives book,
Der Schwangeren Frawē und Hebammen Rosengarten 1529, Augsburg.

12. The birthing room, cover of the midwives' book, *Der Schwangeren Frawē und Hebammen Rosengarten 1529*, Augsburg.

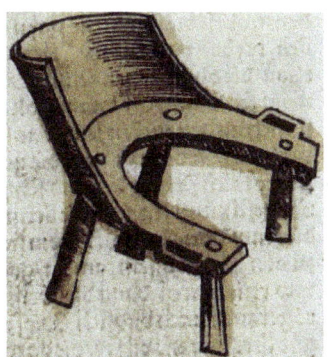

13. A birthing stool, in the midwives book, *Der Schwangeren Frawē und Hebammen Rosengarten 1529*, Augsburg.

14. Maid carrying a bowl, in a late Gothic altarpiece, "Geburt Mariens" by Rueland Frueauf the Younger, 1488.

15. Pröslhof, birthplace of Jacob and Agnes Hutter, in the hamlet of Moos, Puster Valley, South Tirol.

16. Sixteenth century handwriting, July 26, 1530 with bottom heading, "Müllner und Schmidin zu Au predig."

17. Butchering in Augsburg on the square in front of city hall, detail from "Augsburger Perlachplatzes im Winter" by Heinrich Vogtherr the Younger (?), 1540.

18. Seventeenth century farmhouse from the Ziller Valley in, *Museum Tiroler Bauernhöfe*, Kramsach, Austria.

19. Peasant farmer and his wife from the Puster Valley, South Tirol, 1550.

20. Mint tower of Hall in Tirol,
centre for commerce and salt mining where the first coins were struck in 1477.

21. Freundsberg Castle above Schwaz, mining centre in North Tirol.

22. Michelsburg Castle near Moos and St. Lorenzen, Puster Valley, South Tirol, former prison for many sixteenth century Anabaptists.

23. St. Petersberg Castle, west of Innsbruck, Austria, where Anabaptists were imprisoned.

24. Münichau Castle and the Kaiser Mountains, 1913, where Helena von Freyberg held Anabaptist meetings.

25. Pankraz von Freyberg (1508-1565) by Hans Muelich, 1545.

26. Farmer sowing, in the 1560 *Froschauer Bible*, Zurich.

27. Ursula of Essen is flogged at the pillory. She refused to name fellow believers and was burned to death in Maastricht, 1570.
Martyrs' Mirror, 1685.

28. The jailor and Felicitas, a young slave-girl in the early Christian Church in prison. She was executed in Carthage, North Africa, 202 or 203 three days after giving birth.
Martyrs' Mirror, 1685.*

29. Man and woman harvesting grain, from a fifteenth century manuscript owned by Ferdinand I in the 1520s.

30. Woman gives bread to a man, from a fifteenth century manuscript owned by Ferdinand I in the 1520s.

31. The Seventh Seal is opened, four trumpets sound and an angel announces "woe, woe, woe" to the inhabitants of the earth. Revelation, Chapter 8, by Hans Holbein the Younger in the *Froschauer Bible*, 1531.

32. The *Froschauer Bible* of 1560, printed in Zurich.

33. The city hall where Helena von Freyberg was interrogated, detail from "Augsburger Perlachplatzes im Winter," Heinrich Vogtherr the Younger (?)'s view of Augsburg society, 1540.

Illustration Credits

1. Conrad Grebel University College, Rare Book Collection.
2. Detail of majolica stove, 29 x 34 cm, Archivo Fotografico Castello del Buonconsiglio Monumenti e collezioni provinciali, with the consent of Castello del Buonconsiglio Monumenti e collezioni provinciali, Trento, Italy. Copying or reprinting of any kind is expressly prohibited.
3. Photographer, Ulrich Kneise, Eisenach, Germany, with the consent of Fürstlich Hohenzollernsche Sammlungen, Schloss Sigmaringen, Germany.
4. Alpbachtal Seenland Tourismus, Rattenberg, Austria.
5. Giovanni Merola, artist, photographer and graphic designer of Innsbruck, Austria.
6. Plan Sammlung, Stadtmuseum Bozen, Italy.
7. Stadtarchiv, Bozen, Italy
8. Hft. Hohenaschau A 22, Staatsarchiv München.
9. Tourist Information Aschau im Chiemgau.
10. Illustration in MS. 134, fol. 8/ CNRS-IRHT, the Bibliothèque Municipale, Angers, France.
11. Staats– und Stadtbibliothek, Ausgburg.
12. Staats– und Stadtbibliothek, Ausgburg.
13. Staats– und Stadtbibliothek, Ausgburg.
14. Photograph 7000216 of the Österreichische Akademie der Wissenschaften, Institut für Realienkunde, Krems, Austria.
16. Tiroler Landesarchiv, Innsbruck.
17. Painting Nr. 9930 of Heinrich Vogtherr the Younger (?), Kunstsammlungen Stadt Augsburg.
19. Südtiroler Landesmuseum für Volkskunde (South Tirol Museum of Folk Traditions), Dietenheim/Bruneck, Italy.
24. Dr. J. M. Eder, *Schloss Münichau bei Kitzbühel Tirol Seine Geschichte und Sein Verfall* (Wien: Aus der Kaiserlich-Königlichen Graphischen Lehr- und Versuchsanstalt, 1915), Tafel 1, Seite 17.
25. Staatliche Kunsthalle Karlsruhe, Germany.
26. Conrad Grebel University College, Rare Book Collection.
27. Etching of Jan Luyken in Thieleman J. van Braght, *Het Bloedigh Tooneel of Martelaers Spiegel der Doopsgesinde of Weereloose Christenen, Die om 't getuygenis van Jesus haren Salighmaker geleden*

hebben ende gedood zijn van Christi tijd of tot desen tijd toe. Den Tweeden Druk. Amsterdam: Hieronymus Sweerts, …, 1685: II. Mennonite Library and Archives, Bethel College, Kansas, USA.

28. Etching of Jan Luyken in Thieleman J. van Braght, *Het Bloedigh Tooneel of Martelaers Spiegel der Doopsgesinde of Weereloose Christenen, Die om 't getuygenis van Jesus haren Salighmaker geleden hebben ende gedood zijn van Christi tijd of tot desen tijd toe.* Den Tweeden Druk. Amsterdam: Hieronymus Sweerts, …, 1685: II. Mennonite Library and Archives, Bethel College, Kansas, USA. *Perpetua, with whom Felicitas was in prison, wrote their story in the oldest piece of Christian literature written by a woman. See, Mary T. Malone, *Women in Christianity Volume I: The First Thousand Years* (Ottawa: Novalis, 2000), 106.
29. *Tacuinum Sanitatis Manuscript*, NB 28.258-B (Cod. Ser. Nov. 2644, fol. 44r) Used with permission of Österreichische Nationalbibliothek, Bildarchiv, Wien, Österreich.
30. *Tacuinum Sanitatis Manuscript*, NB 1.001-B (Cod. Ser. Nov. 2644, fol. 64v). Used with permission of Österreichische Nationalbibliothek, Bildarchiv, Wien, Österreich.
31. Conrad Grebel University College, Rare Book Collection.
32. Conrad Grebel University College, Rare Book Collection.
33. Painting Nr. 9930 of Heinrich Vogtherr the Younger (?) Kunstsammlungen Stadt Augsburg.

Photographs by Linda A. Huebert Hecht – 15, 18, 20, 21, 22, 23.

Appendix I

1. Sample Interrogation Questions, May 12, 1530, the Jörg Schmid Household

2. October-November 1530, The Value of the Nickinger Property, More Details

3. October 31, 1530, The Possessions of the Former Judge and His Wife, Inventory

4. Abbreviations and Values for Sixteenth Century Money, Wages, Prices

5. Hymn of Dorothea/Anna Malerin and Anna/Ursula Ochsentreiberin

6. Hymn of Ursula Hellrigel of the Ötz Valley and Annelein of Freiberg

7. Helena von Freyberg, "Confession (as follows) on Account of Her Sin," 1540s

1. May 12, 1530, List of Questions for Jörg Schmid, His Wife, Daughter, Labourer

Part A : The Innsbruck government instructed Peter Praunegger, territorial judge of Sonnenburg to take over from the judge of Ambras who captured the Anabaptists imprisoned in Ellenbögen, namely, Jörg Schmid, his wife, his daughter Ursula and his labourer. They were to be transferred to the castle of Vellenberg and questioned on the following matters: where the three leaders whom they named were staying, how they were dressed, what they looked like, by what signs they could be recognized, and what persons they had baptized in Ambras and the neighbouring districts. If the prisoners would not give this information, torture was to be used. If they showed genuine remorse, they could be pardoned.

Part B: *Questions which were asked of Schmid and his wife:*
... who brought them into the Anabaptist sect, who baptized them and when, also where and in whose presence it occurred.

What they believed about infant baptism, the holy sacrament of the altar and the intercession of saints since they had become part of the sect and whether they still believed this.

If they carried out their Christian practice of going to confession and taking the holy sacrament recently during Easter and if so where.

Where they had stayed since joining the Anabaptists and who had given them refuge.

Which persons, both women and men, in this city and the surrounding region were part of their sect and had been rebaptized.

If they wanted to desist from the sect, were remorseful and wanted to do penance.

2. October-November 1530, The Value of the Nickinger Property, More Details

Located on the property were: 2 cows, each worth 4 G for a total of 8 G, an old horse with a colt, appraised at 4 G, all of which had been sold through the territorial judge for 5 G. Ernst Pranndt handled this matter, received this money and would settle the account. Also, there was a pig, worth 1 G, and all the household goods, bed linens, chests, dishes, kettles, pans, all sorts of fruit and measuring utensils, were appraised at 6 G 24 Kr. This Michel Rauch had sold for 5 G and settled the account. Also, there were: 69 stär (a 20-30 liter measure) of oats, 1 stär appraised at 12 Kr for a total of 13 G 48 Kr, which Ernst Pranndt had received and would settle the account; 29 stär rye, 1 stär appraised at 24 Kr for a total of 11 G 63 Kr; 2 stär wheat, 1 stär appraised at 30 Kr for a total of 1 G; 34 lb butter, 1 lb appraised at 12 G for a total of 1 G 21 Kr 3 Vr, also received by Ernst Pranndt who would settle the account. Also present were 7 young cows which Balthasar Nickinger had sold to two farmers in Stanns, but which Ernst Pranndt, the present territorial judge (had taken) and sold for 28 G. The hay and straw, 10 cart-loads, was appraised at 6 G and was left there for Lorentzen Mylbacher who bought the property.

3. October 31, 1530, The Possessions of the Former Judge and His Wife, Inventory

The following list is the inventory of what Hanns Obinger, ... his wife Ursula and their two children - who accompanied him when he secretly left the territory (of Tirol) .... - left behind in their house.

Appendix

First of all (there were): a trough containing husked grain and linseed, an old empty trough, 2 old vats with a bit of flour in them, a pair of horseshoes, 2 harnesses, a pair of boots, 20 to 30 litres (1 stär) of millet in a vat, 7 sickles, a grain bin containing 12 (stär) of iron rings and other old vats. In the basement there were: a bench and several wooden bowls.

In the kitchen there were: 6 husking bowls, …, 2 three-footed iron stands, a hook and chain for hanging vessels above the stove, a measuring container, a grater, 3 chopping utensils, a notched agricultural tool, a barrel and a carrying basket, 13 wooden lids, 3 water containers, 3 ladles, a honey pot, 3 empty containers for cottage cheese, a salt barrel, a pointed saw, 3 hoes, a small wagon, an auger, a flat hoe, a wooden hoe, a scythe, 2 wooden containers for whetstones, 4 whetstones, a flint, a carrying bowl, a spoon for frying, a frying pan, 3 pots, a tub for mixing, an iron spool, 2 rakes, 5 small chests and a milk pail. Also, there were: an instrument for patching, a tool for gathering hay, an iron shovel, a husking fork, 3 tools for working flax, 2 winches, 3 stands for hay, a grinding tool, a whetstone, a weaving tool, a post and weaving bench, 3 cutting benches, a bench for shredding or carving, 10 bundles of raw (unspun) flax, a table, a (large) chest, a small chest, 2 bedsteads, 1 spear, 2 honey pots, 2 harnesses, a meat cleaver, a plane and an anvil to sharpen the scythe.

In the storage room there were: a good chest, a small chest, a cradle, a carpenter's clamp, a grain tool, a grating iron, a wooden frame for bread, an old vat, 2 iron wagons, 2 plows, 2 harrows, 2 cows, a calf, 5 hens, a rooster, hay and straw as needed by such a farm, 3 beehives, 2 large wooden vats, one full of cabbage, 2 benches (for sitting), a chair, a table against the wall, a bread trough, 3 distaffs, a water barrel, 4 cabbage knives, 2 cabbage shovels, and a box with letters including 9 letters with seals.

This inventory was completed October 30 with the help of the chaplain of Breitenbach (and four other men) … all from the district of Rattenberg….

4. Abbreviations and Values for Sixteenth Century Money, Wages, Prices

G Gulden, Pd Pounds, Kr Kreuzer, Vr Vierer.
1 G = 60 Kr or 5 Pd, 1 Kr = 5 Vierer, 1 Pd = 12 Kr, 1 Vierer = 4 (Berner) pennies.
1 Gulden (fl. = Florentiner coin) = 60 Kreuzer[1]

Wages in the early 1500s
Bricklayer – 9 Kr per day (in 1526); annual salary 46.8 G (6 days/week)
Bricklayer's journeyman – 6 Kr per day
Carpenter – 10.20 Kr per day (in 1526); annual salary 53.04 G (6 days/week)

Carpenter's journeyman (Geselle) – 8.15 Kr per day
Day labourer – 6.20 Kr per day[2]
Household maids – 2 Kr per day[3]
Employee of the city (*Stadtknecht*) of Hall – annual salary 20 G per year[4]
Executioner in Hall (1528) – 100 G annually
Executioner in Meran (1525) – 80 G annually[5]
Civil servants, eg. Pilgram Marpeck – 150 G annually in Augsburg
Mining judge in Rattenberg, eg. Pilgram Marpeck – 130 G[6]

Food, tool and Clothing Prices in the early 1500s
One pound of pork meat – 1.40 Kr; one pound of beef – 1.05 Kr; butter – 2.31 Kr; wheat, one kilogram – approximately 1 Kr; rye, one kilogram – .87 Kr[7]

The following prices are all in Kreuzer.
"A sheep cost 29 to 34; a pound of fish, 6 to 8; a hen, 4 to 5; one pound of cheese, 2; one measure of wine, 2; one measure (star) of salt, 18; thirty eggs, 5; one pair of shoes, 8; one blanket, 1 gulden; a hatchet, 10; a crock, 10; rustic linen cloth for a shirt, about 42; woollen cloth for an overcoat (Loden) 64 to 72."[8]

5. Hymn of Dorothea/Anna Malerin and Anna/Ursula Ochsentreiberin*

1. On the day of our Lady, Christ brought together his little lambs. He congregated them quickly in Mils in the green woods.
2. But the wolf came running and scattered the lambs in the valley. They ran very quickly and loudly cried out to God.
3. Then the shepherd came and clearly proclaimed the Word of God to them. He taught them well. May God ever and in all eternity reward him.
4. Now would you like to know what happened? With God's spirit the Holy Gospel was clearly proclaimed, how Christ fed his disciples on the mountain.
5. Now we wish to utter complaints to God in heaven that they wish to banish the word of God from the whole world. We will never buy the word of God for money.
6. And because we will never buy it for money we must leave wife and children. Mark this well. We will not give the priests any money.

7. The Gospel now is clear as day, and causes great grievance and anguish to the monks and priests. [It says that] they should never be great lords.
8. And God will not put up with it any longer; the truth is taken into the whole world. The [monks and priests] do not think this is good. They shear the sheep and suck the lifeblood out of them.
9. And since they never can succeed they make up many lies, [such as] the baptism which Jesus commanded his dear disciples (to practise) is wrong.
10. Now take note of what we have written: infant baptism was instituted for money. That is why they shed much innocent blood.
Amen

*Translated by Linda A. Huebert Hecht in "Wives, Female Leaders and Two Female Martyrs from Hall," in *Profiles of Anabaptist Women*, 192.

6. Hymn of Ursula Hellrigel of the Ötz Valley and Annelein of Freiberg*

Ausbund, the 36th Song

Another Song of Annelein of Freiburg, Who was Drowned and then Burned, 1529

To the tune of "In You I Have Hoped, Lord."

1. Everlasting Father in heaven,
I call on you so ardently,
Do not let me turn from you.
Keep me in your truth
Until my final end.

2. O God, guard my heart and mouth,
Lord watch over me at all times,
Let nothing separate me from you,
Be it affliction, anxiety, or need,
Keep me pure in joy.

3. My everlasting Lord and Father,
Show and teach me,
Poor unworthy child that I am,
That I heed your path and way.
In this lies my desire.

4. To walk through your power into death,
Through sorrow, torture, fear and want.
Sustain me in this,
O God, so that I nevermore
Be separated from your love.

5. Many travel along this road,
The cup of suffering lies there,
And also many untrue teachings
Which try to turn us away
From Christ our Lord.

6. To you I raise up my soul, Lord,
I depend on you in misfortune,
Do not let me come to harm,
That my enemy not stand over me
On this earth.

7. They have imprisoned me.
I wait, O God, with all my heart,
With very great longing,
When finally you will awake
And set your prisoners free.

8. O God, Father, make us like
The five virgins of your kingdom,
Who were prudently careful
To wait for the bridegroom,
With his chosen flock.

9. Eternal king of heaven,
Feed us and quench our thirst
In a spiritual way

With your food of truth
Which never perishes

10. If you withhold your food from us
Everything is lost and useless.
Without you we bring forth nothing.
Through grace we trust in you,
It will not fail us.

11. I do not doubt God's power.
His judgments all are true.
He will not abandon anyone
Who stands firm in the faith,
And stays on the true paths.

12. Be comforted you Christians and rejoice,
Through Jesus Christ forevermore,
Who gives us love and faith.
God comforts us through his holy word,
On that we should rely.

13. I entrust myself to God and his church.
May he be my protector today,
For the sake of his name.
May this come to pass, Father mine,
Through Jesus Christ, Amen.

*Translated by Pamela Klassen in "Ursula Hellrigel of the Ötz Valley and Annelein of Freiburg," in *Profiles of Anabaptist Women*, 199-201.

7. Helena von Freyberg, "Confession (as follows) on Account of Her Sin," 1540s[9]

Beloved in God, I ask you through God's will that you hear my accusation of myself, and the recognition of my guilt, in writing, since I truly cannot speak of it with my mouth without turning red with shame. For flesh and blood have refused to confront it, sought escape where possible and remained silent when I have tried for a long time in the past to deal with it. And so flesh and blood must for this (and can no longer avoid it)[10] be disgraced due to its malice and trickery. The devil has covered me over many times, and distorted the light and made me white while I was black, and perverted the Holy Spirit into a spirit of the flesh. This is what the devil does in all spiritual things. He presents himself as if he were white as an angel (and very humble). But God my Lord is even stronger and deprives him of his power and might (Matthew 12)[11] through Jesus Christ, His beloved Son. To Him be honour and praise. Amen.

First of all: I confess and acknowledge my guilt from the bottom of my heart before God and all his saints in heaven and on earth, how I have transgressed[12] and incurred guilt in the matter which has now been revealed to me by God's grace through the goodness of the Holy Spirit through the mercy and goodness of God my Lord and Father. God does not neglect to discipline his wicked quarrelsome child; unfortunately I have rebelled against God and as a result I have lost the grace of the Holy Spirit.

The fruit of the Spirit, patience, righteousness, gentleness, humility, kindness, true love, faithfulness, peace, self-discipline (Galations 5), can no longer can be seen in me, which mocks true faith and the Word of God.

From the bottom of my heart I am guilty of great impatience before godly discipline and punishment, which has resulted in the bitterness of my heart and in many unfruitful, irresponsible words and behaviour, inwardly and outwardly. Also, I confess that I have carelessly sworn by the name of God and in disobedience to the Holy Gospel, have not followed its rule, the teachings of Christ my Lord (and Redeemer) where he says, learn of me, I am gentle, patient and humble from the bottom of my heart (Matthew 11). He was patient and did not object when injustice was done to him (1 Peter 2), and yet I do not want to suffer because of my guilt. This is far from the mind of Christ, which a Christian should also have; for children of the Heavenly Father should have His nature. Christ teaches us to leave ourselves and the life of self behind (Luke 9), not to seek ourselves, and to follow him faithfully, in simplicity and uprightness, like a child without falseness or deceit.

I also confess that my prayer is not righteous, for I do not gladly allow the Lord's will to happen to me, in that I resist what goes against my will or wants to break it.

I am guilty from the bottom of my heart, of not being genuinely god-fearing, of not having God constantly in my sight. In that I lack the godly wisdom (Psalm 110, Ecclesiastes 1) that comes from the fear of God (Proverbs 9). I exhibit this in my walk; I barely grow or increase in the body of Christ, as an old woman in the faith should,[13] so that I feel worthless and shameful before God and His own. I am weak, miserable, lukewarm and tired in my watching and praying (Acts 3). Wherefore all my trouble has befallen me (Matthew 24). In this I have only myself to blame and no one else.

I confess myself to be guilty and to have failed completely in loving God first and my brother. I have broken the command of God, wherein the whole law is contained (Matthew 7), that is, in forbearance and kindness (Luke 10). For love has no evil passion, and is neither contrary nor complaining, neither boastful nor puffed up, is not undisciplined, bitter or ever angry (1 Corinthians 13). Love endures and forbears all things, and trusts that all will go well, has no evil suspicion, does everything for the best according to the prompting of the Holy Spirit (1 Corinthians 10), and also does not seek its own advantage. In all this I have failed and broken faith.

I wanted to teach and discipline my brother, but I was not teachable or amenable to discipline myself (Matthew 7). I have sought the twig in him, and not seen the beam in my own eye. Also, I have been troublesome in the way I have acted toward my brother and foremost in my great impatience, with which I caused anger and impatience, from which regretfully no good thing followed and happened. Thus the fault is mine alone and falls on me and no one else.

Especially I have transgressed and become guilty concerning the dogs, those in civil authority [Hundt],[14] about which I was spoken to in the beginning; according to my understanding and intention it was not a sin according to the evangelical order. I have resisted on this point with impatience and tactlessness in word and deed. I forcefully wanted to retain the freedom which I thought I had, not wanting to be restricted or compelled, seeking my own good to the detriment of my neighbour, which caused my brother to stumble, resulting in his vexation. In this I did not take into consideration the love of or the good of my brother, and have loved the creature for its own sake. This I confess before God and his own. I have been completely uncooperative and impatient toward those who have resisted me in this. I have often wanted to separate myself from them. In all of this I confess, that I have done wrong, above all with the dogs, those in civil authority (having an improper attitude and excessive conduct). Unfortunately, I have not been able to understand it otherwise until now, but God has revealed it to me, through His holy, charitable Spirit, to whom be praise eternally. Amen.

Thus, I am guilty from the bottom of my heart of committing a sin and becoming indebted to God and my brothers and neighbours, both knowingly and in ignorance as God my Lord knows best for me, inwardly and outwardly. Because of me the name of God has been blasphemed. Consequently, many evil, careless, unfruitful, and blasphemous words have been said before God.

I confess before God, that I well deserve every punishment because of my transgression[15] and guilt, yes probably even more than He has given me, and am worthy only of humiliation, disgrace and ridicule. Surely it would not have been a wonder, for all that I have deserved from God, if He had readily allowed me to perish. But God acts as a faithful father to his angry, quarrelsome child, and punishes me until I become aware of my sin. Due to the great love of God (through Christ) I have experienced grace and compassion (which will speak for me at the judgement) (James 2); to God be given thanks eternally.

So I am in the same position as the lost son. I have uselessly squandered what my Lord and God the Father (in grace) has given me, yes have used it unfruitfully. I say, I am no longer worthy to be called His child (Luke 15), and I say along with public sinners, "God, be gracious and merciful (Luke 18) and forgive me, needy as I am, my sin and transgression.[16] Provide for me (poor soul that I am) a perfect and fitting repentance in all yieldedness [Gelassenheit],[17] humility and self-denial, through the holy blood of Jesus Christ." For I am sorry from the bottom of my heart; God knows what I have done. Therefore I also ask His holy congregation, especially here at Augsburg, whom I have offended greatly, in particular Pilgram and Valtin,[18] to forgive and pardon what I have done against you, for which I am sorry from the bottom of my heart as I have already mentioned and as God knows.

And now however, the consolation and assurance in the shedding of the holy blood of Jesus Christ my God and Lord, promise sanctification and reconciliation. (For He says that in the hour in which sinners sigh in their hearts over their sins, they are forgiven.) To this I cling in faith, that my sins are forgiven through Jesus Christ, which prepares me for death. This I say in praise, honour and thanks for God's immense grace and compassion, to whom be praise, honour and laud, from eternity to eternity. Amen.

I ask and plead to God from the depths of my heart through Jesus Christ and through the intercession of the saints[19] and children of God and His holy congregation (whom the Lord knows). I ask them from the bottom of my heart (and it is also my wish) that they would pray on my behalf (to God) for help and strength, that in future I may withstand all that is opposed to God and end my life following God's will, to the honour and praise of His holy name. Amen.

Thus, I yield myself to the discipline and punishment of God my heavenly father, His holy congregation and Christian church as long and however much, as is pleasing to the Holy Spirit. May the will of God be done in me according to His grace (along with all those who desire it and who are in need). Amen.

This is my will and final decision at present. May God the Lord require of me whatever He wills. I forgive, (forget), and pardon from the bottom of my heart those *whom I suppose to have done things against me. I ask God also to forgive and pardon them, yes that God would give them grace to help them recognize their sin (as I have done through God's grace). Amen.*

Praise be to God [20]

1. Matthias Schmelzer, "Geschichte der Preise und Löhne in Rattenberg vom Ende des 15. bis in die 2. Hälfte des 19. Jahrhunderts" (unpublished Doctoral dissertation, Leopold-Franzens University, Innsbruck, 1972).
2. *Ibid.*, 402, 419.
3. *Hutterite Beginnings*, 378, n.16.
4. This information is from Dr. Romedio Schmitz-Esser, archivist for the city of Hall in Tirol in 2007.
5. Moser, *Die Scharfrichter*, 147, 185.
6. Klaassen and Klassen, *Marpeck*, 63, 289.
7. Schmelzer, "Geschichte der Preise und Löhne," xxiii f.
8. Heinz Noflatscher, "Alltag des Kanonikus" in *Quellen zur historischen Wohnkultur, Denkmalpflege in Südtirol* (Bozen: Landesdenkmalamt, 1988), 325-26, cited in *Hutterite Beginnings*, 378, n. 16.
9. Minor revisions to this text were made by the author and by John Rempel, editor of the English edition of the *Kunstbuch*, in which it will be reproduced. See Chapter Two, March 7, 1528 for Helena's story.
10. Brackets ( ) enclose parts of the text in the same way as they appear in the original.
11. Helena's Scripture references are only to chapters. The sixteenth century Bible did not include verses. In the original handwritten copy of her "Confession" Helena included Scripture references in the margins, relating them specifically to what she was writing. They are included here in brackets within the text.
12. "Transgression" is used where Helena uses the word "vergriffen."
13. Helena calls herself an old woman meaning she had been an Anabaptist for a long time, since 1527.
14. Parentheses [ ] refer to German words in the original text. In Hans Fink, *Tiroler Wortschatz an Eisack, Rienz und Etsch* (Innsbruck: Universitätsverlag Wagner Ges. M.B.H., 1972), 134, "Hundt" is defined as "der Gemeindediener, mancherorts noch heute 'Gemeindehund'

genannt." ("Dog" is defined as a member of the local government, in many places still called the 'local government official' today.) In a letter of February 4, 2004, Dr. Matthias Schmelzer related to the author that Dr. Rudolf Tasser, a language expert for the Tirolian dialect whom he consulted, confirmed Fink's interpretation and stated that this use of the word dog for a local government official, civil servant or person serving the local community, is still used today in many places in Tirol among the older generation. Helena's reference to dogs indicates that she was most likely writing this confession because she recanted. Helena gave a private and short form of the recantation in front of the viceroy of Innsbruck in Tirol in 1534. Johann Loserth refers to the latter official as the "Statthalter" of Innsbruck. See Chapter Two, n.135. See also Klaassen and Klassen, *Marpeck*, 256-57. Copies of the "Bittschrift" and letters of negotiation written for Helena which refer to her recantation are located in the Münich archives. See Chapter Two, n. 129.
15. Here Helena uses "Missetat" for transgression.
16. Here Helena uses "Übertretung" for transgression.
17. This is a central concept in Anabaptist theology and spirituality. Such humility does not result in a loss of personal self.
18. Helena is referring here to Pilgram Marpeck and Valtin Werner.
19. Heinold Fast, discoverer of the *Kunstbuch,* suggests that Helena's reference to saints refers to the prayers of fellow believers on her behalf in the same sense as in the New Testament in Romans chapter 15:30 and in II Corinthians chapter 1:1, 11.
20. Helena ends with the Latin words "Laus Deo."

Appendix II

The third volume of Anabaptist court records collected by Prof. Grete Mecenseffy with the assistance of Dr. Matthias Schmelzer was published in 1983 and provides documents for the years 1532 to 1564. In this third volume, comprehensive indexes were added for the 1983 records as well as for those of 1972. One of these indexes lists the pages for every person who was named and/or arrested on suspicion of being Anabaptist for the five-year time period 1527 to 1531.[1] Using this index for this five year time period (the same time period as used for the women in this book) all the men were counted, both Anabaptist members and those suspected of being Anabaptist, both those whose names are included and those who are unnamed in the 1972 Anabaptist court records.[2]

The total number of men named in the 1972 court records is 687 whereas the total number of women named in these same records (all listed in the "Index of Women's names" at the back of this book) is 418. Both of these numbers are conservative estimates. When the names of a number of women and/or men are not given and there is no indication of how many of each there are, two entries were made for the women and two for the men although there might have been more than two for each group. In cases where the word several (in German "etliche")[3] is used in the court records, the number of women or men listed as unnamed was two or three to represent the whole group. Altogether then, 1,105 men and women, a very significant number, were named in regard to the Anabaptist movement of Tirol in this early time period. A few details of men's involvements in the Anabaptist movement follow.

Beginning January 2, 1527 Ferdinand I issued mandates or decrees to all the local rulers and judges instructing them on how to deal with Anabaptists. His goal of course was to eliminate all Anabaptists in his territory. A year later, on

---

[1] Mecenseffy, *Quellen zur Geschichte der Täufer XIV.Band Österreich III. Teil* (Gütersloh, Gerd Mohn, 1983), 790-791.

[2] In cases where several Anabaptist men are referred to but their names are not given, they are included on the list as n.n. meaning "no name" and the page number on which they are first mentioned. The use of "n.n." to represent persons whose names are not included is used by Claus-Peter Clasen in his article: "The Anabaptist Leaders: Their Numbers and Background Switzerland, Austria, South and Central Germany 1525-1618," *Mennonite Quarterly Review* XLIX, 2 (April, 1975), 122-64.

[3] Whenever German words such as used here: "etliche" they will appear in the text in brackets.

January 24, 1528, Ferdinand's message to Innsbruck, the seat of his government, stated that despite the latest mandate issued just days earlier on January 16, the number of Anabaptists in his territory was said to have risen to 1000. This was of great concern to Ferdinand since it indicated that local authorities were ignoring his decrees. Specifically, government officials were to search out the key leaders and agitators ("Radelsfuehrer") who were stirring up the people and secondly, to find out by what distinctive signs and words of greeting Anabaptists recognized each other. If this information could not be obtained through normal ("guetlich") questioning, the interrogations should include torture.[4] Ferdinand's fears were not exaggerated. The court records of 1972 indicate that in actuality Anabaptist membership did not increase to over 1000 in all of the territory until 1531, as the numbers given above for the participation of both women and men confirm. Nevertheless, Ferdinand repeatedly issued mandates to the local authorities between 1527 and 1531.

The men involved in the Anabaptist movement of Tirol were classified using the same five categories as for women's participation, namely: Believer, Missioner, Lay Leader, Indirect Participant and Martyr. As with the women, the majority of the men were in the first category, that of Believer, which indicated only that the person had been re-baptized. For men the total number of Believers was 511 and for women 279.

In the second category of participation, that of Missioner – a person who proselytized – included nine men whereas the women had one more in this category – ten. This is definitely not the case for the third category of Lay Leader who were persons exercising informal leadership based either on their own calling or affirmation from members of their group. The comparison of male and female leaders is quite interesting. However, for the male leaders, the numbers need to be adjusted appropriately as follows. Twelve male leaders became martyrs and in order that they not be counted twice they were counted only as martyrs. The number of male Lay Leaders who did not become martyrs was 31, making the actual number of male Lay Leaders (31+12) 43, almost twice the number of female Anabaptist leaders, which was 21 (counting both Lay Leaders and Missioners together). Given the patriarchal norms of sixteenth century society – men were the head of the family and household and in charge of matters both private and public – it is not surprising that there were nearly half as many female as male Lay Leaders.

Male Lay Leaders are mentioned very early, on January 2, 1527, in the very first document of the 1972 court records. By November of that year the government was sending out instructions regarding a number of male leaders, namely: Hans Hut who, coming from Bavaria in the North, had introduced the

---

[4] TA 1972, 65: 23-29.

Anabaptist message to northern Tirol; the former monk Leonard Schiemer who alone had already baptized 92 persons in various Austrian territories by this time for which he was executed January 14, 1528 in Rattenberg; and the former priest Hans Schlaffer executed with Leonhard Frick soon thereafter on February 4, 1528.

In November 1527, Hans Hut baptized Ursula Nehspitzer Binder and her husband Eucharias Binder and sent them out to preach in Salzburg. They were a missionary couple and Ursula was the first female Missioner. Not until January 1528 is the first women leader named, the Gallpuechlerin, not by herself but together with her two sons-in-law Adam and Ulrich Kobl. Ulrich was a strong male leader in southern Tirol who associated with Georg Blaurock, the man who brought Anabaptism from Switzerland to South Tirol. The whole Kobl family was a staunch household of Anabaptist believers even involving their two maids and their male servant.[5] However, there is no evidence that Anabaptist women leaders were baptizers. Seemingly that remained the domain of male Anabaptist leaders.

The fourth category, Indirect Participant, refers to men and women who were indirectly involved in Anabaptism. That is, they were arrested either because they were sympathizers of the movement or arrested along with an Anabaptist family or household or they provided food and lodging for Anabaptists. Perhaps they had even allowed a meeting to take place in their home. Indirect Participants were usually released if questioning proved they were not Anabaptists. But all prisoners, including Indirect Participants were expected to give the names of Anabaptists they knew. The number of female Indirect Participants was 23 whereas the number of male Indirect Participants was 45, almost twice the number for women.

Of interest among the male Indirect Participants are a judge and his secretary. This is the only case where the name is included of the male court secretary whose job it was to document the proceedings of the court. His name was Mang Kalgruber and he worked for the judge in Kitzbühel, Georg Perger.[6] Both the judge and his secretary openly sympathized with Anabaptists. The report of July 8, 1528 states there were 36 newly imprisoned Anabaptists in Kitzbühel who had "fallen again." That is, at their first imprisonment they had recanted but then rejoined Anabaptism and now were arrested a second time. Judge Perger had told them he did not believe adult baptism was "against God" but that Anabaptists had to desist from their beliefs because "it was the will of

---

[5] TA 1972, 66: 28-30; 81: 5-6; 10-13.
[6] TA 1972, 149: 22-31. In the 16th century the secretarial work of the court was done by men like Mang Kalgruber.

the government."[7] This of course was unacceptable to the central government who made certain the prisoners understood that their baptism as well as their return to the movement were heretical acts which put their souls in danger of damnation.[8] It is the only time that a judge and his court secretary were suspected of Anabaptist leanings. Following this incident Georg Perger agreed to conduct his duties according to the government mandates since he continued to receive orders from Innsbruck during 1529 through February 1531.

In a number of cases younger men and women were among the Anabaptist prisoners or those ordered to be arrested. They would either be young men working as labourers for farmers, young women working as maids in a household or younger members of an Anabaptist family. However, there is one case in particular where a boy ("ein Knabe") reported the name of an Anabaptist woman to the local judge and the boy's word was taken as authoritative. The boy told the judge in the town of Freundsberg that he had heard Gilg Klein's wife say "in a short time she had made six new Christians." She was arrested on the basis of the boy's testimony and was to be questioned in front of a jury. If no serious crime became apparent, she could be released from prison on the usual requirement of a guaranty (a payment of money) that she would desist from Anabaptism.[9] It is quite unusual that the word of an underage boy was accepted as valid in court.

The Anabaptists who sacrificed the most for their new found faith were those condemned to death, the martyrs. If a man or woman's only crime was re-baptism and they were not involved in proselytizing or baptizing, they were usually let go on the condition that they recant and swear an oath ("Urfehde"). However, for anyone arrested a second time there was no mercy. The number of female martyrs between 1527 and 1531 was 77, in itself a high number. Again, since there were more men than women named as a whole during this time period, one would expect the number of male martyrs to be higher. However, at 86, the number of male martyrs is not that much higher than that of the female martyrs. These figures illustrate that the equality of men and women in the criminal court extended also to martyrdom.

Not everyone attended their local church every Sunday but, often the one time of year they would attend was Easter. Thus, in Springtime the number of arrests and executions increased, since those who had not gone to confession and taken the sacrament at Easter were suspected of being Anabaptist. On May 12, 1529 in the town of Rattenberg east of Innsbruck, 17 Anabaptists were executed, an unusually high number. The protocol of the town council stated:

---

[7] *Ibid.*
[8] TA 1972, 150:11-13.
[9] TA 1972, 229:21-27; 230:30-31.

"never before have so many persons been executed all at once."[10] The majority in this group, 10, were women and seven were men. The question is, did such extreme measures succeed in preventing people from joining Anabaptism. The central government had already been informed that more than 100 men and women had been put to death since 1527. On May 29, the same judge who had ordered the execution of the 17 Anabaptists was instructed from Innsbruck to use torture in interrogating the remaining prisoners in jail in the town of Rattenberg. The government wanted to know the names and occupations of all the Anabaptists in the nearby mining town of Schwaz whose number apparently had reached 800, this in light of the fact that Schwaz's total population was 1200.[11] It had also been reported that there was an Anabaptist woman leader in the region who held a register of 800 Anabaptist names.[12] No wonder Ferdinand feared a revolt of the people. As the historian James Stayer has said, "Potentially, Anabaptism threatened to become the religion of Tirol. It was no mere sect that the government might have safely ignored."[13] Obviously, both male and female Anabaptists were not afraid to die. The authorities in both Rattenberg and Kitzbühel were astounded that the Anabaptists were not frightened by their fate.[14] They were only concerned about their sins, living simply and in peace with one another. They had no intention of revolting against the government as had happened in the Peasant War of 1525.[15]

As in all the other categories, when taken chronologically men became martyrs in Tirol at an earlier date than Anabaptist women. As already mentioned, early in 1528 key leaders were executed, namely, Leonard Schiemer on January 14 soon followed by Hans Schlaffer and Leonard Frick on February 4.[16] At this early stage the government assumed that by executing the key leaders they would eliminate the Anabaptist movement but this government policy failed. The strength of Anabaptism lay in its broad membership among all groups and classes of people in Tirol – both male and female – and in the high number of ordinary people who joined the movement. Just two weeks after Schiemer was executed, on January 28, two such 'ordinary people' a man named Hanns Schneider and a woman named Apollonia Niedermair were in prison on

---

[10] TA 1972, 228:21.
[11] TA 1972, 243:6-8.
[12] TA 1972, 239:25-27.
[13] James M. Stayer, "Anabaptists and Future Anabaptists in the Peasants' War," in *Mennonite Quarterly Review* 62, (1988), 131.
[14] This sentence is translated from: "Erstaunliches Verhalten der Wiedertaeufer, die kein Entzetzen vor dem Tode haetten, habe sich in Kitzbühel und Rattenberg gezeigt." TA 1972, 240:14-16.
[15] TA 1972, 235: 36-39.
[16] TA 1972, 60: 34; 64: 27-28.

suspicion of being Anabaptists. Discussion of their case was delayed until April of that year when the government ordered their execution. By this time Hanns's wife Eva had chosen to become an Anabaptist and all three were condemned to death. Thus, Eva and Apollonia were the first two female Anabaptist martyrs of Anabaptism in Tirol.[17] Hanns Schneider was the first Anabaptist man to be executed who was not a leader.

There were differences in the method of execution for Anabaptist women and men. Men were either executed by the sword or burned at the stake. The method of execution for men depended on whether they chose to die as 'good Christians' by confessing their sin and taking communion before their execution. In doing the latter they could be re-instituted in the church, die by the sword and be buried in consecrated ground, that is, in the church cemetery.[18] Otherwise they were condemned to the death of a heretic, were burned at the stake and buried outside the church cemetery. For women the primary method of execution was drowning. However, for some staunch female believers drowning was not punishment enough and they too suffered the death of being burned at the stake.

By mid 1529 Ferdinand had to admit that the Anabaptists were not planning to rebel. These people were unwavering in their decision to remain Anabaptists. As we have already seen, often they recanted and then rejoined their co-religionists. Ferdinand speculated that people became Anabaptists because they were simple-minded ("ainfalt") and did not understand what they were doing, especially if their only crime was re-baptism.[19] In any case, with the increasing number of Anabaptists, a new method of dealing with them was undertaken, that of re-education. On July 24, 1529 fourteen Anabaptists had been arrested, all except one having been baptized by Jacob Hutter (future leader of the Hutterites). The local warden was told that for ten of them, four women and six men, "...in the presence of the local governor, a competent priest was to instruct them thoroughly on two articles of faith in particular, namely, the holy sacrament and baptism."[20] The priests had to be knowledgeable and intelligent in order to convince the Anabaptists to rejoin the church.

Attempting to re-convert Anabaptists was no easy task. The prisoners whether male or female were well grounded in their faith and the priests had to know their theology well. The number of arrests decreased somewhat in 1530 and 1531 but the instructions to local authorities to send capable priests into

---

[17] TA 1972, 66: 30-33; 117: 19-20; 23-30.
[18] TA 1972, 396: 25-28.
[19] TA 1972, 231:6-7. Since it was a societal norm that women were the weaker sex and not as knowledgeable as men, it was acceptable for women to admit they became Anabaptists out of ignorance or "ainfalt."
[20] This is translated from: TA 1972, 264: 1-3. See also TA 1972, 263: 11-14.

the prisons to re-convert the prisoners occurred a number of times. By the end of 1529, on December 25, Christmas Day to be exact, a reward of 40 Gulden was offered to anyone who reported the name of an Anabaptist leader who was brought to prison.[21]

Also during 1530-1531 the government focused on confiscating the properties of those Anabaptists who had fled or had been executed. Anabaptists interpreted the words of Christ in the Gospel of Luke literally that said they must leave their family behind including their children and even give up their own life in order to be a disciple of Christ.[22] Some Anabaptists fled to Moravia without their children although some children were later brought to their parents by other Anabaptists. Moreover, unless the parents had appointed a guardian ("Vormund") to care for their children, money from the sale of their property went to support any underage children they left behind. In addition to appropriating the salaries of men who fled, the treasury in Innsbruck received monies that were "over and above the court costs."[23] At first the king received half the value of confiscated Anabaptist properties but the treasury in Innsbruck reduced this amount to one third by February 1531. The amount of money the king earned from confiscating Anabaptist men's salaries and from the sale of Anabaptist properties illustrates that the majority of Anabaptists in Tirol were better-off farmers.[24]

In 134 cases husbands and wives were both Anabaptists. In some of these cases the whole family and household was involved in Anabaptism with the majority of the family members being Believers and others giving them their support. There were a number of interdependent family networks: the family of Ulrich Kobl, the Taurer and Nickinger families and the family of Peter Egger the baker. On the other hand, many times two, three or more men are named together in one record with no mention of family members and few details of their involvements.[25] Were they single men or men who did not want their

---

[21] TA 1972, 321: 10-13.
[22] Luke 14 verse 27 states: Whoever comes to me and does not hate father and mother, wife and children, brothers and sisters, yes, and even life itself, cannot be my disciple. New Revised Standard Version of the Bible.
[23] See Linda A. Huebert Hecht, "Anabaptist Women and Their Families in Tirol, 1527-1531: Dispelling the Myth of Poverty," in *Sisters: Myth and Reality of Anabaptist, Mennonite, and Doopsgezind Women ca. 1525-1900*, ed. Mirjam van Veen, Piet Visser, Gary K. Waite, Els Kloek, Marion Kobelt-Groch, Anna Voolstra, (Leiden: Brill, 2014), 66. See also, TA 1972, 266:13-1.
[24] This theme is discussed in Huebert Hecht, "Anabaptist Women and Their Families in Tirol, 1527-1531," 63-87.
[25] Cristan Plumen, Rueplen Lackner am Lehen, Woelfl Kogler are named in TA 1972, 151: 35-36. Wolfgang von Moos, Martin von Nock and Kneusser, a leader, are named

families to be endangered by Anabaptist involvements? However, many times Anabaptist men are also named in the records as guardians for family and household members, namely, their wives, sisters, mothers or maids.

The preliminary statistics discussed above answer some of the questions about men's participation in the early Anabaptist movement of Tirol. They expand on the women's stories in this book and perhaps will encourage further research on both male and female Anabaptist participation.

Linda A. Huebert Hecht, M.A.
Independent Scholar
Waterloo Ontario
February 2023

---

in TA 1972, 182: 35-183: 2. Hans Prunner, Wolfgang Wantler, Martin Blindmueller are Anabaptists who are to be pardoned. See TA 1972, 283: 18-20.

Bibliography

Primary Sources

Mecenseffy, Grete. *Quellen zur Geschichte der Täufer XL. Band Österreich I. Teil.* Gütersloh: Gerd Mohn, 1964.

_____ *Quellen zur Geschichte der Täufer XIII Band Österreich II. Teil.* Gütersloh: Gerd Mohn, 1972.

_____ ed. with Matthias Schmelzer, *Quellen zur Geschichte der Täufer XIV. Band, Österreich III. Teil.* Gütersloh: Gerd Mohn, 1983.

Van Braght, Thieleman J. *The Bloody Theater, or Martyrs' Mirror of the Defenseless Christians Who Baptized Only upon Confession of Faith, and Who Suffered and Died for the Testimony of Jesus, Their Savior, from the Time of Christ to the Year A.D. 1660*, Translated by Joseph F. Sohm. Scottdale, PA: Herald Press, eighth edition 1968.

Secondary Sources

Abbott, Leona Stucky. "Anabaptist Women of the Sixteenth Century." Unpublished M.A. Eden Theological Seminary, 1979.

Andergassen, Leo. "Die Altarwerke Bartlmä Dill Riemenschneiders." In *Renaissancealtäre und Epitaphien in Tirol Schlern-Schriften 325*. Innsbruck: Universitätsverlag Wagner, 2007.

Anderson, Bonnie S. and Judith P. Zinsser. *A History of Their Own, Women in Europe from Prehistory to the Present* Vol. I. New York, N.Y.: Harper and Row, 1988.

Bainton, Roland, *Women of the Reformation in Germany and Italy.* Minneapolis, MN: Augsburg Publishing House, 1971.

Barrett, Lois Y. "Ursula Jost and Barbara Rebstock of Strasbourg." In *Profiles of Anabaptist Women Sixteenth-Century Reforming Pioneers* ed. C. Arnold Snyder and Linda A. Huebert Hecht, 273-287. Waterloo, ON: Wilfrid Laurier Press, 1996.

Bender, Harold S. "Status of Women." *Mennonite Encyclopedia* IV. Scottdale, PA: Herald Press, 1959. 972-74.

Bender, Harold S., Nanne van der Zijpp, Cornelius Krahn, Marilyn G. Peters, Anneke Welcker and M. M. Mattijssen-Berkman. "Women." *Global Anabaptist Mennonite Encyclopedia Online*. 1989. www.gameo.org

Bernard, Paul P. "Heresy in Fourteenth Century Austria." *Medievalia et Humanistica* 10 (1956).

Boulding, Elise. *The Underside of History: A View of Women through Time*. Boulder, CO: Westview Press, 1976.

Boyd, Stephen Blake. "Pilgram Marpeck and the Justice of Christ." Unpublished, Doctor of Theology, Harvard University, Cambridge, MA., 1984.

_____ *Pilgram Marpeck His Life and Social Theology*. Durham: Duke University Press, 1992.

Breit, Stefan. *450 Jahre Aschauer Markt, 1555-2005*. Prien: Gemeinde Aschau i. Chiemgau, 2005.

Burkhardt, Ferne. "Dialoguing with the pope, Mennonite World Conference delegation dialogues with Catholic Leaders, present concerns over 'ecclesial communities'." *Canadian Mennonite Magazine* 11, 23 (Nov. 26, 2007): 16-18.

Catholic Encyclopedia at www.newadvent.org/cathen.12565a.htm.

Chrisman, Miriam U. "Women and the Reformation in Strasbourg 1490-1530." *Archive for Reformation History* 63 (1972): 143-68.

Clasen, Claus-Peter. *Anabaptism A Social History, 1525-1618 Switzerland, Austria, Moravia, South and Central Germany*. Ithaca: Cornell University Press, 1972.

_____ "The Sociology of Swabian Anabaptism." *Church History* 32 (1963): 150-80.

_____ "Executions of Anabaptists, 1525-1618 A Research Report." *Mennonite Quarterly Review* XLVII, 2 (1973): 115-1521.

_____ "The Anabaptist Leaders: Their Numbers and Background, Switzerland, Austria, South and Central Germany 1525-1618." *Mennonite Quarterly Review* XLIX, 2 (April 1975): 122-64.

_____ "The Anabaptist Leaders." *The Anabaptists in South and Central Germany, Switzerland, and Austria their names, occupations, places of residence and dates of conversion: 1525-1618. Mennonite Quarterly Review* (1978).

Collis, Louise. *Memoirs of a Medieval Woman, The Life and Times of Margery Kempe.* New York, NY: Harper and Row, 1964.

Cross, Claire. "'Great Reasoners in Scripture': the Activities of Women Lollards 1380-1530." *Medieval Women*, ed. Derek Baker. Oxford: Basil Blackwell, 1978: 359-380.

Davis, Natalie Zemon. "City Women and Religious Change." In *Society and Culture in Early Modern France, Eight Essays.* Stanford, California: Stanford University Press, 1975. 65-95.

Dyck, Cornelius J. "Elisabeth and Hadewijk of Friesland." In *Profiles of Anabaptist Women Sixteenth-Century Reforming Pioneers,* ed. C. Arnold Snyder and Linda A. Huebert Hecht, 359-364. Waterloo, ON: Wilfrid Laurier Press, 1996.

Ennen, Edith. *Frauen im Mittelalter.* München: C.H. Beck, 1985.

Epp, Marlene and H. Julia Roberts. "Women in the Chronicle of the Hutterian Brethren." In *Profiles of Anabaptist Women Sixteenth-Century Reforming Pioneers,* ed. C. Arnold Snyder and Linda A. Huebert Hecht, 202-221. Waterloo, ON: Wilfrid Laurier Press, 1996.

Farmer, Sharon. "Persuasive Voices: Clerical Images of Medieval Wives." *Speculum, A Journal of Medieval Studies* 61, 3 (July 1986): 517-543.

Fast, Heinold. ed. *Ostschweiz.* Zurich: Theologischer Verlag, 1973.

Fink, Hans. *Tiroler Wortschatz an Eisack, Rienz und Etsch.* lnnsbruck: Universitätsverlag Wagner Ges. M.B.H., 1972.

Friedmann, Robert. "Schiemer, Leonhard (d. 1528)." *Global Anabaptist Mennonite Encyclopedia Online.* 1959. www.gameo.org

_____ "Schützinger, Simon (16th century)." *Global Anabaptist Mennonite Encyclopedia Online.* 1959. www.gameo.org

_____ John Hofer, Hans Meier and John V. Hinde. "Hutterian Brethren (Hütterische Brüder)." *Global Anabaptist Mennonite Encyclopedia Online.* 1989. www.gameo.org

Forster, Ellinor. "Verfolgung und Vertreibung—ein Blick ins frühneuzeitliche Rechtsystem." In *Verbrannte Visionen? Erinnerungorte der Täufer in Tirol,* ed. Astrid von Schlachta, Ellinor Forster, Giovanni Merola, 18-25. Innsbruck: Innsbruck University Press, 2007.

Gehman, Dale D. with files from Brian Doerksen, "Swiss churches reconcile, Brian Doerksen witness to historic forgiveness." *Mennonite Brethren Herald* 46, 11 (November 2007): 21.

_____ "In the shadow of Trachselwald Swiss of all denominations gather to celebrate the Year of the Anabaptists and focus on Jesus' Sermon on the Mount." *Canadian Mennonite Magazine* 11, 20 (Oct. 15, 2007): 16-17.

"German Mennonites, Catholics see common ground in peace." *Courier*, 22, 4 (2007): 10.

Gisman-Fiel, Hildegund. *Das Täufertum in* Vorarlberg. Dornbirn: Vorarlberger Verlagsanstalt, 1982.

Glimpses #201: "In Switzerland and America, A 500-Year Wound That Had to be Healed" Christian History Institute chi.gospelcom.net/GLIMPSEF/Glimpses2/glimpses201.shtml

Gold, Penny Shine. "Male/Female Cooperation: The Example of Fontevrault." In *Distant Echoes, Medieval Religious Women Volume One,* ed. John A. Nichols, and Lillian Thomas Shank, 151-168. Kalamzoo, MI: Cistercian Publications Inc., 1984.

Gregory, Brad S. *Salvation at Stake Christian Martyrdom in Early Modern Europe.* Cambridge, MA: Harvard University Press, 1999.

_____ "Soetken van den Houte of Oudenaarde." In *Profiles of Anabaptist Women Sixteenth-Century Reforming Pioneers,* ed. C. Arnold Snyder and Linda A. Huebert Hecht, 365-377. Waterloo, ON: Wilfrid Laurier Press, 1996.

Grimmelshausen, Hans Jakob Christoph. *Der Abenteuerliche Simplicissimus.* published 1669. In John Horsch. *The Hutterian Brethren 1528-1931 A Story Of Martyrdom and Loyalty,* 67. Republished: Cayley, Alberta: Macmillan Colony, 1985.

Gross, Leonard. *The Golden Years of the Hutterites The Witness and Thought of the Communal Moravian Anabaptists during the Walpot Era 1565-1578.* Revised ed. Kitchener, ON: Pandora Press, 1998.

Haude, Sigrun. "Anabaptist Women—Radical Women?" In *Infinite Boundaries, Order, Disorder and Reorder in Early Modern German Culture,* ed. Max Reinhart, 313-28. Kirksville, MO: Sixteenth Century Journal Publishers Inc., 1998.

_____ "Gender Roles and Perspectives Among Anabaptist and Spiritualist Groups." In *A Companion To Anabaptism and Spiritualism, 1521-1700,* ed. John D. Roth and James M. Stayer, 425-66. Leiden: Brill, 2007.

Harder, Helmut. "Affirmations and concerns A personal reflection on meetings with the pope and Catholic officials to discuss Christian unity." *Canadian Mennonite* 11, 23 (Nov. 26, 2007): 17.

Hecht, Linda A. Huebert. "Faith and Action: The Role of Women in the Anabaptist Movement of the Tirol, 1527-1529." Unpublished Cognate Essay, MA, University of Waterloo, 1990.

_____ "Women and religious change: The significance of Anabaptist women in the Tirol, 1527-29." *Studies in Religion* 21, 1 (1992): 57-66.

_____ "An Extraordinary Lay Leader: The Life and Work of Helene of Freyberg, Sixteenth Century Noblewoman and Anabaptist from the Tirol." *Mennonite Quarterly Review,* LXVI 3 (July 1992): 312-41.

_____ "Helena von Freyberg of Münichau." In *Profiles of Anabaptist Women Sixteenth-Century Reforming Pioneers,* ed. C. Arnold Snyder and Linda A. Huebert Hecht, 124-139. Waterloo, ON: Wilfrid Laurier Press, 1996.

_____ "Wives, Female Leaders and Two Female Martyrs from Hall." In *Profiles of Anabaptist Women Sixteenth-Century Reforming Pioneers,* ed. C. Arnold Snyder and Linda A. Huebert Hecht, 187-194. Waterloo, ON: Wilfrid Laurier Press, 1996.

_____ "Review of the Literature on Women in the Reformation and Radical Reformation." In *Profiles of Anabaptist Women Sixteenth-Century Reforming Pioneers,* ed. C. Arnold Snyder and Linda A. Huebert Hecht, 406-415. Waterloo, ON: Wilfrid Laurier Press, 1996,

_____ "Anabaptist Women in Tirol who Recanted." In *Profiles of Anabaptist Women Sixteenth-Century Reforming Pioneers*, ed. C. Arnold Snyder and Linda A. Huebert Hecht, 156-163. Waterloo, ON: Wilfrid Laurier Press, 1996.

_____ "Anna Gasser of Lüsen." In *Profiles of Anabaptist Women Sixteenth-Century Reforming Pioneers*, ed. C. Arnold Snyder and Linda A. Huebert Hecht, 140-155. Waterloo, ON: Wilfrid Laurier Press, 1996.

_____ "Finding Connections: Reflections on the lives of 16th Century Anabaptist Women." *Sophia Magazine* 7, 2 (Spring 1997): 12-13

_____ "Anabaptist Women: Faith Hidden Until the Time of Harvest." *Sophia Magazine* 9, 3 (Fall 1999): 8-9.

_____ "A Brief Moment in Time: Informal Leadership and Shared Authority Among Sixteenth Century Anabaptist Women." *Journal of Mennonite Studies* 17 (1999): 52-74.

_____ "Speaking up and Taking Risks Anabaptist Family and Household Roles in Sixteenth-Century Tirol." In *Strangers at Home Amish and Mennonite Women in History,* ed. Kimberly D. Schmidt, Diane Zimmerman Umble, Steven D. Reschly, 237-258. Baltimore, MD: The John Hopkins University Press, 2002.

_____ "Helena von Freyberg Woman of Noble and Spiritual Stature." *Profiles of Mennonite Faith* Church Bulletin Insert of the Mennonite Brethren Historical Commission. Series 22 (Winter 2003).

_____ "Confession of Guilt Helena von Freyberg." In *Jörg Maler's Kunstbuch: Writings of the Pilgram Marpeck Circle*, ed. John D. Rempel, 505-512. Kitchener, ON: Pandora Press, 2010.

_____ "Anabaptist Women and Their Families in Tirol, 1527-1531: Dispelling the Myth of Poverty." In *Sisters, Myth and Reality of Anabaptist, Mennonite, and Doopsgezind Women ca. 1525-1900*, ed. Mirjam van Veen, Piet Visser, Gary K. Waite, Els Kloek, Marion Kobelt-Groch, Anna Voolstra, 63-87. Leiden: Brill, 2014.

_____ and Hanns-Paul Ties. "Research Note: The Tirolian Anabaptist Artist Bartlme Dill Riemenschneider and the Anabaptist Women in His Household, 1526-1549. *Mennonite Quarterly Review* 92 (July 2018): 439-461.

Hege, Christian and N. van der Zijpp. "Mandates." *Global Anabaptist Mennonite Encyclopedia Online*. 1957. www.gameo.org

Hellrigel, Ursula. "The 36 th Song, Another Song of Annelein of Freiburg, Who was Drowned and then Burned, 1529." Ausbund, Seventeenth Century Swiss Hymnbook. Translated by Pamela Klassen. In *Profiles of Anabaptist Women Sixteenth Century Reforming Pioneers*. ed. C. Arnold Snyder and Linda A. Huebert Hecht, 199-201. Waterloo, ON: Wilfrid Laurier Press, 1996.

Hildebrand, Bodo. *Erziehung zu Gemeinschaft Geschichte und Gegenwart des Erziehungswesens der Hutterer*. Bamberg: Centaurus-Verlagsgesellschaft Pfaffenweiler, 1993.

Holsey, Virginia Wiles. "Philippians 2:5-11: A Paeon to Submission or a Call for Confidence?" *Mennonite Central Committee Women's Concerns Report*, Report 89 (March-April 1990): 10.

Hutter, Jacob. *Brotherly Faithfulness Epistles From a Time of Persecution*, Translated by the Hutterian Society of Brothers Rifton. NY: Plough Publishing House, 1979.

Hutterian Brethren. ed. *The Chronicle of the Hutterian Brethren*, Vol. I. Translated by the Hutterian Brethren. Rifton. NY: Plough Publishing House, 1987.

Hutterite Brethren. *Die Lieder der Hutterischen Brüder.* Cayley, AB: Macmillan Colony, 1974.

Irwin, Joyce L. *Womanhood in Radical Protestantism 1525-1675.* New York, N.Y.: E. Mellen, 1979.

Jecker, Hanspeter. "Die Hinrichtung einer Täuferin in Rheinfelden—die letzte im frühneuzeitlichen Europa?" *Mennonitische Geschichtsblätter* 54 (1997): 76-88.

Juette, Robert. *Poverty and Deviance in Early Modern Europe.* New York, NY: Cambridge University Press, 1994.

Jung, Martin H. *Frauen des Pietismus, Zehn Porträts.* Gütersloh: Gütersloher Verlagshaus, 1998.

Kalmar, Laura. ed. "Persecution of Christians high in 2007." *Mennonite Brethren Herald* 47, 2 (February 2008): 16.

Klaassen, Walter. *Michael Gaismair: Revolutionary and Reformer.* Leiden: E. J. Brill, 1978.

_____ *Living at the End of the Ages Apocalyptic Expectation in the Radical Reformation.* Lanham, MD: University Press of America Inc., 1992.

_____ "Who can be called an Anabaptist?" *Mennonite Weekly Review.* (October 17, 2005): 6.

_____ and William Klassen, *Marpeck: A Life of Dissent and Conformity.* Lancaster, PA: Herald Press, 2008.

Kieckhefer, Richard. *Repression of Heresy in Medieval Germany.* Philadelphia: University of Pennsylvania Press, 1979.

Kobelt-Groch, Marion. *Aufsässig Töchter Gottes Frauen im Bauerkrieg und in den Täuferbewegungen.* Frankfurt/Main: Campus Verlag, 1993.

_____ "Hille Feicken of Sneek." In *Profiles of Anabaptist Women Sixteenth-Century Reforming Pioneers.* Translated by Linda A. Huebert Hecht. ed. C. Arnold Snyder and Linda A. Huebert Hecht, 288-297. Waterloo, ON: Wilfrid Laurier Press, 1996.

_____ "Divara of Haarlem." In *Profiles of Anabaptist Women Sixteenth-Century Reforming Pioneers.* Translated by Walter Klaassen. ed. C. Arnold Snyder and Linda A. Huebert Hecht, 298-304. Waterloo, ON: Wilfrid Laurier Press, 1996.

Koch, Gottfried. *Frauenfrage und Ketzertum im Mittelalter: die Frauenbewegung im Rahmen des Katharismus und des Waldensertums und ihre sozialen Wurzeln.* Berlin: Akademie Verlag, 1962.

Köfler, Gretl and Michael Forcher, *Die Frau in der Geschichte Tirols.* Innsbruck: Haymon-Verlag, 1986.

Kogler, Klaus. *Stadtbuch Kitzbühel, Bd. III, Baugeschichte, Kunstgeschichte, Theatergeschichte, Schlösser.* Kitzbühel: E. der Stadt Kitzbühel, 1970.

Ladurie, Emmanuel LeRoy. *Mountaillou, The Promised Land of Error.* Tranlated by Barbara Bray. New York, N. Y.: Vintage Books, 1978.

Lerner, Robert E. *The Heresy of the Free Spirit in the Later Middle Ages.* Berkeley: University of California Press, 1972, 230, n. 7.

Lewis, Charles. "Christians under the gun, Olympic-focused China rounds up dissidents, new report says." *National Post* (June 11, 2008): A3.

Lichdi, Elfriede. "Katharina Purst Hutter of Sterzing." In *Profiles of Anabaptist Women Sixteenth-Century Reforming Pioneers.* Translated by Linda A. Huebert Hecht. ed. C. Arnold Snyder and Linda A. Huebert Hecht, 178-186. Waterloo, ON: Wilfrid Laurier Press, 1996

Littell, Franklin Hamlin. *The Origins of Sectarian Protestantism, a Study of the Anabaptist View of the Church.* New York, N. Y.: Macmillan, 1964.

Loewen, Harry. "The Role of Women in the Mennonite Brethren Church." Unpublished sermon, Elmwood Mennonite Brethren Church, Winnipeg, Manitoba (Mother's Day), May, 1986.

Loserth, Johann. "Der Anabaptismus in Tirol Von Seinen Anfängen Bis Zum Tode Jakob Huters (1526-1536), Aus den Hinterlassenen Papieren Des Hofrathes Dr. Josef R. von Beck." *Archiv für Osterreichische Geschichte* 78, 1 (1892).

_____ and Robert Friedmann. "Tyrol (Austria)." *Global Anabaptist Mennonite Encyclopedia Online.* 1959. www.gameo.org

_____ Robert Friedmann and Werner O. Packull. "Hans Hut (d. 1527)." *Global Mennonite Encyclopedia Online.* 1987. www.gameo.org

Malone, Mary T. *Women and Christianity* Vol. III. Ottawa: Novalis, 2003.

Mack, Phyllis. *Visionary Women Ecstatic Prophecy in Seventeenth-Century England.* Berkeley: University of California Press, 1992.

Marr, M. Lucille. "Anabaptist Women of the North: Peers in the Faith, Subordinates in Marriage." *Mennonite Quarterly Review* LXI, 4 (October 1987): 347-62.

Martens, Helen. "Women in the Hutterite Song Book (*Die Lieder der Hutterischen Brüder*)." In *Profiles of Anabaptist Women Sixteenth-Century Reforming Pioneers,* ed. C. Arnold Snyder and Linda A. Huebert Hecht, 222-243. Waterloo, ON: Wilfrid Laurier Press, 1996.

McDonnell, Ernest W. *The Beguines and Beghards in Medieval Culture.* New York, NY: Octagon Books, 126, n. 81 (1969).

McCullough, Brian. "Redefining Normal Christianity, A Glimpse Into The Persecuted Church," *Mennonite Brethren Herald,* (Nov. 2007): 16-17.

Mecenseffy, Grete. "Anabaptists in Kitzbühel." Tranlated by Elizabeth Bender from *Stadtbuch Kitzbühel,* IV. Kitzbühel, 1971, 155-63. *Mennonite Quarterly Review* 46, No. 2 (April 1972): 99-112.

_____, Robert Friedmann and Richard D. Thiessen. "Ferdinand I, Holy Roman Emperor (1503-1564)." *Global Anabaptist Mennonite Encyclopedia Online.* 2007. www.gameo.org

"Mennonite-Catholic dialogues, MWC delegation receives warm welcome in Rome." *Courier* 22, 4 (December 2007):10-11.

Meyer, C. "Zur Geschichte der Widertäufer in Oberschwaben" *Zeitschrift des historischen Vereins fuer Schwaben und Neuberg I*, 1874, 245, cited in Walter Klaassen, *Michael Gaismair; Revolutionary and Reformer*. Leiden: Brill, 1978, 107.

Muir, Elizabeth Gillan. *Petticoats in the Pulpit The Story of Nineteenth-Century Methodist Women Preachers in Upper Canada*. Toronto, ON: The United Church Publishing House, 1991.

Moser, Heinz. *Die Scharfrichter von Tirol, Ein Beitrag zur Geschichte des Strafvollzuges in Tirol von 1497-178*. Innsbruck: Steigerverlag, 1982.

MWC release. "Pope greets Mennonites: a first in church history." *Mennonite Brethren Herald* 46, 12 (December 2007): 8. See also http://mwc.cmm.org/

New Catholic Encyclopedia 9. New York, N.Y.: McGraw-Hill, 1967-96, 200.

Noflatscher, Heinz. "Alltag des Kanonikus." *Quellen zur historischen Wohnkultur, Denkmalpflege in Südtirol*. Bozen: Landesdenkmalamt, 1988, 325-36, cited in Werner O. Packull, *Hutterite Beginnings: Communitarian Experiments during the Reformation*. Baltimore: John Hopkins University Press, 1995.

Oyer, John S. "Mecenseffy, Grete (1899-1985)." *Mennonite Quarterly Review*, 60 (January 1986): 104.

_____ "Mecenseffy, Grete (1899-1985)." *Global Anabaptist Mennonite Encyclopedia Online*. 1988. www.gameo.org

_____ "Recantation," *Global Anabaptist Mennonite Encyclopedia Online*. 1989. www.gameo.org

_____ *"They Harry the Good People Out of the Land" Essays on the Persecution, Survival and Flourishing of Anabaptists and Mennonites*, ed. John D. Roth. Goshen, IN: Mennonite Historical Society, 2000.

Packull, Werner O. *Hutterite Beginnings: Communitarian Experiments during the Reformation*. Baltimore: John Hopkins University Press, 1995.

_____ *Hutterer in Tirol: Frühes Täufertum in der Schweiz, Tirol und Mähren,* Translated by Astrid von Schlachta. Innsbruck: Universitätsverlag Wagner, 2000.

_____ *Peter Riedemann: Shaper of the Hutterite Tradition.* Kitchener, ON: Pandora Press, 2007.

_____ *Mysticism and the Early South German Austrian Anabaptist Movement 1515-1531.* Scottdale, Pa.: Herald Press, 1977.

_____ *Die Hutterer zwischen Tirol und Amerika Eine Reise durch die Jahrhunderte.* Translated by Astrid von Schlachta. Innsbruck: Universitätsverlag Wagner, 2005.

Peachey, Paul. *Die soziale Herkunft der Schweizer Taeufer in der Reformationszeit, eine religionssoziologische Untersuchung.* Karlsruhe: Heinrich Schneider, 1954.

Peters, Marilyn G. "Women," *Mennonite Encyclopedia V.* Scottdale, PA: Herald Press, 1990. 933-934.

Pipkin, H. Wayne and John H. Yoder. ed. and translators *Balthasar Hubmaier Theologian of Anabaptism, 1528.* Scottdale, PA: Herald Press, 1989.

Pries, Edmund. "Anabaptist Oath Refusal: Basel, Bern, and Strasbourg, 1525-1538." Unpublished PhD dissertation, University of Waterloo, 1995. [now published under the same title by Pandora Press, 2023]

Rendall, Jane. *The Origins of Modern Feminism: Women in Britain, France and the United States 1780-1860.* London: Macmillan Education, 1985.

Rischar, Klaus. "Der Missionar Eucharius Binder Und Sein Mitarbeiter Joachim März." *Mennonitische Geschichtsblätter* 25, 20 (1968): 18-26.

_____ "Research Notes, The Martyrdom of the Salzburg Anabaptists in 1527" *Mennonite Quarterly Review* 43, 4 (October 1969): 322-327.

Roth, Friedrich. *Augsburgs Reformationsgeschichte, 1531-1537 bezw. 1540, Bd. II.* München: Theodor Ackermann, 1904.

Roth, Willard and Gerald W. Schlabach. *Called Together to be Peacemakers: Report of the International Dialogue between the Catholic Church and Mennonite World*

Conference 1998-2003. Abridged ed. The Bridgefolk Series. Kitchener. ON: Pandora Press, 2005.

Ruether, Rosemary and Eleanor McLaughlin, ed. *Women of Spirit, Female Leadership in the Jewish and Christian Traditions.* New York, NY: Simon and Schuster, 1979.

Sachs, Hanelore. *The Renaissance Woman.* Translated by Marianne Hertzfeld. New York, N.Y.: McGraw-Hill Book Company, 1971.

Schäfer, Dieter. *Aufstieg, Fall und Ruhm des Pankraz von Freyberg.* Prien am Chiemsee: Ecora-Verlag, 1996.

Schäufele, Wolfgang. "The Missionary Vision and Activity of the Anabaptist Laity." *Mennonite Quarterly Review* 36, 2 (April 1962): 99-115.

_____ *Das Missionarische Bewusstsein und Wirken der Täufer, Dargestellt nach oberdeutschen Quellen.* Lemgo: Neukirchener Verlag des Erziehungsvereins, 1966.

Schiess, Traugott. *Briefwechsel der Brüder Ambrosius und Thomas Blaurer, 1509-1548.* Freiburg i. Br.: Friedrich Ernst Fehsenfeld, 1908.

Schlachta, Astrid von. *Hutterische Konfession und Tradition (1578-1619) Etabliertes Leben Zwischen Ordnung und Ambivalenz.* Mainz: Verlag Philipp Von Zabern, 2003.

_____ *Die Hutterer zwischen Tirol und Amerika Eine Reise durch die Jahrhunderte.* Innsbruck: Universitätsverlag Wagner, 2006.

_____ "Die Geschichte der Täufer in Tirol ein Begleiter durch die Austellung." In *Verbrannte Visionen? Erinnerungs Orte der Täufer in Tirol.* ed. Astrid von Schlachta, Ellinor Forster, Giovanni Merola, 8-47. Innsbruck: Innsbruck University Press, 2007.

Schmelzer, Matthias. "Geschichte der Preise und Löhne in Rattenberg vom Ende des 15. bis in die 2. Hälfte des 19. Jahrhunderts." Unpublished Doctoral dissertation, Leopold-Franzens University, Innsbruck, 1972.

_____ "Jakob Huters Wirken im Lichte von Bekenntnissen gefangener Täufer." *Der Schlern Monateschrift für Südtiroler Landeskunde* 63 (November 1989): 596-618.

_____ "Elisabeth von Wolkenstein of Uttenheim." In *Profiles of Anabaptist Women Sixteenth-Century Reforming Pioneer.* Translated by Linda A. Huebert Hecht. ed. C. Arnold Snyder and Linda A. Huebert Hecht, 164-177. Waterloo, ON: Wilfrid Laurier Press, 1996.

Schwarz, Kaspar. *Tirolische Schlösser, Heft I, Unterinntal, I Teil* (Innsbruck: Verlag der Wagner'schen Universitäts Buchhandlung, 1907.

Segl, Peter. *Ketzer in Österreich, Untersuchungen über Häresie und Inquisition im Herzogtum Oesterreich im 13. und beginnenden 14. Jahrhundert.* Paderborn: Ferdinand Schöningh, 1984.

Shaher, Shulamith, *The Fourth Estate A History of Women in the Middle Ages*, trans. by Chaya Galai. New York, N.Y.: Methuen, 1983.

Snyder, C. Arnold. "Word and Power in Reformation Zurich." *Archive for Reformation History*, 81 (1990): 263-85.

_____ *Anabaptist History and Theology: An Introduction.* Kitchener, ON: Pandora Press, 1995.

_____ *Anabaptist History and Theology: Revised Student Edition.* Kitchener, ON: Pandora Press, 1997.

_____ and Linda A. Huebert Hecht, ed. *Profiles of Anabaptist Women Sixteenth-Century Reforming Pioneers.* Waterloo, ON: Wilfrid Laurier Press, 1996, seventh impression 2008.

_____ "The Swiss Anabaptist Context." In *Profiles of Anabaptist Women Sixteenth-Century Reforming Pioneers,*" ed. C. Arnold Snyder and Linda A. Huebert Hecht, 18-24. Waterloo, ON: Wilfrid Laurier Press, 1996

_____ "South German/Austrian Anabaptist Women." In *Profiles of Anabaptist Women Sixteenth-Century Reforming Pioneers,*" ed. C. Arnold Snyder and Linda A. Huebert Hecht, 70-81. Waterloo, ON: Wilfrid Laurier Press, 1996.

_____ "The North German/Dutch Anabaptist Context." In *Profiles of Anabaptist Women Siixteenth-Century Reforming Pioneers,"* ed. C. Arnold Snyder and Linda A. Huebert Hecht, 246-257. Waterloo, ON: Wilfrid Laurier Press, 1996.

_____ "Magdalena, Walpurga and Sophia Marschalk von Pappenheim." In *Profiles of Anabaptist Women Sixteenth-Century Reforming Pioneers,"* ed. C. Arnold Snyder and Linda A. Huebert Hecht, 111-123. Waterloo, ON: Wilfrid Laurier Press, 1996.

_____ and Linda A. Huebert Hecht, "Ursula Hellrigel of the Ötz Valley and Annelein of Freiburg." In *Profiles of Anabaptist Women Sixteenth-Century Reforming Pioneers,"* ed. C. Arnold Snyder and Linda A. Huebert Hecht, 195-201. Waterloo, ON: Wilfrid Laurier Press, 1996

_____ "Introduction." In *Sources of South German/Austrian Anabaptism*. Translated by Walter Klaassen, Frank Friesen, Werner O. Packull, xiii-L1. Kitchener, ON: Pandora Press, co-published with Herald Press, 2001.

Sprunger, Keith L. "God's Powerful Army of the Weak: Anabaptist Women of the Radical Reformation." In *Triumph Over Silence, Women in Protestant History,* ed. Richard L. Greaves, 45-74. Westport, CT: Greenwood Press, 1985.

Stayer, James M. "The Anabaptists." In *Reformation Europe: A Guide to Research*, ed. Steven Ozment, 135-159 St. Louis: Center for Reformation Research, 1982.

_____ "Anabaptists and Future Anabaptists in the Peasants' War" *Mennonite Quarterly Review* LXII, 2 (April 1988): 99-139.

_____ *The German Peasants' War and Anabaptist Community of Goods*. Kingston, ON: McGill-Queen's University Press, 1991.

_____ "The Passing of the Radical Moment in the Radical Reformation." *Mennonite Quarterly Review* LXXI, 1 (January 1997): 147-52.

Stolz, Otto. *Rechtsgeschichte des Bauernstandes und der Landwirtschaft in Tirol und Vorarlberg*. Bozen: Verlag FerrarIi - Auer A. G., 1949.

Strauss, Gerald. *Law, Resistance, and the State, The Opposition to Roman Law in Reformation Germany.* Princeton, NJ: Princeton University Press, 1986.

Stuard, Susan. "The Dominion of Gender: Women's Fortunes in the High Middle Ages," In *Becoming Visible, Women in European History*, 2nd ed, ed. Renate Bridenthal, Claudia Koonz, Susan Stuard, 153-172. Boston: Houghton Mifflin, 1987.

Thomas, Keith. "Women in the Civil War Sects." *Past and Present* 13 (1958): 42-62.

Ties, Hanns-Paul. "Bartlmä Dill—der Maler und Wiedertäufer, Neues zum Leben und zum Werk des wichtigsten Südtiroler Renaissancekünstlers." *Dolomiten,* 25/26, 2 (2006): 439-461.

Valerio, Adriana. "Women in Church History." In *Women, Invisible in Church and Theology*, ed. Elizabeth Schüssler Fiorenza and Mary Collins, 63-71. *Concillium* 182. Edinburgh, T. and T. Clark, 1985: 63-71.

Waite, Gary. "Women Supporters of David Joris." In *Profiles of Anabaptist Women Sixteenth Century Reforming Pioneers*, ed. C. Arnold Snyder and Linda A. Huebert Hecht, 316-335. Waterloo, ON: Wilfrid Laurier Press, 1996.

Waldhof, Renate and Julia Walleczek. "Alle Wege führen nach Mähren—welchen wählt man?" In *Verbrannte Visionen? Erinnerungorte der Täufer in Tirol,* ed. Astrid von Schlachta, Ellinor Forster, Giovanni Merola, 155-159. Innsbruck: Innsbruck University Press, 2007.

Wall, Victor. "Beugungsgottesdienst in Filadelfia Hinführung aus geschichtlicher Perspektive." *Mennoblatt* (1 Mai 2008): 3-4.

Walker, Williston and Richard A. Norris, David W. Lotz, Robert T. Handy. *History of the Christian Church, Fourth Edition.* New York, NY: Charles Scribner's Sons, 1985.

Wappler, Paul. *Die Täuferbewegung in Thüringen von 1526-1584.* Jena: Fischer, 1913.

Warnicke, Retha M. "Lady Mildmay's Journal: A Study of Autobiography and Meditation in Reformation England." *The Sixteenth Century Journal* XX, 1 (April 1989): 55-68.

Weber, Max. *The Sociology of Religion*. Translated by Ephraim Fischoff. Boston: Beacon Press, 1922.

Weber, Marianne. "Eheideal und Eherecht." In *Frauenfragen und Frauengedanken Gesammelte Aufsätze,* ed. Marianne Weber. Tübingen: Verlag von J. C. B. Mohr (Paul Siebeck), 1919.

_____ *Max Weber on Charisma and Institution Building, Selected Papers*, ed. S. N. Eisenstadt. Chicago, IL: University of Chicago Press, 1968.

Wenger, John C. and C. Arnold Snyder. "Schleitheim Confession." *Global Anabaptist Mennonite Encyclopedia Online*. 1990. www.gameo.org

Whiteley, Marilyn Färdig. "Modest, Unaffected, and Fully Consecrated: Lady Evangelists in Canadian Methodism" In *Changing Roles of Women within the Christian Church in Canada*, ed. Elizabeth G. Muir and Marilyn Whiteley. Toronto, ON: University of Toronto Press, 1995.

_____ "Deaconess Redefined: Seeking a Role for Women in the Holiness Churches of Ralph Horner." In *Historical Papers 1999 Canadian Society of Church History*, 73-86.

Widmoser, Eduard. *Tirol A Bis Z*. Innbruck: Südtirol-Verlag, 1970.

Wiesner, Merry E. "Women's Defense of Their Public Role." In *Women in the Middle Ages and the Renaissance: Literary and Historical Perspectives,* ed. Mary Beth Rose, 1-27 Syracuse, NY: Syracuse University Press, 1986.

_____ "Frail, Weak, and Helpless: Women's Legal Position in Theory and Reality." In *Regnum, Religio et Ratio: Essays presented to Robert M. Kingdon*, ed. Jerome Friedman, 161-169. Kirksville, MO: Sixteenth Century Publishers, 1987.

_____ "Nuns, Wives, and Mothers: Women and the Reformation in Germany." In *Women in Reformation and Counter-Reformation Europe, Public and Private Worlds*, ed. Sherrin Marshall, 8-28. Bloomington: Indiana University Press, 1989.

_____ *Women and Gender in Early Modern Europe.* Cambridge, England: Cambridge University Press, 1993.

Winkelbauer, Thomas. "Die Rechtliche Stellung der Täufer im 16. und 17. Jahrhundert am Beispiel der habsburgischen Länder." In *Ein Thema— zwei Perspektiven Juden und Christen in Mittelalter und Frühneuzeit*, ed. Eveline Brugger and Birgit Wiedel, 34-66. Innsbruck: Studienverlag, 2007.

Wolkan, Rudolf. *Die Lieder der Wiedertäufer, Ein Beitrag zur deutschen und niederländischen Literatur-und Kirchengeschichte*, 16-17. Nieuwkoop, B. De Graaf, 1965 [1903].

Yamasaki, April. "Trust God's Leadership." *Rejoice! Daily Devotional Readings, June, July, August 2008* (Monday June 16), Winnipeg, MB: Kindred Productions, 2008.

Index of Women's Names

Names and categories of Anabaptist Women in Austria, 1527-1531

be=believer; la=lay leader; mi=missioner; ma=martyr; ip=indirect participant; followed by the page number where the woman is first named.

Women categorized as Indirect Participants may not have been re-baptized. Often, they were accused because of Anabaptist family members or persons they assisted.

Women's names often end with 'in'.

The letters n.n. meaning "no name" are used where a woman's name is not given, with the page number where she is first named in the court records, followed by her category and the page number where she is named in this book. These women are not named in the index of TA 1972.

A

Agnes, widow from Erspan,	be, 118
Ameiser, Waldpurga,	be, 101, 115, 126, 151
Ampos, Hanns, wife,	be, 75
Ampos, Sebastian, mother,	be, 75
Angstwurm, Dorothea,	ip, 73
Anna, Goldschmidt's maid,	be, 186
Artzatin of Weissach, Cristina,	ma, 74
Aschelpergerin,	be?, 157

B

Baderin, Gilg,	ma?, 30, 36
Bärbel from Rettenberg,	be, 45, 157
Bair, Magdalena,	ma, 82
Binder, Ursula Nehspitzin,	mi, 29, 34, 35, 51
Blacksmith's wife,	be, 127
Blacksmith's wife, preacher,	la, 48, 49, 144, 161, 209

Blaurock, Els (wife of Jörg),   be, 9, 42, 61
Breidl, Schuester's cook,   be, 186

C

Carpenter's wife in Hall,   be, 190
Craft, Hanns, wife,   be, 57
Crenseisen, Heinrich, wife,   be, 146, 173
Cristina from Scheyern,   be, 78
Crown Administrator's wife,   be, 31, 32, 34, 197
Crown Administrator's wife (old), be, 75

D

Dänckl, (Stablmüller), W., wife,   be, 122
Dörrer, Walpurga,   be, 172

E

Egger, Ursula,   be, 133, 151
Egger, Cristina,   be, 99, 109
Egger, Peter, daughter,   be, 190
Egger, Anna,   la, 50, 53, 72
Erler, Gregori, wife,   be, 121
Ess, Sebastian, wife,   be, 60
Ess, Sebastion, maid,   be, 60

F

Feichtner, Hans, wife,   be?, 197
Fleischacker, Jörg, wife,   la, 77
Fleischacker, Jörg, daughter,   ip, 77
Fleischacker, Jörg, daughter,   ip, 77
Forchner, Elspeth,   ip, 144, 157
Fras's wife,   be, 47, 80, 82
Frawnholtz, Agnes,   be, 133, 148, 163-64
Frewoltin, Barbara,   be, 128
Freyberg, Helena von,   la, 9, 32, 44, 46, 49, 50, 51, 62-9, 78, 149, 247-51
Frick, Dorothea,   be, 43, 72

Frischmann, Hanns, daughter,   be, 180, 188
Fundnetscher, Lienhard, wife, be, 46, 82, 152
Furtnerin, Elisabeth,   be, 162
Futterreith, Magdalena,   ma?, 126, 129

G

Gärber, Christoff, wife,   be, 127
Gärber, Dorothea,   be, 83, 107
Gärberin,   be, 190
Gärn, Juliane,   ip, 110
Gallin,   la, 77
Gallpüchlerin,   la, 30, 42, 53, 59, 83
Gallpüchlerin, daughter,   ip, 59, 61
Gamper, Rosina,   ma?, 129
Ganntzler, Margreth,   be, 163
Ganntzler, Elspeth,   be, 163
Gasser, Anna,   be, 30, 42, 61, 101, 109, 113, 114, 120, 152
Gasserin's maid, Agatha,   be, 101, 107, 112
Gasserin's maid, Lucia,   be, 109, 120
Gasteiger, Anna,   ma, 121, 151
Gasteiger, Barbara,   ma, 107, 129, 131
Gengl, Blasius, wife,   ip, 113
Gesslerin, Elsbeth,   be, 74, 79
Gesslerin, Katharina,   be, 74, 79
Ghreuter, Andre, wife,   be, 187
Glenerin, Margreth,   be, 46, 76
Greiner, Hans, wife,   be, 77
Gret, Cristan Dauxerin's maid, be, 159
Greth, a maid,   be, 159
Gross Enngerle,   be, 75
Gross Enngerle, daughter,   be, 75
Gschälen's, maid,   ma?, 129
Gschäll, Anna,   be, 126, 149, 170-71, 184-85
Gschäll, Margarethe,   ip, 130-31

H

Hanns in the valley, Ursula,	be, 45, 154
Has, Bartlme, wife,	be, 113
Häselerin,	ip, 133
Held, Jörg, wife,	be, 59
Hellrigel, Hanns, wife Anna,	be, 180, 188
Hellrigel, Georg, wife Anna,	be, 173
Hellrigel, Georg, mother Else,	be, 173
Hellrigel, Ursula,	ma, 24, n.58, 216, 245
Heuberger, Ursula, mother,	ma?, 128, 129
Heuberger, Anna, widow,	ma?, 128, 129
Höls, Margreth,	be, 135
Huber, Wolfgang, wife,	be, 190
Hueben, Margarethe,	be, 144, 151, 158
Hülbn, Michel in the, wife,	ma, 99, 110
Hutter, Agnes,	be, 32, 103, 107, 134
Hutter, Balthasar, wife,	be, 121

J

Jacoben, Herr (priest), wife,	be, 57

K

Kaiser, Ruprecht, wife,	be, 187
Kassian, Agnes,	be, 118
Kassian, Katharina,	ma, 118
Katharina at the Kolbenthurn,	be, 190
Katharina, Kramerin/shopkeeper,	ma, 173-74
Katt, Margreth,	be, 133
Katzingerin, Kunigund,	be, 133
Kellen, Anna Fundnetscher,	be, 187
Kerschpaumer, Mathes, wife,	ma, 75, 149
Kirchmair, Walburg,	be, 135
Klein, Gilg, wife,	mi, 54, 100, 115
Klinglerin, Magdalene,	be, 159
Kob, Simon, wife,	ma, 129-30

Kobl, Margret,	be, 30, 42, 73, 79-80, 149, 152
Koblin maid, Bärbl,	ip, 80
Koblin maid, Els,	ip, 79
Köberl, Susanna,	be, 125, 128
Körner, Barbara,	be, 162
Kofler, Lienhard, widow,	be, 118, 123
Koler, Jacob, maid Anna,	be, 98, 109
Kollis, Peter, daughter,	be, 156
Kramer, Peter, wife,	be, 77
Krätlerin, Anna II,	be, 74, 151
Krätlerin, Anna I,	be, 73-74, 151
Kreutzerin,	la, 43, 77
Kuen, Ursula,	be, 99, 125

L

Lackner, Leonhard, widow,	ip, 117
Laittner, Elisabeth,	be, 157
Landbergerin,	mi, 32, 34, 51
Lanntringer, Bernhard, wife,	be, 155
Lanntringer, Bernhard, mother,	be, 155
Lanntringer, Cristina,	ma, 167
Lautterwein, Hanns, wife,	be, 57
Lehner, Margreth,	be, 165
Lentz, Cristan, mother,	be, 187
Leonhardt of Viltz, wife,	ip, 146, 164
Leopold, Hans, wife,	be, 57
Lercher, Barbara,	ma, 172, 198
Letta, Hanns, wife,	be, 118
Letzelter, Hans, wife,	be, 76-7, 168
Lindner, Ulrich's wife,	ip, 113
Lindterspacher, Georg, wife,	ip, 148-49, 164
Lucas, wife,	be, 57
Luntzbegkerin, Cristina,	ma, 133

M

Magdalena of Hallerndorf,	be, 156
Magdalena, maid of Rattenberg,	be, 135
Maria from the Nons,	be, 162
Mair, Elisabeth,	be, 110
Mair, Anton of the village, sister,	be, 165
Mair, Anton of the village, wife,	ma, 149, 165
Mair, Katharina,	be, 181, 189
Mair, Christoff (Stoffl), wife,	be, 113-14, 119-20
Mairhofer, Balthasar, wife,	be, 197
Mairhofer maid,	ip, 197
Maler, Barbara,	be, 107, 181, 189
Maler, Caspar, wife,	mi, 49, 54, 79
Maler, Dorothea/Anna,	ma, 101, 102-03, 107, 126-27, 244-45
Margreth, the Kobin's sister,	ma?, 129.
Manngl's wife	ma?, 129
Marpeck, Gilg, wife,	ip, 186
Marx in the pasture, wife,	be, 156
Maurer, Hans, wife,	ma, 55, 128
Maurfoglin,	be, 77
Mayr, Melchior, wife,	ma, 159
Mayrl, Margareth Frönerin,	ip, 120
Messerschmied, Mathias, wife,	mi, 29, 30, 32, 33-4, 51, 183, 197
Messerschmiedin from Hall,	be, 61
Miner in Schwaz, wife,	ip?, 157
Miner's wife,	be?, 186
Miner's wife's daughter,	be?, 186
Miterspacher, Elisabeth,	be, 163
Mittenmair, Lienhard, daughter,	be, 162
Moser, Mathes, wife,	be, 112
Mügin, Valtin,	be, 157
Müller, Dorothea,	be, 118
Müllerin, Ursula (old),	be, 121
Müllner, Peter, daughter,	be, 127

N

n.n.55a, young woman,	be, 58
n.n.55b, a cook,	be, 58
n.n.55c, a maid,	be, 58
n.n.55d, mother of maid,	be, 58
n.n.55e, chaplain's cook,	be, 58
n.n.55f, innkeeper, wife,	be, 57
n.n.56a, city judge, wife,	be, 58
n.n.56b, mayor, wife,	be, 58
n.n.56c, two cooks,	be, 57
n.n.56d, two cooks,	be, 57
n.n.56e, a young woman,	be, 57
n.n.56f, a maid,	be, 57
n.n.57a, shoemaker, wife,	be, 58
n.n.57b, wife,	be, 58
n.n.96a, maid,	be, 70
n.n.113a, maid,	be, 72
n.n.113b, maid,	be, 72
n.n.120a, several women,	be, 72
n.n.120b, several women,	be, 72
n.n.137a, four women,	be, 73
n.n.137b, four women,	be, 73
n.n.137c, four women,	be, 73
n.n.137d, four women,	be, 73
n.n.138a, one woman,	be, 74
n.n.138b, 1 of 3 women,	ma, 74
n.n.174a, mother,	ma, 81
n.n.174b, daughter,	ma, 81
n.n.175a, 3 women executed,	ma, 81
n.n.175b, 3 women executed,	ma, 81
n.n.175c, 3 women executed,	ma, 81
n.n.177a, woman,	be, 81
n.n.184a, two pregnant women,	be, 83
n.n.184b, two pregnant women,	be, 83
n.n.190, woman/Schiemer,	ma?, 109

Addition

n.n.95a, Freyberg maid,	be, 63
n.n.95b, Freyberg maid,	be, 63
n.n.95c, Freyberg maid,	be, 63

n.n.193a, two women,   ma, 110
n.n.193b, two women,   ma?, 110
n.n.223a, 2 poor women,   ma, 114
n.n.223b, 2 poor women,   ma, 114
n.n.227a, three women,   be, 115
n.n.227b, three women,   be, 115
n.n.227c, three women,   be, 115
n.n.237a, 10 women executed,   ma, 116
n.n.237b, 10 women executed,   ma, 116
n.n.237c, 10 women executed,   ma, 116
n.n.237d, 10 women executed,   ma, 116
n.n.237e, 10 women executed,   ma, 116
n.n.237f, 10 women executed,   ma, 116
n.n.237g, 10 women executed,   ma, 116
n.n.237h, 10 women executed,   ma, 116
n.n.237i, 10 women executed,   ma, 116
n.n.237j, 10 women executed,   ma, 116
n.n.239, woman leader,   la, 117, 189
n.n.278, a woman,   be, 125
n.n.280a, 2 women of Hall,   ip, 124
n.n.280b, 2 women of Hall,   ip, 124
n.n.287, woman Plattner baptized, be, 128
n.n.297, woman pardoned,   be, 131
n.n.380a, pregnant woman,   be, 160-61
n.n.380b, pregnant woman,   be, 160-61
n.n.394, three women,   be, 162
n.n.415 Bavarian women,   be, 166
n.n.449 women in Gschäll house, be, 184
n.n.472a women drowned,   ma, 188
n.n.472b women drowned,   ma, 188
n.n.472a wives who fled,   be, 189
n.n.472b wives who fled,   be, 189
n.n.474a two women,   be, 190
n.n.474b two women,   be, 190

n.n.498 women at cave meeting, be, 197
n.n.502, women in Sterzing, be, 199
Naterin, ma, 173
Neschgartin, Margreth, be, 190
Nickinger, Balthasar, wife, be, 149, 166-67, 242
Nickinger's old mother, ip, 149, 154, 166-67
Nickinger, Balthasar, 1st sister, be, 149, 165, 167
Nickinger, Balthasar, 2nd sister, be, 149, 167
Nickinger, L. Katharina, wife, be, 149, 162
Nickinger, L. Katharina, sister, be, 149, 162, 165
Niedermaier, Apollonia, Nock, ma, 43, 47, 58-9
Martin's wife, ma, 45, 82, 151
Nüssler, Scholastica, be, 157

O

Ober, Margreth, ma, 165
Oberhöller, Michel, wife, be, 185
Oberhofer, Michel, wife, ip, 81
Obermauer, Martha, be, 156-57
Oberwiser, wife, ip?, 156
Obinger, Ursula, be, 147, 167, 242
Obinger, Gilg, wife, be, 190
Ochsentreiber, Anna/Ursula, ma, 102-03, 126, 244-45
Ochssennfurtterin, ip, 34
Ortner, Dorothea, ma, 119
Ottilia of Tuna, be, 78

P

Pästler, Margreth be, 190
Palpatscher, Florian, wife ip, 81
Paneyder, Cristina be, 124
Passerin be, 98, 108
Penntz, Lamprecht, wife be, 44, 75-6
Pentzel's daughter be, 83
Pernhappel, Barbara be, 46, 75, 77
Pinzgauer, Ursula, be, 158-59

Planer, Andre, wife,   be, 121
Platten, Lienhard, wife,   be, 72, 73
Platzfassin,   be, 156
Pletzer, Hans, wife,   be, 70
Pölt, Paul, wife,   ma, 172
Porst, Marx, wife of,   be, 165, 180, 188
Praun, Katharina,   be, 126-27
Praun, Martin, wife,   be, 191
Prewin,   be, 156
Pünnter, Anna,   be, 173-74

R

Raderin of St. Lorenzen,   be, 118
Ragermacher maid,   be, 191,
Räss, Briccius, wife,   be, 181, 189
Reck, Han, daughter,   be, 115
Regina, martyr's widow,   ip, 146, 166
Reichlerin,   be, 190
Reschl, Barbara,   be, 133
Riederin, Anna,   be, 128
Riedhofer, Hanns, wife,   be, 57
Riemenschneider, B. D., maid, ip, 60, 61
Riemenschneider, B. D., Katharina, be, 60, 61
Riemer, Veit, wife,   be, 51, 77
Riemer, Caspar, wife,   be, 77
Riemer, Pangratz, wife,   mi, 77
Rinnerin, Anna,   be, 79, 151
Rospuchlerin, Äfferlin,   be, 75
Rotvelderin,   ma, 115
Rueff, Hanns, wife,   be, 57

S

Sackmann, Anna,   be , 107, 112, 119-20
Sailerin, Ursula,   be, 72

Index

Sallman, Ziprian, wife,	ip, 197
Schäntl, Jacob, wife,	ip, 47, 82
Schaider, Anna (Weissach),	be, 163
Scheffelmacher, Balthasar, wife,	be, 159
Schesserin, Helene,	be, 78
Scheuring, Hans, wife,	ma, 113, 151
Schleiffer, Uetz, wife,	be, 57
Schlosserin,	ip, 70
Schmid, Jörg, wife,	be, 157, 241-42
Schmid, Ursula,	ma, 173, 198, 241
Schmid, Valtein, wife,	ma, 146, 171
Schmid, Wolfgang, widow,	ip, 187
Schneider, Anna,	ma, 173
Schneider, Caspar, wife,	be, 121
Schneider, Eva,	ma, 43, 47, 58
Schneider, Hanns, wife,	be, 58
Schneider, Magdalena,	ma, 119
Schneider, Melchior, wife,	be, 54, 82, 119
Schneider, Wilhelm, wife,	be, 157
Schneider, Wolfgang, wife,	ip, 102, 122, 152
Schneyder, Matheus, wife,	be, 57
Schröffl, Margarethe,	be, 190
Schueler's maid,	be, 128
Schuester, Jacob, wife,	be, 157
Schützinger, Barbara,	be, 43, 70-1, 147-48, 210, 213
Schuster, Katharina, widow,	ma?, 129
Schuster, Regine,	ma, 165
Schwaiglin, Katharina,	be, 100, 119, 133
Schwartz, Caspar, two sisters, a,	mi, 54, 100
Schwartz, Caspar, two sisters, b,	mi, 54, 100
Schwaykofer, wet nurse,	be, 182, 191
Schwaykofer, mother,	be, 182, 191
Schweitzer, Jörg, wife,	be, 110, 151
Silberin,	la?, 53, 83
Smit, Liennhart, wife,	be, 57

Sneider, Bernhard, wife,   be, 75
Spitzhamer, Leonhard, wife,   be, 149, 171-72
Spitzhamer's maid,   be, 43, 56, 70
Springenfell, Bartlme, wife,   be, 56, 70
Staindl, Leonhard, wife,   ma, 167
Stainer, Margarete,   ma, 162
Stainperger, Thomas, wife,   be, 119
Steffan's wife, innkeeper,   be, 79
Steiner, Dorothea,   be, 133
Stocker, Katharina,   be, 184
Strael, Wolfgang, wife,   ma, 45, 82
Streicher, Katharina,   ma, 55, 103, 108, 134-35, 144, 159
Sumerer, Hans, wife,   be, 197
Sunschwennter, Cristina,   be, 133, 151

T

Taurer, Andre, maid,   be, 61-62
Taurer, Andre, wife,   be, 61-62
Taurer, Cristan, maid,   be, 61-62, 78
Taurer, Cristan, wife,   be, 61
Taurer, Hans, maid,   be, 70
Taurer, Hans, wife,   be, 70
Taurer, Paul, wife,   ma, 169
Taurer, Peter, wife,   ip, 70
Taurerin, Elsbeth,   be, 75
Tegerseer, Hanns, wife,   ma, 169-70
Tillen, Ursula,   be, 121
Tischler, Benedikt, wife,   ma, 119
Tollinger, Jörg, widow,   be, 134
Tonauer, Magdalene,   ma, 156
Treibenreif, Sigmund, maid,   be, 60
Treibenreifin   be, 61, 152
Torgglerin, Katharina   be, 48, 80
Tückhls, Margarethe   be, 190
Tyschler, Peter, wife,   ip, 34

Index 291

U

Ungelter, Jacob, wife,	be, 57
Urscher, Erhardt, wife,	be, 180, 185, 186, 187, 197, 213
Urstetterin, Lenntz,	be, 107, 179, 186

V

Vasser, Jörg, wife,	be, 36, 146, 169
Velcklehner, Barbara,	mi, 75, 110-11, 153
Velcklehner, Hans, sister,	mi, 53, 73
Vest, Balthasar, wife,	ma, 55, 103, 108, 132
Veytstetter, Dorothea,	be, 164
Veytstetter, Barbara,	ma, 133, 164
Viltzurner, Hans, wife,	ip, 79, 153
Vischer of Liesfelden, wife,	be, 72
Vischer, Erhardt, wife,	be, 180, 187
Vischer, Lienhard, wife,	be, 126, 170
Vitzthum, Lorenz, wife,	ip, 81, 152
Vogellehner, wife,	be, 156

W

Wagensail, Lucas, wife,	be, 154, 192
Wagner, Katharina,	be, 133
Wald, Magdalena,	be, 119
Waldner, Mathis, wife,	la, 53, 83
Waltsamin of Wattens,	ip, 78
Waltzenpergerin, (coinmaker),	be, 199
Weber, Hanns, wife,	be, 58
Weber, Jörg, wife,	be, 188
Weiss, Helena,	be, 189
Weiss, Magdalena,	ma, 180, 188
Weissach, wife of,	ip, 163
Weissach, Margreth,	be, 163
Weissenhofer, wife,	be, 58
Weissenpurgerin, Ursula,	be, 162
Weltzenberger, Anna,	ma?, 112, 153

Weltzenberger, Magdalena,	ma, 129
Weltzenbergerin, Martha,	be, 46, 70
Wennter, Hanns, wife,	be, 57
Wennter, Hanns, daughter,	be, 58
Werd, Margarethe,	ip, 133
Weylmesserin, Barbara,	be, 131
Widinger, Barbara,	be, 156
Widinger, Cristina,	be, 156
Widmauer, Katharina,	be, 133, 151
Wilthueter, Leonhardt, wife,	ip, 172
Wiser, Dorothea,	be, 118, 123
Wiser, Margreth (Old Wiserin),	be, 118, 123
Wiser, Margarete, daughter,	be, 162
Wolf, Margreth,	ma, 60, 61, 173-74
Wolfgang in the Ried, Barbara,	be, 148, 163
Wolfram, Elisabeth,	be, 45, 83, 111-12
Wolfram, Magdalena,	ip, 111
Wolkenstein, Elisabeth von,	la, 9, 44, 45, 48, 49, 53, 104, 106, 154, 182, 192-96
Wynnter, Martha,	be, 35

Z

Zägeler, Elspeth,	be, 112, 163
Zehentnerin, Ursula,	
Ziegler, Cristina,	be, 191

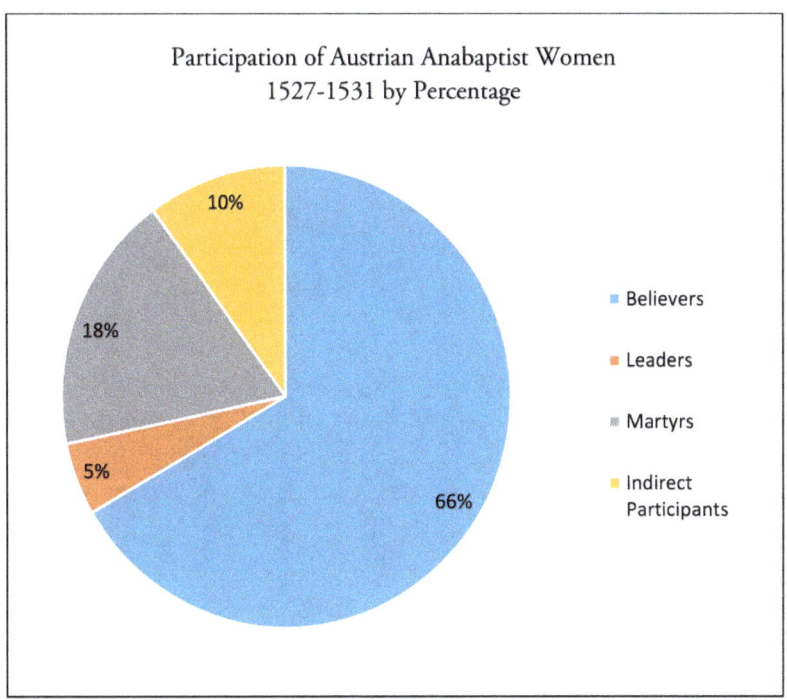

Created by the author, August 21, 2023.

Please note: the Leaders category of five percent (21 in number) represents two similar groups of women: 10 Missioners and 11 Lay Leaders.

Index of Selected Names and Topics

Ambras, 127, 241-242

Amish, 11, 17

Amon, Hans, 104, 126, 171, 193, 211

Anabaptism: baptism and recantation were individual choices, 1, 60, 207; beginnings, 3-6; emphasis on voluntary membership, 7; and the Great Commission, 4; how it came to Tirol, 29-31; how it continued, 209-213; lay nature of, 8, 48, 150; meaning of the word, 1, 4-5; and the medieval Waldensian sect, 8; a popular grass roots movement, 30; as renewal, 7-8, 183; restitution of New Testament church, 30; stages of development and institutionalization, 7-8, 51-53, 204, 206; teachings and beliefs, 5, 36, 77, 79, 107, 111, 156, 179, 185-86, 215, 244-45, 247-51; for its nonviolent nature *see* nonresistance. *See also* apocalypticism, community of goods, Bible, faith, Lord's Supper, priesthood of all believers, sacraments and, religious movements

Anabaptists, direct descendants today, 11, 17

Annelein of Freiburg, 245-247. *See also* Ursula Hellrigel

Anngst, Bartlme, judge in Rattenberg, 56, 154, 170

Anticlericalism, 4-5, 6, 7; expressed in a hymn, 244-45; the holy cross was only a piece of wood, 36; in Klausen, 30, 33

Apocalypticism (end times): the prophet Daniel, 35; the seven seals, 35, 237; influence on Ursula Binder, 29, 34-35, 51

Aschau im Chiemgau, 68. *See also* Hohenaschau

Au, in the forest of Bregenz, *see* Bregenz and Feldkirch

Augsburg, 29, 34, 35, 66, 150, 182; Anabaptism in, 51, 52, 57, 69, 250; booklet brought from, 33; butchering in, 230; city hall of, 238; Diet of, 182; Helena von Freyberg interrogated in, 67-69; midwives book from, 226, 227; salary of Pilgram Marpeck in, 244

Auspitz, 71, 103, 147, 210

Austerlitz, 104, 171, 210

Authority: divine inspiration gives inner, spiritual authority, 8-9; from God, 101; an inner call to exercise gifts, 8, 49; and religious freedom, 207. *See also* priesthood of all believers

Bainton, Roland H., 11
Ban, *see* discipline
Baptism: of adults (believers'), 1, 4-5, 11, 145, 203-04; a criminal act, 4; infant baptism, 4-5, 245; infant baptized by God, 122; voluntary, 7. *See also* Zurich
Baptist denominations, 11
Bavaria, 3, 57, 63, 65, 68, 69, 70, 71, 110, 150, 166
Bender, Harold S., 7
Berne, Switzerland, 42
Bible: biblical knowledge of women, 98; biblical reform, 4; Gospels in the vernacular, 8, 31, 34, 121, 197; interpretation by the illiterate, 8, 101; New Testament, 7, 8, 31, 104, 182, 191, 206; readings by women, 31, 32, 33, 34, 43, 50, 77, 191, 193; Scripture alone, 4
Blaurock, Jörg, 4, 9, 30, 32, 42, 59, 61, 104, 130, 192, 215
Books, *see* heretical literature
Boulding, Elise, 10 n. 53, 50
Bozen, 3, 31, 42, 47, 57, 59, 60, 81, 99, 107, 173, 224; first Anabaptist martyrs in, 58
Bregenz, 3, 45, 73-74, 161
Breitenberg, 83, 129, 215
Brenner Pass, 1, 105
Brethren in Christ, 11
Brixen, 3, 29, 31, 34, 36, 57, 67, 117-18, 134, 183, 194, 195, 196, 197, 209
Brixlegg, 56, 73, 102, 119, 122, 171-72
Bruck am Ziller, 128, 160, 162, 166, 167, 172
Bruneck, 3, 57, 182

Caspar von Schwenckfeld, 69
Categories of participation, 11, 204. *See also* leadership of Anabaptist women and, martyrs
Cathars: in the Anabaptist court records, 141. *See also* religious movements

Index 295

Children: ages given, 81, 144, 146, 162, 164; accompanied parents to meetings, 186; began work at age seven, 71 n.154; care they received in Moravia, 211; eight, largest family discussed, 152; fled with their parents, 167, 173, 210, 242; foster children, 170; had to pay for the family property, 171; inheriting money, 99, 110, 119, 126, 147, 149, 160, 164, 166, 170, 171; left by parent who fled or was martyred, 10, 70-71, 75, 79, 81, 99, 110, 121, 122, 125, 132, 142, 154, 158, 159, 163, 167, 168, 171, 172, 185, 189, 198; mothers allowed to return to their children, 99, 109, 111, 153; not considered adults until age 16, 145; parents of, arranged for their care, 145; re-united with parents, 145; supported from common treasury if abandoned, 105; underage meant between three and seven years of age, 71. *See also* pregnancy and childbirth

Chronicle of the Hutterian Brethren, 102, 145, 148, 215

Church of the Brethren, 11

Church: visible, gathered, 5; underground church today, 17

Citizens, 13, 71, 103, 112, 125, 126, 173; carrying no weapons meant disenfranchisement, 42, 44, 46

Civil authorities: duties of the crown administrator, 31 n. 18; referred to as dogs, 249;
sympathetic to Anabaptists, 6, 37, 46, 47, 58, 78, 81, 108-09, 111, 120, 173-74, 179, 180-81, 182, 190, 197-98, 199; tensions between central and local rulers, 6, 14, 184. *See also* Ferdinand I, Archduke

Clasen, Claus-Peter, 15, 49, 209

Clergy *see* anticlericalism and, Roman Catholic Church (of the sixteenth century)

Coburg, 34, 35

Commoners, 3, 30; angry when Anabaptists sing, 128; being led astray, 180; support for Anabaptists 143, 144, 209

Communion, *see* Lord's Supper

Community of goods, 32, 105, 124, 141, 148, 208; among Hutterites in Moravia, 71, 104, 147-48, 210, 212, 213. *See also* mutual aid

Conformity, *see* recantation

Constance, 3, 66

Court records, 12-16, 33, 49, 203, 204, 205, 210

Crown Administrator *see* civil authorities
Crucifixion, painting of, 222

Danube River, 105
Daughters, *see* young women
Death: burial in sacred ground, 67, 180. *See also* martyrdom
Decrees (mandates) *see* Ferdinand I, Archduke
Deutschnofen, 47, 81, 82, 190
Dirks, Elisabeth, 54, 106, 206, 209
Discipleship, 5, 7, 49
Discipline: the ban in the Hutterite community, 147; forgiveness in Anabaptist congregations, 52, 69, 247-251; of older children who agreed with their parents, 145
Dowry, 147, 148, 163, 164

Economics: Anabaptists who were better off, 121, 146, 148, 163, 205; income of carpenters and bricklayers 46, 99, 146, 243, 244; income of a civil servant, 65 n.123, 244; income of a noblewoman, 69; money values, 243-44. *See also* community of goods, mutual aid and, property and goods
Education: universal among Hutterites, 212. *See also* literacy and, Roman Catholic Church (of the sixteenth century): attempts to dissuade female Anabaptist prisoners Egalitarianism, 7-9, 206-08. *See also* authority, freedom and, leadership of Anabaptist women
Eisack River, 3
Ellmau, 153, 160, 163, 164
Emigration to Moravia, 105, 143-44, 179 184
Eppan, 65
Etsch: river (Adige), 3; territory of, 60
Evangelization *see* leadership of Anabaptist women: in mission work
Execution *see* martyrdom
Exile (banishment) of Anabaptist women *see* punishment

Faith: alone, 4; took priority over family and children, 154; faith courage and commitment of Anabaptist women, 215. *See also* freedom and, Anabaptism: teachings and beliefs

Family: evangelization in, 10, 31, 53; threatened by women's central involvement, 10. *See also* marriage and, children
Family networks *see* the women in the Gallpüchler, Gasser, Kobl, Nickinger, Sackman, Taurer, and families and households
Feeble-minded, 72
Feldkirch, 144, 161, 179
Felicitas, martyr in the early Christian church, 235
Ferdinand I, Archduke: absolute power and control of the estates, 6; decrees (mandates) of; 1, 5, 12-13, 31, 41-45, 47, 50, 67, 99, 100, 106, 142-45, 150-51, 179, 180, 184; Diet of Speyer, 99, 116, 143; petitions submitted to his children, 131; policy changes, 14, 98, 102, 179; threats, fines and admonitions to local authorities, 47, 143, 144, 161-62. *See also* Hapsburg
Feudalism: fiefs, 130, 165 n.61; land tenure in Tirol, 6
Financial records, *see* property and goods
Forgiveness, see discipline
Freedom: Christian, 208; spiritual, 7. *See also*, authority and, women, Anabaptist: making choices
Freundsberg, 57, 107, 115, 154, 181, 182, 188, 189-90, 191, 232
Freyberg, Pankraz von, 63, 69-70, 234
Froschauer Bible, 221, 234, 237
Fuchs, Christoff, 65, 66, 114, 160

Gasser, Barbara, 114
Gelassenheit, *see* yieldedness
Government *see* civil authorities
Grace of God, 5, 247; in Helena von Freyberg's confession, 248-51
Graz, 43, 79
Grembs, Veronica, 193
Gries, adjacent to Bozen, 3
Grumbach, Argula von, 203
Gufidaun, 3, 29, 31, 32, 34, 36, 79, 114, 124, 144, 145, 159, 172, 183, 197-98

Hall in Tirol, 3, 34, 72, 102, 105, 109, 112, 126, 128, 132, 143, 198, 231, 244, 245

Hapsburg monarchy, 5, 105. *See also* Ferdinand I

Haude, Sigrun, 204

Heretical literature, pamphlets and books, 29, 33, 191, 182, 192, 197, 208

Heretical movements, 7. *See also* religious movements

Hertenberg, 72, 73, 75-76, 79, 111

Hiding places *see* meetings

Hohenaschau Castle, 63, 65, 69, 70, 150, 225

Hoheneck, 74, 79

Holy Spirit: basis for biblical interpretation in the unlearned, 101; divine inspiration gave women the freedom to speak, 8-9, 49, 208; in Helena von Freyberg's confession, 69, 248-250; named in Anabaptist greetings, 9, 208; part of Anabaptist teaching, 186; significant for women's participation, 8-9. *See also* authority

Humour, Casper Maler's wife speaks about the sacrament, 79.

Hut, Hans, 29, 34, 35, 51

Hutter, Jacob: Elisabeth von Wolkenstein his follower, 31, 182, 193; hatmaker by trade, 31; married Katharina Purst, 104, 211; in Moravia, 147-48, 204, 210; in Tirol, 32, 45, 71, 103-04, 118, 121, 124, 135, 152, 157, 171, 192, 210, 213

Hutterite Songbook, 102

Hutterites: beginnings in Tirol, 104, 210; descendants of Anabaptists in Tirol, 11, 205-06, 212; and the Jerusalem model of the church, 213. *See also* community of goods, *Chronicle of the Hutterian Brethren* and, Moravia

Hymns, Anabaptist: about women from Tirol, 102-03; in the *Ausbund*, 215, 245; one written by a woman, 216, 245-47; sung in prison, 103, 128

Iconoclasm, 117

Innsbruck, 2-3

Jost, Ursula, 9, 52, 55

Kaltern, 166, 189

Kampner, Elizabeth, 215

Karneid, 81

Kempe, Margary, 150
Kitzbühel, 3, 150.
Klassen, William, viii, 87, 90, 92, 219, 251, 252.
Klaassen, Walter, xiii, xv, xviii, 18, 20, 27, 37, 39, 87, 90, 92, 137, 251, 252.
Klausen, 3, 183
Kolsass, 73, 158
Kramsach, 184, 230
Kufstein, 3, 65
Kunigspergerin, 68
Kunstbuch, Das, 69; Helena von Freyberg's confession in, 247-51
Kurtatsch, 81, 108, 110, 134, 180

Land tenure *see* feudalism
Lang, Matthias, 64, 133
Laws *see* women: legal position in the sixteenth century
Lawyers, 130-131, 132
Leadership of Anabaptist women, 48-55, activities of, 50; as baptizers, 50-51; charismatic, 7, 9, 48, 206; as mediators, 55, 69; lay nature of, 7-8, 48, 150; in leading congregations and meetings, 43, 50, 64, 77; and martyrdom, 55; in mission work, 35, 53-54, 64, 67, 100, 115; negative attitudes towards, 54-55; in networks, 50, 53-54, 83, 119; numbers involved in, 11, 48-49; in preaching, 53, 72, 77, 144, 161, 205; as prophets, 9, 52, 53, 55; as self-appointed, 48; serving communion, 55; spiritual call and gifts for, 49; as teachers, 34, 35, 50, 51, 54, 69, 182; wives of male leaders, 55. *See also* apocalypticism, authority, Bible: readings by women and, marriage: wives as co-workers with husbands
Leifers, 83, 129, 198
Liechtenstein, Christoff Philipp von, 62, 70-71, 134, 159
Liechtenstein, Wilhelm, 47, 58, 80, 81, 82, 108-09, 110, 173-74, 180
Literacy, 33, 34, 43, 49-50, 51, 77, 98, 205, 208, 212; illiterate, spirit filled believer a truer exegete of Scripture, 9; majority of the population illiterate, 4. *See also* Bible: readings by women
Lord's Supper, 43, 44, 54, 55, 64, 71, 83, 112, 121, 153, 163, 174, 183, 192, 193, 194, 197, 208; partaking both bread and wine, 5, discussed by Jörg Zaunring, 5; woman in Styria explains communion, 79
Lüsen: home of Anna Gasser, 114

Luther, Martin, 4, 6, 30, 31, 34, 37, 48, 63, 101; views on women, 54
Lutheran movement, 79, 174, 192, 197; nobility in 70, 203; referred to as a sect, 65, 111, 114, 161; sources for, 15. *See also* Protestant leaders

Maids *see* occupations and employment
Maler, Jörg, 68
Malone, Mary T., 52
Mantz, Felix: first Anabaptist martyr in Zurich, 4
Mantz, mother of Felix: meeting took place in her home, 4
Marpeck, Pilgram, 32, 42, 63, 66, 69, 171, 244
Marriage: influence of a spouse, 55; modern ideal of, 206-07; leaving property, spouse and children, 145, 180, 185, 189, 203, 245; role and duties of wives 9-10; wives as co-workers with husbands, 50, 53, 55. *See also* children: left by parent who fled or was martyred and, exile (banishment) of Anabaptist women
Martyrdom, 100; burned at the stake, 74, 75, 119, 134, 166, 198, 208, 211, 235, 245; by the sword, 181, 188, 209; conducted in secret, 143; cost of executions, 81, 103, 132; drowning, 181, 188; first female martyrs in Tirol, 43, 58-59; last known execution in Tirol, 209; mass executions in Rattenberg, 99, 115-16; numbers of, 55, 97-98, 184; in the Reformed Church, 11
Martyrs' Mirror, 11, 12, 16, 98, 102, 108, 215, 235
Mecenseffy, Grete, 12, 13, 15, 16, 210, 214
Meetings of Anabaptists, 8; in caves, 155, 183, 197; in forests, 123, 126, 143, 144, 158, 192, 209, 213; in homes, 33, 36, 66, 68, 121, 131, 143,182, 188, 193; at night, 128, 174, 179, 186; numbers attending, 180, 183, 185-86, 197-98; in a pit, 198; in vacant houses, 184; sermons at, 179-80, 185-86
Mennonite Brethren, 11
Mennonites, 18
Meran, 3, 244
Michelsburg 146-47, 156, 157, 190; castle of, 232; Agnes Hutter 'fell again' in the district of, 134; Bishop of Brixen capture Anabaptists in district of, 118,
Mils: Anabaptists met in forest near, 123, 126, 244
Miners *see* occupations and employment: miners

Monastic institutions and individuals: Beguines; celibate ideal; convents; Franciscan court preacher; Sonnenburg nunnery

Money values, *see* economics

Moos, hamlet of, birthplace of Agnes Hutter: 134, 228

Moravia, 147-48; 205-06, 210-212; route to, 105. *See also* Hutterites

Moser, Heinz, 98

Münster, city of, 68, 211

Mutual aid: gift of   money to prisoners, 65; providing food and lodging, 31, 47, 50, 64, 67, 71, 80, 82, 121, 144, 157-58, 181, 187, 188, 189, 193, 214. *See also* community of goods and, property and goods: money from property given to leaders

Mysticism, 87 note 53.

Networks, *see* leadership and family networks

Neuhaus Castle at Gais, 192, 213

Nicodemism, *see* recantation

Nonresistance: nonviolent nature of Anabaptism, 17, 30, 33 n. 24, 99, 116; staff bearers, 104. *See also* punishment: carrying no weapons

Numbers of participants *see* women, Anabaptist: numbers and percentages

Oath *see* recantation

Occupations and employment: one artist, 60; 3 bakers, 72, 75, 190; 5 blacksmiths, 127, 145, 161; 2 booksellers; 2 carpenters; a city judge, 58; a civil servant (judge), 42, 244; coin-maker, 198; 6 cooks; 1 former court secretary, 81; 2 crown administrator's wives, 34, 75; 2 cutlers, 33, 157; a goatherd, 32; a hatmaker, 31; 5 innkeepers, 57, 79, 80, 130 186; many maids, 10, 79, 112; a mayor, 57; 4 millers, 121, 149, 161, 171; a number of miners, 77, 110, 157, 168; many peasant farmers, 97, 205; 2 shoemakers, 58, 135; a shopkeeper, 169; a silversmith, 99; a stone mason, 135; 5 tailors, 35, 57, 116; and a water carrier in the mines (former monk), 36

Ötz Valley, 3, 165, 189, 216

Pacifism, *see* nonresistance

Packull, Werner O., xiii, xix, 18, 19, 38, 39 87, 104, 175, 210, 218.

Paraguay, reconciliation event in, 17

Pardon for accused Anabaptists, 43-44, 46, 60, 77-78, 82, 106, 111, 126, 144, 159, 196, 204, 242; for those who were not leaders 42,

70-71, 72-73, 110, 208; granted by the king's children, 131; new requirements for, 159; none for two poor women, 114; not a deterrent, 98-99, 109; penance required for, 76, 155-56; a second pardon granted, 114, 189. *See also* relapsed Anabaptists

Paulle, Hans Mair, wife, 193, 214

Peasant farmers: illustrations of, 231, 236; majority of Anabaptists in Tirol engaged in farming, 10; practice of transhumance, 97. *See also* commoners

Peasants' War, 6, 30; women in the, 59, 61

Penance *see* recantation: and penance and pardon: penance required for.

Persecution: of Christians today, 17-18; commemorated in Anabaptist hymns, 102; everyone needed in new religious movements, 8, 206; high points in Tirol, 97, 106, 145, 205, 209; severe in sixteenth century Tirol, 16-18

Pflaurenz, 121, 155

Pietism, 7

Poverty of Anabaptists: indebtedness, 147

Pranndt, Ernst, judge in Rattenberg, 166, 167

Pregnancy and childbirth, 11, 150-54: a birthing room, 227; a birthing stool, 227; corporal punishment while pregnant, 46, 114; decrees regarding, 150-51; giving birth while fleeing, 213-14; humane treatment for, 161; midwives, 121, 226; miscarriage, 113, 152; more moderate punishment during, 152; mothers nursing infants, 121, 152, 211; and Roman law, 105-06; wet nurse who baptized a child, 122, 152; wet nurses, 121, 151, 182, 191.

Priesthood of all believers, 4, 48

Property and goods, 13-14, 55, 73, 75, 80, 81, 99, 110, 122, 125-26, 129, 130-32, 142, 151, 158, 180, 185; confiscations of nobility's, 62, 63, 66, 194, 197, 198; discussion of properties and financial inventories, 71, 144-150, 159-160, 163-74, 242-43; government expenses for Anabaptist, 145, 146, 151, 160, 163, 164, 165, 167, 181, 199; money from property given to leaders, 187, 197; seventy-two percent of Anabaptists owned over 50 Gulden, 205. *See also* marriage: leaving property, spouse and children and, community of goods

Prösels Castle, 111, 187

Proselytization *see* evangelization

Protestant leaders: Ambrosius Blaurer in Constance, 66; who met with Helena von Freyberg in Augsburg, 68. *See also* Martin Luther

Punishment of Anabaptists: bail, 46, 79, 83, 112, 113, 115, 120, 165, 172; carrying no weapons, 42, 44, 46; corporal, 42, 46, 56, 74, 76-77, 82, 98, 108, 109, 114, 120, 145, 152, 235; death sentence, 13, 14, 41, 42, 43; exile (banishment), of Anabaptist women, 9, 34, 42, 61, 67, 68, 71, 99, 109, 142; fines, 42, 144, 157, 159, 180, 188; guaranty required for release, 64, 65, 120, 150, 161; loss of property; 13-14, 145; no fear of; 100, 142; payment of court expenses, 70, 75, 111, 190; sparse diet in prison, 47, 70, 75, 81, 152, 155. *See also* Ferdinand I, Archduke: decrees (mandates) of, recantation, trial and imprisonment of Anabaptists: in the criminal court

Purst, Katharina, wife of Jacob Hutter, 104, 211

Puster Valley, 3, 6, 42, 54, 57, 100, 103, 104, 116, 121, 124, 129, 147, 171, 182, 187, 192, 210, 228, 231, 232

Radfeld, centre adjacent to Rattenberg, 126, 128, 146, 165, 167, 169, 173

Rattenberg, 168

Rauch, Michel: conducted inventories of Anabaptist property, 160 n. 51

Rebstock, Barbara, 9, 55

Recantation, 13, 14, 42, 43-44, 60, 109, 115, 124, 156, 183, 214, 242; long and short forms, 44; oath (affidavit) of, 44, 60, 84 n. 12, 89 n. 93, 111, 196; as occasional conformity or Nicodemism, 45; and penance, 46, 75, 81, 111-12; penance format, 76, 155; public versus private, 45, 66-67, 76, 156, 196; the reason for Helena von Freyberg's confession, 252; repeating word for word, 158-59, 196; spoken from the pulpit 45; texts, 75-76, 154-55, 195-96. *See also* pardon

Reconciliations with Anabaptists: and the Reformed Church, 17

Re-education of women, *see* Roman Catholic Church (of the sixteenth century): attempts to dissuade female Anabaptist prisoners

Reformation, 3-6

Reformed Church: Calvin's views on women; martyrs in the, 11

Refugees, Anabaptist, *see* emigration

Reischach, 118, 144, 157

Relapsed Anabaptists (fallen again, rejoined the movement), 13, 107, 134, 173, 184, 188, 189, 214

Religious movements: Christianity, the Beguines, Cathars, Hussites, Lollards, Waldensians, Anabaptists, Pietists, Quakers, Methodists, the Holiness movement, 7; in Canada, 7

Rettenberg, 73, 123, 157, 158, 190, 191

Riemenschneider, Elisabeth, 60

Ritten plateau, 59

Rodeneck, 42, 124

Roman Catholic Church (of the sixteenth century): attempts to dissuade female Anabaptist prisoners, 14, 98, 123, 188, 194, 195, 205; belief in Mary the Mother of God, 77, 114, 214; Bishopric of Freising, 3; clergy to admonish the people, 143; decree from Salzburg, 41; lack of spiritual care for the people, 3, 23 n. 41; reinstatement in the Roman Catholic Church: church *see* recantation. *See also* anticlericalism, commoners, iconoclasm, monastic institutions and individuals, and, entries for Brixen, Salzburg and Trent regarding bishops there.

Roman Catholic Church (of today): reconciliation with Anabaptists, 16

Rosenau, 68

Rottenburg, 156

Routes of escape, *see* Moravia

Sacraments: mass, Anabaptist belief in, 5; the seven, listed in interrogation questions, 194

Saints: as idolatrous, 77; Margaret, for pregnant women, 74, 150. *See also* Roman Catholic Church (of the sixteenth century): belief in Mary the Mother of God

Salzburg: bishopric, centre of, 3; Binder couple captured there, sent to do mission work, 29, 34-35; decree made about exiled wives, 34

Sarnthein, 107, 179, 185, 186, 213

Schlachta, Astrid von, xvi, 18, 19, 25, 38, 137

Schmelzer, Matthias, xix, 183, 251

Schwaz, 3, 36, 41, 58, 98, 101, 117, 118, 125, 147, 162, 181

Sickness and disease, 51, 70, 100, 119, 146, 164, 165

Simons, Menno, 51

Simple-mindedness, 100-01, 114. *See also* legal position of women

Single Anabaptist women, 100, 134, 164. *See also* occupations and employment: maids and, young women

Snyder, C. Arnold, xiv, xvii, 19, 20, 37, 38, 39, 55, 86, 92, 137, 216, 217, 218, 219.

Social status: nobility weaker in Tirol, 6; special treatment for noblewomen, 63, 195

Sonnenburg, Puster Valley, 6, 128, 132, 155, 241

Sources for Anabaptist research *see* court records and, *Martyrs' Mirror*

St. George, 3; rents paid to monastery and abbey of, 163, 166, 167, 172; Anabaptists from, spent time in Elisabeth von Wolkenstein's home

St. Lorenzen, 3, 118, 232; Anabaptist widow in, 187; Wölfl preached in Bader home located in, 36

St. Petersberg: Anabaptists in district of, 72, 75, 120, 125, 156, 165, 173, 180, 188; Ursula Hellrigel imprisoned in castle of, 216, 233

Stainer, Anna, 193

Stams: women baptized by Jörg Vasser here and Anna Egger evangelized nearby, 72

Sterzing, 3; Anabaptist miners and their wives in, 102, 110; Anabaptists in, 110, 113, 157, 189; Anna Gasser's daughter in, 114; the court preacher to come there, 182; end of 1531, Anabaptists still meeting in large numbers, 183, 199; Katharina Purst worked as a maid, 104

Styria: female Anabaptist leaders in, 43, 48, 49, 51, 54, 77, 79; women baptized by Leonard Schiemer in 58;

Swiss Anabaptism, *see* Zurich

Taufer Valley, 3, 49, 82, 183, 192

Theology debated by Anabaptist women, 68, 86 n. 35, 186, 195, 206

Ties, Hanns-Paul, xvii, 89, 95

Tirol: geography of, 2-3

Toblach, 121, 124-25, 134

Torture and the threat of torture: in interrogations of Anabaptist women, 13, 103, 105-108, 128, 132, 135, 142, 174, 214, 242; unsure if it should be used for women, 181, 189-90; local judge and jury against it, 107; mentioned in Ursula Hellrigel's hymn, 246; not used for nobility, 193, 194; Roman law, 105; used more often for those who rejoined, 106

Transgressions, of Anabaptist women *see* women, Anabaptist: writings of Trent; urban centre of, 3; bishop of, 60; bishopric of, 80

Trial and imprisonment of Anabaptists: court secretaries, 15, 108, 132, 142; in the criminal court, 13, 14; different treatment for nobility, 65,

193, 195; expenses for, 103, 132; held in secret, 143, 165; interrogation questions; 5, 13, 60, 106, 127-28, 193-94, 241-42; the jury, 13, 103; juries who refused to condemn prisoners, 100, 190; petitions submitted for Anabaptists, 36, 46, 56, 66, 67, 71, 73, 75, 77, 78, 79, 81, 83, 110, 111, 115, 119, 125, 126, 130-31, 133, 153, 156, 159, 187, 190, 191, 198; petition to the estates, 60. *See also* pardon for accused Anabaptists, punishment of Anabaptists and, torture and the threat of torture

Ursula of Essen, 235
Uttenheim, 45, 82, 104, 183, 193, 196, 213

Vienna, 29, 35, 57
Venice, Anabaptist fleeing south toward, 80
Vintschgau, 3
Völs, 47, 53, 54, 82, 111-12, 118-19, 129, 186, 187, 198
Vorarlberg, 3; Anabaptist preachers in, 161

Wages and income, *see* economics
Waldensians: the only successful medieval sect in Austrian regions, 8. *See also* Religious movements
Wangen, 59 n. 90, 61, 83, 120, 153
Wattens, 78, 112, 126, 131, 159, 163
Weapons, *see* nonresistance
Weber, Marianne, 206-207
Weber, Max, 7, 206
Welsberg, 103, 116-17
Widows, 50, 53, 69, 78, 102, 105, 117, 118, 123, 125, 128, 129, 134, 146, 157, 158, 165, 187, 204, 209, 211
Wiesner, Merry E., 8, 208
Wipp Valley, 3
Wölfl, the radical, corner preacher, 9, 29, 31-33, 34, 36, 51, 182, 183, 192, 197
Wolkenstein, cook, 193-94
Women, Anabaptist: historical memory for, 3; integrally involved in the movement, 9-12; legal position in the sixteenth century, 105-06; making choices, 1, 5, 11, 14, 18, 55, 63, 101, 114, 151, 154, 184, 203, 207, 209,

215; motivations, 99-100, 206-209; numbers and percentages of, 6-7, 97-98, 184, 203-05; persevering, 58, 69, 98, 102, 103, 107, 112, 128, 132, 134-35; recurring pattern of greater participation in the beginning, 6-9; social position in the family, 47, 204; speaking publicly, 208; writings of, 52, 247-51. *See also* Anabaptism: baptism and recantation were individual choices and, hymns, Anabaptist: written by women

Yieldedness (Gelassenheit), 52, 69, 208, 250

Young women, 10, 57, 58, 72, 77, 78, 100, 101, 104, 107, 112, 115, 125, 142, 163, 172. *See also*, occupations and employment: maids

Zurich: first baptisms in, 4, 17, 30

www.ingramcontent.com/pod-product-compliance
Lightning Source LLC
Chambersburg PA
CBHW070230230426

43664CB00014B/2258